THE OVERMOUNTAIN MEN
Battle of King's Mountain • Cumberland Decade
State of Franklin • Southwest Territory

Pat Alderman

Illustrations

Bernie Andrews • Kenneth Ferguson
Edyth Price • John Alan Maxwell
Robert Pannell • William Bowman

The Overmountain Press

JOHNSON CITY, TENNESSEE

Cover Design by Bernie Andrews

Original Copyright 1970
Reprinted with Index 1986
ISBN 0-932807-16-X
Copyright © 1986 by The Overmountain Press
Printed in the United States of America
6 7 8 9 0

Early Tennessee History
1760-1795

General Contents

This volume is a compilation of a series of booklets planned by the author to cover succeeding periods of history. Only the first two sections were published separately (*The Overmountain Men* in 1958 and *One Heroic Hour at King's Mountain* in 1968); although type was subsequently set and layouts prepared for the separate printing of remaining portions. In 1970, the compilation was accepted and published verbatim by The Overmountain Press, using original layouts furnished by the author. In this second edition, a great portion of the text was typeset again. An index was added and some passages were reworked for clarity; however, no major alterations were considered, so that the author's style is preserved in these presentations he labeled ''history made interesting.''

Clifford Maxwell

John B. (Pat) Alderman
1901-1984

THE OVERMOUNTAIN MEN

THE
CHEROKEE INDIAN

The Cherokee Indian is closely linked with the story and settlement of Tennessee and the white man's expansion westward. They were the original southern mountaineers, and custodians of the wilderness. The Indian's love and worship of nature did not allow him to slash trees or kill without reason. To him, every stone, tree, and animal contained a spirit and had a purpose in life; and his love and care of the open country was part of nature's balance.

The geographical location of the Cherokee nation, with the natural mountain barriers, along with their greatly superior numbers, made them a power among southern Indians. Their Tribal Council was made up of delegated Chiefs chosen from the Seven Clans. This body, though the supreme law, did not have absolute authority. The women also selected their clan leaders who had strong voices in the Nation's Councils. The chosen leader of the Women's Council became the "Beloved Woman" and was greatly respected and revered among the Cherokees. This loosely knit tribal organization worked almost like a democracy with

each town a self-governing body. Clan membership was indicated by distinctive headdress, as was their rank and position in the clan. There were three geographical divisions of the Nation: The Lower Towns, The Middle Settlement, and The Overhill Country.

The Cherokee language does not include a word that means *Cherokee*. It seems that the English started using this name about 1708. The Cherokee Indians called themselves *Ani-Yunwiya*, which means *The Real People*. They are descendants of the northern Iroquois Tribe.

The Cherokee's original claims of land stemmed from the "Smokies" and extended into portions of several present day states including the northern parts of Alabama, Georgia, and South Carolina, western North Carolina and Virginia, the southern portion of West Virginia and the eastern portions of Tennessee and Kentucky. The extent of their territorial claims is very indefinite as there were no fixed boundary lines.

Whiskey and guns were introduced by the white man shortly after 1700. Smallpox brought to them from a slave ship anchored at Charleston wiped out nearly half the nation. This hundred year period, 1700 through 1800, was one of great disaster for the Indian people. They were not prepared by knowledge or experience to cope with the forces pressing against them. They faced the encroachment of their country bewildered and confused, totally unprepared for what lay ahead in the coming stream of events.

There were few large towns and no fortresses among the Cherokee when first seen by the Overmountain pioneers. Their towns were settlements of crude huts and wigwams scattered along the banks of creeks and rivers. There was not much order or regularity in their arrangement. Each village was usually located

near good springs and convenient to favorite fishing and hunting grounds. Near each dwelling was a section of cleared ground where the women raised vegetables such as corn, beans and potatoes, and tobacco. Their garden tools were sharp pointed sticks, wooden hoes and rakes fashioned by hand until the iron implements were brought in by the white traders.

THE CHEROKEE MEDICINE MAN used the Booger Masks, pictured above, along with rattles, conjuring stones, various herbs and barks to scare away evil spirits.

POTTERY, such as pots, pans, jugs, and jars for domestic purposes, were made from local materials by adept hands.

WAR IMPLEMENTS and tools were homemade until the white man introduced the iron tomahawk, gun, and metal spear points.

The Cherokee relics pictured on this page are part of a numerous collection that can be seen at the MUSEUM OF THE CHEROKEE INDIAN, Cherokee, N.C. These pictures are used through the courtesy of The Cherokee Historical Association.

THE COUNCIL HOUSE is the center of political and religious life of the Cherokee. A seven sided building, each side represents one of the seven clans. The seats are raised one above the other for benefit of clan members. The sacred altar fire is in a cleared area in the center. The principal Chief's seat occupies the central place back of the Sacred Fire.

CORN was the Cherokee's chief produce and their main dependence. Here Mrs. Mollie Sequoyah is shown in the reconstructed village, grinding corn in a large wooden mortar, using the heavy wooden pestle to pound the grains into meal.

The Cherokee Historical Association in Cherokee, N.C., has reconstructed a Cherokee village of 200 years ago so that posterity may know how the Cherokee Indians lived before the white man came to the wilderness. Here, in this village, Cherokee Indians show how the community life existed during that period, actually demonstrating their customs, arts and crafts. This log structure is one of several progressive types shown in the *Oconaluftee* village at Cherokee.

THE HOT HOUSE, or "Sweat House," a smaller structure close beside the regular dwelling, was made of poles and chinked with mud. It was sometimes partly covered over with earth. The one small opening was used for entering or leaving the place. Entrance shown in insert at top right. A fire was kept continually and the heat became so great at times that clothing could scarcely be borne. This structure was used in coldest weather.

INSIDE and OUTSIDE views of HOT HOUSE, and other scenes in Oconaluftee, *the reconstructed Cherokee Indian Village of 200 years ago in Cherokee, North Carolina. Photos by John Parris, used courtesy of The Cherokee Historical Association which sponsors the Cherokee Indian drama,* Unto These Hills, *The Museum of the Cherokee Indian and the* Oconaluftee.

1756 — FORT LOUDOUN — 1760

Fort Loudoun was erected on the banks of the Little Tennessee River near the mouth at Tellico. The Cherokees gave the English some seven hundred acres of land for this purpose. The fort was named in honor of Earl of Loudoun, appointed Commander-in-Chief of the American armies, 1756. Construction was begun in the fall of that year under the command of Captain Raymond Demere. It was garrisoned in the summer of 1757 under the command of Captain Paul Demere, younger brother of Raymond. The plan of the Fort followed the European 18th century pattern. It was one of a chain of forts built on the western frontier by the English during the French-Indian war. Both the French and English courted the friendship of the Cherokees in their struggle to gain control of the rich Tennessee and Ohio valley territory. Many incidents led to the breaking of friendly relations between Cherokees and the British. During the early part of 1760, the Indian warriors began closing in around the Fort and total siege was instigated. The garrison eventually, starved to submission, surrendered August 1760. Later, the Cherokees destroyed the Fort.

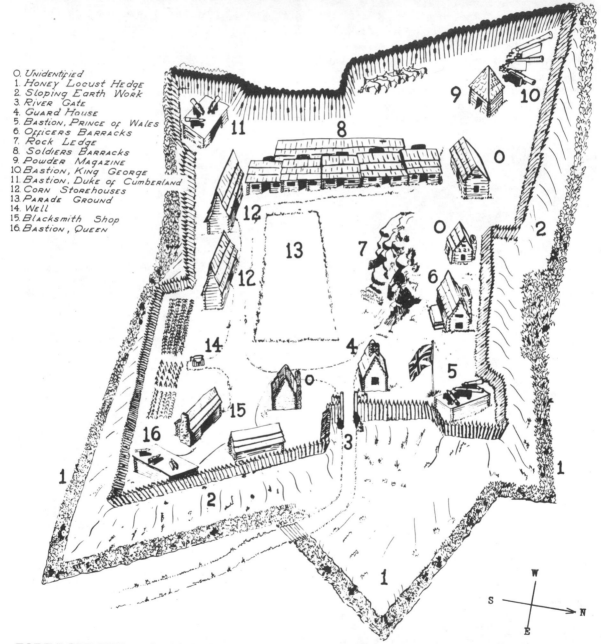

0. Unidentified
1. Honey Locust Hedge
2. Sloping Earth Work
3. River Gate
4. Guard House
5. Bastion, Prince of Wales
6. Officers Barracks
7. Rock Ledge
8. Soldiers Barracks
9. Powder Magazine
10. Bastion, King George
11. Bastion, Duke of Cumberland
12. Corn Storehouses
13. Parade Ground
14. Well
15. Blacksmith Shop
16. Bastion, Queen

FORT LOUDOUN on the Little Tennessee River, a pictorial restoration based on archeological investigation. Drawn by Garvin M. Colburn for Elsworth Brown, March 11, 1957.

Fireplaces of the soldiers' barracks.

Partially reconstructed palisade wall. Well in foreground.

Cast iron plates and forks discovered during excavation.

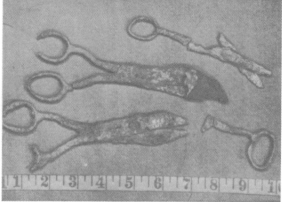

Scissors and shears found while digging around old foundations.

Outside view of a completed segment of Fort wall.

New stone work on old foundations of the interior structure of the Fort.

Pictures used through courtesy of Elsworth Brown, Director of Research, Fort Loudoun Association, and Paul Kelley, Superintendent of Restoration.

5

NANCY WARD

Nancy Ward, one of the greatest among Tennessee's celebrated women, was born in July 1740 at Chota, capital of the Cherokee Nation. Her mother is said to be Tame Doe of the Wolf Clan and sister of Attakullakulla, called "Little Carpenter," Peace Chief of the Cherokee. Nancy's brother, named Long Fellow, was an influential Chief and ruled over seven towns. Dragging Canoe, son of Attakullakulla and cousin of Nancy, usurped Oconostota as war chief and led repeated attacks on settlers.

Nancy Ward died in 1822. She was buried close by her home near Benton, Polk County, Tennessee. The Nancy Ward Chapter of the D.A.R., Chattanooga, erected a marker at her grave.

Nancy first married King Fisher of the Deer Clan. They had two children, Catherine and Little Fellow. Nancy accompanied King Fisher on the warpath against the Creeks in North Georgia. In this *Battle of Muskogee*, King Fisher was killed. Nancy took up her husband's gun and fought as a warrior. After the victory, Nancy was given the title of *Ghighau* or *Beloved Woman* in recognition of her bravery. The *Beloved Woman* title was one given the principal woman in the female councils and endowed her with power to speak in the council of the Chiefs. Her badge of authority was a swan's wing.

Nancy later married Brian (Bryant) Ward, an English trader from South Carolina. They had two children, Elizabeth, (called "Betsy") and Nannie. Betsy married Colonel Joseph Martin. Nannie is said to have married Richard Timberlake, descendant of Henry Timberlake. Joseph Martin, later acting as Virginia's agent to the Cherokee, found this marriage beneficial in his dealings with the Indians.

Brian Ward later returned to South Carolina, where he lived with his white family on the banks of the Tugaloo River in the Pendleton District. On occasion, Nancy Ward visited him and his white family and was received with respect. William Martin, son of Joseph Martin, who lived near the Wards and saw her on these visits, says: "She was one of the most superior women I ever saw." (Draper Mss.)

Nancy Ward, the Prophetess and Beloved Woman of the Cherokees, played an important role in the story of Tennessee. She was friendly to the white man and, with her power of life and death, was responsible for saving the lives of many settlers. Her position in the Council gave her knowledge concerning the treaties and dealings between Indians and white men. She befriended James Robertson on the occasion of his visit to the Overhill Towns in 1772. Learning of Dragging Canoe's plans for the wholesale attack on the Watauga and Holston settlements she was able, with the help of some of her people, to slip Isaac Thomas and three others out of the Indian towns. She asked John Sevier and Arthur Campbell to spare the towns of Hiwassee. Like her prominent uncle, Attakullakulla, she was a strong advocate of peace between the two races.

Without the timely warning by Nancy Ward, most of the settlers of the Watauga, Holston, and Carter's Valleys could have been surprised by the Indians and killed. Without these settlements there would not have been an Overmountain Men's Army to defeat Ferguson at King's Mountain. Without that victory the story of America could have been different.

RACE TO CHOTA

(Many legendary stories are told of Nancy Ward; the one related here seems to be the most popular and universally known.)

Brian Ward, an English trader, was traveling through the Overhill Country about the time the Cherokees captured Fort Loudoun. Great celebrations over their victory were in progress in all the Indian towns and villages. A party of warriors captured Ward and brought him before the Chiefs and accused him of being an English spy. They demanded that he should run the gauntlet of almost certain death. Two rows of warriors would face each other; the victim would be forced to run through the corridor, trying to avoid the flaying war clubs and spears slashing at him. Just as they were about to begin this sport, Nancy Ward appeared on the scene. Using her power as *Ghighau* and wearing the emblem of her authority, the swan's wing, she halted proceedings and suggested a race to Chota, some twenty miles distance, between young Ward and the Cherokee braves. This appealed to their sport-loving nature, and the Chief decreed that the race would be run three suns hence. Ward would be given about a half-mile start. If Ward could reach Chota, Town of Sanctuary, safely, his life would be spared. The stakes were high. The warrior returning with Ward's scalp would be made a chief.

The sun of the third day arose on a large crowd gathered for the event. They were perched on hills along the route for a panoramic view of the race to Chota. Nancy and her Uncle Attakullakulla had coached Ward the best they could on how to make the race. Nancy had gone on to Chota to be near at the finish.

The warriors are all set—Ward has reached his starting point—the signal is given—the race is on. Ward, young and fleet of foot, strong of heart, spurred on by the yelling hordes behind him, splurges ahead—he goes ten miles without breaking his stride—he begins to hear the yells of the warriors gaining on him—nearer and nearer they come—Ward goes another five miles—his strength is now beginning to ebb—his steps are getting weaker and shorter. He glances over his shoulder and sees the nearest braves closing the distance fast. With a renewed urge he races on—another agonizing mile—two miles—his stride is weakening fast—another look and he sees only two or three braves left in the race: one is ahead of the others and still gaining on him. Can he keep going? His breath is coming in sobs—dimly he sees the people ahead—Chota—only yards to safety. He hears the gasping breath of the last remaining warrior close behind—and those yards seem like miles. Yard after yard he struggles, his body weaving, every gasp an agony. He can almost feel the hot breath of the brave on his back as he staggers, stumbles and falls—just feet away from the line and safety of Chota. The victorious warrior raises his tomahawk to strike, a look of triumph on his face, when suddenly, from out of the throng of witnesses, a woman rushes in. She shoves the exhausted warrior aside and half carries, half drags, the unconscious Ward across the victory line to Chota and safety.

For days Ward was sick with a fever brought on by the extreme exertion of the race. Nancy Ward, his savior, administered herbs and healing potions. He responded and recovered. Brian Ward won his life and Nancy his love. They were married Indian fashion and lived many years together. Ward was accepted by the Cherokees after his union with Nancy.

HISTORIC LONG ISLAND

1. The Island
2. Island Flats and Fort
   Patrick Henry (beyond the ridge)
3. Bay's Mountain
4. Tilthammer Shoals
5. Tilthammer Rock
6. Indian War Path
7. Sluice of Holston River

This picture and legend taken from *Historical Sketches of Holston Valley* by Thomas W. Preston, used by permission of the family.

LONG ISLAND

This beloved Long Island was a sacred sanctuary to the memory of the Cherokee. The flames of many council fires had lighted its horizon as war and peace pacts were sealed. It was a neutral ground where the Cherokee met the Chiefs of the north, east, and west, to council and smoke the pipe of friendship. Then came the desecration by white man; first Fort Robinson, built by Colonel Byrd in 1760, the greedy covetousness of the 1770's that finally pushed the Indian off. The constant encroachment of the white man on Indian land gave the Red man cause for retaliation. Long Island was one of the last pieces of land ceded by the Cherokees. We reprint the oration delivered by "The Tassel" as paraphrased in *William Tatham, Wataugan* by Williams. This oration was made at the Long Island Treaty, 1777.

SPEECH

"You say: Why do not the Indians till the ground and live as we do? May we not, with equal propriety, ask why the white people do not hunt and live as we do? You profess to think it no injustice to warn us not to kill our deer and other game from the mere love of waste; but it is very criminal in our young men if they chance to kill a cow or a hog for their sustenance when they happen to be in your lands. We wish, however, to be at peace with you, and to do as we would be done by. We do not quarrel with you for killing an occasional buffalo, bear or deer on our lands when you need one to eat; but you go much farther; your people hunt to gain a livelihood by it; they kill all our game; our young men resent the injury, and it is followed by bloodshed and war.

"This is not a mere affected injury; it is a grievance which we equitably complain of, and it demands a permanent redress.

"The Great God of Nature has placed us in different situations. It is true that he has endowed you with many superior advantages; but he has not created us to be your slaves. *We are a separate people!* He has given each their lands, under distinct considerations and circumstances; he has stocked yours with cows, ours with buffalo; yours with hog, ours with bear; yours with sheep, ours with deer. He has indeed given you an advantage in this, that your cattle are tame and domestic while ours are wild, and demand not only a larger space for range but art to hunt and kill them; they are, nevertheless, as much our property as other animals are yours, and ought not to be taken away without our consent, or for something equivalent."

9

D. BOON CILLED
A BAR 1760

Daniel Boone, noted pioneer trailblazer, was about 26 years old when he first ventured from his Yadkin Home in North Carolina, across the mountains in search of new hunting grounds. The first indication of his presence in the Overmountain Country was an inscription found on a tree some six miles north of the present Johnson City, Tennessee, just off the Kingsport Road. The tree was blown down during a storm about 1920. A Boone Trail Marker, erected by the State D.A.R., indicates the location.

The picture at left is a copy of an actual photograph of the tree. The original hangs in the lobby of the Washington County Courthouse, Jonesborough, Tennessee. Below is the artist's conception of Boone carving the inscription after shooting the "bar."

BOONE WATERFALL

These two pictures of the Boone Waterfall show how the bed of the stream could change over a period of years. The view at the top was taken around the turn of the century, and hangs in the lobby of the Washington County Court House; the scene at the bottom was taken in 1957. The waterfall is on Boones Creek, just down the hill from Boones Creek High School.

LEGEND

One of the favorite hand-me-down stories of upper East Tennessee is the one of Daniel Boone hiding under this waterfall from the Indians. The occasion was during one of his frequent hunting trips in the 1760's.

Boone, while out hunting, discovered Indians on his trail. Not wanting to lead them to his camp, he headed in a fast trot to a nearby waterfall that he knew about. Barely had he concealed himself under its ledge and curtain of water, when the Indians arrived fast on his tracks. Not seeing Boone and finding no tracks leading away from the creek, the frightened and superstitious Indians hastily fled the vicinity, believing that Boone had been turned into an invisible spirit and was hovering around.

Photo by Jimmy Ellis

THE LONG HUNTERS

The Long Hunter period of the 1760's was one of adventure and exploration. During this ten-year period, the frontier farmers, who were hunters by necessity, used the meat for food and pelts for trade. They traveled far and deep into the mountain wilderness. Land companies were soon employing these hunters as guides for their surveyors, in plotting new country for settlement or speculation. Daniel Boone was employed by the Henderson Company on more than one occasion for such work.

Boone and other hunters, returning home from these early hunting trips into the Overmountain country, soon spread the news of the wonderful land across the hills. They told of the thundering herds of buffalo, furred animals of all kinds, forests full of deer. Many adventuresome young hunters were soon packing their traps and provisions and heading for this uninhabited hunter's paradise. They would remain on these hunts for a year or more and, because of their long stay or absence, were called *Long Hunters*. Rifles, hunting knives, traps, blankets, dogs and a pack horse made up their equipment. These hunters lived and hunted much in the same manner as the Indians. Their customary dress was the long hunting shirt, leather breeches and leggins, moccasins and a cap made from a small animal's skin. The pelts brought back were used for barter and trade. A good hunter could make more on a year's hunt than he could farming.

One of the early groups was headed by Elisha Walden in 1761. On their first trip they explored as far as the Carter's Valley country, and on a later trip (1763) went deeper into the Cumberland territory. Ramsey says there were fifteen in the party. Williams lists some of the names as follows: Henry Skaggs, William and John Blevins, Charles Cox, William Pittman, William Harilson and one Newman. Walden's Ridge and Walden's Creek were named for Elisha Walden. Another party of four—Benjamin Cutbird, John Stewart, John Baker and James Ward—traveled all the way to the Mississippi River in 1766. Williams' *Dawn of Tennessee Valley* records many well known personalities and groups that traveled and hunted in the new country during this *Long Hunter* decade. The reports brought back by these hunters did much to stimulate the flow of pioneers who were soon to cross the mountains.

WILLIAM BEAN

Photo by Jimmy Ellis

Captain William Bean moved his family into the new country early in the year 1769. He built a cabin on a point between Boones Creek and Watauga River, just above the mouth of the creek. Ramsey says that Bean had camped here while hunting with Boone and was familiar with the country. The cabin was hidden from the river by high rock formations and thick growth. Water was plentiful from the creek and springs.

William and Lidia Bean are credited with being the first permanent settlers in the new country, now the State of Tennessee. It was here that Russell Bean, first white child of Tennessee, was born. William Bean was acquainted with military training of the time and held a Captain's rank in the Virginia Militia. He was a born leader and a man of means. His name appears frequently in the organization and affairs of the Watauga Association and Washington County. Many relatives and friends from Virginia soon settled around Bean. Among them were John and George Russell, brothers of Mrs. Bean, William Jr., and John Bean, William's sons and others.

The marker pictured above was placed on the original site by the Sevier Chapter of the D.A.R. The stone pillow holding the marker was constructed from rock out of the original Bean cabin chimney. This picture was made before the waters of Boone Lake covered the original site. Below is the artist's conception of the Bean cabin as it might have been in the year 1769.

THE PIONEER SETTLERS

Things were rather quiet and uneventful during the early days of the Watauga, Holston and Nolichucky settlements. Little trouble was had with the Cherokees, who legally claimed the land the settlers occupied. The reason for this was that the Cherokees were in no condition to protest these settlements by force, for in 1769 they undertook to conquer the Chickasaws, their one-time ally who lived in West Tennessee. The Chickasaws met and defeated them, plundered their camps, killed about half their warriors and chased the rest of them home. After this sore defeat the Cherokees were so busy licking their wounds, and mourning their dead, that they had lost their sting and became militarily impotent. By the time they had recovered from this terrible defeat, the Overmountain settlements had their roots in the ground and could adequately defend themselves.

At this time a constant stream of people was crossing the mountains from Virginia and the Carolinas—some fleeing the King's wrath, some seeking freedom and a place to make a home. Others were fleeing justice. The narrow buffalo trails used by the early pioneers allowed travel only by horse or foot. On the crude racks of the pack horses they could bring only such things as the iron parts of hoes, axes, plows, some cooking utensils, seed for planting and a few extra pieces of clothing. The long trail was arduous and demanded great physical endurance and stability. The men walked, carrying their guns. Women with small babies rode horseback, and older children helped drive the cows and other domestic animals.

THE CABIN HOME

When a suitable place had been located, they would clear the land and build a one-room log cabin with a lean-to at the back. Cracks were chinked with mud. At first cabins had only a dirt floor, later a puncheon floor made by fitting split logs together with the flat side up. More industrious pioneers would laboriously hand-saw thick boards for the floor. Roofs were made of broad split boards held in place by long poles fastened down with wooden pegs. The large fireplace was made of rock. It served as the family cook stove, as well as providing heat and light. The chimney was made of rock or small poles laid box fashion and chinked and lined with mud. Beds were made of small trees hewn and fitted together. Ticking stuffed with grass or straw served as a mattress. Tables and stools were made of split logs or clapboards with peg legs. Deer antlers and wooden pegs along the wall furnished hangers for clothing, tools and guns.

THE WOMEN

The women, strong and self-reliant, milked, gardened, cooked, carded the wool, spun the yarn, and wove the thread into cloth on hand-made looms. They used nature's dyes for colors. A hopper in the yard held ashes for making soap. This is the way of life that the Beans, Robertsons, Browns, Carters, Boones, Crocketts and the host of other pioneers knew, as they carved their homes and communities out of the rugged wilderness of the Overmountain country.

IB 15
FIRST SETTLERS

About 1½ miles west and north of here, in Carter's Valley, Joseph Kinkead and John Long, first known pioneers to what later became Hawkins County, settled in 1769-70. The valley is named for Col. John Carter, who first settled here and later became a prominent member of the Watauga Settlement.

TENNESSEE HISTORICAL COMMISSION

JAMES ROBERTSON

Early in 1770, James Robertson left his home in Wake County, North Carolina, and crossed the mountains. He followed the trail of Boone and other *Long Hunters* through the present towns of Boone, North Carolina, Zionville, Trade, Shouns and down Roan Creek into the valleys of the Watauga River. Ramsey says he found one John Honeycutt living in a hut located near where Roan Creek empties into Watauga River. Honeycutt furnished him food and accommodation and most likely a description of the country thereabout. Robertson located on the "Old Fields" lands, formerly tilled by the Indians and now the present townsite of Elizabethton. This rich valley land was especially adaptable to his taste. He cleared the land and planted corn. While the corn was making a crop, Robertson built a log cabin and corn crib. We can assume that Robertson scouted the surrounding area, since he had promised neighbors and kinsmen back home that he would find locations for them. It is very likely that he saw the Beans on this first trip.

LOST ON THE MOUNTAIN

On Robertson's return trip he lost his way during a heavy rainstorm. He tried blazing his way and found himself going in a big circle. When he reached terrain his horse could not navigate, he unbridled the animal; and for fourteen days he wandered, lost and desperate. His gunpowder was wet and useless for shooting any game for food. Robertson subsisted on berries and roots. The story is told that on one occasion he watched two male bears fighting, fearful that they might attack him in his weakened condition. With no weapon or means of protecting himself, he spent many uneasy nights. Time after time he thought the end had come. Two weeks after he became lost, two hunters found him by accident and gave him food and a horse to get back to the settlement. Except for this chance discovery, James Robertson might have died of starvation and exposure, leaving Tennessee robbed by fate of one of her most colorful pioneers.

OVER THE MOUNTAINS

James Robertson moved his family into the new country sometime during the year 1771. The exact date of his departure seems cloudy. Some historians say that it was before the Battle of Alamance, others say afterward. Some say there were sixteen in the party. Others say there were sixteen families. We do know that during this year Robertson and his group headed west, trying to leave lands under British control. Williams lists (as members of the party that came over the mountains) three brothers of James Robertson—Charles, Mark, and Jonathan—and Mrs. Robertson's brother, William Reeves. The Robertson settlement along the Watauga was the nucleus of the Watauga Association that became Washington District, Washington County, State of Franklin and the State of Tennessee. James Robertson was a predominating personality, respected by his fellowman. His leadership held the infant community together.

Other settlers who were to play important roles in events to come included: Henry Lyle, Joshua Houghton, Mathew Talbot, Joseph Tipton, James Denton, Isham Irby, Edward Lucas, Henry Rice, Joseph Duncan, John Jones, Isaac Ruddle, Andrew Greer, Baptist and John McNabb, Henry Massengill, George Reeves, Jesse Benton, George Gray, Michael Hyder, John Williams, Archibald Taylor, David Hughes, John Cox, Richard White, William Blevins, the Rheas, the Laws, the Longs, the Kincaids and a host of others. Most of these arrived about the same time as James Robertson, or soon after, and were part of the Watauga Association and the original Overmountain Men.

OVERMOUNTAIN SETTLEMENTS

The first permanent settlements during the early 1770's and their leaders were: the Watauga, James Robertson; Carter's Valley, John Carter; Holston, Evan Shelby, Sr.; Nolichucky, Jacob Brown.

THE WATAUGA was the first of these settlements. The pioneers, finding the country good, cleared sections in the valley of the river and along the tributary streams. The various land grants name many of these streams: Doe River, Stoney Creek, Roan Creek, Buffalo and Gap Creek, Sinking Creek, Brush Creek, Boones Creek and others.

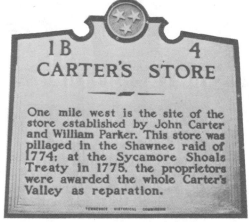

CARTER'S VALLEY was named for John Carter, pioneer trader and storekeeper, who set up a store in that section to catch the Indian pelt trade. Carter's partner was Joseph Parker. The store proved so popular with the Indians that the traders living in the Overhill Towns complained that this store hurt their own business. The Chiefs warned Carter and Parker to move out. They did not obey and the store was soon looted by Indians. Carter moved to Watauga, Parker soon abandoned the store and returned to Virginia. John Carter was a member of the Carter and Trent firm located on the James River in Virginia. They maintained several establishments for barter and trade.

SHELBY'S FORT was a stockade erected around his trading post for protection. This store was a gathering post for the area and numbered among its customers Daniel Boone, Valentine Sevier (father of John), James Robertson, William Williams, William Bean, John Cox and many other well known pioneers. It was at Shelby's Fort that the various companies mustered for the Lord Dunsmore Campaign in 1774.

Evan Shelby, Sr., and wife, Lelita Cox, were the parents of seven children: Isaac, Susannah, John, James, Evan Jr., Moses and Catherine.

The family moved to the Holston country during 1771-1772 and settled at Sappling Grove, changed later to King's Meadows. The estate had some 1250 acres covering much of the present town of Bristol, Tennessee. Few campaigns are mentioned during the 1770 decade that do not include a Shelby.

The marker at right was erected by the Volunteer Chapter of the D.A.R., Bristol, Tennessee, on the original site of the Fort between Locust and Anderson Streets.

THE NOLICHUCKY settlement was started in 1771 by Jacob Brown and a group of Regulators from North Carolina. Williams suggests that Wm. Closin (Clawson) and William Clark were two of these pioneers. Clark was later a representative to the North Carolina Assembly.

JACOB BROWN'S SETTLEMENT

The first permanent settler in the Nolichucky Valley was Jacob Brown, who arrived with his party in 1771. He set up a store and blacksmith shop on the north bank of the river, about midway between the present towns of Erwin and Jonesborough.

Brown leased a large tract of land from the Indians for the price of ten shillings and a few trade goods. He then leased this land to settlers. In 1775 he secured deeds to the land from the Transylvania Company, which had purchased the territory from the Indians. The Cherokee were always friendly toward Brown; and the story is told that Brown and a Chief were camping together one night, when the Chief dreamed Brown had given him a dog and gun. Indian custom said that such a dream must be fulfilled, so Brown parted with the items. Later, Brown contrived a dream in which the Indian Chief had given him a large tract of land, and when told about it the Chief reluctantly agreed but said, "No more dreams."

The oak tree, under which Brown leased two tracts of land from the Indians. (Tree destroyed by storm, May 10, 1958.) Photo by Clifford Maxwell

The rich Nolichucky River bottoms afforded good farming and grazing; and many settlers obtained leases from Brown, whose grants covered much of the finest lands of the present Washington, Greene and Unicoi counties.

Jacob Brown was a member of the Watauga Association and likely the fifth commissioner. Prominent in all the affairs of the new country, he fought under John Sevier in many Indian campaigns, and was an officer in the Battle of King's Mountain.

Brown's descendants say that he was accidentally killed while crossing the river in a boat near his home, when the paddle hit his gun and set off the charge into his body. However, historians say he was killed while hunting on Spivey in Unicoi County. Many direct descendants live in Tennessee.

TRYON'S PALACE

The restoration of Tryon's Palace, the first Capitol seat of North Carolina, was made possible by the late Mrs. Maude Moore Latham of Greensboro, North Carolina. The trust fund provided by Mrs. Latham, with the appropriation of a large amount from the General Assembly, permitted the restoration of this magnificent building. The picture at the bottom of the page is a recent photo of the restored palace in New Bern, North Carolina.

Tryon Palace was so called for William Tryon, appointed Royal Governor of North Carolina in 1765. He came into office almost with the Stamp Act, and was associated with the noted English law and levy. About a year after taking office, Tryon asked the Assembly to vote 15,000 pounds for the purpose of erecting a Capitol building that would also serve as a home for the Governor. This building was to be located in New Bern, North Carolina. Construction began in 1767, and the Tryon family moved in during 1770 even before completion. This extra tax burden for the sumptuous building, added to the already overtaxed inland farmers, fanned into flame an already burning resentment. The poor man had to pay the same amount of taxes as the rich coastal planter. The heavier populated, wealthy counties of the sea coast controlled the Assembly, since they had five representatives per county. The counties in the central and western section, with less population and very small income, had only two representatives from each county and were out-voted in all legislative matters. Thus, the Palace became a sort of symbol of the unequal taxes and representation between the western and eastern settlements.

Governor Tryon's residence in the Palace was short-lived as he was moved on to New York soon after the *Battle of Alamance*. Josiah Martin was appointed in his place. Governor Martin tried to administer the affairs of the State in a hard-fisted form of authority that made matters worse. His plan of rule or ruin, trying to enforce the laws of the English Parliament and collect the taxes, brought a showdown in May, 1775. The Assembly, anxious to cooperate with the provincial congress, defied his order and met to elect delegates. Martin tried to dissolve the Assembly. Failing this, he fled for safety to a British war vessel anchored nearby. (The Royal Government having broken down, the Provincial Government promptly moved into the vacated Capitol Palace.) Thus Tryon's Palace became the first permanent Capitol of Independent North Carolina, and so remained until 1794.

Tryon's Palace was also the seat of Government of the Territory, now the state of Tennessee, from 1777 until 1790 when the Overmountain country became *The Territory of the United States, South of the Ohio River*. William Blount was the Territorial Governor. The one exception was a four year period, 1784-1788, during the existence of *The State of Franklin*.

Governor Tryon and the Regulators in one of their Stormy Meetings.

THE REGULATOR BATTLE GROUND

The above drawing of the Battlefield was made about 1853. This picture and the etchings of Governor Tryon and the Regulators are used through courtesy of the State Department of Archives and History, Raleigh, North Carolina.

THE REGULATORS

The Regulators were Carolina frontiersmen who rose up against the corrupt practices of government officials. Their cause was just, and the complaints serious. They had very little say-so in government matters. To correct the situation, they asked local officials to meet with them, discuss and regulate the legal fees, tax levies and other grievances. The officials refused.

The North Carolina Governor was appointed by the Crown; and he in turn appointed the sheriff from the freeholders, according to who paid the highest rent for the job. The other county officials were appointed by the Governor and his council. When the western counties were organized, sheriffs, lawyers, clerks and other appointed officials swooped down on the defenseless settlers who were unable to protect themselves. Scarcity of money and ignorance of the law made them easy game for the crooked officials, who collected the high fees and pocketed half the money.

The Regulator movement was a result of such conditions; but having no intelligent leadership, they became a mob. Receiving no satisfaction from the courts, they broke them up and destroyed the records, abused attorneys and judges. The result, Governor Tryon called out the Militia.

BATTLE OF ALAMANCE
MAY 16, 1771

A. GOV. TYRON AND PROVINCIAL CAMP
B. FIRST POSITION
C. SECOND POSITION
D. REGULATOR CAMP AND BATTLE
E REGULATORS IN FLIGHT

The Battle of Alamance lasted two hours. The leaderless Regulators were no match for Governor Tryon's trained militia. Nine were killed on each side and many were wounded. The rebellion was crushed. Many took the oath, others fled across the mountains. It was a misguided battle, but the first shots of freedom had been fired.

WATAUGA ASSEMBLY

The first free government in America, independent of any other state or colony, was established and administered by the Overmountain Men. These first settlers of the Watauga and Nolichucky Valleys thought they had built their cabins within the boundaries of Virginia, but learned they had settled on lands claimed by the Lord Granville family, part of the Royal Government of North Carolina. Many of them, having recently fled the oppression of the English domination in the Carolinas, wanted no further part of it. Seeing that there was no law or order of organized form, they proceeded to set up their own judicial and civil body. Their *Articles*, simple but adequate, were fashioned after the Virginia laws. Haywood says in his *History of Tennessee*, "In May 1772 the Settlement of Watauga, being without government, formed a *Written Association of Articles* for their conduct. They appointed five commissioners, a majority of whom was to decide all matters of controversy, and to govern and direct for the common good of all the people." This five-man commission was made up of John Carter, James Robertson, Charles Robertson, Zachariah Isbell, the fifth not certain. Williams suggests the fifth member might have been Jacob Brown. The Commission settled questions of debt, probated wills, recorded deeds, determined rights of property, issued marriage licenses and hanged horse thieves. This government was entered into by the consent of all the people and continued nearly six years. Unfortunately, the *Written Articles* have not been preserved.

The formation of this government was a fundamental necessity, created solely to provide self protection and legal needs of a people far away from any form of authority. Their government, as well as their homes, furniture and other essentials, was handmade to fit the need of a people seeking a way of life.

SETTLERS LEASE LAND FROM INDIANS

James Robertson and John Bean leave for the Overhill Towns to treat with the Indians for a lease arrangement to the Watauga lands. (Scene from the Erwin Drama *Overmountain Men*.)

The Wataugans, finding they were not in Virginia as thought, faced a serious problem of getting title to the lands they had settled. The lands they had cleared and built cabins on were part of the Lord Granville grant and under jurisdiction of the English authority of North Carolina. The Granville land office had closed, and the North Carolina government had no authority to issue grants on the Granville tract. Also, the British Government had issued a proclamation forbidding further settlement in the Overmountain country, and the Cherokees had a prior claim. Action was needed, so a meeting of the family heads was called to discuss the situation. A lease plan with the Indians, who claimed the land, was worked out. James Robertson and John Bean were delegated to visit the Indian towns and treat with the Chiefs. Their mission was successful and a ten-year lease was arranged. A big celebration with the Indians was planned at Sycamore Shoals, near the present town of Elizabethton, Tennessee.

HISTORIC TREES

Trees have always played an important role in the course of history. They have served as landmarks, period markers, the sanctuary for the early church, the justice hall of the court, the execution chamber for criminals, and the romantic shade for young love. Many prominent trees are mentioned in the history of the Overmountain people. Among them: The Boone Bar Tree, The Brown Trade Tree, The Spencer Tree, the Oak where Blount held court, and others.

To the right is the historic Sycamore Tree in Elizabethton under which the first court of the Watauga Association was held in 1772. The tree stands near the old covered bridge.

KILLING INDIAN ENDANGERS LEASE

After the Cherokees leased the lands to the Watauga settlers, a great race was planned. People gathered from all over the territory for the celebration. As friendly relations existed between Indians and settlers, many Indians were present. During the day, William Crabtree from Wolf Hills watched for an opportunity to start trouble. Late in the afternoon, from cover, he shot and killed an Indian named "Cherokee Billie." This infamous act frightened the Indians, who hastily left for their homes.

The Wataugans were alarmed at this needless killing. They knew the whole settlement would suffer should the Indians seek revenge. James Robertson was again called on to make the long trip to the Overhill towns in an attempt to pacify the Cherokees. Accompanied by William Falling, he visited the Chiefs at Chota. In the big council meet, Robinson explained that his people were horrified at such a deed and that the crime was committed by an outsider. He promised that the culprit would be punished when caught. The Indians, pleased at the white man's condescension and loss of face, accepted the apology. Many of the young braves and clan members of Cherokee Billie's family angrily demanded revenge, but the older chiefs, wanting to keep peace, were responsible for averting a bad situation.

BERNIE
ANDREWS

TRANSYLVANIA AGREEMENT

IA 52

TRANSYLVANIA PURCHASE

In this valley, March 17, 1775, the Transylvania Company, led by Richard Henderson, John Williams, Thomas and Nathaniel Hart, bought from the Cherokee, led by Chief Oconostota, all lands between the Kentucky and Cumberland Rivers. Over 20 million acres sold for 2000 Pounds Sterling and goods worth 8000 Pounds.

The biggest private or corporate real estate transaction in United States history took place at Sycamore Shoals, March 17, 1775. A consideration of silver and goods, amounting to about ten thousand pounds, was given the Cherokees for this vast tract of land. Twelve hundred Indians are said to have attended.

Desirous of establishing colonies on the Kentucky and Cumberland Rivers, Richard Henderson made arrangements with the Indians to purchase the lands between the Kentucky and Cumberland Rivers. A big treaty was planned at the Watauga settlement. A delegation of Indians traveled to North Carolina to see the promised goods. Their report to the towns, of the vast store of riches, was soon greatly exaggerated. The braves and their families, anticipating great wealth, began gathering in the vicinity of the treaty grounds a month before the date set. The Henderson Company arranged with the Wataugans to furnish corn and beef to feed the ingathering horde. After many days of counseling and pow-wowing, the signing ceremony took place March 17, 1775. The Watauga Association, taking advantage of the opportunity bought all the lands they had formerly leased and more. John Carter and his partner were awarded most of Carter's Valley, for losses suffered by Indian debts and the looting of their store. Jacob Brown obtained deeds to his vast Nolichucky empire.

The Cherokees signed away a vast empire to the Transylvania Company at the Sycamore Shoals Treaty, March 17, 1775. During the weeks of discussions between Colonel Richard Henderson and the Chiefs, many sessions of pipe smoking took place. On one of these ocassions Dragging Canoe disrupted the meeting with his dramatic speech opposing the transaction. Attakullakulla, Oconostota, Willanaugh, Onistositah and other leading Chiefs overcame the opposition aroused by this outburst and the deeds were signed. As the grants were being passed, Dragging Canoe, with a dramatic gesture, voiced a prophetic warning — ''You have bought a fair land, but there is a cloud hanging over it. You will find its settlement dark and bloody'' — a prophecy that events in the years ahead proved all too true for both redman and white man.

THE CHIEF SPEAKS

The Sycamore Shoals Treaty discussions lasted several days. Maneuvers were attempted on both sides to get the advantage. After each pow-wow, the Chiefs would withdraw for their customary Council before conceding a point. During one of the meetings between Colonel Henderson and the Chiefs, Dragging Canoe, who was against ceding lands to the whites, entered the Chiefs circle and entreated them in a pathetic speech to stop the treaty. (Following is a reprint of the paraphrased version from Williams' *Dawn of Tennessee Valley*, as taken from Haywood's *History of Tennessee* published in 1823.)

THE ORATION

''The orator began with the very flourishing state in which his nation once was, and spoke of the encroachments of the white people, from time to time, upon the retiring and expiring nations of Indians who left their homes and seats of their ancestors to gratify the insatiable desire of the white people for more land. Whose nations had melted away in their presence like balls of snow before the sun, and had scarcely left their names behind, except as imperfectly recorded by their enemies and destroyers. It was once hoped that they would not be willing to travel beyond the mountains, so far from the ocean, on which their commerce was carried on, and their connections maintained with the nations of Europe. But now that fallacious hope had vanished; they had passed the mountains, and settled upon Cherokee lands, and wished to have their usurpations sanctioned by the confirmation of treaty. When that should be obtained the same encroaching spirit would lead them upon other lands of the Cherokees. New cessions would be applied for, and finally the country which the Cherokees and their forefathers had so long occupied would be called for: and a small remnant which may then exist of this nation, once so great and formidable, will be compelled to seek a retreat in some far distant wilderness, there to dwell but a short space of time before they would again behold the advancing banners of the same greedy hosts; who, not being able to point out any further retreat for the miserable Cherokees, would then proclaim the extinction of the whole race. He ended with a strong exhortation to run all risks and to incur all consequences, rather than submit to any further dilacerations of their territory. But he did not prevail and the cession was made.''

The Chiefs disregarded Dragging Canoe's plea and the deeds were signed. On the day of the ceremonial signing, Dragging Canoe, pointing westward, said, ''A dark cloud hangs over that land known as *The Bloody Grounds*.'' Coming events were to prove this prophecy all too true.

The Indian's oration loses much of its natural beauty and expression during the process of interpretation. Its force and dignity cannot be adequately portrayed by the English words necessarily used in the translation. Many of the Cherokee Chiefs were great orators and could deliver flowery and impassioned speeches on occasion.

SETTLEMENT GROWS

The Watauga Association opened a land office the 1st of April 1775, to handle the patents on the lands along the Watauga, New and Holston Rivers that had been purchased from the Indians at the Transylvania Treaty. Charles Robertson was named trustee, James Smith, clerk, and William Bailey Smith, surveyor. Grant deeds were issued to the Watauga Association members, and other tracts sold to newcomers. One such grant was made to Robert Young for lands now occupied by the Veterans Administration, Johnson City, Tennessee. Below is a picture of the restored cabin as it stands today on the original site.

Photo by Clifford Maxwell

ISAAC LINCOLN

Another patent was made to Isaac Lincoln, great uncle of Abraham Lincoln, Civil War President. This grant, dated November 18th, 1775, was for a section of land lying on the east side of Doe River, near the James Robertson tract. Isaac Lincoln later obtained most of the James Robertson holdings, after Robertson moved to the Big Creek settlement. Isaac Lincoln and Daniel Boone were related.

In Abraham Lincoln's autobiographical sketch, he wrote that before his father was of age he passed one year as hired hand with his Uncle Isaac on Watauga, a branch of the Holston River. The year was 1798. Abraham's father, Thomas Lincoln, lived alone that year in a log cabin at the foot of Lynn Mountain. It is said that Thomas did not get along very well with his uncle, who was hard to please. Otherwise he might have settled on the Watauga instead of returning to Kentucky. Isaac Lincoln and his wife are buried in the vicinity of Elizabethton, Tennessee. Three branches of the Lincoln family settled in Greene County.

Headstone of Isaac Lincoln's grave located in a field some four miles up Watauga River from Elizabethton, Tennessee.

DANIEL BOONE MOVES TO KENTUCKY 1775

The above reproduction of the G.C. Bingham painting of "Daniel Boone Escorting a Band of Pioneers into the Western Country" is used through the courtesy of Washington University of St. Louis, Missouri.

THE REVOLUTION REACHES WATAUGA

New arrivals brought word of the happenings back east, where the spirit of independence was at high pitch. The Overmountain people would naturally join the Revolution movement in their desire to be rid of British rule and also obtain clear titles to their lands, which were a part of the Lord Granville Grant.

The settlers in the Long Island area had taken the name *Pendleton District* and successfully petitioned the Virginia Assembly to be made part of that Colony. Following suit, the Wataugans, now *Washington District*, sent a similar petition to Virginia; but this Assembly, conscious of the North Carolina claim, turned them down. Discouraged by the Virginia act, the Watauga Settlers met and voted to apply for adoption into provincial North Carolina. A petition, written by William Tatham, July 5, 1776 and signed by over 100 heads of families, was sent to this Assembly.

Meanwhile, in England, plans were underway to subdue the unruly colonists. They planned to attack the southern settlements first, as many Tories (British sympathizers) were settled in the South and the Cherokee Indians, English allies, were well situated at the back door of the colonies. English agents already living in the Overhill towns were busy stirring up ill will toward the Americans. The British forces under Colonel Clinton and Admiral Parker sailed for America. In April more than sixty horse loads of lead and powder were delivered to the Cherokees by Henry Stuart, deputy English agent. Cameron and Stuart began a definite campaign to force the settlers of the Nolichucky and Watauga Valleys to move. In May, the Chiefs, meeting in council, stated that any claim by these settlers that the Cherokees had sold these lands to them was false and they desired them to move. Letters were exchanged and Isaac Thomas, white trader, was the bearer. These communications caused much uneasiness. The Wataugans, allowed only twenty days to make this removal, were determined to protect their possessions. They began immediately to strengthen their forts and build others. In the meantime, a general campaign against the Indians was being organized by the Virginia and North Carolina authorities, but the Cherokees struck before much was done.

EARLY FORTS

With the threat of war getting closer, the Overmountain pioneers speedily pushed the building of new forts and strengthening those already started.

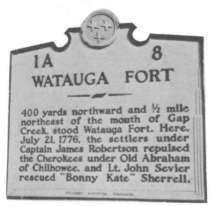

WATAUGA FORT, also named Fort Caswell, was located near the present town of Elizabethton. No description of the Fort is available other than it was a group of cabins arranged in rectangular shape, connected by stockade walls of sharp pointed poles set firmly in the ground, and within reach of its guns was a courthouse and jail.

EATON'S STATION, sometimes called *Heaton's Station*, was built by Amos Eaton near Reedy Creek about five miles east of the present city of Kingsport. Here the various companies of Militia assembled for the Battle of Island Flats.

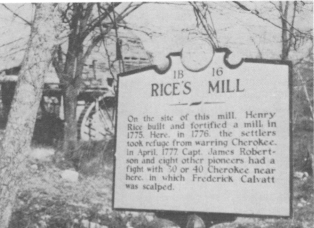

PATTERSON'S MILL and RICE'S MILL were two of the Carter's Valley forts that housed settlers during the Raven's raid. These forts were located on sites west of the present town of Church Hill.

FORT PATRICK HENRY, erected 1776, was located about 200 yards below the upper end of Long Island. It was approximately 100 yards square with stockade walls on three sides. On the fourth and river side, the deep water and steep bank served as a safe barrier. Bastions were located at each corner. A building in the center held military stores and served as official headquarters. From here Colonel Christian launched his campaign against the Indians.

SHELBY'S FORT was located in the environs of the present city of Bristol, Tennessee.

ANOTHER SHELBY'S FORT was on Beaver Creek, two miles south of the Virginia line.

JACOB WOMACK'S FORT was erected on the south side of the Holston, about two miles east of the present town of Bluff City. Jacob Womack, a descendant of the Duke of Albemarle family, fought with John Sevier on many campaigns. He was a member of the Watauga Association.

JOHN SHELBY'S FORT was on the Holston, about five miles east of the present Bluff City.

KING'S MILL STATION was at the mouth of Reedy Creek, built by James King.

FORT LEE was located on Limestone Creek near Nolichucky. It was destroyed by Indians during the 1776 raid.

FORT WILLIAMS was in the Telford community, its exact location unknown.

DRAGGING CANOE PLANS WAR

Dragging Canoe, sullen and angry, had returned home from the Sycamore Shoals Treaty determined to run the whites off Indian lands. He accused Attakullakulla, his father, Oconostota, and the other aging Chiefs of being too old to hunt or fight, therefore willing to give lands of their fathers away. The young Chief, tall of figure, face pock-marked from smallpox, and dominant in character, practically took over the War Chief's role. He went up and down the nation beating the war drum and stirring up resentment toward the encroaching whites. In this he was aided and abetted by Cameron, the English agent living in the Nation. This turn of events fitted into the British strategy of inciting the Cherokees to attack the settlers when the time came. Thus conditions were moving swiftly toward open hostilities.

While this fateful course of events was in progress, there turned up in the Cherokee towns during May 1776, Indian representatives from the northern tribes of the Mohawks, Ottawas, Nancutas, Delawares, Shawnees, and others of the Iroquois Confederation. They came with the purpose of drawing the Cherokee and other Indian Nations into the overall British campaign against the Americans. The plan was for the English troops to attack the colonies from the sea side and the Indians to fight the settlers from the rear.

These talks further aroused the disgruntled Chiefs who were ready to take up the war hatchet. Ammunition had arrived from Florida and the plan of attack was prepared. The immediate objective of the Cherokees was to run the settlers out of the Nolichucky, Watauga, Long Island and Carter's Valley settlements. Old Abram would take about 300 warriors and attack the Nolichucky and Watauga people. Dragging Canoe would take another force of like number and march into the Long Island country. Raven with a small force would move into the Carter's Valley section and, after destroying that settlement, move on into the Virginia territory, killing and burning. The Indian women were busy parching corn and meal and preparing food for the march. Guns, spears, bows and arrows were put in readiness. The customary rituals were observed, especially the sacred black drink ceremony. The Cherokees were again headed for the warpath.

NANCY WARD SENDS WARNING

Nancy Ward, "Beloved Woman" of the Cherokee Council, was greatly concerned at the prospect of a war that could end in nothing but tragedy for her people and inflict needless death and suffering on her white friends. As a member of the Council, she could learn the plans of the War Chiefs and warn the settlers. She must do this secretly and by means of the white traders in her town. These traders had been told to stay in their houses during the councils. Nancy Ward outlined the plan of attack to Isaac Thomas, and arranged for his escape from the Indian nation along with William Falling, Jarrett Williams and one other. Most likely members of her clan aided in this effort, as horses were necessary in making the long trip to the settlements.

Thomas and the other traders left the Cherokee towns the night of July 8th, 1776. They arrived at the first settlement on the Nolichucky the morning of July 11th. John Sevier was in charge of constructing Fort Lee, on Limestone Creek near its junction with the Nolichucky, when Thomas arrived with the message from Nancy Ward. Sevier immediately wrote a note for Thomas to carry on to the other forts. Riders were sent out at once to warn the scattered settlers to gather inside the stockades. The alarmed people of the Nolichucky fled, leaving only about fifteen men under Sevier to defend the unfinished fort. Knowing this force insufficient, Sevier and his command fell back to the Watauga Fort.

BATTLE OF ISLAND FLATS

On reaching the Nolichucky settlements, the Indians found most of the cabins deserted. In their haste to catch up with the fleeing settlers, they did not bother the growing crops or animals left behind by the white people. Finding the unfinished Fort Lee (later Gilliespie) on Limestone Creek deserted, they destroyed it. The main force divided here. Dragging Canoe led his forces on toward Long Island, while Old Abram continued his march toward Watauga.

Warned by the message brought by Isaac Thomas, five companies of Militia assembled at Eaton's Station near Long Island. Captain James Thompson was in command. A complete report of the battle was made to Colonel William Preston by Captains James Thompson, James Shelby, William Buchanan, John Campbell, William Cocke and Thomas Madison.

The Fort command decided to meet the Cherokee force in the open, rather than wait for them in the station, thinking that the Indians might bypass the Fort and destroy their homes, crops and livestock. The two forces, about equal in number, met on Island Flats (now part of the City of Kingsport). In a fierce, hard fought battle, much of it fought in close quarters in hand-to-hand combat that lasted about an hour, the Indians were defeated. Many warriors were killed or wounded, among them Chief Dragging Canoe with a broken thigh. The Indian force fled in confusion carrying their wounded from the field.

This was the first battle of the Revolution west of the mountains, and its success gave the white man confidence that he could meet the Indians on equal terms in a fight and hold his own. To the Cherokee, this battle meant loss of faith in their prowess against the white. The depressed braves began to lose their old time confidence in their own valor.

At the Battle of Island Flats the Cherokee Warriors, under Dragging Canoe, were surprised at the unexpected attack by the Militia. The well organized resistance was not anticipated. They never fully recovered from this defeat.

SIEGE OF FORT WATAUGA

(FORT CASWELL)

The division of warriors, under Old Abram of Chilhowie, followed along the foot of the mountains toward Fort Watauga, sending small groups out on scouting trips to pick up any whites they could find. Mrs. William Bean was seized. Most of the settlers had already fled to the Fort, where about seventy-five men, according to one of the defenders, were under the command of Captain James Robertson, Colonel John Carter, Lieutenant John Sevier and other able officers.

The Cherokees made a sudden and fierce assault in the early morning of July 20th, but it was repulsed by the defense with heavy loss. The Indians laid siege to the Fort for about two weeks, keeping up occasional gunfire from a safe distance. They removed those killed and wounded to their camp on the Nolichucky.

The first attack was about daybreak. Some of the women had gone outside the Fort to milk when they saw the Indians. Their screams, while running for the gate, aroused the defenders in time to beat back the surprise attack and allow them to enter the Fort. In this party was Catherine Sherrill, a tall, athletic young woman. Seeing that the Indians had blocked her way to the Fort gate, she made a turn to reach the stockade on another side, resolved as she afterwards said, "to scale the Fort wall. The bullets and arrows came like hail; it was now leap or die, for I would not live a captive."

The hand of a man reached down to aid her over the wall. That man was John Sevier, whom she married some four years later. It was said that Catherine (Bonnie Kate) Sherrill could out-run, out-shoot and out-ride any man in the settlement.

Another heroine was Ann Robertson, sister of James. With the aid of other women she climbed the stockade wall and poured boiling water, from the wash pots, on a group of braves trying to set fire to the Fort wall. Amid the shower of bullets and arrows, Ann was wounded but stayed at her post until the scalded Indians gave up and scampered back to safety.

During the siege, bands of warriors were making raids in other directions and taking what captives they could find. Finally, in discouragement, after hearing of Dragging Canoe's defeat, Old Abram raised the siege and returned home. Shortly after the siege was lifted, Captain Evan Shelby arrived with a company of rangers to aid the people in the Fort and help drive the Indians out of the area.

INDIANS CAPTURE MRS. WILLIAM BEAN

Mrs. William Bean, the wife of an early pioneer, was captured by Indians as she was hurrying on horseback to the safety of the Watauga Fort. She was taken to their camp on the Nolichucky river, where Indian warriors threatened to kill her. The Chiefs wanted information about the settlements which they planned to attack; so they forced Samuel Moore, another white captive, to question Mrs. Bean on the location of all forts and stations, how many soldiers in each, how much powder and lead they had, and if they could be starved out.

Mrs. Bean convinced the Indians that the forts were strong enough to withstand any attack because they had large forces and plenty of food in storage. Old Abram, the Indian Chief who led the attack on the Fort, finding the settlers ready for him and not taken by the surprise attack, gave up the fight.

Mrs. Bean and Moore were taken back to the Cherokee towns in the Overhill country. Moore was cruelly tortured to death in the town of Tuskegee, while Mrs. Bean was taken to Togue where she was condemned to be burned. She had given up all hope as she was bound to the stake and the fire lighted, when suddenly Nancy Ward appeared and scattered the burning embers and stomped out the fire. After untying Mrs. Bean, Nancy turned to the subdued warriors and remarked: ''It revolts my soul that the Cherokee warrior stoops so low as to torture a squaw.'' Lydia Bean stayed with Nancy Ward and taught the Indian squaws how to make butter and cheese before she was returned to the settlement.

CHRISTIAN CAMPAIGN AGAINST CHEROKEES

The Christian campaign against the Cherokees was not one of retaliation. The authorities of Virginia, Georgia and the Carolinas had anticipated that the Cherokees, under the influence of Stuart and Cameron (English agents), might cooperate with the British forces. The Christian plan was to destroy the Indian nation, should they fight on the side of the British.

Colonel Christian met the various companies of militia at Fort Patrick Henry, September 1776. His army was all infantry except (one company of light horse) commanded by Captain John Sevier. Reverend Charles Cummings and Joseph Rhea, from the vicinity of present Abingdon, Virginia, accompanied the troops as chaplains.

As Christian's forces advanced on the Indian towns, there was a sharp debate in the councils of the Chiefs, who were divided on what course to pursue. Many of the older chiefs were for appeasement. Dragging Canoe, leader of the war faction, backed by Cameron and Stuart, was in favor of withdrawing to the Hiwassee area and fighting. The elder Chiefs prevailed, and Nathaniel Gist was sent to talk with Christian and arrange terms. A treaty was made by the older Chiefs, but Dragging Canoe and the unruly Chiefs with their followers withdrew to Chickamauga Creek, near the present city of Chattanooga. Colonel Christian was generous in his dealings with the Indians, which did not please many of his command. A big treaty signing was planned to be staged at Long Island, during 1777.

WASHINGTON COUNTY

The Battle of Island Flats and the siege of Fort Watauga by the Cherokees, British allies, made the Wataugans realize that the fight for freedom and liberty had begun in earnest. Their dream of establishing an independent colony, similar to those in the East, must wait. They felt their number too few to fight both foes. They needed to be joined with a stronger state. The North Carolina Provincial Government had taken over after the collapse of British rule, so the Overmountain people sent a petition to them asking to become a part of that State. Ramsey's *Annals of Tennessee* carries the document in its complete text with the names of the 113 signers. The date of origin, not on the document, was July 5, 1776. Across the back of the document was inscribed, "Received August 22, 1776." The Petition was written by William Tatham and signed by John Carter, Chairman.

The Petition outlines the activities of the Watauga Association past and present, why it was organized, how it functioned in legal and civil matters. It outlined the military strength and organization of the Overmountain men. It stressed the willingness of the western people to share in the glorious cause of liberty. Much of the original background of the Watauga Association can be garnered from this document.

No record has been found of any legislative action in annexing the Territory, now the state of Tennessee. It is assumed that none was deemed necessary by the Assembly, as North Carolina considered these lands part of that state. Ramsey further states that Charles Robertson, John Carter, John Hale, and John Sevier were among those attending the North Carolina Provincial Assembly that met in Halifax, North Carolina, November and December, 1776. They were appointed from the Washington District. It was at this convention that the Constitution and Bill of Rights were adopted. A proviso was inserted in the Bill of Rights (quote from Ramsey), "That it shall not be so construed as to prevent the establishment of one or more governments westward of this State by consent of the Legislature." This clause has a definite Overmountain flavor.

The house in which the North Carolina Assembly met in November 1776 at Halifax, North Carolina. Here the Constitution and Bill of Rights were adopted. Representatives from the Watauga Association attended this session. (Courtesy North Carolina State Department of Archives and History.)

The Watauga Association, which for a period assumed the name of Washington District, carried on very much in the same manner as it had been functioning since organization. It was not until the legislative session in New Bern, North Carolina, April 1777, that specific action is noted. The name Washington County was officially designated. Twenty-seven Justices were appointed. Among those twenty-seven names were many of the same men who had served in official capacity in the Watauga Association. The Justices were sworn in individually, February 1778. They formed the first Court in Washington County and its first session was held in the home of Charles Robertson, who lived in the Sinking Creek section of the present Johnson City. The second session was held in the home of Mathew Talbot.

JOHN SEVIER

John Sevier was a rugged, aggressive individual who feared neither man nor beast. A born leader, he opportunely arrived on the Watauga scene as a most dramatic episode of American history was about to unfold. The westward flow of civilization symbolized opportunity to young Sevier, who rebelled against the restrictive, conventional shackles of the eastern ruling class. His courage and prowess in politics and battle soon made him a frontier hero.

John Sevier was clerk and, afterwards, magistrate of the Watauga Association. Shrewd in knowledge of land and barter, he acquired large holdings. He came to Watauga with the rank of Captain; was a defender of Fort Watauga, 1776, and that same year accompanied Colonel Christian on his campaign against the Cherokees; represented Washington County in the North Carolina Assembly; was first clerk of the Washington County Court; Colonel of the militia and one of the main leaders in command at the Battle of King's Mountain; fought thirty-five Indian campaigns without a single defeat; the only governor of the State of Franklin; the first elected governor of Tennessee.

Sevier was a hospitable personality who enjoyed entertaining his neighbors from miles around at frequent "you all come" get-togethers. Whole beefs would be barbecued on these occasions to feed the crowd. There would be singing, dancing and horse racing.

John Sevier's father and mother, Valentine II and Joanne Goad, were parents of nine children: John, Robert, Valentine III, Joseph, Abraham, Bethenia, Elizabeth, Sophia and Polly. John, the oldest, was born in 1745. He received limited book education but learned the knack of farming, trading, and storekeeping, working with his father. Young John was five feet nine inches tall, well-knit symmetrical frame, handsome face and well-mannered. His magnetic personality attracted friends readily. John Sevier and Sarah Hawkins were married when they were about sixteen years old. They acquired a tract of land in upper Virginia and started a town that was called New Market. In 1773 John Sevier, with his father and brothers, moved to Keywood, near the Shelbys. Valentine III, already living in that settlement, and John had made several trips to the Holston and Watauga settlements before moving. In 1775, John Sevier acquired land grants in the Watauga Valley, and it has been assumed that he moved there sometime during that year. He settled in the Nolichucky Valley during 1777. Descendants of Jacob Brown say that Sevier first lived in a cabin owned by Brown on the north side of the Nolichucky.

PLUM GROVE has been marked as the Nolichucky home site of John Sevier. The Seviers are thought to have moved there during 1777-1778. Pictured on the next page is the limestone chimney (still standing) that was part of the original building. The chimney has two fireplaces, one for each floor. Their height indicates that the first floor was near ground level and the second floor about seven or eight feet above the first. The lintel shows very early structure. Plum Grove is known today as the Jackson Farm. Henry Jackson, many years back, made this statement to a neighbor, "When the original house was torn down I saw the name of one of John Sevier's brothers scratched in the mortar and the date of occupation."

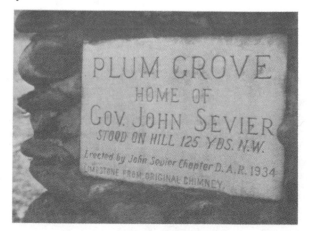

MT. PLEASANT HOME

The building below has been identified as Mt. Pleasant, home of the Seviers. This house was located across the river from the Plum Grove site. Much of Sevier's correspondence during State of Franklin days carried a Mt. Pleasant heading. The structure indicates a later and more elaborate building than the Plum Grove chimney shows. William places Sevier in the Mt. Pleasant house in 1781 when ex-Governor Caswell and family were guests. The house was torn down about 1908.

THIS MANTEL, removed from the Mt. Pleasant home of John Sevier in 1905, is in the possession of Mr. and Mrs. T.K. Broyles who live near the Plum Grove site. Mr. Broyles paid fifty cents for the mantel.

Photo by Jimmy Ellis

DAVID CROCKETT

In 1777 a band of Indians, said to be followers of Dragging Canoe, attacked the family of David Crockett, who lived in the environs of the present town of Rogersville. David Crockett, his wife, and several of the younger children were killed. Joseph was seriously wounded. Another son, James, deaf and dumb from birth, was taken back to the Indian towns where he lived for eighteen years. He was discovered and ransomed by John Crockett, his brother and father of the famous Davey Crockett.

WILLIAM COCKE

William Cocke was one of the impetuous, ambitious and controversial personalities of the early Overmountain days. Shelby and Cocke had differences during the muster at Shelby's Fort for the Dunmore War of 1774. During that same year, Cocke and James Robertson tarred and feathered a British recruiting officer for making slurring remarks about the Watauga people. William Cocke was employed by Richard Henderson to enlist axmen and purchase supplies for Daniel Boone's party, moving into Kentucky in 1775. He commanded a company of militia at the Battle of Island Flats, and fought in many Revolutionary and Indian campaigns.

William Cocke was a lawyer. He tried to oust John Sevier as the first clerk of Washington County court in 1778. A strong advocate of the State of Franklin, he became one of the first U.S. Senators from the state of Tennessee.

1B 34
MULBERRY GROVE
About 2½ miles south, now under water, William Cocke had his plantation. A veteran of the Revolution and the War of 1812, he served in the legislatures of Virginia, North Carolina, Franklin, Transylvania, Territory South of the River Ohio, Tennessee and Mississippi. He was U.S. Senator from Tennessee, 1796 to 1805.

JONESBOROUGH ESTABLISHED 1779

More and more settlers were pushing through the Shenandoah Valley of Virginia and over the hills from the Carolinas into the new country, now Tennessee. A permanent settlement seemed a certainty. Charles Robertson was appointed senator from Washington County, and Jesse Walton and Henry Clark representatives to the lower House of the North Carolina Assembly. They were instrumental in pushing through legislative action for the selection of a permanent site for a Washington County Courthouse, greatly needed

WILLIE JONES.
Member of the Continental Congress

for handling records and holding court. The bill was introduced by Jesse Walton, to whom much credit is due for the establishment of the new County Seat. Jonesborough, chartered by the North Carolina legislature, was founded January 17, 1779, thus becoming the oldest town west of the mountains. The town was named in honor of Willie Jones (pronounced Wylie) of Halifax, North Carolina, a man of prominence and wealth. He came from one of the aristocratic families of the state, and cut a big figure in the social and political life of the times. Strangely enough, he was one of the most radical leaders in the fight for independence. Jones was popular with the people and had a large following. He advocated recognition of the Overmountain people and remained their constant friend.

Jesse Walton, John Woods, George Russell, James Stewart, and Benjamin Clark were commissioned to lay out and supervise the building of the town. The area was surveyed and laid off in lots which were numbered. The purchaser could buy as many lots as desired at $100 each. On a stated day the numbers of the lots, appearing on chart, taken from Washington County records (see page 40), were drawn in a public lottery. The names of those obtaining lots, and the number of lots they bought, are found beneath the Jonesborough town plot.

Building restrictions were stipulated. "Every grantee of any lot shall within three years build on same one brick, stone or well framed house, twenty feet long and sixteen feet wide, and at least ten feet in the pitch, with a brick or stone chimney. If the owner shall fail to build and finish thereon, as before described, then such lots shall be forfeited."

As most of the county officials lived out in the county on their farms, the growth of the town was slow. The first session of court actually held in Jonesborough was May 24th, 1779 in a private home. No description has been found of the first courthouse used in Washington County. A new courthouse was eventually built on the town lot set aside for that purpose, and with it the whipping post, the stocks or pillory necessary for punishment in the early days. A description of this courthouse is found in the county records.

"The Court recommended that there be a courthouse built in the following manner to wit: 24 feet square, diamond corners and hewed down after the same is built up, nine feet above the upper floor, and each floor to be neatly laid with plank. The roof to be of joint shingles neatly hung with pegs; a justices' bench, a lawyer's and clerk's table, also a sheriff's box to sit in."

"The Court ordered that Colonel Charles Robertson be allowed fifty pounds current money for building the courthouse in the town of Jonesborough."

Above is a chart taken from the records in the Register of Deeds Office in Jonesborough, County Seat of Washington County, showing how the town was to be laid off. The lots were purchased by subscription and, on an appointed day, a public drawing was held. Williams has included a list of the purchasers in *Tennessee During the Revolutionary War* as taken from "American Historical Magazine" (Nashville), v. 224. The list is as follows, with the number of lots each subscriber purchased: "Robert Sevier, 1; Major Reynolds, 3; David Hughes, 2; Nathaniel Evans, 1; Martin Maney, 4; Jas. Allison, 8; Peter McClure, 2; John Allison, 2; Jesse Bounds, 2; Captain Stephen Cole, 2; Captain Charles Holliway, 2, since sold to Jesse Walton, now sold to Christopher Taylor May 2, 1785; Wm. Noddy (Snoddy), 1; James Ray, 1; Richard Minton, 2; Colonel Andrew Belford (Balfour), 4; James Reese, 4; Spruce McCay, 2; John Gilliland, 2; James Lackey, 2; John Woods, 2; John Yancey, 1; James Stuart, 10; Jesse Walton, 9."

The first session of the Washington County Court, held in the environs of the present Jonesborough, was May 24, 1779, "at a place appointed for the courthouse". A private home was used, perhaps a log cabin structure similar to the one pictured above by the artist.

Later, the court recommended that a courthouse be built with a justices' bench, a lawyer and clerk's table, and a sheriff's box. Charles Robertson was allowed fifty pounds for erecting this building. Above is the artist's conception of Jonesborough's first Courthouse.

CHRISTOPHER TAYLOR HOUSE

Above is the artist's drawing of the Taylor house, as it might have looked when first built. The house is located about one mile west of Jonesborough. Christopher Taylor owned a big tract of land, kept a stable of race horse, claimed the finest and fastest hounds in the country. Taylor built the house about 1777-1778.

On the right is a picture of the Christopher Taylor house taken January 1958. Note the stone chimney.

DUNGAN'S MILL

Dungan's Mill was built by Jeremiah Dungan in 1778. The mill has since been in continuous operation on the same site and by a descendant of Dungan. To the right is the original Dungan home built during the 1770's. Jeremiah Dungan was a stone mason and his masonry is still in good repair. These two pictures, taken some years ago, furnished through the courtesy of George St. John, present owner-operator of the mill.

42

PIONEER CHURCHES

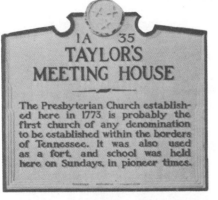

During the first years of the Overmountain settlements, the pioneers heard only an occasional sermon by an itinerate preacher. One such preacher, traveling through the territory sometime during 1772-1773, was called upon by Mrs. James Robertson to baptize her young children and those of her neighbor, Mrs. Daniel Boone.

TAYLOR'S MEETING HOUSE was first called the "Meeting House" and is the first known building erected for religious services. It was located some four miles west of the present town of Blountville. It was a definite point used in property grants and laying off early roads. Judge Williams suggests that probably all denominations worshiped here during those first years, as the settlements were too thin for the organization of any one denomination. Any passing preacher was called on to hold services.

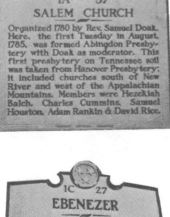

BUFFALO RIDGE BAPTIST CHURCH has been accepted by historians as the first organized church body in Tennessee territory. Tidence Lane moved from North Carolina in 1776 to the Watauga Settlement and established a church of Baptist faith on Buffalo Ridge and was its first pastor. The Church has since moved from its original location to Gray Station. The marker at left is on the original site, which is a graveyard.

SALEM CHURCH was organized in 1780 by Samuel Doak of the Presbyterian faith. Three log buildings were erected on the site of the present Washington College Academy: one for a dwelling, one for a church and one for a school. Samuel Doak and John Sevier were good friends and Sevier was a supporter of Doak's school and church, but there is no record that John Sevier was a member of any church.

EBENEZER METHODIST CHURCH organized in 1790 was located on a site about one mile and a half from the present village of Chucky. Earlier, in the year 1783, there was a circuit rider named Jeremiah Lambert who traveled through the Holston Settlement as a missionary by appointment.

SINKING CREEK BAPTIST CHURCH is perhaps the oldest church in Tennessee occupying its original location and foundation. It is the oldest church in Carter County and contributed much to the spiritual life of the early settlers.

BUFFALO RIDGE BAPTIST CHURCH

Below is the artist's conception of Buffalo Ridge Baptist Church building at the time of its erection 1778-1779.

The pioneer preacher brought religion and education to the frontier settlements. Preaching in log churches, homes, under brush arbors or wherever a group could gather, he would deliver a simple message with an emotional appeal that found a warm reception. His small supply of leather-bound books were circulated among the scattered homes. The preacher would often serve as a doctor. He received no pay, and made his living in the same manner as the other settlers. The influence of these dedicated men is still felt in the mountainous section of Tennessee, known throughout the country as the heart of the Bible Belt.

SAMUEL DOAK

During 1778, a young preacher who was to cast a great influence on the spiritual and educational life of the new country, began preaching in Washington County, Virginia. Later he moved to the fork country of the present Sullivan County, Tennessee. Then following the flow of settlers to the southwest, Doak traveled through the present Washington County (Tennessee) on horseback with his gun, Bible and books. The legend is told that Doak, while riding along a horse trail, came upon a group of settlers felling trees for a clearing. Learning that he was a preacher they asked him to speak to them. They gathered the available people together for the service. His horse was his pulpit and the woods his sanctuary. A mutual liking and fellowship arose and they induced Samuel Doak to settle in their midst. Obtaining a grant of land, and with the aid of neighbors, Doak erected three log buildings: a home, a church and a school.

Samuel Doak was born in August, 1749, in Augusta County, Virginia. His parents were Samuel and Jane Mitchell Doak. Young Samuel made a profession of religion at the age of sixteen and began his education that same year. A man named Alexander was his teacher. Later this school was moved to Lexington, where it eventually became Washington and Lee University. Determined to become a minister, Doak continued his studies at West Nottingham Academy, Colora, Maryland. Young Samuel so desired an education that he offered his portion of the family estate for funds to continue in school. His father reluctantly agreed. By doing his own cooking in company with another student and doing assistant teaching work, he finally graduated from this school. In 1773, at the age of twenty-four, he entered the College of New Jersey, now Princeton University. Graduating in 1775, he accepted a position as tutor in Hampton Sydney College. During this same year, he married Esther Montgomery. Doak remained in this work for two years and also continued his ministerial studies. He was ordained as a preacher in October 1777. Challenged by the frontier life, he soon moved into the Holston settlement, then on to the community where he made his permanent home.

Many experiences of danger and hardship were encountered by the Doaks in the new country. Tradition relates that on one occasion, when Samuel Doak was away from home to obtain family supplies, Mrs. Doak, seeing some Indian warriors approaching the cabin, was able to slip into nearby concealment with her infant son. From here she watched the Indians plunder and burn their cabin home. After dark, she made her way to a nearby blockhouse to await the return of her husband.

Doak's rifle was always near at hand during the church services. On one or more occasions, he is said to have stopped the service and chased Indians. Bishop E.E. Hoss said of Doak: ''He feared God so much that he feared nothing else and would have made a fit chaplain for a regiment of Cromwell's Ironsides, a man of influence on the early history of the state.'' History is still recording the effect this noble character had on the lives of the early settlers and their descendants.

Samuel Doak was above average height and had a large muscular body. He manifested a very stern, grave appearance, was a man of great intellect and good common sense. He chose service rather than riches. Many churches that Doak organized dot East Tennessee today.

DOAK'S "LOG COLLEGE"

WASHINGTON COLLEGE

1A   30

← 1.7 miles →

First established as Martin Academy by the Rev. Samuel Doak in 1780. It was later called Dr. Doak's Log College and in 1795 received its present name on motion by John Sevier. Dr. Doak died in 1829, at the age of 80, and is buried on the campus.

One of the three log buildings erected by Samuel Doak was used by him as a private school, the first educational institution established west of the mountains. In April 1783, Doak received a charter from North Carolina Assembly to maintain a classical school. It was named "Martin Academy" in honor of Governor Alexander Martin of North Carolina. Both Governor Martin and Samuel Doak were graduates of West Nottingham Academy in Maryland. The school was again chartered as "Martin Academy" by the State of Franklin, March 1785. Being the only school in the new country, it was natural that it flourished and became the educational center of the Overmountain people. The frontier settlers affectionately called it "Doak's Log College."

In 1795, the school was chartered as Washington College by the Territory of the United States South of the Ohio. The first graduating class consisted of two: John Whitfield Doak, son of Samuel, and James Witherspoon, who received A. B. degrees. Many great leaders and personalities received their education under Doak's tutelage, including such notables as Dr. J. G. M. Ramsey, great Tennessee historian; L. C. Haynes; N. G. Taylor; Z. B. Vance and a host of others. The sons and daughters of John Sevier received their education here, as well as the children of many other frontier families.

Samuel Doak, preacher and teacher, lived a life of service. History records that his students loved and revered him. His imprint of idealism, character and high morals is still in evidence. He burned the torch of learning and kindled the spirit of evangelism in the hearts of the Overmountain men and women. His students and their descendants were destined to blaze the emblem of new statehoods in the western trek.

COLONEL JOHN CARTER

The picture of the Carter home, below, was taken in 1958. The Carter Mansion was built sometime during 1780, just months before the death of Colonel John Carter. His son, Landon, ably assumed the responsibilities of his father and became one of the prominent leaders during the political upheavals of the 1780 decade. Carter County was named in honor of Landon Carter. Elizabethton was named in honor of Landon's wife, Elizabeth Maclin Carter.

Colonel John Carter, a trader and merchant, was a member of the Carter-Trent mercantile firm of Virginia. This company maintained branch trading posts at many strategic points. Colonel Carter was benefactor of William Tatham, who started as clerk with the firm in 1769, at one of their posts on the James River. Tatham was one of the colorful figures that emerged from the rugged life of the frontier. After Carter and Parker's store was looted in Carter's Valley, Carter moved to the Watauga and is thought to have established a store there. John Carter was chairman of the Watauga Association, the Washington District, and the first Court of Washington County. He was the first state senator to represent the district in the North Carolina assembly.

LANDON CARTER was tutored for college by William Tatham. He attended Liberty Hall (now Davidson College) in North Carolina. Equipped by education, training and experience, Landon Carter was well prepared to assume the roles of leadership that fell his lot in the years to come. In military matters he served in many campaigns. He and John Sevier were close friends, and their lives were closely linked in this most spectacular episode of Tennessee history.

SULLIVAN COUNTY ESTABLISHED 1779

During the fall session of the North Carolina Assembly in 1779, an act was passed to form a new county. A portion of Washington County, embodying much of the Holston settlement, was designated. John Sevier, Isaac Shelby, and John Chisholm were named as a commission to run the line dividing the two counties. The new county was named Sullivan in honor of General John Sullivan. The boundary lines generally began at Steep Rock Creek, ran along the dividing ridge to the head of Indian Creek, thence along the ridge dividing the waters of Watauga and Holston, to the mouth of Watauga, then to the highest part of Chimney Top Mountain at Indian boundary. This county took in much land formerly part of Virginia.

The first session of Sullivan County court was held in the cabin home of Moses Looney, near Eaton's Station. The Justices were: Isaac Shelby, David Looney, Anthony Bledsoe, George Maxwell, John Anderson, Joseph Martin, Henry Clark, Samuel Smith, Gilbert Christian, John Duncan and William Wallace. Nathan Clark was elected sheriff and John Rhea, clerk; John Adair, entry taker; and Ephraim Dunlop, attorney. Isaac Shelby was commissioned as Colonel of Sullivan County Militia; Henry Clark, Lieutenant-Colonel; David Looney as major and John Shelby second major. The second session of the court was held in the home of James Hollis.

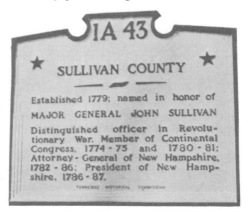

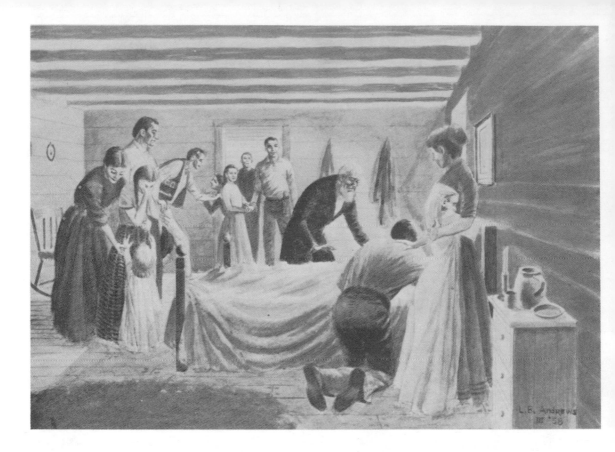

Sarah Hawkins Sevier, daughter of Joseph and Sarah Marlin Hawkins, born in Shenandoah County, Virginia, 1746, died in Washington County, Tennessee, 1780. She had an unusual education and great strength of character. Married at fifteen, she was for the nineteen creative, formative years of his (Sevier's) life the greatest single factor in his spectacular early rise to fame and fortune. A wise, capable, understanding wife and mother who commanded her husband's post in his absences, she made the hazardous journey down the Shenandoah Valley in December 1773, with seven children under eleven years of age. The mother of ten, she gave five fighting sons to the protection and building of Tennessee, finally giving her life during an Indian uprising.

The location of the grave of Sarah Hawkins Sevier is unknown. It has been indicated that she was buried in the vicinity of Telford Station. It is believed that the Seviers were living at the Plum Grove home at the time of her death. The children of John and Sarah Sevier, and the dates of their birth, are: Joseph 1762, James 1764, John Jr. 1766, Elizabeth 1768, Sarah Hawkins 1770, Mary Ann 1772, Valentine 1773, Richard 1775, Rebecca 1777, Nancy 1779. Sarah Hawkins Sevier seems to have been a rather quiet, retiring personality of noble character, who tended to her family's needs and stayed out of the limelight. The Seviers were married very young and she was not over 35 at the time of her death. The ruggedness of the frontier and the constant worry of danger for her children and husband could have been a contributing cause. Also, 1779-1780 was known as the "Cold Winter" and exposure could have brought on pneumonia. Her death left John Sevier with a large family of children to look after, as well as many other dependants. The oldest girl, Elizabeth, age 12, was rather young to assume the responsibility of such a large household.

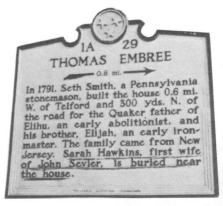

The Thomas Embree marker located on Highway 11-E about a mile from the Embree house states that Sarah Hawkins Sevier is buried nearby. No definite location has been established.

48

SPENCER'S TREE

Thomas Sharp Spencer was one of a group of settlers who moved to Henderson's Cumberland Settlement during 1778. The majority of this group became dissatisfied and returned to Kentucky; but Spencer, liking the country, stayed. He made his home in a large hollow tree. More of a hunter than a farmer, Spencer spent much of his time trapping and hunting. He was a man of giant-like stature and had very big feet. The story is told that while on one of his trips; he passed the cabin of one of De Monbreum's French trappers. His huge feet left their imprint in the soft soil near the cabin. The trapper, frightened at seeing these footprints, thought he was living in a forest filled with giants. Without looking for a boat, he swam the river and wandered for days until he reached another French settlement on the Wabash.

It is said that when Spencer's friend Halliday decided to return to Kentucky, Spencer broke his knife in half and gave one piece to Halliday who had lost his own. Spencer preferred stopping fights rather than starting them. One day while separating two men who were fighting, he was struck by an onlooker who wanted to see the fight. Spencer picked the man up, held him over his head, walked over to a nearby fence and tossed him over. The culprit, somewhat shaken and subdued, spoke, "Mr. Spencer, if you'll oblige by throwing my horse over to me, I'll be goin'."

SHELBY'S CHICKAMAUGA RAID

The Chickamaugas, living at the foot of Lookout Mountain (Chattanooga), were causing much concern by their frequent raids on settlers. Dragging Canoe and other Chiefs, prodded by Cameron, were carrying out their threat of a bloody ground.

A company of militia numbering about 600, under command of Colonel Evan Shelby, left Big Creek Fort April 10, 1779, on a campaign to subdue the Chiakamaugas. They went by river route on boats built and financed by Isaac Shelby.

The Chickamauga Indians, surprised by this sudden unexpected approach by water, fled to the hills. Shelby's men burned Dragging Canoe's town and eleven others. About 20,000 bushels of corn, many pelts and several horses were captured.

At the conclusion of the campaign one company, under Montgomery, continued down the Tennessee by boat to join Colonel George Rogers Clark. The remaining force, under Shelby, destroyed their boats and returned to the settlements on foot.

JAMES ROBERTSON PLANS CUMBERLAND SETTLEMENT

The Cumberland Settlement really began in 1777 during the Long Island Treaty. This occasion brought together James Robertson, John Donelson and Richard Henderson where plans were discussed and made for the adventure. At the close of the Treaty, Donelson returned to his home in Virginia and began preparation for moving to Big Salt Lick. James Robertson, George Freeland, Zachariah Wells, James Healey, William Neely, Edward Swanson, William Overall, Mark Robertson and a negro slave made the trip to the present site of Nashville in 1778-1779 to look the situation over. They planted seed corn brought along and put up a fence to protect it from the animals. Robertson, with some of the pioneers, went by canoe into the Illinois country to purchase supplies and horses. On this trip, he obtained from George Rogers Clark a 3000 acre grant Clark owned in the Cumberland. Leaving men to watch corn, stock and cabins, Robertson returned to his home on the Holston to make final arrangements for moving.

James Robertson and the men took the stock and went the Kentucky route, while Donelson with the women traveled by boat. With the horses, cows, hogs and sheep forming a caravan, they followed a route indicated in Williams' *Early Travels in Tennessee Country.* "The route made a great bend through the Kentucky country. The main stations it passed through after leaving Cumberland Gap were: Whitley's Station on to Dick's River, Carpenter's Station on Green River; thence along the north side of Green River to Robertson's Fork, down same to Pittman's Station; then crossing same at Elk Lick; passing Blue Spring and Dripping Spring to Big Barren River; thence up Drake's Creek to a bituminous spring; thence to Red River; thence into Carolina (Tennessee), passing Mansker's Lick; then to French Lick." The extreme cold winter made the trip difficult. The caravan of men and animals reached the Cumberland River, across from Big French Lick, Christmas week of 1779. Finding the river frozen solid, they drove the stock across the ice on Christmas day. Thus the Cumberland Settlement, which was to become a center of western expansion, had its beginning. James Robertson and the men began erecting cabins and clearing sections, preparatory to the arrival of their families journeying with Donelson by boat.

THE DONELSON RIVER TRIP

The most colorful exploit of all pioneer experience was that of Captain John Donelson's boat trip, with the women, by river route to the Cumberland Settlement. They left Fort Patrick Henry on December 22, 1779, but because of excessive cold and ice, they made only about three miles and were forced to tie up until the middle of February. The rains set in, making the handling of the boats difficult. Some sank, and had to be raised and repaired. They finally camped near the present town of Loudon, where they repaired boats and secured food. Here more boats joined the fleet, bringing the total up to thirty. Also, while in camp here a negro slave died of frostbite infection, and a baby was born.

As the voyagers passed through the Chickamauga towns, the Indians began to attack. One group of boats, with smallpox epidemic aboard, had dropped behind. The Indians captured these boats and killed or made prisoners of all the occupants. Several hundred warriors died of smallpox as a result of this raid. Later, another boat overturned with all the supplies; as rescue came, Indians began firing from the shore. During the melee, Nancy Grover grabbed the helm of one boat to steer, was hit in the thigh, but kept at her post until help arrived. Another boat, stuck at the "Boiling Pot" and thought lost, showed up days later with some people missing, including the newborn baby.

They docked at Muscle Shoals, expecting to meet James Robertson and go overland from there. Finding no sign, they continued on through the hazardous shoals and down the river. From here the flow was gentler and the Indians bothered them only occasionally. March 15th they reached the mouth of the Tennessee and the high water of the Ohio. As these boats were not suited for upstream travel, many of the men gave up in despondency and drifted downstream rather than undertake the difficult task of poling upstream. Some of the women had to take men's places in manning the boats. After much hardship, they camped at the mouth of the Cumberland long enough for the men to secure meat by hunting, and the women to gather herbs and salad to replenish their exhausted food supply. The flow of the Cumberland being gentle made the difficult poling upstream somewhat easier. A few of the boats tried crude sails which helped. April 12th they reached Red River, where Moses Renfroe and others left to form a settlement in that valley. The upstream pull was so tedious and slow, they did not arrive at French Salt Lick (site of Nashville) until April 24th. Here, they were met by James Robertson and the men in a happy reunion after a most tragic and hazardous trip. Rachel Donelson, daughter of Captain John Donelson, was one of the passengers. She afterwards married Andrew Jackson. The beginning of the Cumberland Settlement had its full share of blood and sweat.

FORT NASHBOROUGH

FORT NASHBOROUGH FIRST AVE. & CHURCH ST. NASHVILLE, TENN.

THE CUMBERLAND ASSOCIATION

Donelson's flotilla of boats arrived at Big French Lick (Nashville) April 24, 1780. Colonel Richard Henderson had already put in motion the necessary machinery for getting an organized form of government set up in the new settlement. The Compact, most likely worked out jointly by Henderson and Robertson, was phrased to aid the Transylvania Company in handling their land grants to the new settlers. This territory was part of that purchased from the Indians by the Henderson Company at the Sycamore Shoals Treaty in 1775. (This big land deal at the Watauga Treaty was later repudiated by the North Carolina Assembly. Henderson's Company was given some 200,000 acres of land in the Powell Valley section as recompense.)

The Cumberland Pact, in its general form, was somewhat similar to that of the Watauga Association, which James Robertson was instrumental in formulating some eight years previous. At a later session, May 13th, the written pact was adopted and signed by two hundred fifty-six of the white settlers. Of this group only one man had to make his mark. Two of Richard Henderson's brothers were signers.

A single copy of The Compact, minus the first page, was found years later by Putnam who reproduced the text in his *History of Middle Tennessee*. It provided for a court of twelve members and outlined their duties and functions in legislative and legal matters. One of the stipulations included binding all signers to abide by the decision of the twelve-man court, without benefit of appeal to the far away courts of North Carolina. Another was that all males over sixteen be subject to military service, but it also gave them permission to hold land grants at that age. The members of the court were selected from the eight settlements that made up the Cumberland group. These stations, similar to present town and county districts, were: Manskers Lick, Bledsoe's, Asher's, Stone's River, Freeland's, Eaton's, Fort Union and Nashborough.

Nashborough was named for General Francis Nash of Hillsboro, North Carolina, who was killed in the battle of Germantown in 1777. He was a close friend of Colonel Richard Henderson.

OVERMOUNTAIN MEN IN CAROLINA DURING EARLY 1780

During the first months of 1780, some 400 Watauga and Holston frontiersmen, under the commands of Major Charles Robertson and Colonel Isaac Shelby, went to the assistance of Colonel Charles McDowell. The British had overrun most of South Carolina, and the threat of a full scale invasion loomed over North Carolina. McDowell sent a company under Shelby to take Thickety Fort, garrisoned by a detachment of Ferguson's men. This was done without firing a shot. Another skirmish was against Major James Dunlap at Cedar Springs. Dunlap's forces were about to be defeated when Ferguson came to his aid. Outnumbered, the Overmountain men retreated, using hit and run tactics, much to Ferguson's disadvantage. He abandoned the chase after four or five miles.

A later battle of importance was that of Musgrove's Mill. McDowell again sent Shelby and Robertson, with a detachment of troops, to join Colonel Williams for this engagement. They had to slip around Ferguson's main force to reach their objective. By strategy, they drew the loyalist forces of Colonel Innis into ambush. After a terrific battle lasting nearly an hour, the enemy retreated, badly defeated. The men were ready to return to McDowell's headquarters, when a messenger arrived with the news of Gate's disastrous defeat at Camden. Knowing that Ferguson might be closing in for a battle any hour and that no help was available, Shelby thought it best to lead his men to the safety of the mountains. Pursued by Ferguson for some sixty miles, the men, existing on green corn and peaches found along the way, slipped homeward through the mountain passes and out of Ferguson's range.

JOHN SEVIER MARRIES "BONNIE KATE"

During the eventful year of 1780, John Sevier was burdened by many problems, military and civil. Left a widower by the death of Sarah Hawkins, and with a household of ten children, ranging in ages from Nancy, a babe in arms, to Joseph, a young man of 18, he decided to remedy the home situation. He cast a romantic eye to a near neighbor's daughter, Catherine Sherrill, whom he had pulled over the fort wall at Watauga during the Indian attack some four years earlier in 1776. Samuel Sherrill and his family had moved from the Yadkin River in North Carolina and settled in their home, known as "Daisy Fields." Sevier courted and married Catherine "Bonnie Kate" Sherrill, August 16, 1780.

Catherine Sherrill, an already prominent figure on the frontier settlement, was stepping into a future filled with tragedy, romance, and exciting experiences. She spent her honeymoon mending and making uniforms for the Sevier boys to wear to the King's Mountain Battle. She is one of Tennessee's romantic personalities, the first lady of the State of Franklin and later the first lady of Tennessee.

Scene from "The Overmountain Men" historic drama produced in Erwin, Tennessee, 1952-1953. All the cast in this production were natives of Erwin.

TREATY OF SYCAMORE SHOALS, MAR. 17, 1775

The Chiefs Of The Cherokees To Rich Henderson and Co.

This Indenture, made this   day of   of the year of our Lord one Thousand Seven Hundred and Seventy-five, between Oconistoto, Chief Warrior and first representative of the Cherokee Nation or tribe of Indians and Attacullaculla and Savanooka, otherwise Coronoh, Chiefs appointed by the Warriors and other head men to convey for the whole Nation, Being the Aborigines and sole owners by occupancy from the Beginning of time of the lands on the waters of the Ohio River from the mouth of the Tennessee River up the said Ohio to the mouth or emptying of the Great Canaway or New River, and so across by a Southward line to the Virginia line by an intersection that shall strike or hit Holston River six English miles above or Eastward of the Long Island therein and other land or territorys thereunto adjoining, of the one part; and Richard Henderson, Thomas Hart, Nathaniel Hart, John Williams, John Luttrell, William Johnston, James Hogg, David Hart, and Leonard Hendley Bulloch, of the Province of North Carolina, of the other part;

WITNESSETH, that the said Oconistoto for himself and the rest of the said Nation of Indians, for and in consideration of Ten Thousand Pounds Lawfull money of Great Britain, to them in hand paid by the said Rich Henderson, Thomas Hart, Nathaniel Hart, John Williams, John Luttrell, William Johnston, James Hogg, David Hart, and Leonard Hendley Bulloch, the Receipt Whereoff the said Oconistoto and his whole Nation do and for themselves and their whole people hereby acknowledge, have granted bargained, sold, aliened, enfeoffed, Released & Confirmed & by these presents do Grant, bargain & sell alien, enfeoff, Release & Confirm unto the said Rich Henderson, Thomas Hart, Nathaniel Hart, John Williams, John Luttrell, William Johnston, James Hogg, David Hart, and Leonard Hendley Bulloch, their heirs and assigns forever, all that Tract, Territory, or Parcel of Land.

Beginning on the Holston River where the course of Powel's Mountain strikes the same, hence up the said River as it meanders to where the Virginia line crosses the same, thence along the line run by Donelson & Co. to a point Six English Miles Eastward of the Long Island in the said Holston River, thence a direct course towards the Mount of the Great Canaway until it reaches the top ridge of Powel's Mountain, thence Westward along the said ridge to the Beginning.

and also the Reversion and the Reversions, Remainder and Remainders, Rents and Services thereoff and all the Estate Rights, Title Interest, Claim, and Demand whatever of them, the said Oconistoto and the aforesaid whole band or Tribe of People of, in, and to the said premises, and of, in, and to Every Part and Parcel through, To Have and to Hold the said Messuage & Territory and all the singular the Premises above mentioned with the appurtenances above mentioned, unto the said Rich Henderson, Thomas Hart, Nathaniel Hart, John Williams, John Luttrell, William Johnson, James Hogg, David Hart, and Leonard Hendley Bulloch, their heirs and assigns in Severalty & Tenants in Common and not as Joint Tenants, that is to say:

One eighth part to Rich Henderson, his heirs and assigns forever;
One eighth part to Thomas Hart, his heirs and assigns forever;
One eighth part to Nathaniel Hart, his heirs and assigns forever;
One eighth part to John Williams, his heirs and assigns forever;
One eighth part to John Luttrell, his heirs and assigns forever;
One eighth part to William Johnston, his heirs and assigns forever;
One eighth part to James Hogg, his heirs and assigns forever;
One sixteenth part to David Hart, his heirs and assigns forever;
One sixteenth part to Leonard Hendley Bulloch, his heirs and assigns forever;

To the only proper use and behoof of them, the said Rich Henderson, Thomas Hart, Nathaniel Hart, John Williams, John Luttrell, William Johnston, James Hogg, David Hart, and Leonard Hendley Bulloch, their heirs and assigns forever, under the yearly rent of four pence or to be holder of or the Chief Lord or Lords of the feds of the Premises by the rents and Services thereoff due and of right accustomed; and the said Oconistoto and the said Nation of themselves do covenant and grant to the said Rich Henderson, Thomas Hart, Nathaniel Hart, John Williams, John Luttrell, William Johnston, James Hogg, David Hart, and Leonard Hendley Bulloch, their heirs and assigns, that they, the said Oconistoto and the Rest of the said Nation or People now are lawfully and rightly seized in their own right of a good Fee Simple or and in all and singular of the said Messuage and premises above mentioned and of all and every part and parcel thereof with the appurtenances without any manner of conditions, mortgages, limitation of use or uses, or other matter, cause or thing to alter, change, charge or determine the same, and also the said Oconistoto and the aforesaid Nation now have good right, full power, and lawful authority in their own fight to Grant, Bargain and Sell and Convey the said Messuage and Premises above mentioned with the appurtenances unto the said Rich Henderson, Thomas Hart, Nathaniel Hart, John Williams, John Luttrell, William Johnston, James Hogg, David Hart, and Leonard Hendley Bulloch, their heirs and assigns; and they shall and may from time to time hereafter peaceably and quietly have hold, occupy, possess, and enjoy, all and singular the said premises above mentioned to be hereby granted with the appurtenances, without the lest trouble, interference and molestation in occupation and denial of their right thereto, by the said Oconistoto and the rest of any part of the said Nation their heirs and assigns and of all and every other person whatsoever, claiming or to claim, by, from, or under them, or any of them; and further, that the said Oconistoto, Attacullacullah, Savanooka, otherwise Coronoh, for themselves and in behalf of their whole Nation and their heirs and all and every other person or persons and his and their heirs, anything having or claiming in the said Messuage, Territory, or any part thereof, by, from, or under them, Shall and will at all times hereafter at the Request and Cost of the said Rich Henderson, Thomas Hart, Nathaniel Hart, John Williams, John Luttrell, William Johnston, James Hogg, David Hart, and Leonard Hendley Bulloch, their heirs and assigns forever, make, do and execute, or cause or procure to be made, done, or execute, all and every further and other lawful and reasonable Grants, Acts, and Assurances in the Law whatsoever for the further better and more perfect granting, conveying, and assuring of the said premises hereby granted with all appurtenances unto the said Rich Henderson, Thomas Hart, Nathaniel Hart,

John Williams, John Luttrell, William Johnston, James Hogg, David Hart, and Leonard Hendley Bulloch, their heirs and assigns forever according to the true intent and meaning of these presents, and to and for none other use, interest, or purpose whatsoever:

And lastly, the said Oconistoto, Attacullacullah, Savanooka, otherwise Coronoh, for themselves and the whole Nation aforesaid, have made, ordained, constituted, and appointed, and by these presents do make, ordain, constitute and appoint Joseph Martin and John Sevier their true and lawful Attorneys, jointly and in either of them severally, for them and in their names unto the said Messuage, Territory, and Premises and Appurtenances hereby granted, conveyed, or mentioned, or to be granted or conveyed, or unto some part thereof in the name of the whole, to enter in full and peaceable possession and Seizen thereof, for them and in their names to take and to have such possession and seizure to thereafter seize and hold the lawfull and peaceable possession and Seizure thereoff or of some part thereof in the name of the whole unto the said Rich Henderson, Thomas Hart, Nathaniel Hart, John Williams, John Luttrell, William Johnston, James Hogg, David Hart, and Leonard Hendley Bulloch, or their certain attorney or attorneys in their behalf, to Give and Deliver to hold to them, the said Rich Henderson, Thomas Hart, Nathaniel Hart, John Williams, John Luttrell, William Johnston, James Hogg, David Hart, and Leonard Hendley Bulloch, their heirs and assigns forever according to the purpose, true intent, and meaning of these presents, Ratifying, confirming, and allowing all and whatsoever their attorneys or either of them shall do in the premises.

In Witness Whereof, the said Oconistoto, Attacullacullah, Savanooka otherwise Coronoh, the three chiefs appointed by the warriors and other head men to sign for and in behalf of the whole Nation, hath hereunto Set their Hands and Affixed their Seals, the day and the year above written.

OCONISTOTO (His Mark)
ATTACULLACULLAH (His Mark)
SAVANOOKA
(Otherwise Coronoh) (His Mark)

Signed, Sealed, and Delivered, in the presence of

WM. BAILEY SMITH	LITTLETON BROOKS
GEORGE LUMPKIN	JOHN BACON
THO. HOUGHTON	TILMAN DIXON
VALENTINE SEVIER	THOMAS PRICE

This copy of the Treaty is thought to be that section of land granted to John Carter and Robert Lucas in Carter's Valley in compensation for goods stolen from them by Indians. Covers site of the present town of Rogersville.

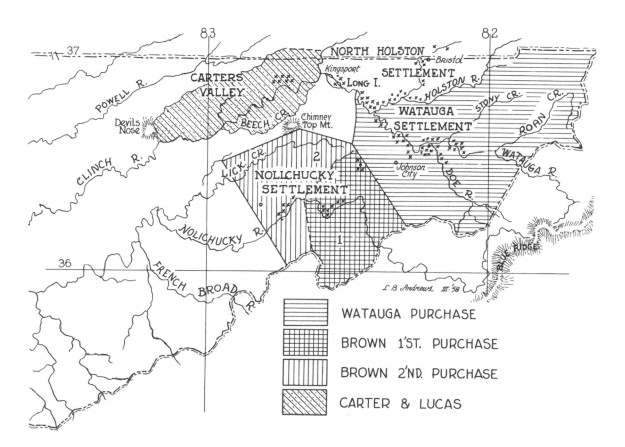

PETITION TO NORTH CAROLINA — JULY 5, 1776

To the Hon. the Provincial Council of North Carolina:

The humble petition of the inhabitants of Washington District, including the River Wataugah, Nonachuckie, &c., in committee assembled, Humbly Sheweth, that about six years ago, Colonel Donelson, (in behalf of the Colony of Virginia), held a Treaty with the Cherokee Indians, in order to purchase the lands of the Western Frontiers; in consequence of which Treaty, many of your petitioners settled on the lands of the Wataugah, &c., expecting to be within the Virginia line, and consequently hold their lands by their improvements as first settlers; but to their great disappointment, when the line was run they were (contrary to their expectation) left out; finding themselves thus disappointed, and being too inconveniently situated to move back, and feeling an unwillingness to loose the labour bestowed on their plantations, they applied to the Cherokee Indians, and leased the land for a term of ten years, before the expiration of which term, it appeared that many persons of distinction were actually making purchases forever; thus yielding a precedent, (supposing many of them, who were gentlemen of the law, to be better judges of the constitution than we were,) and considering the bad consequences it must be attended with, should the reversion be purchased out of our hands, we next preceeded to make a purchase of the lands, reserving those in our possession in sufficient tracts for our own use, and resolving to dispose of the remainder for the good of the community. This purchase was made and the lands acknowledged to us and our heirs forever, in an open treaty, in Wataugah Old Fields; a deed being obtained from the Chiefs of the said Cherokee nation, for themselves and their whole nation, conveying a fee simple right to the said lands, to us and our heirs forever, which deed was for and in consideration of the sum of two thousand pounds sterling (paid to them in goods,) for which consideration they acknowledged themselves fully satisfied, contented and paid; and agreed for themselves and their whole nation, their heirs, &c, forever to resign, warrant and defend the said lands to us, and our heirs, &c., against themselves, their heirs, &c.

The purchase was no sooner made, than we were alarmed by the reports of the present unhappy differences between Great Britain and America, on which report, (taking the new united colonies for our guide,) we proceeded to choose a committee, which was done unanimously by the consent of the people. This committee (willing to become a party in the present unhappy contest) resolved (which is now on our records) to adhere strictly to the rules and orders of the Continental Congress, and in open committee acknowledged themselves indebted to the united colonies their full proportion of the Continental expense.

Finding ourselves on the Frontiers, and being apprehensive that, for the want of a proper legislature, we might become a shelter for such as endeavored to defraud their creditors; considering also the necessity for recording Deeds, Wills, and doing other public business, we, by consent of the people, formed a court for the purposes above mentioned, taking (by desire of our constituents) the Virginia laws for our guide, so near as the situation of affairs would admit; this was intended for ourselves, and was done by the consent of every individual, but wherever we had to deal with people out of our district, we have ruled them to bail, to abide by our determinations, (which was, in fact, leaving the matter of reference,) otherways we dismissed their suit, lest we should in any way intrude on the legislature of the colonies. In short, we have endeavored so strictly to do justice, that we have admitted common proof against ourselves, on accounts, &c, from the colonies, without pretending a right to require the Colony Seal.

We therefore trust that we shall be considered as we deserve, and not, as we have (no doubt) been many times, represented, as a lawless mob. It is for this very reason we can assure you that we petition; we now again repeat it, that it is for want of proper authority to try and punish felons, we can only mention to you murderers, horse thieves and robbers, and are sorry to say that some of them have escaped us for want of proper authority. We trust, however, that this will not long be the case; and we again and again repeat it, that it is for this reason we petition to this Honorable Assembly.

Above we have given you an extract of our proceedings, since our settling on Wataugah, Nolachuckie, &c., in regard to our civil affairs. We have shown you the causes of our first settling and the disappointments we have met with, the reason of our lease and of our purchase, the manner in which we purchased, and how we hold of the Indians in fee simple; the causes of our forming a committee, and legality of its election; the same of our court and proceedings, and our reasons for petitioning in regard to our Legislature.

We will now proceed to give you some account of our military establishments, which were chosen agreeable to the rules established by convention, and officers appointed by the committee. This being done we thought it proper to raise a company on the District service, as our proportion, to act in the common cause on the sea shore. A Company of fine riflemen were accordingly enlisted, and put under Captain James Robertson, and were actually embodied, when we received sundry letters and depositions, (copies of which we now enclose you,) you will then readily judge that there was occasion for them in another place, where we daily expected attack. We therefore thought proper to station them on our Frontiers, in defence of the common cause, at the expense and risque of our own private fortunes, till farther public orders, which we flatter ourselves will give no offence. We have enclosed you sundry proceedings at the station where our men now remain.

We shall now submit the whole to your candid and impartial judgement. We pray your mature and deliberate consideration in our behalf, that you may annex us to your Province, (whether as County, district, or other division,) in such manner as may enable us to share in the glorious cause of Liberty; enforce our laws under authority, and in every respect become the best members of society; and for ourselves and constituents we hope, we may venture to assure you, that we shall adhere strictly to your determinations, and that nothing will be lacking or any thing neglected, that may add weight (in the civil or military establishments) to the glorious cause in which we are now struggling, or contribute to the welfare of our own or ages yet to come.

That you may strictly examine every part of this our Petition, and delay no time in annexing us to your Province, in such a manner as your wisdom shall direct, is the hearty prayer of those who, for themselves and constituents, as in duty bound, shall ever pray.

John Carter, Chn.	Zach Isbell,	Jacob Brown,	George Rusel,
Charles Robertson,	John Sevier,	Wm. Been,	Jacob Womack,
James Robertson,	Jas. Smith,	John Jones,	Robert Lucas,

The above signers are the Members in Committee assembled.
Wm. Tatham, Clerk, P.T.

Jacob Womack,	James Easley,	John I. Cox,	Joud. Bostin, sen.,
Joseph Dunham,	John Haile,	John Cox, jr.,	Henry Bates, jun.,
Rice Duncan,	Elijah Robertson,	Abraham Cox,	Will'm Dod,
Edward Hopson,	William Clark	Emanuel Shote,	Groves Morris,
Lew. Bowyer, D.Atty,	his	Thomas Houghton,	Wm. Bates,
Joseph Buller,	John X Dunham	Joseph Luske,	Robert Mosely,
Andw. Greer,	mark	William Reeves,	Ge. Hartt,
his	Wm. Overall,	David Hughes,	Isaac Wilson,
Jaob X Mitchell,	Matt. Hawkins,	Landon Carter,	Jno. Waddell,
mark	John Brown,	John McCormick,	Jarret Williams,
Gideon Morris,	Jos. Brown,	David Crocket,	Oldham Hightower,
Shadrach Morris,	Job Bumper,	Edward Cox,	Abednago Hix,
William Crocket,	Isaac Wilson,	Tho's Hughes,	Charles McCartney,
Thos. Dedmon,	Richard Norton,	William Roberson,	Frederick Vaughn,
David Hickey,	George Hutson,	Henry Siler,	Joseph McCartney,
Mark Mitchell,	Thomas Simpson,	Frederick Calvit,	Mark Robertson,
Hugh Blair,	Valentine Sevier,	John Moore,	Joseph Calvit,
Elias Pebler,	Jonathan Tipton,	William Newberry,	Joshua Houghton,
Jos. Brown,	Robert Sevier,	Adam Sherrell,	John Chukinbeard,
John Neave,	Drury Goodan,	Samuel Sherrell, Junr.	James Cooper,
John Robinson,	Richard Fletcher,	Samuel Sherrell, Ser.,	William Brokees,
Christopher Cunningham	Allexander Greear,	Ossa Rose,	Julius Robertson,
Jas. Easley,	Joseph Greear,	Henry Bates, Jun.,	John King,
Ambrose Hodge,	Andrew Greear, jun.,	Jos. Grimes,	Michael Hider,
Dan'l Morris,	Teeter Nave,	Christopher Cunningham, sen.	John Davis,
Wm. Cox,	Lewis Jones,	Joshua Barten, sen.,	John Barley.

Originally Washington District included a portion of what is now Western North Carolina. It covered the lands acquired by the Wataugans and Jacob Brown under deeds from the Cherokees in 1775, extending eastward to the Blue Ridge rather than the Allegheny range.

WATAUGA RIVER: Site where first permanent Overmountain settlements were made; first free and independent government in America was organized here in 1772. The name Watauga comes from the Creek word ''Wetoga'', meaning broken waters.

WASHINGTON COUNTY LISTS OF TAXABLES 1778-1801

This Washington County Tax List is taken from Washington County, Tennessee, Records, as transcribed by Mary Hardin McCown, Vol. 1. The Washington County Lists of Taxables 1778-1801 was privately published in 1964, Johnson City, Tennessee, by Mrs. McCown.

1778. Valentine Sevier, Sheriff, Dr. to the County Court of — The Following Taxes Collected from the several— (torn)—The County Aforesd. 1778. (To wit.)

Assest by James Maulden, Josiah Hoskins & John Higgans. Retd to Benjn Willson, Esqr.

Abbott, Elijah	Curtis, Joshua	Higgans, John	Shelly, Philip
Arnold, John	Davis, John	Holdway, Timothy	Sweeton, Edward
Asher, Charles	Denny, Samuel	Hoskins, E----	Tate, Samuel
Asher, Charles	Durram, Nathn.	Hoskins, Jesse	Tidwell, George
Asher, John	Flannary, William	Hoskins, John	Tidwell, John
Asher, Thomas	Garrott, Amos	Hoskins, Josiah	Ward, Benjamin
Asher, Wm.	Gentrey, Joseph	Hoskins, Ning	White, Richard
Brown, Zekel	Griffin, William	Maulden, A--on	Willson, Benjamin, Esq.
Bunton, Andrew	Grimes, Henry	Maulden, James	Willson, Richd
Certain, James	Grimes, John	Morgan, Leonard	Wooldridge, Richard
Certain, Jo---	Hatherley, Hueins	Oweings, James	
Coleson, James	Hatherley, George	Polestone, Jonas	
Collett, Richard	Hatherley, Samuel	Pains, Henry	
Coward, James	Hicks, David	Renolds, Wm.	
Curtis, David	Hicks, David	Sawyer, William	

Assest by Henry Lyle, Samuel Henry & William McNabb. Retd to Jno, McNabb, Esq.

Arthurr, Matthew	Doddy, Howell	Lain, Lewis	Robertson, Julis
Barksdill, Clevers	Dugger, William	Little, Jonas	Sevier, Robert
Brown, John	Dunging, Jeremiah	McNabb, Baptist	Sevier, Valentine, Sr.
Brown, Wm.	Gilleland, John	McNabb, David	Sevier, Valentine
Carter, Emanuel	Gooding, Drury	McNabb, John, Esqr.	Shelby, John, Esqr.
Carter, John, Esqr.	Greer, Joseph	McNabb, Wm. Esqr.	Stuart, James
Casedy, John	Gris'm, James	Millican, James	Talbert, Hail
Chamble, Jacob	Henry, James	Moore, John	Talbert, Matthew
Cocke, Wm.	Henry, Samuel, Senr.	Nave, Teter	Talbert, Matthew, Jr.
Cooper, Patience	Hickey, David	Odull, John	Taylor, Isaac
Culberson, Joseph	Hider, Michael	Overall, William	Tipton, Joseph
Culberson, Samuel	Hodge, Ambrose	Parker, Wm.	Ward, William
Cunningham, Christopher	Houghton, Joshua	Pearce, James	Wray, James
Cuningham, Chriso. Jr.	Houghton, Thomas, Esq.	Reeves, George	Young, Robert, Senr.
Denton, James	Hughs, John	Reeves, Jorden	Young, Robert, Jnr.
Denton, Joseph	Jones, Lewis	Reeves, William	
Denton, Samuel	Kenner, John	Robertson, Charles	

Assest by Benja. Cobb, Solomon Smith, Wm. Asher. Retd to John Chisolm, Esqr.

Bayley, William	Cox, Abraham	Masengill, Henry, Sr.	Smith, Samuel
Cawood, John in Viga.	Cox, John	Masengill, Henry	Stout, Hosea
Chasons, Charles	Gris'om, Wm.	Matlock, John	Top, Roger (Virga)
Choate, Austin	Hill, John	Maxsey, Jesse	Underwood, Samuel
Choate, Edward	Hutton, Samuel	Odull, Caleb	Vawter, Jesse in Virga.
Choate, Richard	Little, Mathias	Roach, Jorden	Weaver, Christian
Choate, Thomas	Little, Valentine	Ryley, John	Webb, Jonathan
Cobb, Arthur	Mallock, James	Shells, Arnol.	
	Masengill, Henry, Sr.		

Assest by ----, Retd to Wm. Been, Esqr.

Abbott, James	Bridges, Edward	Cobb, William & Pharoh	Dunkin, Charles
Adcocks, Leonard	Calliham, Joel	Cooper, James	Duncome, Elizabeth
Anthony, William	Calliham, John	Crawford, John	Duncome, John
Bayley, John	Carrole, Delany	Davis, Nathan	Duncome, Joseph
Bean, Jesse	Cavil, Alexr.	Davison, Joseph	Dunkin, John
Been, John	Chis'm, John	Dillingham, Vachworth	Fain, Samuel
Been, Robert	Choate, Christopher	Dixon, Clement, Senr.	Fletcher, Richd.
Been, Wm. Esqr.	Clark, John	Drake, Benjamin	Fletcher, Thomas
Benn, Wm. Junr.	Clark, Henry	Drake, John	Gambrel, Bradley

Gotcher, Henry
Gray, George
Hickky, Henry
Hollis, James
Hufman, Jacob
Hufman, Peter
Hunt, Uriah
Jonachin, Thomas
Kelley, James
Laird, Moses
Lucas, Robert, Esqr.

McMahon, John B.
McMahon, John B.
Martin, George
Masengill, Michael
Morey, Morgan
Mitchell, Joab
Parker, Charles
Renfro, Peter
Rice, John
Richardson, George
Richardson, Henry

Richardson, Mary
Russell, George, Esqr.
Russell, George
Russell, John
Russell, John
Stringer, William
Thompson, Absolum
Thompson, Andrew
Thompson, Andrew
Thompson, Charles
Titsworth, Isaac

Titsworth, Thomas
Vance, John
Walker, Danl.
Walker, James
Walker, Richard
Ward, Demsey
Wheeler, John
White, John
Whitter, James
Williams, Tho.
Young, Wm.

Assest by ----, Retd to Mchl. Woods, Esqr.

Atkins, Charles
Bayley, Robert
Bond, Jesse
Brown, Jacob
Brown, John
Cannon, Wm.
Chosewood, Alexr.
Crawford, Samuel
England, Charles
England, John
England, Joseph

English, Joseph
English, Wm.
Gibson, Benja.
Gibson, Humphrey
Isbell, Godfrey
Isbell, Zacha.
Johnston, Benjamin
Johnston, Wm.
Jones, James
Jones, Philipp
Leech, Joseph

Lewis, Surrel
McAdams, James
Nave, Henry
Nave, John
Oneal, John
Pinson, Aaron
Pinson, Joseph
Pinson, Thomas
Reding, John
Roase, Hosea
Shurley, Edward

Shurley, John
Shurley, Thomas
Smith, Edward
Smith, John
Thornton, Wm.
Tipton, Jonathan
Tipton, Jonathan
Trevillian, Richd.
Vaich, Jeremiah
Webb, Martin
Woods, Michael

Assest by Saml. Williams. Retd to Zacha. Isbell, Esqr.

Robert Box & Frances Hughes
Baits, Henry, Senr.
Baits, Henry, Jr.
Bond, Charles
Border, Michael
Box, Edward
Box, James
Clark, William, Esqr.
Clauson, William
Conway, Philip

Dunham, Joseph
Earnest, Henry
English, Joseph
Evans, John
Evans, Thomas
Hair, Daniel
Hightower, Oldum
Holley, Jonathan
Ireby, Isom
Isbell, Zachariah, Esq.

Murphy, Patrick
Price, Thomas
Reed, George
Rice, Edward
Rice, Leonard
Seduxas, Emanuel
Sevier, John
Sherrill, Philip
Sherrill, Samuel
Sherrill, Samuel, Jr.

Underwood, George
Vance, John
Waddell, John
Walton, Jesse, Esqr.
    do   do
Williams, Benjamin
Williams, Joshua
Wood, John

Assest by ----, Retd to Jacob Womack, Esqr.

Allison, Charles
Allison, John
Allison, Robert
Allison, Wm.
Anderson, Barnaba
Angland, Adren
Arrington, Charles
Bacon, Michael
Barker, Thomas
Bird, Jonathan
Blackburn, Robert
Blackwell, John
Blair, Hugh
Bradley, James
Brown, Thomas
Buchanan, James
Bullard, John
Bullard, Joseph
Burleson, Aron
Burleson, Thomas
Campbell, Alexr.
Campbell, David
Campbell, William
Carrack, John
Chambers, David
Chambers, John
Chambers, William
Coal, Solomon

Craduck, David
Denton, Jonathan
Dunham, Daniel
Dunham, Henry
Dunham, John
Dunham, Ruebin
Edwards, Evan
English, James
Fowler, Joseph
Gentry, Charles
Gentry, Robert
Gest, Benja.
Gest, Joseph
Gibson, John
Gillihan, John
Gillaspy, Thomas
Gozach, Sandofer
Grymes, James
Hamilton, Francis
Hamilton, Isiah
Hamilton, Jacob
Handley, Samuel
Hobson, Edward
Howard, John
Hudson, George
Hughes, David
Hutton, William
Johnson, Isaac

Jones, Henry
Karr, George
Kenedy, Daniel
Lyle, Samuel
McCartney, Charles
McCartney, James
McCord, David
McNamee, Peter
Magahah, Farill
Martin, Andrew
Martin, Joseph
Martin, Josiah
Michael, James
Miller, James
Moore, Moses
More, Moses
Mulchy, Phillip
Morrison, John
Murray, James
Murrow, Alexr.
Nelson, Elisha
Nelson, Southey
Nelson, William
Patterson, John
Pinson, Aaron
Pinson, John
Posey, David

Pyburn, Benjamin
Randol, James
Rawlings, Asael
Ritchie, John
Ritchie, William
Roberts, Edmund
Robertson, -----
Robertson, John
Scott, Thomas
Sherrill, Adam
Shurley, Robert
Stepheson, James
Story, William
Taylor, Christopher
Trimble, John
Trimble, William
Weaver, Samuel
Wilson, -----
Williams, Jarret
Webb, John
Willson, Adam
Willson, Isaac
Willson, Joseph
Willson, Robert
Womack, Jacob
Woods, Bartholomew
Wray, Joseph

RESUME

(This brief pictorial sketch of early Tennessee History is not intended as a source of research, but rather as a medium of calling attention to some of the highlights of that period of the early settlement up to the Battle of King's Mountain. The sketches by the artist are based on available descriptions and knowledge of the site. The dates, names and places are as accurate as available research materials have indicated.)

Following the pattern of history, the conflict between the white man and the red man was inevitable. It is needless to blame either race. The frontiersman, accustomed to overcoming any obstacle that stood in his way, thought of the Indian as an inferior being who claimed vast uninhabited lands that he did not use. The pioneer would not, or could not, understand the Indian's viewpoint or philosophy. Thus the ever surging tide of settlers kept pushing and crowding the red man further and deeper behind the mountain barriers. The Indian resentful of broken treaties and continuous encroachment on his ancestral lands and way of life, struck back in the only way he knew. He fought with a savage brutality, following his own fierce standards of warfare. This aroused the anger of the white man, who, tolerating no opposition, hit back with a fury inspired by fear.

The frontier hunters and pioneer explorers, following the Indian and buffalo trails, crossed over the mountains to the beautiful valleys of the Watauga, Holston and Nolichucky Rivers. The glowing descriptions and tales, told by these early travelers on their return, lured many adventuresome persons to move their families into the Overmountain Territory. These first permanent settlers sought peaceful living with the Indians, but the unrestrained greed on the part of land speculators and the unscrupulous actions of some, in their disregard of Indian rights, caused trouble. Boundary agreements were not respected. This gave the Indians cause for anger.

Along with the good people, there also came a lawless element. The leaders of the infant settlement, recognizing the need for an organized society, called the heads of the families together and formed the "Watauga Association." This government lasted until the Revolutionary conflict forced the settlers to become part of a larger state. Changing the name to "Washington District," they were accepted into the jurisdiction of North Carolina. That Assembly changed the name to "Washington County." During the Revolutionary War years, the Overmountain settlers were North Carolinians. After the war, when North Carolina ceded the territory to the United States Government, the Overmountain people organized their own state. The leaders petitioned the United States Congress to be accepted into the union as "The State of Franklin." They missed becoming the 14th state by one vote. During the latter part of 1789 the territory was accepted by the United States Government, becoming, "The United States Territory South of the River Ohio." In 1796 the Territory finally achieved statehood as "Tennessee," the 16th state. The Watauga settlers lived under six different governments during this 24-year period, 1772-1796.

The pioneer mountaineers of Western North Carolina and East Tennessee played an important role in the Revolutionary battles of the South. A company of Volunteers fought in the first "Battle of Charleston," May, 1776. They won the first battle west of the mountains, "The Battle of Island Flats." They fought in the "Battle of Boonesborough" and many other engagements vital to the successful outcome of the conflict. The men under William Campbell and Charles Robertson were the last to fire guns in the "Battle of Guilford Court House." General Greene, thinking this battle lost, sounded a retreat. The mountaineers had moved back into a wooded area where bayonets were useless. When Cornwallis charged them, their deadly fire inflicted heavy casualties with their Indian style of fighting. Even in their apparent victory, the English lost over a third of their army. General Cornwallis described this fight as the bloodiest battle of the war. General Greene in a letter written from his South Carolina camp on the Pee Dee River said (Quote from Williams' *Tennessee During The Revolution*, Appendix G): "The back-country people are bold and daring in their make, but the people of the seaboard are sickly and indifferent militia." This Battle at Guilford Court House broke the back of the English campaign in the south; Cornwallis practically retreated to Wilmington. There were some 700 Overmountain Men in the last "Battle of Charleston." During the Revolutionary War these rugged mountaineers participated in battles fought in Georgia, South Carolina, North Carolina, Kentucky, Indiana, and Tennessee. It has been told that a company was present at the final surrender of Cornwallis at Yorktown. The title "Volunteers" was deserved even then.

The Overmountain Men fought on two battle fronts during this war. The Indians, British allies, threatened at their back, while the English troops were successfully moving toward the mountain barrier. These sturdy men helped turn the tide of battle. Because of the Indian alliance with England, many pioneers felt that the Cherokees had forfeited their claims on the Overmountain lands. This feeling was not entertained by all the people. Many of the American leaders tried to maintain a just dealing with the red man, but greed and the successful fight for freedom against the Royal government were elements that worked against the Indians.

The sequel of this story will continue in the forthcoming pictorial book, *The State of Franklin*. This next book will originate from Greeneville, Tennessee, the permanent Capitol of that unusual state.

ONE HEROIC HOUR AT KING'S MOUNTAIN

October 7, 1780

"The Battle that changed the course of American history"

THE OVERMOUNTAIN MEN

Pat Alderman   Verna Alderman

We come ov-er the high moun-tain looking for the prom-ised land

Dim trails ev-er lead-ing west-ward Nar-row steep and treach-er-ous

Sun and moon beat down up-on us Dan-ger lurks on ev-ry hand Brave men

Nev-er look-ing back-ward as we fol-low un-known trails Ov-er the hills

Down thru the vales fol-low-ing the riv-ers fear-less on our way peo-ple seek-ing

free-dom lands to build a home West-ward and on-ward to lands un-known

Like specters from out of nowhere came an army of patriots and pioneers. It was not an army by military standards. It had no uniforms; its guns, though not obsolete, were a hodge-podge variety of flintlock and musket, each weapon exhibiting extreme degrees of durability and class but each weapon and owner were an independent entity. Esprit de corps was a strange expression to these people, but yet the competence and pride that each man felt toward his own ability and the ability of his comrade in arms, without the fatal complacency, was an awesome factor for the British.

But this little army that wasn't an army destroyed a superior force in material and number, and then, like the miracle army it was, faded into the mountain mists.

The apparition the British saw at King's Mountain October 7, 1780 was no apparition at all, but an integrated force of flesh and muscle and sinew, wedded to one common purpose and directed by the destiny of a growing nation.

The Revolutionary War from beginning to end was very unmilitary; and by contemporary standards its battles were mere skirmishes.

But never was a call to arms more eloquent, no appeal so fraught with logic, no cause more drastic, no victory more demanding, no challenge more inspiring, than the Tory threat to the peace and independency of America.

The results have reverberated down through the years and each succeeding generation of descendants of those mighty men takes increasing pride in the contribution their glorious ancestors played in uniting this nation.

Moral issues were at stake — and independence. A vision from the mountain top had given them an insight of greatness; and although they were a combination of heterogeneous cultures seeking a free and independent democracy, they fought as great men and left a great imprint on history.

The battlefield was their hearthstone. Clear of mind, pure of thought, determined and resolved, these sturdy people met the enemy and he was theirs. And by their conduct on that memorable day, the foundation of a great government was laid.

The patriotic half of young America who fought and supported the War was endowed with a broad outlook. The other half was opposed to the fight for freedom and the attendant responsibilities of self-rule that it would impose.

They feared reprisals and recriminations by the British; they resented the privations and loss of income from a long and tedious fight. They were non-committal to the patriots and attempted an attitude of neutrality where the British were concerned. A third of the population of the new America were out-and-out Tories. Congress did not have the ability or authority to wage this war. It was in reality a fight between thirteen individual Colonial States against the trained professionals of England. The Patriots had to fight a three-front war: one against their Tory neighbors; a second with the Indians, allies of the British, who threatened their rear; and, of course, the Loyalist regiments, commanded and supplied by the Royal Empire.

The New England and the Southern phases of the Revolutionary War were entirely different in cause and intent. All thirteen States had differing interests. Their unity was geographical and not political. Their one common bond was liberty and freedom from English oppression.

Thus the year 1780 was almost a disastrous and overwhelming one for Congress and the Americans. The war in the New England States was at a stalemate. The British had moved into the South and were fast overrunning Georgia and the Carolinas. General Cornwallis and his growing army seemed invincible. No organized resistance seemed possible. Then, Saturday afternoon, October 7, 1780, about three o'clock, came a thunderbolt that changed the course of history.

The King's Mountain victory looms with even greater significance when viewed through international intrigue of 1778-1783. France and Spain were secretly helping America, not because of brotherly love or friendship, but to hurt England. Benjamin Franklin and Silas Deane were earnestly seeking open allies to aid their struggling country. The victory at Saratoga, and Franklin's persuasive arguments, overrode the one hundred and fifty years of enmity the French had for the colonists. French leaders saw a selfish opportunity to embarrass England on another front, and, at the same time, protect French possessions in North America. They agreed to furnish troops, ships and money. But, had the French leaders realized their support of republicanism would hasten the fall of their own monarchy, they would have perhaps joined forces with England and helped destroy America.

Spain would not espouse the American cause, Florida Blanca, the Spanish Minister, hated England and all Americans. One of Spain's conditions in their alliance with France, was the agreement that the Mississippi Valley would be Spain's. All during the dismal year of 1780, Blanca was pressuring Congress, through the French Representative, for a cession of at least part of the Mississippi Valley.

The successful campaign of the British in the south caused the government of Lord North to project the forming of the Carolinas, Georgia, and the Bahamas into a separate Colonial Territory. The rule of international law was: "Hold by Force." Each of the powers wanted to control as much territory as possible.

During all this back stage maneuvering, Franklin kept selling the advantages to be obtained by helping America. His personal magnetism won the support needed and so some prominent men — Lafayette and de Kalb, French officers; Pulaski and Kosciuszko from Poland; and German von Steuben — became great names in American history. They, like Franklin and Deane, were aware of the growing strength and vitality of the young republic. But few of the world leaders realized that the loose federation of states would one day grow into a strong union that would influence the policies of the world.

| Marquis De Lafayette | Barron de Kalb | Count Pulaski | Thaddeus Kosciusko | Baron von Steuben |

Now quoting from Bancroft, "we come to the series of events which closed the American contest and restored peace to the world...France was straining every nerve to cope with her rival Britain in the four quarters of the globe; Spain was exhausting her resources for the conquest of Gibralter; but the incidents which overthrew the Ministry of Lord North and reconciled Great Britain to America, had their springs in South Carolina."

The King's Mountain battle was not the most strategic victory of the Revolutionary War, but it was the most decisive. One year and twelve days afterwards, General Cornwallis surrendered in Yorktown, Virginia. The men of this Ghost Legion constituted the last effective resistance to the British onslaught. These Overmountain frontiersmen were not trained soldiers, and military discipline was practically unknown. They belonged to small local companies of pioneer settlers, organized under their own leader, to protect the frontiers from Indian raids. Their one common interest was family and home. Every man and officer fought for himself, and the best officers were those who fought best; they were leaders rather than commanders. When fighting was in progress the officer was expected to be up front. Failure to do this would indicate cowardice, and he would be removed from command by acclamation rather than court-martial. When a leader thought a campaign was needed for the common good, he would send riders to summon the men to prearranged muster ground. They would come mounted and equipped at their own expense, expecting no government pay. Living in their primitive independence, behind their tall mountain barrier, they had scant knowledge of the war raging along the eastern seaboard.

These frontiersmen were sons of frontiersmen, accustomed to the rugged life of the new country. They were courageous souls, daring and eager as they ventured along the unfamiliar trails leading westward. The wide expanse of mountains, hills and valleys, covered with virgin forests and teeming with wild game, challenged their pioneer spirits. This unhampered wilderness freedom, far removed from royal rulers and their taxes, was to their liking. These bold, resolute men were self-reliant. They were independent, individualistic, and not always inclined to respect or observe the niceties of the soft life. Living on the outskirts of civilization, their law was to have and to hold. They depended on the forest and streams for their sustenance. They would pitch a fight, scalp an Indian or wrestle ("rassel") a bear at the drop of a hat.

This mountaineer force did not dress in the general military fashion of the day. The long fringed hunting shirt was worn by most of the pioneer army, and was usually made of dressed deer skin, very Indian in looks and use. It was made with an opening in front with plenty of overlap. A leather or wampum type belt fastened around the waist would hold it together, and at the same time make a wallet or pouch in which to carry food and other essentials. From scabbards, attached to the belt on either side, hung a tomahawk and knife. The pants were either made of skins or homespun. Leggins and moccasins, made of leather and sewed with strips of deer skin, protected legs and feet. Lighter clothing, made in same fashion out of homespun or linsey, was worn in the warmer months. During the winter the summer clothing was worn under the skin garments for extra warmth. Caps were made of animal skins; hats of beaver hides or pressed animal hair.

These are the Americans that arose to the need of the hour. Needing a government, they organized the Watauga Association and administered it. This was the first organized political body, free and independent of any other state, in America. When their freedom was threatened they came out of the hills to fight. They had no staff, quartermaster, commissary, surgeon, or chaplain. A shot pouch, tomahawk, knife, powderhorn, knapsack, blanket and rifle constituted his outfit. The earth was his bed, the sky his cover, the creeks and rivers his source of water.

These are the soldiers that made up the unknown army that defeated Colonel Ferguson on King's Mountain, October 7th, 1780. The British timetable was broken, the Tories were frightened and Patriots were given time to reorganize. This is why King's Mountain is important in America's Revolutionary War history.

THE WAR IN REVIEW

Monument to the Signers of the Mecklenburg Declaration at Charlotte, North Carolina.

The King's Mountain victory signaled the turning point of the Revolutionary War in the South. After six long years of conflict, the fortunes of the Patriots hung in the balance. Nothing but faith and hope sustained the American cause during this dismal war. From the first battle at Lexington to the surrender of Cornwallis at Yorktown, it was a desperate fight. Congress had little power and less credit. Inadequate leadership and treachery from the inside were almost fatal.

Among the events that led up to the war with England were: The Stamp Act; the Riot in New York; The Boston Massacre; the Battle of Alamance; the Tea Parties; the Five Intolerable Acts imposed by England to punish Massachusetts; and the Taxation Without Representation. Instead of subduing the Patriots, these unjust acts and levies pushed them further away from the mother country. When the final breaking point came, many of the colonies pulled away and set up their own government. Virginia was the first. Others soon followed. They elected representatives who formed the first Continental Congress. This body met in Philadelphia on September 5, 1774.

The battles at Lexington and Concord during April 1775; the Mecklenburg Declaration of Independence at Charlotte, May 20th; the capture of Ticonderoga and Crown Point by Ethan Allen and the Green Mountain Boys, also in May; and the battle of Bunker Hill in June, were the opening guns of the long seven-years war that was destined to change the history of the world.

Patriots in every colony made ready to fight. Militia companies were formed in every settlement. They collected arms and ammunition and hid them in places of rendezvous.

The British placed General Gage in command, and sent in troops and naval reinforcements to put down the rebellion. The charter of Massachusetts was annulled — the port of Boston closed. The war had begun.

Ethan Allen and the Green Mountain Boys Capture Fort Ticonderoga

On July 3, 1775, General George Washington assumed command of the American Armies. He was hampered throughout the war with insufficient troops, desertions, and discontent. Unconquerable faith supported him throughout those dreary, desolate years. Integrity of purpose, and his understanding of the attitudes and prejudices of the people, aided him in uniting them in the objectives of their venture. Washington himself was the embodiment of the cause of freedom. His unselfish loyalty forced upon the people the realization that they and the new America were one. He reflected the true idealism of the Union and the Patriot.

When Virginia revolted, Governor Dunmore fled to the safety of a British warship and attempted to wage

George Washington takes command of the American Armies.

war on the Virginia Colony from this vantage point. His force was badly defeated December 9th in the Battle of the Great Bridge. In retaliation, Dunmore caused the town of Norfolk to be burned New Year's Day, 1776. As active resistance spread, the Royal Governors from New Hampshire to Georgia fled to the safety of the British Navy. The King's Government collapsed and the Whigs took over, setting up their own Provincial Assemblies. They drilled and armed local companies of minutemen. Paper money was issued. Conditions were moving fast forward declaring independence.

The Americans who opposed the King called themselves "Whigs". The name was taken from the Liberal Party of England. This group had long opposed the conservative "Tory" element or Party. The Patriots adopted this name and became known as the party that supported the revolt.

Those who supported the King's cause were called "Tories". The colonists who adhered to this belief composed about one-third of the population in the new country. They fell into several classes. One was the sect that opposed war of any nature. Another segment, unfamiliar with the issues at stake, was satisfied with existing conditions. They felt that England would soon subdue the Rebels and so preferred not to get involved.

The worst of the lot was that group of Tories, existing in every community, who made the name hated. Their whole effort in the war was for selfish, personal gain; and they saw in the conflict a possible way of acquiring their neighbors' property with legal sanction. They did not mind the killing, robbing, and plundering required to gain their objective. They visualized the rich reward for their faithfulness to the Crown. They turned from seemingly honest men to criminals, and they would betray a neighbor who had been their friend. They were much more dangerous than the armies in the battlefields.

The British used the Tories as they did the Indians. When they were through with them, they forsook these allies and left them homeless, friendless and without help. They literally turned their backs on them because they despised them. Many of the generous Americans helped their treacherous neighbors many times after the war was over. The Revolutionary War would have been over two or three years earlier but for this group of Tories.

A North Carolina Whig

With the Tory element stronger in the South, the British command made plans for a campaign in that direction. Governors Martin, of North Carolina, and Campbell, of South Carolina, thought the subjection of these two states would be a simple matter. Both had fled the colonies for the safety of a British warship, and together they planned a coastal invasion. A Highland Scottish settlement along Cross Creek (now Fayetteville, North Carolina), loyal to the Crown, answered Martin's appeal. The Scotchmen assembled some two thousand strong under General Donald McDonald, and marched to join Clinton on the coast. Learning this, the Patriots met the Tories at Moore's Creek Bridge February 27, 1776, and completely defeated the kilted force. The rebel forces in Eastern North Carolina were under the commands of Colonels James Moore, Alexander Lillington and Richard Caswell. Clinton, unable to land his force, withdrew.

Moore's Creek Battleground

For several months, General Washington had confined the English Army under General Howe, who had replaced General Gage, in Boston. Unable to make a direct assault because of a shortage of ammunition, Washington resorted to subterfuge. Howe, thinking he was outmanned, evacuated Boston on March 27th. He left behind a great amount of military supplies which were quickly taken over by the Americans. In addition, much needed food, left behind by the British, was also appropriated.

During this campaign, the first American flag was flown — the Grand Union. It contained thirteen stripes — seven red and six white — representing the thirteen colonies. The white cross of Saint Andrew and the red cross of Saint George were shifted to the upper lefthand corner of the staff. This indicated that the colonists had not yet declared independence. John Paul Jones first flew this flag from his battleship, December 3, 1775. Previously the British ensign had been flown in the colonies.

The next move of the British was against Charleston, South Carolina. General Clinton and Colonel Cornwallis with a strong command, and the support of a fleet of forty warships under Admiral Peter Parker, attacked the Palmetto Log Fort on Sullivan Island, June 28th, 1776. This fort was commanded by Colonel William Moultrie and four hundred thirty-five men. Isaac Motte and Francis Marion were his first and second officers. The British fired their three hundred cannons all day with little effect. Most of the shots would sink harmlessly into the soft logs or sand. The Americans, with only twenty-eight rounds of ammunition for their thirty cannons, had to make every shot count. Moultrie had instructed his gunners to wait until the gun smoke cleared from the British ships, then take careful aim before firing. The Bristol, Flag Ship of Admiral Parker, was hit on the quarter-deck. Governor William Campbell, Admiral Parker and Captain Morris were all severely wounded. Over two hundred Tars were killed and wounded during the contest. Several ships went aground, and one blew up when a Patriot shot hit her powder storeroom. At sundown, the crippled British Fleet retired without doing any significant damage to Charleston and its valiant defenders. Why no move was made by three thousand regulars who were landed on Long Island, has always been a mystery.

Lord Clinton

Sergeant Jasper rescues Flag at Fort Moultrie.

Colonel Moultrie had placed a regiment of sharpshooters, under Colonel Isaac Huger, on James Island. These men in rifle pits were his second line of defense. Among the men of this force was a platoon of Overmountain men under Lieutenant Felix Walker. During the day of the battle, the citizens of Charleston watched the progress of the fight from vantage points, including house tops. They knew their safety and welfare depended on those determined perspiring men in Fort Sullivan.

Colonel Moultrie was flying a beautiful flag over the Fort. It was blue with a white crescent, and the motto LIBERTY was emblazoned across its length.

During the battle, a shot from one of the British guns cut the flag staff, and it fell outside the Fort wall, on the battle side. Sergeant Jasper, seemingly unafraid of the shots flying all around, clambered down and regained the flag. Back inside the Fort wall, using a halberd or sponge stick for a staff, Jasper soon had the flag flying over the Fort again. A big cheer was raised by the watching populace for this brave performance, and Governor Rutledge awarded Sergeant Jasper a sword in recognition of his valor. Jasper accepted the sword but refused a Lieutenant's commission. He was killed in a later battle.

Colonel Moultrie had eleven men killed and twenty-six wounded. Some historians have rated this battle as one of the three decisive victories of the Revolution. The Moore's Creek and Fort Moutltrie victories saved the South from invasion for some two years.

On July 2, 1776, Richard Henry Lee made a motion in Congress that the "united colonies are, and of a right ought to be, free and independent states." To give form to this motion, Congress adopted on July 4th, "The Declaration of Independence," written by Thomas Jefferson of Virginia. This paper is perhaps the most important political instrument ever written. By its virtue, each colony became a state.

Among the many events of the year 1776 was the Cherokee Uprising against the Overmountain men; the Battle of Long Island; the loss of New York to the British; the defeats at White Plains and in Canada; the destruction of the Lake Champlain Fleet; the British recapture of Crown Point and Newport, Rhode Island; and Washington's surprise victory over the Hessians in Trenton on Christmas Day. Thus the historic year of 1776 was a gloomy one, despite victories at Princeton, Bennington, Stillwater and Saratoga. Losses at Brandywine and Germantown brought into the open the animosity of some of the command toward Washington. Several members of Congress were loud in their clamor against Washington's conduct of the war. They wanted him to drive the enemy from Philadelphia immediately. But General Washington, knowing how weak his army was, did not dare let the enemy know his weakness.

A plot by a French officer, General Conway, assisted by Gates and many other jealous officers, made a desperate attempt to discredit Washington and place Gates as Commander-in-Chief. The victory at Saratoga was cited as a comparison of their ability. Gates never gave credit to the small companies, led by their individual commanders, that won Saratoga. Gates wanted to retreat. It was men like Daniel Morgan who saved the day. Gates lied out of the situation; Conway resigned and apologized. Washington was too well respected and loved for the loyal members of Congress to do anything as foolish as replace him. This was known as "the Conway Cabal."

Burgoyne surrenders to Gates after Saratoga.

Winter at Valley Forge

On November 15 "The Articles of Confederation," providing a form of government for the United States, was adopted by Congress; but these did not go into effect until after the war because the thirteen colonies had to ratify the document.

The winter at Valley Forge can well be called the Valley of Despair. This moral scar on American political history was a direct result of jealousy, corruption and duplicity. Many of the congressmen, and some of the highly-ranked military officers, were jealous of George Washington and his loyal command. They were willing to do anything to hurt the General.

Even though it was a minority group, their selfish acts brought a period of desperation to the fighting Patriots of America. Using bribery in the right places, these traitors had wormed their way into responsible positions. They filled their own pockets, while handling government supplies and contracts. Frequently they sold the supplies, intended for our troops, to the British for higher prices. Sometimes they would destroy food, clothing and other supplies rather than accept the paper money issued by the government. Many of the appointed commissary officers would let food, clothing and tents rot in barrels on road sides, if they could not see a profit for themselves. The suffering at Valley Forge and other sections meant nothing to these mercenaries.

Soldiers at Valley Forge went hungry, shoeless, blanketless, and many shelterless because of this situation. General Washington had caused many shelters to be built from the trees of the area, but not near enough could be put up before the winter storms had made such work impossible. Soldiers often had to share one ragged suit between them. Valley Forge will always be a symbol of American patriotism at its noblest and purest form.

Then came spring and a pledge of help from France. With this turn of events, new recruits swelled Washington's force. General Clinton, who had succeeded Howe, evacuated Philadelphia. Washington followed and attacked Clinton near Monmouth, New Jersey June 28, 1778. Clinton continued his retreat to New York. The American Army set up camp at White Plains, pinning Clinton's forces to the seaboard.

Meanwhile, the Tories and Indians were invading the Wyoming Valley of Pennsylvania, plundering, burning and killing. At night, these invaders would torture their prisoners with savage devices. They followed this destruction of homes and settlements on through Cherry Valley located in New York State. This savage Tory-Indian force was led by Colonel John Butler. In all sections of the country, such warfare was carried on by some of the Tories and Indian renegades. This savage and useless cruelty hurt the King's cause. It created a lasting hostility in the hearts of the Americans in all thirteen States. The Indian's alliance with England became a tragic affair for them.

NORTHWESTERN CAMPAIGN

British Agents in the southwest and northwest territories, were busy inciting the Indians to attack the frontier settlements of Tennessee and Kentucky. In the northwest, the English had posted garrisons at Kaskaskia on the Mississippi; Cahokia, across the river from St. Louis; Vincennes on the Wabash; and Fort Detroit on Lake Erie. Colonel George Rogers Clarke secured backing and authority from Patrick Henry, Governor of Virginia, for a

Indian Massacre from McGee History by Victor Perard

campaign into the northwest territory. Captains Joseph Bowman, Leonard Helm, William Harrod and Major William B. Smith were commissioned to enlist several companies from the Kentucky and Holston Settlements. The place of muster was the Falls of the Ohio. Colonel Clarke found a much smaller force than he expected. When the type and extent of the proposed campaign was revealed to the enlisted men, desertions were many.

Undaunted, Colonel Clarke captured Kaskaskia July 4, 1778, without bloodshed. Shortly afterward, Vincennes was occupied in like manner. Colonel Henry Hamilton, Lieutenant Governor of Canada, regained possession of the Garrison at Vincennes, December 1778. With a force of one hundred thirty men, Colonel Clarke set out to attack Vincennes. The Patriot force had to travel through miles of rough country, often crossing icy streams waist deep. They recaptured

George Rogers Clarke

Vincennes on February 23, 1779. Colonel Henry Hamilton, called the hair (scalp) buyer, was captured, along with his force and a big store of supplies intended for the Indians. Colonel Clarke's conquest of the northwest saved that territory for America. Without this successful undertaking, the Canadian line could well have been the Ohio River, instead of being along the Great Lakes.

Another campaign of equal importance to the Tennessee settlers was the Chickamauga Campaign, commanded by Colonel Evan Shelby. Some six hundred men embarked on boats from the mouth of Big Creek on the Holston River in April 1779. The streams, swollen by spring freshets, made for a fast trip to the Chickamauga towns. The surprise attack on this Indian country was a complete success. The Indians fled to the hills and forests. Large stores of supplies, furnished by the English for the attack on the Tennessee settlers, were captured. Many of the towns were burned.

Captain John Montgomery, sent to the northwest with Colonel Clarke, was with this force at the capture of Kaskaskia. Captain Montgomery was sent back to the Holston Settlements to recruit more troops. During the winter months of 1778-1779, Captain Montgomery had enlisted one hundred fifty men for a year's service. Colonel Shelby, planning the Chickamauga Campaign and needing more men, asked the aid of this force. Governor Patrick Henry ordered Captain Montgomery and his men to participate with Shelby. At the close of this mission, Captain Montgomery and his men continued the trip by boat. They rejoined Colonel Clarke in the northwest. Montgomery, promoted to Colonel, was placed in charge of the Kaskaskia district for a period. Captain James Shelby, son of Colonel Evan Shelby, accompanied Colonel Montgomery with sixteen men. Captain Shelby was placed in command of Fort Patrick Henry at Vincennes.

These two campaigns stopped, for the time being, the large-scale Indian attacks on the settlers of Tennessee and Kentucky, as planned by the English agents. These two ventures proved most important in the course of events that followed.

Montgomery County in Tennessee was named for Colonel Montgomery. The county seat was named Clarkesville in honor of Colonel George Rogers Clarke.

THE WAR MOVES SOUTH

General George Washington, unable to obtain sufficient money or supplies for an active campaign, determined to contain General Clinton to the seaboard. Because of the short term enlistments and shortage of supplies, the American force had again dwindled to less than five thousand men. A month's pay would barely purchase one good meal, and better clothing could be had at home. The American currency was almost worthless, and Congress did not have sufficient influence and strength to make a move.

General Clinton, having failed in the campaign against the northern states, turned his attention again toward the South. He sent Colonel Campbell with three thousand troops to attack Savannah, Georgia. He soon proceeded to overrun and plunder Georgia. Pleased with this foothold, Clinton sailed south to personally

THE SIEGE OF CHARLESTON.
After the picture by Chappel.

direct the campaign. With a strong fleet and an army of thirteen thousand, Clinton laid siege to Charleston. Two months later, on May 12, 1780, General Lincoln surrendered. Lincoln never had sufficient supplies or troops to withstand a siege. When the British entered Charleston, they, with their Hessian mercenaries, pillaged the city. The homes of the Patriots were taken over or burned. Property was taken from any person thought to have anti-royalist sentiments. South Carolina suffered more than any other state during the Revolutionary War.

General Clinton, quickly taking advantage of the defeat of Lincoln's army at Charleston, sent British detachments in all directions. He wanted to subdue the Patriots and demonstrate to the people that it was much better to take the oath of allegiance than to fight. Placing General Cornwallis in charge, with instructions to finish off South Carolina and then move on into North Carolina and Virginia, Clinton returned to New York.

The British and Prussian officers were more interested in filling their own pockets than reuniting the Empire. Thus, the Whigs of the southland faced loss of life, family, property and possessions in the savage raping, wholesale ransacking and reign of terror that followed.

Colonel Abraham Buford and four hundred Virginians, arriving too late to assist Colonel Lincoln in the defense of Charleston, had turned and started back toward North Carolina. Colonel Banastre Tarleton was sent in pursuit and overtook them near Waxhaw, South Carolina. When Colonel Buford saw the hopelessness of the battle, he asked for quarter for his men. Tarleton, wanting to make them an example for the rest of the South, cut them down without mercy or regard of their surrender request. One hundred thirteen were killed outright. Fifty were cut and maimed so badly that they could not be moved. Only fifty-three men were taken prisoners. Less that two hundred were able to escape. This was the type of butchery practiced by Tarleton and his dragoons. The battle cry of the South became "REMEMBER BUFORD AND HIS QUARTERS".

Tarleton's massacre of the Buford Company at Waxhaw, South Carolina

Thomas Sumpter   **Francis Marion**   **Andrew Pickens**

But the South was not that easily taken. Small partisan groups, under leaders chosen from their own members, made fringe war on the English. They would plough by day and fight by night. This type of warfare slowed up the British in their Southern campaign. Among the outstanding leaders were Francis Marion, Thomas Sumpter, Andrew Pickens, Elijah Clarke, Charles McDowell, Andrew Hampton, Benjamin Cleveland, Joseph Winston and many others. Congress finally sent help. A sizeable force under General Gates, who was appointed to take Lincoln's place, composed of various militia groups, was assembled. Two thousand men came from Delaware and Maryland, and they were joined by several companies of militia from Virginia and North Carolina. Gates had been appointed Commander-in-chief by Congress, against Washington's advice. Gates took charge in midsummer at Hillsborough. General Richard Caswell, appointed by the assembly as Major General of the North Carolina militia, joined Gates' force with his command.

In August, Gates moved his army into South Carolina to meet Cornwallis. On the night of August 16th, the advance guards of both armies stumbled into each other. A sharp exchange of shots occurred. Both generals waited until daybreak to give battle. At first dawn, Cornwallis ordered his men to charge. Gates, a poor general, muddled his plans, lost his head and fled. His men, leaderless and demoralized, fled in every direction. The entire army was either killed, captured or scattered. Gates himself did not stop, except for food and sleep, until he

Gates Defeat at Camden   by Chappel

reached Hillsborough some 200 miles away. The result of this battle proved nearly disastrous to the southern patriots. To the British and Tories it seemed to signal final success.

Colonel Patrick Ferguson, aide to Cornwallis, was sent into the district of Ninety-Six to fortify that garrison and organize the Tories. After arriving with a force of some 200 men, Ferguson made this garrison his headquarters. He had the British Mandate read to the people of that section: "We come not to make war on women and children but to relieve their distress." This sounded good to the Tory-inclined. They flocked to the British standard in large numbers. Companies and regiments were organized. Fort Ninety-Six was so named because it was ninety-six miles from the Indian town of Keowee, located just across the river from Fort Prince Charles. Prince Charles was near Keowee River, some ten miles south of the North Carolina line.

The new Tory recruits were thoroughly drilled and disciplined by Ferguson's staff. Small detachments were sent into the surrounding country to recruit others and obtain supplies. These platoons were also on the hunt for Whigs. This instituted a reign of terror in South Carolina and Georgia. Troops under Major Dunlap and Lieutenant Taylor ransacked, plundered, burned and killed. Horses were turned loose on fields

Elijah Clarke

of grain that belonged to the Patriots. Homes were burned, forcing mothers and children to find shelter and food in the forests as best they could. Patriots were shot just because a jealous Tory neighbor had turned their names over to the British leaders.

In Georgia, Colonel Elijah Clarke, commander of a partisan force of the Augusta area, felt forced to disband his company. He and his men decided to wait until more favorable circumstances allowed for renewed fighting against the British. Colonel Clarke, an active patriot leader, figured prominently in the action that took place during the following weeks and months. One of his officers, Colonel John Jones, and some thirty-five recruits, decided to travel north and join the Carolinians. John Freeman was one of the officers, and Benjamin Lawrence served as guide.

They palmed themselves off as Tory recruits enroute to join Ferguson. In the present Greenville, South Carolina, area they heard of the Cedar Springs engagement, and asked to be directed to the defeated Tory detachment, that they might join them in their attempt to regain prisoners taken. A Tory guide volunteered this service. On reaching the Tory encampment about midnight, Colonel Jones surrounded the sleeping soldiers and captured them all. The Tory guide did not know what was taking place until it was too late. The next morning Jones released the prisoners on parole. The captured supplies, ammunition, and guns outfitted his small company; and taking the Tory horses, they forced the unwilling guide to lead them to McDowell's camp.

Fort Prince Charles was located on the east bank of the Keowee River. Colonel Innes, commander of this post, was unaware of the presence of the McDowell force in the area. Innes sent Majors Dunlap and Mills, with a sizeable company, to pursue and capture Colonel Jones and his company of Georgians. Dunlap located the Patriot camp and, thinking he was attacking Jones' small company, charged across the Pacolet River into the unsuspecting Camp of Colonel Charles McDowell. A warning shot by one sentry enabled the Americans to fire on Dunlap's men. Realizing his mistake, Dunlap withdrew across the river. Colonel Andrew Hampton's son Noah was killed in this action, and Hampton blamed McDowell for not putting out more sentries. This was one of three successive night fights: the Cedar Springs attack on Colonel Thomas; Jones' attack on the loyalist camp; and the attack on McDowell by Dunlap and Mills.

McDowell, convinced that Ferguson's invasion threatened the settlements of Western North Carolina, sent for help across the mountains. Messages were sent to Colonel John Sevier and Colonel Isaac Shelby. Sevier had lost his wife, Sarah Hawkins Sevier, in February and could not leave at the time. Also he was unwilling to leave the frontier exposed to Indian attack. Sevier did arrange to send part of his regiment under the command of Major Charles Robertson. Colonel Shelby, delayed because of business in Kentucky, joined McDowell in July with two hundred riflemen. Colonel Shelby was placed in charge of the Overmountain men. About the same time, Colonel Clarke arrived in the area with a company of Georgians. He was looking for the McDowell force but found Sumpter instead.

Fort Anderson, located on Thicketty Creek and commanded by Captain Moore, was headquarters for bands of plundering Tories. Colonel Sumpter directed Clarke to join with Shelby, Robertson, and Hampton for a surprise attack on this Fort. About six hundred mounted riflemen started at sunset and journeyed some twenty-five miles to the Fort which they surrounded at daybreak. Colonel Shelby sent Captain William Cocke to make a demand for the surrender of the stockade. Moore replied that he would defend it to the last man.

Shelby then withdrew and told his officers his plans. He circled the Fort with his men in shooting distance, making ready the attack. This force made such a formidable showing that Moore surrendered without a shot. Ninety-three Loyalists were taken. The Patriots captured two hundred fifty stands of arms and a large store of supplies and ammunition.

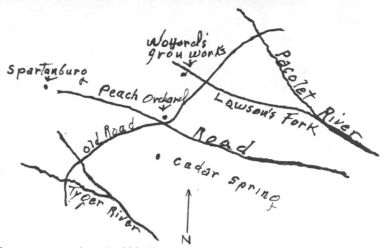

Carrying the supplies and prisoners, Shelby and his men returned to headquarters at McDowell's camp. The McDowell force now numbered 1000; Ferguson's between 1500 and 2000. The Carolina Patriots maintaining camp at Cherokee Ford sent small detachments to harass British troops who were traveling through the countryside enlisting and collecting supplies. Ferguson made several attempts to surprise these groups, but the ever-watchful Americans were never there when the British arrived. They had no fixed camp and were constantly on the move.

On August 7th, Shelby and his men stopped to rest, eat and feed their horses near Fair Forest Creek. Scouts reported the enemy to be one-half mile away. One of Dunlap's Tories accidently fired a gun which warned Shelby's men of the nearness of the British. The Americans withdrew toward the Old Iron Works near Lawson's Ford on the Pacolet and took their positions near Cedar Springs on ground suitable for battle. Major Dunlap soon made his appearance, confident of victory. The severely-fought battle lasted about half an hour. Dunlap's Tory militia waged a terrific fight, but Shelby's and Clarke's well-placed riflemen inflicted heavy losses. Many hand fights occurred during this battle. One was between Colonel Clarke and two Tories. Being a giant of a man, he soon knocked one down and the other fled. The Americans beat back the enemy with heavy losses. Dunlap's fleeing forces came up with Ferguson's main force some two miles from Cedar Springs. The retreating men were reorganized, and the Tories advanced to give battle to the Patriots. Shelby and Clarke meanwhile began a withdrawing, delaying type of action. After several miles of this, Ferguson abandoned the chase.

McDowell, fearing an attack on his camp at Cherokee, moved to Smith's Ford, about ten miles farther south. Colonels Clarke and Shelby remained in camp several days, letting their men get a much needed rest. Several needed to have their wounds treated, and time to mend. Clarke, his son, and Major Charles Robertson were slightly wounded during this battle. The location of this battle site has been much contested. Suffice to say that it was near Cedar Springs or Wofford's Iron Works.

MUSGROVE MILL BATTLE

Scouts reported that two hundred men were stationed at Musgrove's Mill, forty miles from McDowell's Camp. These loyalist troops were placed there to guard the ford across Enoree River. Ferguson was camped about midway between the American camp and Musgrove's Mill. Since Shelby's and Robertson's time of enlistment was about up, they volunteered for this assignment. Colonel Elijah Clarke and his Georgians also asked to take part in the mission. With three hundred mounted riflemen they set out in the late afternoon. They wanted to make most of the trip during the night. This was done for two reasons: secrecy and speed. A night march in August was favorable to the stamina of horses. They also had to slip unobserved past Ferguson's force. They followed a road part of the way, sacrificing possible detection for speed. Among the officers were Captains James McCall, Samuel Hammond, James Williams, Joseph McDowell, Valentine Sevier, and David Vance.

Among the streams crossed on their route were the Pacolet, and Tyger. They passed within four miles of Ferguson's camp, in the Brandon Settlement, and rode all night without stopping. The Americans halted about one mile from Musgrove's Mill and sent scouts to reconnoiter. The scouts ran into a small detachment of Tory scouts returning to camp. In the exchange of shots, two of the Loyalists were killed and others wounded. The Americans, though some were wounded, were able to ride back to the main force. A native Patriot living nearby informed the Americans that several hundred re inforcements had arrived the night before from Fort Ninety-Six, enroute to join Ferguson.

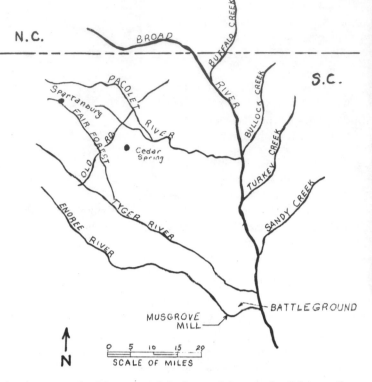

The news of the larger force made a desperate situation for the Mountaineers. The men were weary and their horses were tired because of the long night march of forty miles. But Ferguson, being stationed at their rear, left little room for retreat. They had no choice but to fight. On a timbered ridge about one-half mile from the mill, an improvised breastwork of logs and brush was thrown together. A fence offered some protection. The American lines extended some three hundred yards in a semicircle along the ridge and across the road. The Patriots took their positions, somewhat concealed behind this cover. Shelby took the right wing, Clarke the left, Captain Williams the middle. A corps of twenty horsemen was placed behind each wing for reserves. Later, these came to be needed in the heat of battle.

Meanwhile the arrival of the two remaining Tory scouts at the mill caused much commotion. The Loyalist officers had their headquarters in Edmond Musgrove's home. A hurried council was held. Colonel Innes, in charge of the detachment moving to join Ferguson, was for attacking the rebels at once. Others contended for a delay until more information could be obtained. Colonel Innes prevailed. The British command organized their forces and made ready to catch the "scurvy ragamuffins," as they regarded the Americans. Leaving about one hundred men in camp as reserves, the loyalists crossed the river and advanced. Among the British officers were Major Frazier, in command of the regular detachment stationed at the ford; Captain Abraham De Peyster; Captain David Fanning, who had taken part in the battle of Alamance; and Colonel Daniel Clay, a famous Tory leader of the area.

The American commanders had improvised a plan which was effectively put into action. Captain Shadrack Innman was sent forward with twenty-five mounted men. His orders were to fire upon and provoke the enemy to cross the river and attack. After firing he was to retire, hoping to draw the British into the prepared trap. The strategy worked well. The loyalists eagerly followed, hoping to bayonet the lot. Captain Innman kept up a show of fighting and retreating. About two hundred yards from the mountaineer breastworks, the English formed lines and advanced. Their first shots went over the heads of the concealed Americans. The mountaineers held their fire as ordered. Their leaders had told them to wait until they could count the buttons on the British coats, then sight their object sure.

The British center, against whom Captain Innman made his feigned attack, saw him retire in apparent confusion. Pressing forward with beat of drum and sound of bugle, shouting "Huzza for King George," the British approached to within seventy yards of the improvised breastworks before the Americans met them with a deadly wall of fire. Their superiority in numbers enabled the Loyalists to continue the attack. A strong force, led by Colonel Innes and Frazier, charged Shelby's wing with bayonet and drove them back after a desperate struggle. Clarke sent his reserve to help Shelby. At this critical moment, Colonel Innes fell wounded. Shelby rallied his men, who raised a frontier Indian war yell and charged into the enemy, forcing them back. An attack against Clarke's wing failed to break that line. Many of the British officers fell during these forward charges, and the few that were left could not rally the men. The Americans now advanced from their positions, and with savage yells began chasing and slashing the fleeing militia. It was a melee.

The British-Tory troops were now in a panicked retreat, closely followed by the entire American force who were knocking down the enemy as they caught them. Captain Shadrack Innman was killed during this final charge. The moans and screams of the wounded and dying, and the pursuit of the retreating British by the Indian-yelling mountaineers, over a battlefield covered with a canopy of smoke, was soul shaking. The terrified Loyalists dropped everything and fled for their lives. Their one thought was to escape those yelling, savage devils at their rear.

Some of the British and Tory reserves had climbed on top of Musgrove's house to watch the fun, never doubting the outcome. They thought that the retreating rebel horsemen under Captain Innman constituted the entire American force in the vicinity. They had raised their voices in shouts of victory as the small force seemed to be retreating. Suddenly the whole picture changed! The onlookers were stunned by the tremendous burst of gunfire. The hidden Americans were mowing down the British in their chaotic retreat. Many of this group on the housetop were paroled Tories. They did not want any part of this savage horde. Long before the retreating Loyalists reached the ford, these men had grabbed their knapsacks and headed for Fort Ninety-Six.

The battle lasted about an hour. The remaining Loyalist force, under the command of Captain De Peyster, returned to Ninety-Six that day, fearing that the Americans might make another attack. Only a small detachment was left to bury the dead and care for the wounded.

Musgrove Battle Ridge
                              **Bridge across Enoree River at site
of Musgrove's Mill**

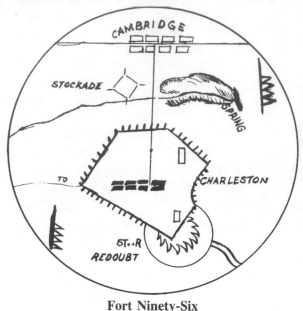

Fort Ninety-Six

The Americans captured around seventy prisoners. It is estimated that about half of the British force was either captured, killed, or wounded. A Tory scouting party arrived soon after the battle. Thinking they might recapture some of the prisoners, they charged across the river to attack the mountaineers, but these gentlemen had departed. On the American side, four were killed and ten wounded. This engagement is thought to have been one of the hardest fought battles with small arms, of any engagement during the southern phase of the Revolutionary War.

At the close of the battle, the mountaineers were anxious to take advantage of the victory, and to continue on to Fort Ninety-Six some twenty-five miles distant. Preparations were being made for such a move when Francis Jones, an express messenger from McDowell's camp, arrived with the news of General Gates' disastrous defeat at Camden. The letter was written by General Richard Caswell, a commanding officer under Gates. The letter, addressed to McDowell and all commanding officers, instructed them to get out of the way before they were cut off. Shelby recognized Caswell's handwriting and knew the news was authentic. McDowell also sent word that he was moving to the vicinity of Gilbert Town.

The situation of Shelby's and Clarke's forces was extremely bad. They were unable to return to McDowell's camp. Gates' southern army was defeated, captured, killed and scattered. The position of Sumpter's forces was unknown. In the rear were Cruger's trained regulars at Fort Ninety-Six, and Ferguson's army on their flank. The Overmountain men had but one choice—to run for their lives. The flush of victory changed to desperate retreat. They decided to take the backwoods route and rejoin McDowell at Gilbert Town. Each prisoner was placed in the charge of three Patriot riders, who were to alternate in carrying him on their horses, and each prisoner carried his gun minus flint. In a short time the entire force was moving, knowing that Ferguson would soon be on their trail in an effort to overtake them.

The mountaineers, burdened with their prisoners, traveled as rapidly as possible toward the northwest and the mountains, leaving Ferguson's position to the right. As expected, a strong detachment of Ferguson's men was in pursuit. Under Colonel Shelby's energetic urging, the wearied men traveled mile after mile with no rest except to water their horses. They ate raw corn snatched from the fields as they rode and now and then, a peach plucked from the trees as they passed under them. During that day and night the mountaineers rode sixty miles from the battlefield. In the course of two nights and one day, these hardy men had traveled one hundred miles on horseback, and fought a battle. All this was done without any food, sleep or rest during hot August weather. Ferguson's men gave up the chase after forty miles. The Americans, with their prisoners, finally reached McDowell's force at Gilbert Town.

The detachment from Ferguson's force came near catching the mountaineers; they came within thirty minutes of the tired Patriots. After locating the spot where the fleeing Americans had stopped to water their horses, they gave up the chase. Their own mounts near exhaustion, and not knowing how far ahead the enemy, they decided to turn back.

The tired men, faces and eyes swollen, kept pushing on to safety. They did not know that Ferguson's men had turned back. Musgrove's Mill Battle and the Musgrove Family are traditional stories that few people outside of South Carolina have taken time to read.

As the leaders rested in camp, they reviewed the events of the past weeks and months. They knew that Ferguson would move up into the western section of South Carolina and North Carolina looking for supplies. They explored the prospect of organizing a volunteer force large enough to cope with the growing Loyalist army. All of the officers and men discussed such a plan and agreed to participate in its execution. These talks were very informal, but it was here that the King's Mountain campaign was born. Colonel Charles McDowell agreed to send word to Colonel Benjamin Cleveland, commander of the Wilkes County Tory fighters, and Major Joseph Winston, who headed a like force in Surry County. Messengers offered their services as "go-betweens" for the Overmountain men and the Patriots of McDowell and other partisan forces.

Restored home of Colonel David Vance, grandfather of Zebulon Vance, Civil War Governor of North Carolina. Many of the events recorded came from the papers of David Vance. He was active in many of the battles preceding King's Mountain.

Three brothers — James, Jack, and Archibald Neal — living in Turkey Cove volunteered to serve from the McDowell group. Colonel Cleveland, when advised of the plan, appointed his brother Robert Cleveland and Gideon Lewis as messengers to Sevier and Shelby. After a much needed rest, most of the volunteer groups returned to their own settlements.

Colonels McDowell and Hampton, with less than two hundred men, decided to remain in the vicinity of Gilbert Town. Soon they would be forced deeper into the mountains by the approach of Ferguson's army. Colonel Clarke and his men headed back toward their homes in the area of Augusta, Georgia. Clarke had hopes of accomplishing a move by an unexpected attack there. Colonel Hampton and Captain James Williams were designated to deliver the prisoners to the authorities at Hillsborough.

Governor Rutledge of South Carolina was at Hillsborough, and Captain Williams, in making his report, conveyed the idea that he, Williams, was in general command during the battle at Musgrove's Mill and was responsible for the victory. He gave Colonels Shelby and Clarke very little credit. As a result of this report, Governor Rutledge gave Williams the rank of Brigadier-General.

Ferguson's move into Western North Carolina forced the small partisan groups deeper into the hills. Tories of this section were flocking to the King's standard. They thought the British were absolute victors. With

Recruiting Tories

the fall of Charleston; the massacre of Buford's men; the total route of Gates' army at Camden; the defeat of Sumpter's force at the mouth of Fishing Creek by Tarleton, a cloud of gloom hung over the country.

Colonel Ferguson, hoping to break up the McDowell-Hampton force, made a surprise attack against them on Bedford's Hill. The engagement, an indecisive one, was bitterly contested by the greatly outnumbered mountaineers. They fought the Loyalists Indian-style and inflicted heavy damage. Major Dunlap of Ninety-Six was wounded during this battle. The Tories suffered such heavy casualties they withdrew.

THE OVERMOUNTAIN PEOPLE

Colonel Charles McDowell and Colonel Andrew Hampton, realizing the impossibility of opposing Ferguson with their small force, led one hundred sixty men across the mountains to the Watauga Settlement. The men built crude huts and lean-tos along the Watauga River, near the mouths of Gap and Buffalo Creeks. The people of the community made sure they had sufficient supplies. McDowell told the Overmountain people of the high-handed methods and destruction of Ferguson. Some of the men left on the other side of the mountains had driven their stock deep into the mountain gorges and caves, in an effort to save their limited supply. Many of the men moved their entire families across the mountains. A few of the men left behind were instructed to take the oath under Ferguson in order to save stock, homes and people.

It was near Watauga River between Gap Creek and Buffalo Creek that McDowell's people built their temporary camp. This location is also near Sycamore Shoals and site of Fort Caswell.

The plight of the Patriots is summed up in a quotation from Theodore Roosevelt's "Winning the West": "Except for occasional small guerilla parties, there was not a single organized body of American troops left south of Gates' broken and dispirited army. All the southern lands lay at the feet of the conquerors. The British leaders, overbearing and arrogant, held almost unchecked sway throughout the Carolinas and Georgia; and looking northward they made ready for the conquest of Virginia. Their right flank was covered by the waters of the ocean, their left by the high mountain barrier-chains, beyond which stretched the intermidable forest; and they had as little thought of danger from one side as the other."

So desperate was the situation, that many of the people were willing to just let the British have Georgia and the Carolinas without a struggle. Why fight against such losing odds? Liberty meant nothing to people of this make-up.

South Carolina Governor John Rutledge was conducting whatever state business he could from Hillsborough, North Carolina. For about three years there was no constituted government in that state. Civil war was rampant. Tories and Whigs were fighting almost constantly. South Carolina furnished more men and money than any other state during the Revolution. It also suffered more. It is said that in the District of Ninety-Six no less than thirty battles were fought. After the war, some fourteen hundred widows and orphans were listed in that area alone.

From Williams' **Tennessee During the Revolution,** we copy a letter from Governor Rutledge, written September 20, 1780.

"Not a man from Virginia is in this State, except about 250 Continentals under Beaufort (Buford), and about sixty of the militia who ran away from the action with Cornwallis, and who have lately been brought to Hillsborough; nor can we hear of any being on the march from Virginia.....Alas! When may we really and reasonably expect that all those things will come to pass."

Gloom and despair prevailed over most of the South. No help was available from General Washington. He had no troops he could spare. State treasuries were exhausted. Many of the partisan groups had to depend on clothing, weapons and ammunition from a slain enemy or a fallen comrade. Often a man without a gun would stay in the background until a weapon was available in this way.

Governor Rutledge of South Carolina

FERGUSON'S THREAT

Colonel Ferguson was riding high with his successful campaign. An energetic officer, he was seeing a victorius end to the war in the South. Visions of a rich reward, as one of the successful conquerors, no doubt filled his mind. Little did he realize that these were false illusions, soon to be destroyed. His mind kept reminding him of the hated backwater men. Those Indian-yelling, bushwacking Overmountain men had been a thorn in his flesh too long. Colonel De Peyster, who had in the meanwhile joined his command, had

**Ferguson's Headquarters
at Gilbert Town**

evidently reported that it was those Indian-yelling mountaineers, that had wrought such havoc at Musgrove's Mill. Ferguson became angry every time he thought of their successes at Pacolet, Thicketty Fort, Wofford's Iron Works, and the worst of all at Musgrove's Mill. He decided to do something about it.

Samuel Phillips, a prisoner of war in the Tory camp, was a distant cousin of Shelby and lived in the Holston settlement. Ferguson, thinking to throw a scare into those uncouth barbarians from the Overmountain country, wrote a message to Shelby and the other leaders. He sent a message by Phillips; Ferguson did not know it but this message proved to be his death warrant. The message read in effect: if he, Shelby, and the other backwater leaders did not desist from their opposition to the British Arms, he would march his army over the mountains, hang their leaders, and lay waste the country with fire and sword.

Colonel Isaac Shelby, upon receipt of this message and having questioned Phillips regarding Ferguson's location and strength, immediately saddled his horse and rode some forty miles to the home of Colonel John Sevier near the Nolichucky River. Sevier had recently married Catherine Sherrill (the Bonnie Kate of Tennessee); and the Seviers were in the midst of a big festival gathering. Neighbors and friends from far and near were present. Horse racing, a barbecue and dancing were in full sway. Upon learning the seriousness of Shelby's visit, the two men withdrew from the crowd and began a three-day conference. The plan, discussed earlier by Shelby, McDowell, Clarke and Robertson, was explored. They canvassed the possible number of men they could muster, and how to finance the campaign. Would the Virginians under Colonel William Campbell and Colonel Arthur Campbell help?

The Pioneer

Old Tilson Water Mill built in the 1840's

Colonel Isaac Shelby: prominent in the early settlement of Tennessee, Indian campaigns, and politics; commanded forces at Thicketty Creek, Cedar Springs, and Musgrove's Mill; declined President Monroe's appointment as Secretary of War; first Governor of Kentucky.

Isaac Shelby

Colonel John Sevier: Clerk and Magistrate, Watauga Association; defender at Fort Caswell, 1776; Clerk of Washington County Court; Colonel of Militia; Governor, State of Franklin; first elected Governor of Tennessee.

John Sevier

A PIONEER MUSTER

September 25th was the date set for the muster at Sycamore Shoals (Elizabethton, Tennessee). Both men sent riders over the countryside to call in their men. Money for the undertaking was secured from John Adair, entry taker for Sullivan County. Adair told the two men, Sevier and Shelby: "I have no authority by law to make that disposition of this money; it belongs to the impoverished State of North Carolina, and I dare not appropriate a cent of it to any other purpose; but if the country is overrun by the British, our liberty is gone. Let the money go too. Take it, if the enemy, by its use, is driven from the country. I can trust that country to justify and vindicate my conduct, so take it." John Sevier and Isaac Shelby gave their personal pledges for its return, should the State of North Carolina so demand. (Adair was given a receipt for its use by North Carolina in 1782.)

The grist mills of Baptist McNabb and Mathew Talbot were busy grinding corn for bread making. The women busied themselves with their looms and needles, making and mending clothes for their menfolk. Mrs. John Sevier spent her honeymoon making suits for the Colonel and his sons. Mary Patton supervised one of the powder mills. Lead for bullets was mined from a hill near the Nolichucky River, in the present Bumpass Cove section of Unicoi County. Every hand turned out to help in the defense of home and country.

On the appointed day, the whole countryside seemed to be gathering for the muster. Most of the men were accompanied by their families. Beef cattle for meat were driven to Sycamore Shoals. So many wanted to go that a draft had to be made. Sevier and Shelby knew that the frontiers were in constant danger from Indian raids, so the very young boys and older men were drafted to stay home to protect the women and children. It was some gathering, as the people arrived from every cove, valley and hillside. Mothers, sisters, sweethearts and children were present to see their menfolk off to battle. This would be the last farewell for some.

Two hundred forty men were selected from Sullivan County to follow Shelby; a like number from Washington County under Sevier. Some two hundred Virginians came with Colonel William Campbell. Colonel Arthur Campbell brought about two hundred more militia of his Virginia Command, and placed them under Colonel William Campbell's command. Already on the grounds were the troops of Colonel Charles McDowell and Colonel Andrew Hampton. Major Charles Robertson was left in charge of the Washington County forces to protect the frontier. Colonel Anthony Bledsoe was placed in command of the Sullivan home force.

On the morning of September 26th, the men gathered in companies, accompanied by their families for a religious service. Colonel Sevier had asked the Reverend Samuel Doak to speak to the men. After the early morning worship, the men started their march up Gap Creek with the battle cry, "The Sword of the Lord and Gideon."

SAMUEL DOAK'S FAMOUS SERMON AND PRAYER

AT SYCAMORE SHOALS MUSTER SEPTEMBER 1780

"My countrymen, you are about to set out on an expedition which is full of hardships and dangers, but one in which the Almighty will attend you.

"The Mother Country has her hands upon you, these American Colonies, and takes that for which our fathers planted their homes in the wilderness—OUR LIBERTY.

"Taxation without representation and the quartering of soldiers in the homes of our people without their consent are evidence that the Crown of England would take from its American Subjects the last vestige of Freedom.

"Your brethren across the mountains are crying like Macedonia unto your help. God forbid that you shall refuse to hear and answer their call—but the call of your brethren is not all. The enemy is marching hither to destroy your homes.

"Brave men, you are not unacquainted with battle. Your hands have already been taught to war and your fingers to fight. You have wrested these beautiful valleys of the Holston and Watauga from the savage hand. Will you tarry now until the other enemy carries fire and sword to your very doors? No, it shall not be. Go forth then in the strength of your manhood to the aid of your brethren, the defense of your liberty and the protection of your homes. And may the God of Justice be with you and give you victory."

"Let Us Pray"

"Almighty and gracious God! Thou hast been the refuge and strength of Thy people in all ages. In time of sorest need we have learned to come to Thee—our Rock and our Fortress. Thou knowest the dangers and snares that surround us on march and in battle.

"Thou knowest the dangers that constantly threaten the humble, but well beloved homes, which Thy servants have left behind them.

"O, in Thine infinite mercy, save us from the cruel hand of the savage, and of tyrant. Save the unprotected homes while fathers and husbands and sons are far away fighting for freedom and helping the oppressed.

"Thou, who promised to protect the sparrow in its flight, keep ceaseless watch, by day and by night, over our loved ones. The helpless woman and little children, we commit to Thy care. Thou wilt not leave them or forsake them in times of loneliness and anxiety and terror.

"O, God of Battle, arise in Thy might. Avenge the slaughter of Thy people. Confound those who plot for our destruction. Crown this mighty effort with victory, and smite those who exalt themselves against liberty and justice and truth.

"Help us as good soldiers to wield the SWORD OF THE LORD AND GIDEON."

"AMEN"

The sermon and prayer of Samuel Doak are used through the courtesy of Mrs. Rollo H. Henley, Washington College, Tennessee. It is taken from the scrapbook of her father, J. Fain Anderson.

Sycamore Shoals Muster, where the Overmountain Men assembled before leaving for the King's Mountain Campaign. The date was September 25, 1780. So anxious were the men and boys to go they had to draft those who were needed to remain and protect the home front. Women and children, boys and girls came to see their husbands, fathers, and loved ones off on this hazardous undertaking. Colonel John Sevier had asked his friend Samuel Doak to conduct services for the men. This picture is a reproduction of a painting by Lloyd Branson. The original hangs in the State Capitol, Nashville. It is used by courtesy of the Tennessee Department of Conservation.

84

THE TRAIL TOWARDS FERGUSON

Shelving Rock

The first night's camp was at Shelving Rock (sometimes called Resting Place) near the present town of Roan Mountain. Under the shelter of this rock, powder, meal and other supplies were stored. Many of the pioneers had their horses shod by John Miller, a blacksmith of that vicinity. A council, held under the rock, made plans for crossing the mountains and a faster march. The herd of cattle was slowing the progress of the men; so it was decided to slaughter and cook sufficient meat

Bright's Branch

Bright's Settlement

for the mountain crossing. The remainder of the herd was driven back to the settlements. Much time was consumed the morning of the 27th with this chore, but it saved time in the long run.

They reached the Bald of Roan Mountain in the afternoon. Here the men ate lunch and drilled in snow, ankle deep. Militia drilling was a new experience for these pioneer Indian fighters. Rolls were called by companies. It was discovered that two men of Sevier's company, with Tory leaning, were not present. The commanding officers decided to change their route. The British might be nearer than they had thought. They turned down Elk's Hollow, following Bright's Trace. This was a trail used by Bright traveling to and from his hunting camp. They camped the second night, September 27th, near the mouth of Bright's Branch where it flowed into Roaring Creek.

Bright's Trace

Grassy Creek

On the morning of September 28th, they followed the Yellow Mountain Trail (Bright's Trace) as it meandered along Roaring Creek to Toe River. They followed this trail along Toe River through Bright's Settlement, to Cathee's Place near the mouth of Grassy Creek, where they camped the third night. This campsite is near the present town of Spruce Pine, North Carolina.

The next day they traveled up the valley of Grassy Creek to Gillespie's Gap on the Blue Ridge. Here it was decided to divide the force in case the British should try to ambush their troops. Colonel Campbell led his men down through the Turkey Cove route, and they camped near Colonel Wofford's Fort. During the night an attempt was made to get information from Henry Gillespie, a Tory living in Turkey Cove.

Gillespie was so far removed from any contact with the war, that he had no useful information. Gillespie and Wofford had taken the oath, under Ferguson, more of necessity that from any sense of allegiance. Gillespie's descendants had a pass issued by Ferguson. They were so ashamed of this paper they kept it hidden for years.

Sevier and Shelby led their men down through the North Cove of Catawba Creek, and camped near Honeycutt's Creek. It was here that Colonel Charles McDowell met with these two commanders who had started the campaign. McDowell reported that scouts placed Ferguson at Gilbert Town, and that Colonel Cleveland and Major Winston were approaching with a force of three hundred fifty men. Charles McDowell, who had left Watauga several days before the Overmountain men, had sent James Blair to inform Cleveland and Winston of the mountaineers' movements. Blair had been wounded by a Tory while on this mission, but was able to reach Cleveland at Fort Defiance. McDowell had also gained the information that Sumpter's men, under the command of Generals Hill, Lacey, and Hawthorne, were close enough to join in the march against Ferguson.

Legend has stated that the Seviers spent the night of September 29th in this cabin. A post office and a school nearby were named Sevier.

On September 30th, the two forces were reunited, and continued on to the Catawba River and along its banks, crossing the Linville River, finally arriving at Quaker Meadows (Morganton, North Carolina). Here at the McDowell home, they were given fresh meat from the hidden beefs driven from the mountain gorges. The McDowell brothers insisted on the use of dry fence rails to build their fires. Many of McDowell's men who had remained behind rejoined the force. During the night Colonel Benjamin Cleveland with the men from Wilkes County, and Major Joseph Winston and his company from Surry County, joined the Overmountain men, bringing the total force to about fourteen hundred.

The ridge in right center separates two creeks. Cane River flows on view side of ridge. Silver Creek flows on the beyond side.

On Sunday morning October 1st, the march was resumed. A good road made for faster progress. During the afternoon, a heavy rain set in. They made camp early in South Mountain Gap, near the head of Cane and Silver Creeks. Pilot Mountain, well-known landmark, could be seen from campsite. Another name for the place is Bedford's Hill. This was near the battle site where McDowell's force was attacked by a force of Ferguson's men a few weeks earlier.

The next day it continued to be wet and rainy, so the army remained in camp. The unaccustomed discipline and restraint caused unrest and occasional fights among the men. This gave the officers much concern. It was generally agreed that a definite military organization must be set up and campaign plans made.

The officers met during the evening of October 2nd for a conference. Colonel Charles McDowell, being the senior officer present, presided. It was brought out that there should be a military head for the entire force. The coming of various companies from several sections resulted in the fact that no one was properly in command of the whole. It was decided that a messenger be sent to headquarters at Hillsborough, North Carolina, to ask General Gates to send a commanding officer to take charge of the entire army.

This proposed delay greatly irked Colonel Shelby, Sevier and their associate officers from across the mountains. It was then proposed that the officers meet daily for consultation, and that one of their number be chosen as officer of the day. This officer was to carry out plans formulated at the staff meeting the preceding day. This plan still did not satisfy Shelby. With Ferguson reported so near, Shelby argued that the combined forces needed a firm leader of known experience—a leader that would pursue the objective with all promptness. All the commanding officers were North Carolinians, save Colonel William Campbell, who was from Virginia. Shelby said he knew Colonel Campbell to be a man of good sense, and sincerely devoted to the cause of his country. Also, Colonel Campbell commanded the largest regiment. Shelby thus proposed Campbell's name for consideration. Shelby closed with the proposal that Colonel Campbell be made the commanding officer, until the designated officer should arrive from headquarters, and that they march at once against the enemy.

It is said that Campbell took Shelby aside and requested his name be withdrawn. Campbell asked Shelby that he, himself, consent to serve in the capacity of commanding officer. Shelby replied that he was the youngest Colonel present, and that he had served under Colonel McDowell, a fine man but slow of action for such an enterprise as this.

Cane Creek

Pilot Mountain

Shelby feared that Colonel McDowell might take offense should he, Shelby, be placed in command over him. Campbell agreed to this reasoning. In the meeting of the staff, this proposal was agreed upon and adopted. Colonel Shelby states that he made the proposal to silence the expectations of Colonel Charles McDowell — a brave, patriotic and good man, but too inactive for such a command. He lacked the tact and efficiency called for in handling a campaign of this magnitude. Colonel McDowell had the tendency to send rather than to lead. Some of the officers expressed the desire that either General William Lee Davidson or General Daniel Morgan be sent to take command of the force. (A conference, concerning the selection of a commanding officer, was held by the Overmountain officers on top of Roan Mountain during their stop there.)

General Daniel Morgan was one of the finest of Revolutionary War officers. He was largely responsible for victories at Stillwell and Saratoga. Gates never mentioned him in his report to congress. His last and outstanding victory was at Cowpens, South Carolina, January 17, 1781. Bad health caused his retirement shortly afterwards. Morganton, North Carolina, was named in his honor.

General William Lee Davidson, from Charlotte, North Carolina, was beloved by all Carolinians and Tennesseans. He was a gallant officer and gentleman. He was assisting Morgan escape with prisoners when killed February 1st, 1781. Davidson County, Tennessee, was named in his honor.

Colonel Charles McDowell, who had the good of the country at heart more than the title to command, submitted gracefully to the decision. McDowell also suggested that, if agreeable, they let him convey to general headquarters the request for a commanding officer. This was warmly approved. A sincere ovation was given McDowell, who was warmed by the grand manner in which this proposition was presented to his fellow officers. He turned his command over to his brother, Major Joseph McDowell. Thus Colonel William Campbell became temporary commander of the army that was on the warpath against Colonel Patrick Ferguson and his Tory Force.

Major Joseph McDowell, commanding Patriots from Burke County, North Carolina

THE "GAMECOCK"

Colonel Thomas Sumpter, nicknamed the "Gamecock", used the title of Colonel but held no commission. The men in his force, at the time of the King's Mountain Battle, were mostly exiles from Loyalist persecution in South Carolina. They just sort of banded together and selected Sumpter as their leader. Many of their homes, including Sumpter's, had been burned and their families were refugees. These men were not receiving any government pay or backing. They were only interested in fighting the British with any responsible group. They furnished their own horses, guns, and equipment. Some would just tag along until they could get a horse and gun from a fallen comrade or a slain enemy.

Governor Abner Nash of North Carolina, through the influence of Governor Rutledge, had given Colonel Williams permission to recruit in North Carolina. Williams made his headquarters in Rowan County. Governor Nash had also promised supplies from the limited commissaries of the state. Colonel Williams promised beef, bread and potatoes, in his

Abner Nash, Governor of North Carolina

call to arms. New recruits, and the addition of a company of South Carolinians under Colonel Thomas Brandon and Major Samuel Hammond, brought Williams' command to the approximate number of seventy; and learning the location of Sumpter's men, Williams moved in that direction. He had been repulsed by Sumpter and his men in an earlier attempt to take over the command. He decided to try again.

Colonel Sumpter, and many of his regular officers, had gone to Hillsborough to confer with Governor Rutledge, regarding Williams' attempt to take over his command. Colonel William Hill was left in charge during this period. Meanwhile, the troops were marching to form a junction with General William Lee Davidson, then in charge of the Salisbury District Militia.

The Sumpter Force, under Hill's command, arrived at the foot of Flint Mountain (presently known as Cherry Mountain) October 3rd. On this same day, Colonel Charles McDowell, enroute to general headquarters, visited these men. McDowell explained the purpose and extent of the mountaineer campaign, and invited the South Carolinians to join in the march against Ferguson. During the same day, Colonels William Graham and Frederick Hambright, and some fifty or sixty men from Lincoln County, North Carolina, joined the Sumpter group. Colonel James Williams again visited the camp and demanded the post of commanding officer. Again he was refused. So strong was the feeling against Williams, that he moved his camp some distance away. Colonel Hill, suffering from a wounded arm received in a recent battle, placed Colonel Edward Lacey in active charge of the force.

In a council, it was decided that Colonel Lacey visit the camp of the Overmountain men, and find out more

about their plans. Also, scouts with recent information regarding Ferguson's location had arrived in camp. Lacey set out, the night of October 5th, and traveled toward Gilbert Town. The night trip was a hard one, but he finally found the camp at Alexander's Ford on Green River.

Flint Mountain, later called Cherry Mountain

The Patriot Army assembled at Bedford Hill before the march to Gilbert Town

The mountaineer army, thinking Ferguson some fifteen miles away at Gilbert Town, made preparation for the conflict. Before breaking camp, Colonel John Sevier assembled the troops for a meeting. Colonels Cleveland, Campbell, Shelby, Sevier, McDowell, Winston and other officers entered the circle of men. With eloquent words of wisdom, the two-hundred-fifty-pound jovial Cleveland spoke first. He told them of the priceless opportunity of service to their country, and a rich heritage to their children. Cleveland also offered the weak-hearted a chance to back out. After a moment for consideration, Major Joseph McDowell, with his personable smile, asked, "what kind of story would they relate when they arrived back home, while their comrades were fighting for their country?"

Shelby then proposed that those who desired to leave step three paces to the rear. Not a man accepted this invitation. A murmur of applause rose from the men, who seemed proud of each other. Quote from Shelby: "I am heartily glad to see you, as a man, resolved to meet and fight your country's foes. When we encounter them, don't wait for the word of command. Let each of you be your own officer and do the best you can, taking every care of yourselves, and availing yourselves of every advantage that chance may throw your way. If in the woods, shelter yourselves and give them Indian play. Advance from tree to tree pressing the enemy, killing and disabling all you can. Your officers will shrink from no danger. They will be constantly with you, and the moment the enemy gives way, be on the alert and strictly obey orders."

With this appeal and advice, the troops were dismissed with directions to be ready to march within three hours. Provisions for two meals were to be prepared and placed in their knapsacks. Colonels Cleveland and McDowell had somehow secured whisky, which they added as a treat for the men.

Breaking camp, they marched down Cane Creek a few miles, and stopped for the night near the home of Samuel Andrews, a loyal Whig. Placing guards around the camp, they slept on their arms. The next morning, October 4th, they continued their march. After crossing Cane Creek several times, the mountain men reached the vicinity of Gilbert Town about nightfall. They learned from Jonathan Hampton that Ferguson and his Tories had left that area, and Hampton told them it was rumored that they were headed southward toward Fort Ninety-Six.

Home of Samuel Andrews built in 1740. Both armies camped near this house: Ferguson, after the Battle with McDowell's men; the Overmountain men enroute to King's Mountain. Andrews lost all of his stock and food supplies to the Tories. He had to hide in the hills for safety.

THE MOUNTAIN CROSSING

Colonel Elijah Clarke, encouraged by the success at Musgrove's Mill, took leave of Shelby and McDowell and returned to Georgia. Recruiting more troops as he led his men along a foothill route, he made plans for a series of harassing attacks against the Loyalist forces in his home settlements. Clarke soon learned of the big stock of supplies stored in the depot at Augusta. These supplies were for the proposed Indian campaign against the settlers of the Watauga and Nolichucky districts. Clarke and his men laid siege to Augusta on September 14th, 15th, and 16th, 1780. This attack would have succeeded but for a party of Cherokee and Creek warriors arriving in Augusta for these supplies. Enraged at having their way blocked in getting the guns and ammunition, they attacked from the rear. Clarke, unable to withstand an attack from both sides, had to retreat. This relief gave Cruger the needed time to arrive with reinforcements from Ninety-Six. Colonel Clarke was forced to run. With his force and some four hundred women, children and old folk (families of his men), he fled toward the mountains.

Several patriots had been taken prisoner by the Tories. Captain Ashby and twelve of his men were hung immediately. Thirteen were turned over to the Indians to be tortured and put to death Indian-style. Colonel Browne, wounded several times during the siege, was determined to wreak his vengeance on any American within reach. Over thirty were hung, tomahawked and shot.

A report of this Battle and its outcome was sent to Colonel Ferguson, who immediately sent detachments out in hopes of intercepting Clarke. Captain Alexander Chesney did get near enough to catch one prisoner and return him to Ferguson. One of the British Lieutenants commented, ''There were several whom they immediately hanged and have a great many more yet to hang. We have now a method that will put an end to the rebellion in a short time, by hanging every man that has taken protection and is found acting against us.''

Colonel Clarke, with remnants of his force, and the four hundred women and children headed for the mountains. They were constantly harassed from the rear by bands of Tories and Indians. His faithful followers were able to ward off most of the attacks and allow the main party to gain the safety of the mountains. The Indian and Tory attackers would fall on the old men and women who were unable to keep pace with the main body. Occasionally, young boys would be captured and taken to the Tory camp.

At night the captured boys would be stripped of their clothes and made to dance between two hot fires until burned to death. Old men would be dismembered, scalped and limbs of their bodies hung on tree branches. The atrocities committed were almost too ghastly to relate. These stories were told to the Overmountain men, by Major Candler and his men, when they arrived at Gilbert Town. Captain Edward Hampton, who was scouting in that part of the country, had informed the Clarke people of the Campaign then in progress against Ferguson.

It took Colonel Clarke and his refugees many days to make the mountain crossing of about two hundred miles. The scant food supplies were reserved for the children. The adults lived entirely on nuts, berries and whatever food could be obtained from the forests. The entire party was near starvation when they arrived in the Nolichucky settlements.

Clarke leads his people across the mountains

The generous people of the Nolichucky and Watauga communities opened their hearts and homes to these refugee Georgian Patriots in distress. Colonel Clarke and his family were received into the Sevier home and remained there until conditions were such that they could return to Georgia.

Colonel Patrick Ferguson

THE ELUSIVE FERGUSON

Colonel Ferguson, receiving Cruger's message regarding Colonel Clarke's defeat at Augusta and consequent retreat toward the hills, immediately left Gilbert Town and marched south in hopes of intercepting the Georgians. He made camp at James Step's place near Green River. Detachments were sent out in several directions in an effort to locate Clarke's route of retreat. It was at the Green River camp that James Crawford and Samuel Chambers, the two Tory defectors from the Overmountain force, joined the Ferguson Camp.

This report, of the large back-water army advancing toward him, rudely awakened the British Colonel from his sense of security. He suddenly realized that his threat of hanging, fire, and sword, had aroused a giant to come after him. Having tarried in this sector longer than planned, in trying to capture Clarke, Ferguson knew that he had to move.

Dispatches were prepared asking for reinforcements. One message, written to General Cornwallis, was sent by Abram Collins and Peter Quinn. Delaying tactics were employed by watching Whigs. Two sons of Alexander Henry followed the Tory messengers. Collins and Quinn saw the Henry boys lurking on their trail. Afraid for their lives, they hid by day, and traveled by night. These maneuvers slowed the messengers to such an extent that they did not reach the camp of Cornwallis until October 7, the day of the battle. Colonel Cruger, in his reply to Ferguson, stated that he did not have half the number requested in his garrison. It was at this stage that Ferguson had the rumor spread that he was marching toward Fort Ninety-Six.

The Tory commander's elusive route and whereabouts caused the Overmountain men some delay and confusion. This was part of the British Colonel's strategy, in trying to work himself out of a difficult situation. He wanted to trap Clarke and his Georgians and he needed time to recall his furloughed men. Ferguson was also probably debating in his mind, should he join Cornwallis in Charlotte or fight the hated Indian-yelling mountaineers.

From the diary of Lieutenant Anthony Allaire of Ferguson's Corps, these entries are noted: October 1, "got in motion at five o'clock in the afternoon and marched twelve miles to Dennard's Ford where we lay 8th September." Monday 2nd, "got in motion at four o'clock in the afternoon and forded Broad River; marched four miles; formed in lines of action and lay on our arms. This night I had nothing but the canopy of heaven to cover me." Tuesday 3rd, "got in motion at four o'clock in the morning; marched six miles to Camp's Ford of Second Broad River, forded it and continued on six miles to one Armstrong's plantation, on the banks of Sandy Run. Halted to refresh; at four o'clock got in motion, forded Sandy Run; marched seven miles to Buffalo Creek; forded it; marched a mile further and halted near Tate's plantation." Friday 6th, "got in motion at four o'clock in the morning, marched sixteen miles to little King's Mountain, where we took up our ground."

The two-day halt at Tate's plantation was most likely made to wait for the furloughed men to report, and to get fresh information from scouts as to the whereabouts of the Patriot army. Messages to Cornwallis indicate this line of reasoning. Colonel Ferguson seemed unaware that none of his messengers were getting through to Cornwallis. He underestimated the calibre of this hardy force of Indian fighters that had crossed the mountains just to fight him.

Mountain on which famous battle was fought.

MESSAGE TO CORNWALLIS: "My Lord: - A doubt does not remain with regard to the intelligence I sent your Lordship. They are since joined by Clarke and Sumpter—of course are becoming an object of some consequence. Happily their leaders are obliged to feed their followers with such hopes; and so to flatter them with accounts of our weakness and fear, that if necessary, I should hope for success against them myself; but numbers compared, that must be doubtful."

"I am on my march towards you, by a road leading from Cherokee Ford, north of King's Mountain. Three or four hundred good soldiers, part dragoons, would finish the business. Something must be done. This is their last push in this quarter, etc."

Colonel Ferguson was evidently expecting more of his furloughed men under Colonel John Moore and Major Zachariah Gibbs to report. Not knowing that his messages were not reaching General Cornwallis on schedule, he had false hopes of his reinforcements. Colonel Banistre Tarleton, recovering from a siege of fever, was unable to lead a platoon. Colonel Cruger's militia from Fort Ninety-Six would not arrive in time to help. Colonel Patrick Ferguson, thinking that reinforcements would come, dreamed grandiose visions of defeating the hated backwater men. He thought that King's Mountain afforded him an ideal spot for such an encounter, and that he could withstand any force the rebels could muster against him. He is reputed to have said that, "God Almighty could not drive him from it."

Part of King's Mountain Range

King's Mountain Range took its name from a family of that name who lived at the foot of the range. King's Creek has the same name origin. The entire range, some sixteen miles in length, extends generally from the northeast in North Carolina, to a southwest direction in South Carolina. Spurs jut out in many directions along its course. The principal elevation is a tower called the "Pinacle". This promontory is nearly six miles from the battleground. Crowder Mountain is the tall hill at the northeast end of the range. The mountain on which the battle was fought is in York County, South Carolina. This promontory is approximately six hundred yards long and about two hundred feet from base to base. The rocky summit of the mountain stands some sixty feet above the surrounding terrain. Its ridge surface, along the six hundred yards, varies from sixty to one hundred feet in width. It is narrow enough that a man, standing on it, can be shot from either side.

A spring on the northwest side furnished sufficient water for the men and horses of Ferguson's army. There were trees to build breast-works, but none were built. About the only thing done of a defensive nature, was to place the wagons and baggage along the northeast ridge of the mountain near his headquarters. Here he waited for the return of his furloughed men who never came. Vainly, he looked for the reinforcements from Cornwallis and Cruger. Instead there came those hated Indian-yelling, vagabond backwater men. Ferguson's exaggerated dependence on the bayonet, and infatuation for military glory, is the only plausible explanation for his remaining on King's Mountain.

The King's Mountain Battleground, showing the north slope of the ridge, on the left, and the original Chronicle marker in the background. Sketched by Benson J. Lossing during his visit to the area on January 8, 1849.

THE GHOST LEGION

Mouth of Cane Creek

Now, back to the Overmountain men at Gilbert Town. The Commanding Officers were greatly dismayed at finding their quarry had fled. Jonathan Hampton, a loyal Whig and son of Colonel Andrew Hampton, told the officers that Ferguson had left several days earlier and headed south. During a staff meeting, called to discuss their next move, Major William Candler with thirty Georgians from Clarke's force, marched into camp. They had no news of Ferguson, as they had traveled a back route.

The Americans, more determined than ever, marched in the direction of Ninety-Six. At Probit's Place, near Broad River, Major William Chronicle with twenty men from Lincoln County, North Carolina, joined the growing army. Each addition was hailed with much enthusiasm. The many small companies, weak by themselves, were becoming a formidable force by uniting together.

Following the same general direction and route they thought Ferguson had followed, this legion of rugged fighters crossed Mountain Creek, and then Broad River at Dennard's Ford. Here they lost sight of Ferguson's trail. Scouts were sent out in every direction to search for information. The Patriots continued on to Alexander's Ford on Green River, crossed and made camp on what was later known as Alexander's farm. Many of the horses were limping, and some of the foot-soldiers were footsore and showing signs of strain, in their effort to keep pace with the march. The leaders were worried and concerned about the situation. They realized that Ferguson, with several days' start, could elude them unless they moved faster.

Alexander's Ford on Green River

In a staff meeting it was decided to select the best riflemen and the best horses, in order to speed up the chase. Most of the night of October 5 was spent accomplishing this task. About seven hundred were chosen. A strong guard, changed every two hours, was posted around the camp. Rumors, picked up by the returning scouts, indicated that Ferguson had marched to Fort Ninety-Six. This stronghold, recently repaired and strengthened, was reputed to be impregnable against an attack by small arms. Not deterred, the mountaineers made plans to move in that direction.

During this all-night session at Green River, Colonel Edward Lacey rode into camp. He had some difficulty gaining access to the Command Officers. The suspicious guards thought he might be a Tory spy. This visit by Lacey was most opportune, as it gave direction and focus to the march. Colonel Lacey told of McDowell's visit to their camp and invitation to join the campaign. He was able to give definite news of Ferguson's general location and strength. One of his scouts, pretending to be a Loyalist, had stayed in the Tory Camp for a day or two. Lacey urged the leaders to push on and engage the British before reinforcements could arrive. Delay might prove fatal to their success. This plan was heartily approved.

Before leaving, Lacey promised to lead his force for a junction with the mountaineers at Cowpens the next day, October 6. On arrival at the South Carolinian camp, about ten o'clock in the morning, he related the prospects of the march against Ferguson to his fellow officers. The reaction was for moving immediately, as they broke camp and began the twenty odd miles trek, toward Cowpens. They arrived there shortly after the mountaineers.

The seven hundred horsemen left the Green River Camp early Friday morning. They traveled to Sandy Plains, and from there followed the ridge road in a southeastern direction. Colonel Campbell had placed the foot soldiers under the commands of Major Joseph Herndon, Major Patrick Watson, Captain William Neal, Captain Richard Allen and other necessary officers. He asked them to follow as speedily as possible as they might be greatly needed in a prolonged battle. It has been well established that some fifty footmen reached the scene of the battle just moments after it was finished. Some historians have insisted that some of the foot soldiers were actually in the battle.

Cowpens was so named because a wealthy English Tory ran a big cattle ranch there and had constructed many pens to herd his cattle. Sanders, pulled out of bed and questioned about Ferguson's whereabouts, was unable to give them any information regarding the Tory force. They had not passed that way.

During the Cowpens stop, the Americans slaughtered several cattle from the Sanders herd. Fires dotted the night as the men roasted the meat. A field of corn was harvested in short order for the horses. This rest and food would be the last that men and horses would get for many long, hard, weary hours. During this stop, a crippled scout named Joseph Kerr caught up with the army. Kerr had passed himself off as a Tory and spent some time in the British Camp. Kerr mixed among the men and gained much information without arousing suspicion. He stated that Ferguson planned to camp on Little King's Mountain. His news heartened the Patriot force and quickened their anticipation of overtaking the enemy.

The estimate of the entire American army, according to Draper, is 1,840 including footmen. The number that left Sycamore Shoals was 1,040 plus or minus a few. This included the Virginians under Campbell, the Sullivan County men with Shelby, the Watauga and Nolichucky Indian fighters with Sevier, and the North Carolinians from Burke County with McDowell. At Quaker Meadows the addition of the Surry Countians with Winston and Wilkes County men under Cleveland brought the total to about 1,390; Candler's thirty Georgians and Chronicle's twenty Lincoln Countians brought the total to 1,440. The addition of the South Carolinians, under Hill, Lacey, Hawthorne, Hambright, Graham and Williams brought the entire force to the 1,840 count.

Two hundred of the best riflemen and horses were selected from the South Carolinians. This brought the total horsemen to something like 910. This mounted force left Cowpens about nine o'clock Friday night, October 6. Shelby says, "it was dark, cold, cloudy and rainy, and that at times a heavy downpour." The roads were difficult to follow in the murky blackness. The scouts, leading Campbell's force up front, took the wrong road, and several companies became lost from the main body. It was morning before the missing men had been located and reunited with their regiment. The plan to cross Broad River at Tate's was discarded for the reason that Ferguson might have guards stationed on the eastern bank. Cherokee Ford, some two and one-half miles south, was thought to be safer. As they approached the river, Enoch Gilmer, a scout, was sent to check on possible sentries. They soon heard him singing "Barney Lynn", the all clear signal. It was daylight when they made the cold wet crossing. Eighteen miles had been covered since leaving Cowpens. King's Mountain was still fifteen miles away.

The cold hard night's travel through rain and slush had made many of the men discontented, grumpy and surly; and the rain still fell. Campbell, Sevier and Cleveland felt that a halt, to let men and horses rest, would help matters. They approached Shelby with this suggestion. He replied, "I will not stop until night if I follow Ferguson into Cornwallis' lines." Without a word of reply, the three officers returned to their places and the march continued.

About seven miles from the river crossing, two Tories were captured at Solomon Beason's house. Beason changed his loyalty as the occasion required. With a little persuasion, the two men told the Mountaineers that Ferguson was camped on Little King's Mountain and agreed to pilot them there. Along the way, two other Tories were captured, and their story corroborated this information. For the first time in several days, this Ghost Legion, composed of several different small companies, had a definite foe ahead on King's Mountain.

Keeping a wary eye in all directions, guarding against a surprise ambush, the army moved onward. Rounding a turn in the road, the leaders saw a familiar horse hitched in front of a house. It belonged to Gilmer, who was scouting ahead of the columns of marching men. Campbell and some of the officers entered the house. They found Gilmer, enjoying a homecooked meal served by two attractive ladies. With a big show of capture and much abusive language, they placed a noose around the scout's neck with angry threats of hanging then and there. Major Chronicle begged Campbell and the other officers, in deference to the ladies, that they not hang the man until they had passed beyond sight of the house. With the rope around his neck, Gilmer was led away by the Americans and

Broad River

released when some distance down the road. The scout related how he had passed himself off as a Tory looking for the British camp, in order to sign up. One of the women told him that she had visited the Tory camp that morning, with chickens for the Commander. She described the location of the camp by saying it was on a King's Mountain ridge, between two creeks where a hunter's camp was set up. Chronicle and Mattox spoke up and said they had used this camp on several occasions, when hunting in that section. They were thus able to give a good description of the terrain and approaches.

With this information, concerning the lay of the land and the position of the Tory camp, the officers withdrew and held a council. The plan of action was mapped out and each Commanding Officer assigned a definite sector of the mountain. Each company was supposed to reach their position before the signal for attack was given. As the rain had stopped at noon, and the sun was shining bright, the spirits of the men brightened with the day.

The officers returned to their various commands and explained the plan of battle and the general arrangements of the troops around the mountain. The men were told that by shooting uphill they were less likely to hit their comrades. Also they would be less likely to be hit by the British, who in shooting downhill would overshoot. Major Chronicle, with Colonel Hambright's permission, had been placed over Colonel Graham's men. Graham was called home to a sick wife.

Two more Tories, captured by Sevier's men, corroborated the earlier information. John Ponder, a messenger bearing a dispatch to Cornwallis, was taken prisoner a short distance from the mountain. This letter was one asking for immediate assistance. The Americans also learned from Ponder that Ferguson, a well-dressed man, wore a duster over his uniform. Colonel Hambright, of German descent, is supposed to have said, "Well poys when you see dot man mit a pig shirt over his clothes, you may know who him is. Mark him mit your rifles."

About a mile from the mountain the men were halted. They had been traveling in single file, or small scattered squads with little order or regularity. Now two definite battle lines were formed. Colonel Campbell, leading one line in double column, was turning to the right. Colonel Cleveland, leading another double column, turned to the left. Major Chronicle and Colonel Hambright's men had been given a position toward the northeastern end of the mountain, to join forces with Major Winston and close up that portion of the line. Thus, as the various companies reached their positions, the mountain was surrounded with a cordon of the best marksmen in the world. No messenger or troops could escape through this band of iron.

The last general command given to the various officers had been, "When you reach your position, dismount, tie your horse, roll coats and blankets and tie them to the saddle." Then the last part of the order, "Put fresh prime in your guns, and every man go into battle resolved to fight until he dies."

BLOOD ON THE MOUNTAIN

Colonel Ferguson had posted picket lines along the crest of the mountain to its southwestern extremity. This was the most approachable area for an attack. These are the men who first sounded the alarm when the Whig army was sighted. The Rangers and best trained Loyalists would be placed here for the main attack. These soldiers, skilled in the use of bayonets, were dressed in scarlet coats. Ferguson depended on these men for his main defense. The Tory troops recruited in the area, lacking bayonets, had been equipped with long knives fitted by the blacksmith to slip over the muzzle of their guns. These knives served in place of bayonets. No breastworks had been erected from the available trees around the mountain. No reinforcements had arrived to strengthen the British army. The furloughed men being collected by Gibbs and Moore had not arrived. None of the famous plundering Tory bands were with Ferguson on King's Mountain. Among those absent were Captains David Fanning, Bloody Bill Bates, Bloody Bill Cunningham and Sam Brown.

Colonel Ferguson, a vain man, could not imagine that it was possible for him to be defeated. He had never met the hated mountaineers in combat face to face. He disregarded the warning of Captain De Peyster and other officers who had experienced a battle with these riflemen. With no preparation, a false sense of security and visions of glory, Colonel Ferguson waited.

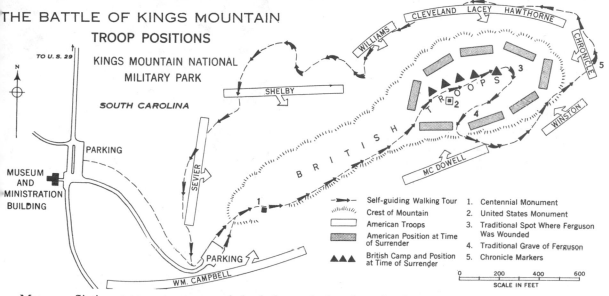

THE BATTLE OF KINGS MOUNTAIN

TROOP POSITIONS

Many conflicting statements are recorded relative to the location of various companies around the battle mountain. The historians of the King's Mountain National Military Park have arranged markers around the mountain in an acceptable manner. With their permission, the author is using their map of location.

Shelby's men had captured a British outpost some distance out, without firing a shot. The main force of mountaineers was within a quarter mile of the Tory position before they were discovered. When the presence of the enemy was reported to Colonel Ferguson, he ordered his men to their positions with beat of drum. The Redcoats fired first on Shelby's men, and he had difficulty in restraining them from advancing. Strict orders had been given not to attack until all commands were in position and the signal given. But the firing from the British had become so regular that Colonel Campbell threw off his coat and yelled at the top of his voice, "Shout like hell and fight like devils." The fierce bloodcurdling Indian yells were taken up by the other companies as they reached their positions and began the attack. Soon the whole mountain was circled with an eerie wail and a burst of gunfire. De Peyster is said to have warned Ferguson of the type of enemy he faced and also remarked, "Those yelling boys are here again."

Cleveland, Chronicle and Winston's men were longer in reaching their positions, as they had a greater distance to travel and the terrain was much rougher. Campbell and Shelby were confronted by the well-trained Rangers, and they bore the brunt of the main attack. This first attack against Campbell and Shelby gave the other officers, who had been delayed, time to reach their positions and open the battle from their sector. As the fight enveloped the mountain, it became volcanic from bottom to top in a sulphuric blaze of thundering guns and smoke.

Colonel Campbell's men were the first to charge up the hill and engage the Rangers. This part of the mountain was steep and rough. The Virginians were met by a fierce charge of fixed bayonets. Many tried to fight it out hand to hand, but guns were no match for sword points, at close range. A fast retreat was made downhill and to the gorge beyond, followed by the Redcoats. Near the foot of the mountain the British Rangers turned and started back to their stations, reloading their guns as they climbed. Ferguson had trained his troops in this style of fighting. By the time the Rangers regained the crest of the incline, Shelby attacked from the other side of the mountain. This gave Colonel Campbell time to reorganize and rally his men for another assault. Campbell's shouted appeal was, ''Boys remember your liberty, come on, do it my brave fellows, another gun, another gun will do it.'' This call, from their leader, seemed to galvanize the Virginians into another spirited attack against the dreaded bayonets.

Almost as Shelby's company retreated, away from the bayonet attack, Campbell and his men would advance up the hill and claim their attention from the other side. This type of charge and counter charge was repeated three times. A description of this part of the fight is given by Captain Chesney, a Tory officer. ''By the time the other Americans who had been repulsed had regained their former stations, and sheltered behind trees poured in an irregular and destructive fire. In this manner the engagement was maintained nearly an hour, the mountaineers flying when there was danger of being charged by bayonet, and returning again as soon as the British detachment had faced about to repel another of their parties.''

When Shelby's men reached the foot of the hill, he would yell, ''Now boys, quickly reload your rifles and let's advance upon them and give them another hell of a fire.'' Finally Colonel Sevier's Indian fighters had inched their way up rock by rock and tree by tree, until they gained the top and held. By hitting the flank of the enemy, it gave Shelby and Campbell sufficient relief, enabling them to close in from their positions. The men, from all three commands, had become intermingled during the uphill assault. The smoke was so thick and heavy at times, the men could hardly see. But above it all Shelby could be heard, ''Shoot like hell and fight like devils.''

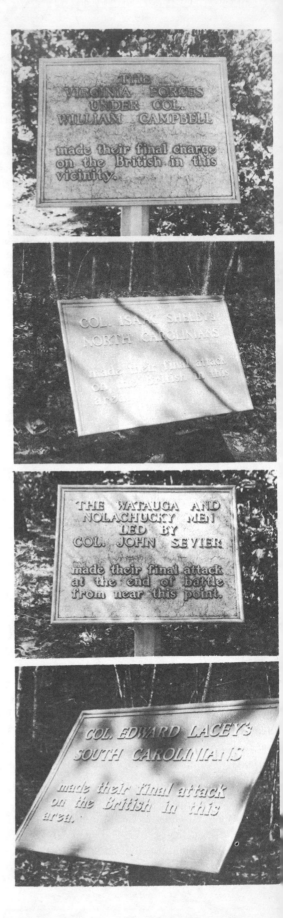

Meanwhile Colonel Lacey and Hawthorne were making a strong push in their quarter. The South Carolinians had better ground over which to reach their assigned position. They arrived at their post before Cleveland. Colonel Lacey had his horse shot out from under him soon after the battle began. The seasoned troops from York and Chester Counties, South Carolina, gave a good account during the attacks in their sector. No record shows that they were faced with a bayonet charge.

Colonel Cleveland's detachment was about ten minutes late in reaching their position. The swampy ground, flooded by the recent rains, made passage difficult. They were fired upon even before reaching their post. During their march they captured an advance picket with very little trouble. Cleveland, admonishing his men during the battle, could be heard by friend and foe. One of his favorite yells was, "Yonder is your enemy, and the enemy of all mankind." Part of the Wilke's County line was charged by Tories wielding the knife bayonets. During the battle, as his men would advance from tree to tree, Cleveland would shout, "A little nearer to them my brave lads, a little nearer." Roebuck, Cleveland's favorite horse, was killed early in the fight. The Colonel, despite his enormous weight and size, kept up with his front lines on foot. One of his men brought another horse before the conflict was over.

Colonels McDowell and Hampton were holding their positions against an onslaught of bayonets and Tory fire. The loud Indian yells, the constant shrill blast of Ferguson's whistle, two thousand blazing guns, the shouted commands of the officers were all intermingled into a grim nightmare. All this, shrouded with a fog of sulphuric gun smoke, seemed to create a chaotic segment of hell.

Major Chronicle and Colonel Hambright led their Lincoln County troops to the northeastern sector of the mountain. They, like Campbell, had drawn one of the rough and steep slopes of the mountain. As they reached their designated position, Major Chronicle, some steps ahead of his men, shouted, "Face to the hill." Chronicle was killed almost immediately from a volley fired by the Tories above. John Boyd, William Rabb and Captain John Mattox were killed about the same time. The men pressed on to the attack under the leadership of Colonel Hambright, Major Dickson, and Captains White, Espey and Martin. They were charged by a company of Tories using the knife bayonets. As had the other commands, they gave ground, then returned to the fight. Colonel Hambright was wounded toward the close of the battle but continued, even as his boot filled with blood.

The sector of the mountain assigned to Major Winston was more difficult to reach than some of the others. It was a very important position, as his men would form the final link in the encircling chain of riflemen. Major Winston and his Surry County fox hunters had left the main force some distance back, to follow a circuitous route to their position. The terrain was rough and unfamiliar, and they made one or two wrong approaches before finding the right spot. Winston's right wing connected with the left wing of Chronicle, and his left wing with the right wing of McDowell. This closed off the last avenue of escape for either Tory soldier or messenger.

Winston's men escaped a direct charge by the Rangers, as they were posted on the other end of the mountain. The Tory Provincials, stationed in this sector, had little inclination to sally against the sharpshooters lurking below. The many stories about the prowess of these backwoods marksmen gave them caution.

Many stories have been told about Colonel James Williams, some good, some bad. Some say he sulked because his superior rank was not recognized by the General Staff. Others say that he was in the middle of the battle, fighting it out with the bravest. Be that as it may, he gave his life for America. We do have the positive statement saying, in the final charge up the hill, Williams and his men were fighting their way up the slope along with the Sullivan forces under Shelby. Step by step he led his men up the hill against the Rangers. His battle cry was, "Come on boys, the old wagoner never yet backed out." During this fierce charge, the horse Williams was riding was shot out from under him. He continued on foot.

The human slaughter was tremendous. The dead and wounded covered the mountain on the slopes and on the flat. Even before the Mountaineers had gained the crest, Captain De Peyster had urged Ferguson to surrender. He knew the odds were hopeless, and to continue was needless slaughter. Ferguson would have none of it; he still felt that in some way he could win. Surrendering to those hated backwater nothings was impossible. Some of the hardest-fought moments of the battle took place after the Patriots gained the crest of the ridge and were closing in on the Rangers.

Colonel Ferguson, finally realizing that his cause was lost, decided to make a desperate effort to break through the Whig lines. With two companions, he made a sally toward Sevier's position on the hill. Wielding his sword in his left hand, he cut and slashed until his sword was broken. The colonel and two of his fellow officers, Colonel Vessey Husbands and Major Daniel Plummer were shot down by the crack riflemen. These Frontiersmen had come a long way just to get Ferguson. Many have claimed credit for firing the fatal shot. Most historians have credited Robert Young with the deed. Regardless, the bullet that felled Ferguson soon brought the battle to an end.

As the Colonel fell from his horse, his foot caught in the stirrup. The frantic horse dragged the fallen commander around the closing circle of Patriots. It is very likely that many shots were fired into the body during this episode. Each viewing Patriot and Tory could have his own version of what he saw during this dramatic moment. The numerous stories about the shooting of Ferguson had their origin from this incident. We must remember that the battle phobia was at its highest pitch when the Scotchman fell. The stories told and retold would add romantic touches and variations down through the years.

Many conflicting stories are told about where and when the mortal wound of Colonel Williams was sustained. An eyewitness, one of Williams' own men, relates that it was after the white flag of surrender was raised that his Colonel was shot.

Captain Abraham De Peyster, second in command, took charge of the British force after Colonel Ferguson fell. With determined action he continued the fight. De Peyster stubbornly yielded ground, as he gradually pulled his troops back to the cover of the supply wagons where a rally was undertaken. This did not last long, as the encircling Americans soon routed them out of this position. The Tories were finally driven into an area some sixty yards long. De Peyster, realizing the contest was hopeless, raised the white flag of surrender.

Many of the Tories had tied white clothes to their gun sticks and held them up earlier in the battle. Ferguson would cut them down as fast as he saw them hoisted. During the last minutes of the conflict, the scared Loyalists were calling for quarters and mercy. The American password during the campaign was "Buford," and the battle-cry, "Remember Buford and his quarters." They had little compassion or mercy in their hearts. The Tories, sensing this, did not know what to expect from those demon mountaineers. James Sevier

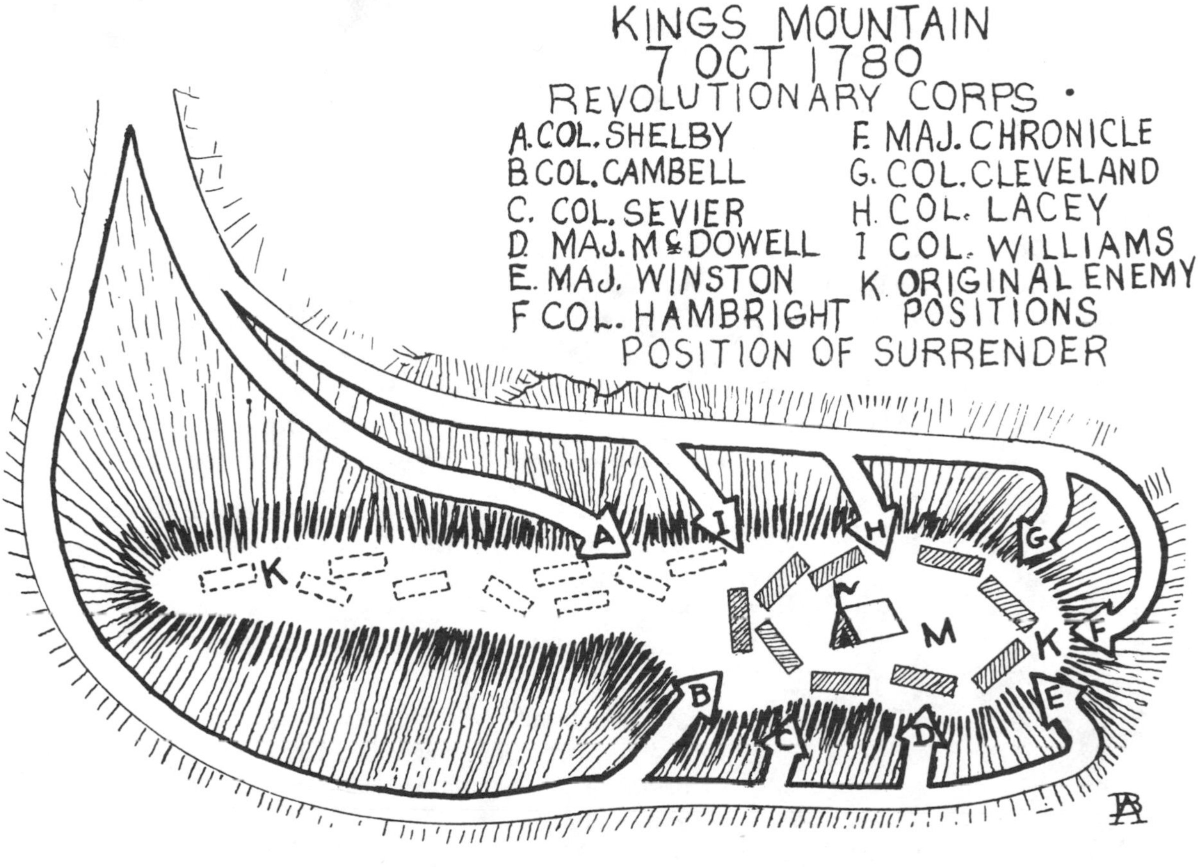

KINGS MOUNTAIN
7 OCT 1780
REVOLUTIONARY CORPS ·
A. COL. SHELBY   F. MAJ. CHRONICLE
B. COL. CAMBELL   G. COL. CLEVELAND
C. COL. SEVIER   H. COL. LACEY
D. MAJ. McDOWELL   I. COL. WILLIAMS
E. MAJ. WINSTON   K. ORIGINAL ENEMY
F. COL. HAMBRIGHT   POSITIONS
        POSITION OF SURRENDER

POSITION OF MOUNTAINEER CORPS
ACCORDING TO DRAPER

had heard that his father, Colonel John Sevier, had been killed. This so enraged him that he kept loading his gun and shooting Tories even after the surrender flag had been raised. It was his Uncle Robert that had been mortally wounded.

Some of the Patriot fighters, coming from various sectors of the battle front and not knowing that the British had surrendered, continued to fire as they approached the huddled group. It must be remembered that there was no general communication between the various companies or individuals, as each detachment and frontiersman fought by themselves with little direction. The mountaineers were out to get the renegades that had been causing them so much misery.

With all escape cut off and nowhere to hide from the deadly fire, the Tories thought they would all be killed. Colonel Shelby rode into the middle of this chaotic situation and ordered the Loyalists to lay down their arms, if they expected mercy. Captain Sawyers suggested separating the prisoners from their guns, many of which were found to be loaded. Some firing was still going on when Colonel Campbell arrived at the surrender area. Campbell immediately ordered the Tory officers to group themselves together, sit on the ground and surrender their swords. Before any of these commands could be carried out, a near tragedy occurred. A small party of Tories, returning from a foraging trip, saw the Patriots and began firing. It was more an act of desperation than an attempted attack. Whigs and Tories alike thought that the expected Tarleton and his dreaded Dragoons had arrived. Tories grabbed their guns and began firing on their captors. The Patriots, under Campbell's orders, began firing on the prisoners. It was a very confused aftermath of the battle. Fortunately, the exchange of shots was brief; but it was costly. It was at this point that Colonel James Williams, riding toward the scene of surrender, is said to have received the mortal bullet wound.

Captain Abraham De Peyster, second in command to Ferguson at King's Mountain. Courtesy New York Historical Society.

The prisoners were marched away from their guns and surrounded by a grim cordon of Whigs. The officers, seated on the ground and bareheaded, extended their swords to any Whig officer near. Colonel Campbell, hatless and coatless, passed among their lines collecting swords. One report says that his arms and hands were full. The British officers could hardly believe that this unmilitarily dressed man could be the Commanding Officer. Many reports as to which officer Captain De Peyster surrendered his sword have been made. The broken sword of Ferguson is another enigma. The small whistle used during the battle was taken by Elias Powell, aid-de-camp to Ferguson. Powell's home was near present Lenoir, North Carolina. Colonel Shelby obtained the longer whistle found in camp.

The granite marker at the grave of Major Patrick Ferguson was given by R.E. Scoggins of Charlotte, North Carolina. Stone mound on grave comes from Scottish custom of placing rock cairns on graves.

Historians, have and will, question Ferguson's choice of King's Mountain to make his stand against the mountaineers. One authority, General Simon Bernard, said, "The Americans, by their victory in that engagement, erected a monument to perpetuate the brave men who had fallen there; and the shape of the hill itself would be an eternal monument to the military genius and skill of Colonel Ferguson, in selecting a position so well adapted for defense; and that no other plan of assault but that pursued by the Mountain Men could have succeeded against him."

From Trevelyan's George III, "The battle of King's Mountain has justly been regarded as the turning point in the war in the Southern States. After the catastrophe the Loyalist party was so cowed and prostrate, that military men serving with Lord Cornwallis began to doubt whether such a party any longer existed."

Expert theories and partisan viewpoints come from many quarters as to who did this or did that at King's Mountain. The important thing is, *The Americans Won*. There is a very narrow difference between defeat and victory, or the turn of events that makes one person a hero and the other a villian.

Legend insists that the two women, in the Ferguson camp at King's Mountain, were part of the staff. Both females, said to be very attractive, had most likely been signed on as maids, serving ladies or cooks. Virginia Sal was killed, during the early part of the battle, while helping a wounded soldier to a tent. After the battle was over, many of the curious crowded around to see the fallen Colonel. Tradition says that his clothing was taken from his body for souvenirs, and his naked body was wrapped in a raw beef hide when placed in the grave. Elias Powell, aid-de-camp to Colonel Ferguson, was granted permission to bury his Commander. Another tradition says that, because of the emergency and press of time, Virginia Sal was placed in the same grave. Virginia Paul, of both fact and fiction fame, was taken prisoner as far as Quaker Meadows (Morganton) before being released to return to the Cornwallis Camp.

Ferguson, considered the villian in this episode, conducted himself bravely during the conflict. He did all that mortal man could in trying to prevent total defeat. He was everywhere; his whistle and shout could be heard in all sections of the battleground. He had put too much trust in the bayonet, which was almost useless against the pioneers with their Indian-style warfare. He had two horses shot from under him before his final dash for freedom and death. Many big IF's pop up, as in every conflict. What would have happened if Tarleton had not been sick and made his appearance during the Battle? What would have happened if Cornwallis had received the messages asking for help? What would have happened if the several hundred furloughed men had returned and opened fire from the rear?

The fate of American independence hung in the balance during this fateful hour. This victory changed the course of the war. It greatly subdued the Tories of the two Carolinas. News of the battle fired the Americans with fresh zeal and encouraged the fragments of the scattered Army to reorganize and rise anew. The appearance of this unknown army from out of nowhere that completely annihilated another army, and then disappeared, was something new in military annals. It was a complete surprise to the British. It upset their timetable and turned a successful campaign into one of retreat. It was three days after the battle before Cornwallis fully learned of Ferguson's disastrous and total defeat. He retreated to Winnsboro, South Carolina. Heavy rains and fever-ridden officers (Cornwallis had the fever himself) delayed further activity for some three months. The attitude and cooperation of the Tories completely changed. They feared retaliation from their Whig neighbors for their misdeeds. They refused to join the British forces or support them. The going was harder. All this gave the Patriots renewed hope and time to reorganize. The tide had turned. For this, Clinton blamed Cornwallis, and Cornwallis blamed Ferguson.

The Chronicle Markers: on the left is the original stone, erected 1815, which was replaced with the newer marker in 1914. These stones mark the graves of Major William Chronicle, Captain John Mattocks, William Rabb, and John Boyd; Patriots killed in the battle.

No accurate tabulation of the number of killed and wounded Americans is available. Several men were detailed for this mission but their count did not agree. This Army, made up of many small companies who kept their own rolls, did not have an official roster to check against. Many of these company rolls have been lost or misplaced. Colonels Campbell, Shelby, and Cleveland, in their signed report for General Headquarters, listed twenty-eight killed and sixty wounded. Statements on pension applications would contradict this total, and some of them could be in error.

Regarding the number in the British Army at King's Mountain, the best available estimates place the number near eleven hundred. The American report says: the daily returns for rations was eleven hundred eighty seven (1187); more than one hundred fifty killed; a like number wounded; eight hundred ten prisoners taken. Each writer, in discussing the totals, finds a different answer. The Tory army seems to have been some larger by count than the American force, but the difference is insignificant.

Fifteen hundred stands of arms and a supply of ammunition were found. The seventeen Tory wagons and other supplies that could not be taken by foot or horseback were burned over the campfires that night. The tent cloth was used in making tandem litters to carry the wounded. Very little food supply was found in the Ferguson camp. One keg of rum taken was used in treating the wounded.

It was good dark before the Americans had finished securing their prisoners. The task of caring for the wounded was an all night job. The most severe cases were placed in tents. Dr. Uzal Johnson, the only surviving doctor, attended Tory and Whig alike. Many of the Patriots with minor wounds doctored themselves, as they were accustomed to doing, with herbs and roots.

The Patriots took turns guarding the prisoners during the long, eerie, uneasy night. The best that can be said, it was a night of horror. The dead were scattered over the hill. The moans and groans of the wounded and dying, crying for help and water, mingled with the fear of an expected attack by Tarleton and his Dragoons, made it a soul-searing experience.

Diorama of Battle can be seen at King's Mountain Military Park

104

From Bancroft's *History of the United States:* ''The appearance of a numerous enemy from the settlements beyond the mountains, whose names had been unknown to the British, took Cornwallis by surprise; and their success was fatal to his intended expedition. He had hoped to step with ease from one Carolina to another, and from those to the conquest of Virginia; and now he had no choice but to retreat.''

From Roosevelt's, *Winning of the West:* ''The victory was of far-reaching importance, and ranks among the decisive battles of the Revolution. It was the first great success of the Americans in the South, and the turning point in the Southern Campaign, and it brought cheer to patriots throughout the Union.''

An early artist's illustration of the King's Mountain Battle. This print from Draper's ''King's Mountain and its Heroes.''

''The Battle of King's Mountain.''   **From a painting by F.C. Yohn.**

THE TRAIL BACK

Tandem Horse Litter by Edith Price

Sunday morning, October 8, about ten o'clock, most of the American force left the mountain battlefield. The fear that Cornwallis would send Tarleton and his Dragoons against them, hurried their departure. The early morning hours were used in constructing tandem horse litters to carry the severely wounded. Nicholas Starnes was placed in charge of the wounded detail during the homeward march. Colonel Campbell dispatched William Snodgrass and Edward Smith to meet the footsoldiers and direct them to a junction with the main force.

The prisoners were directed to carry one or more of the captured guns, minus flint, with physical ability the determining factor in the number of guns carried. Colonel Shelby stood by to see that this order was obeyed. It was necessary to use the flat of his sword on some objectors.

Colonel Campbell and a company of his men remained behind to bury the dead. A similar detachment of Tories was detained to perform a like duty for their fallen comrades. Several long pits were dug and the slain placed in them side by side. Dr. Uzal Johnson, a British surgeon, had stayed behind to give what aid he could to the wounded. After the battle, Dr. Johnson had treated both Whig and Tory wounded. Many people, both friend and foe, had come to the mountain to find out if a husband, son, brother or neighbor had been killed or wounded. Numerous stories and rumors have been handed down from generation to generation regarding the aftermath of the conflict. Fact and fiction have intermingled to such an extent that the two are hard to separate. Needless to say that any carnage, such as happened on King's Mountain, is bound to leave a pitiful past.

The march away from King's Mountain was necessarily slow. Encumbered with seven or eight hundred prisoners, and wounded comrades, the progress of the tired fighters was greatly slowed. Camp was made the night of October 8, near Broad River between Buffalo and Bowen Creeks, twelve miles from the scene of battle. Colonel James Williams died about three miles from the start of the morning march. The footsoldiers met the returning men and helped set up camp. They had obtained some beeves and located a field of sweet potatoes, which gave the men their first good meal since Friday night at Cowpens. Colonel Campbell,

and the two companies with him, came into camp later that night.

It was decided to bury Colonel James Williams here, as it would be almost impossible to take the body home. With full military honors, he was placed in a grave near the mouth of Buffalo Creek.

The grave of Colonel James Williams was later located and the remains moved to a site in the front yard of Gaffney Carnegie Library, Gaffney, South Carolina.

The burial and care of the wounded took up a big portion of the day, but for safety's sake camp was moved some three miles to the north side of Bowen Creek. The leaders hoped to get an early start from here the next morning.

Tuesday morning, October 10, the forces were on the move by good light. They traveled up Broad River, crossing First Broad, Sandy Run, and many other streams as they continued in a northwest direction toward Gilbert Town. They followed the most travelable route leading toward the mountains. Some twenty miles were covered on this march.

The King of England gave land for Brittain Church, built in 1768.

The large body of walking prisoners, strung out in a long thin line, was difficult to guard. Many managed to escape into the forest along the way. Camp was made October 10 near Second Broad River.

Wednesday, October 11, about twelve miles were covered. Camp was made near Gilbert Town on the plantation of Colonel John Walker. A patch of pumpkin, found nearby, was the source of food on this stop. This camp was located about a mile from Brittain Church. The prisoners were placed in bull pens built by Ferguson for Whig prisoners. The Tories were easier to handle here and this respite gave the officers opportunity to handle other complex problems. It was while camped here that the Tory clothing, captured at King's Mountain, was given to the men. One change each was alloted the Tory officers.

Sevier, Shelby and Campbell were faced with a difficult and almost impossible problem in the transportation of their wounded across the mountains. Patriots of that area came to their rescue by offering their homes as havens, until the men were recovered sufficiently to make the trip. Rest and medical care would be available. The records say that Dr. Dobson attended some eighteen of the wounded quartered in Burke County. Most of the day Thursday, October 12, and part of Friday was spent attending this chore. Many individual stories of heroism could be related concerning this chapter of the campaign.

Colonel Campbell and his staff were having other problems that gave them great concern. The Rebels were not treating the captured Tories with the greatest respect. One Tory, taking advantage of an opportunity, threw down his gun and escaped into the woods. Some of his captors found him hiding in a hollow tree. He was dragged out and literally cut to pieces by one of the officers with his captured sword. Many such incidents were happening, causing Campbell to issue a strong order: "I must request officers of all ranks in the army to restrain from the disorderly manner of slaughtering and disturbing the prisoners. If it cannot be stopped by moderate measures, such effectual punishment shall be executed upon delinquents as will put a stop to it."

Another order was directed toward deserting and plundering. Some of the men, hungry, tired, or just plain ornery, were plundering Whig and Tory homes alike. They felt that, having risked their lives in the recent battle, food was due them. Colonel Campbell ordered that "no troops be discharged or released until the prisoners had been delivered to the proper authorities or definite plans for disposal worked out and agreed on by the staff."

Friday, October 13, the army moved to Bickerstaff, sometimes called Red Chimneys. Today the community is called Sunshine. It was here that certain officers of the Carolinas presented complaints to Colonel Campbell. It was stated that among the prisoners were a number of Tories who were robbers, houseburners, parole breakers and assassins. It was also stated that General Cornwallis was responsible for this in his edict, "to subdue the Patriots of South Carolina and Georgia with a cruel hand if necessary." The Southerners who would not take the oath of allegiance were to be treated like criminals.

Whigs who escaped were to be hunted until captured, and their homes burned. In many cases, the women were raped. If a son refused to tell the whereabouts of his father, he was hung. If a wife refused to reveal the location of her husband, her stomach would be ripped open by knife. Tarleton and many of the Tory bandit leaders would force the Tory Americans, under their command, to perform these atrocities. Children, women and old folk were scattered over the countryside, their homes plundered and burned. Many such refugees were found in the woods huddled over a campfire, no food except what they could obtain from the forest. It was felt that if these men were allowed to escape or be paroled, they would continue these deeds. One man told of seeing eleven men hung at Fort Ninety-Six, their only offense being "Whig Rebels."

Bickerstaff Farm where the nine Tories were hung.

Colonel Campbell, on the strength of these complaints, consented to hold court with a copy of North Carolina laws in hand, which stated, "it was legal for two magistrates to summon a jury and hold trial." The law also provided capital punishment. On this basis court was held. A court-martial was ordered. The jury was made up of field Officers and Captains, thus giving the proceedings the status of an orderly court. Witnesses were summoned and examined. The result: thirty-six Tories were convicted and condemned. Right or wrong, the court was legal and handled in proper form.

Some of the Tories brought to trial were released through intercession of neighbors or acquaintances. Among the prisoners were James Crawford and Samuel Chambers. These two men, deserters from Sevier's Corps at Roan Mountain, were released by request of Colonel Sevier. They were told to keep to the straight and narrow and sin no more.

Many of the Patriot officers felt that strong measures were needed to curb the Tory atrocities. This was especially so in the Georgia and South Carolina sections. An eye for an eye was their attitude. If this determined group would set an example, it might halt some of the lawlessness being practiced by the renegades. The officers insisted that they would accept full responsibility for this court action and the executions that might follow. The trials lasted all day and thirty-six were condemned to be hung that night.

A suitable oak tree was selected. For many years this tree was known as "The Gallows Tree." Lines, three and four deep, were formed around the tree, as hand torches lighted the scene. Nine had been hung, three at a time, and the next three made ready when a very unexpected event occurred. Isaac Baldwin was the name of one of the men in the next group to be strung up. He was the leader of a Burke County group of renegade Tories. His reputation of plundering, pillaging and harassing Whigs in that area was well known. As he was waiting for the rope to be placed around his neck, a small lad asked permission to say a farewell to his departing brother. With much crying, wailing and screaming, he made a big show of caressing his brother, as his arms clung in embrace around Isaac's waist. His big show of sorrow and tears completely fascinated the circled soldiers. So intense was their attention, they failed to notice that the young brother, while embracing Isaac, had managed to cut loose the ropes that bound the prisoner's arms behind him. Isaac, free of his bonds, darted through the broken lines of the men and escaped in the darkness. This escape was made through the lines of the best marksmen in the country. They so admired this act of bravery, no effort was made to catch Baldwin. Isaac was killed, shortly after this event, at Bickerstaff's in a fight with a Whig party.

Another man was put in Baldwin's place, and the executioners made ready to continue. Shelby, Sevier and some of the other officers, having a stomach full, put a stop to the hanging. One of the reprieved men told Sevier that he had just received word that Colonel Tarleton, with a strong force, had been sent in pursuit. This was partially true, and easily believed, as such a move had been expected. General Cornwallis, who had received a garbled message of Ferguson's predicament Tuesday, October 10, did send Tarleton to his aid. Tarleton reached a point, near King's Mountain, where full news of the disaster reached him. About the same time a message from Cornwallis, who had also learned the bad news, recalled Tarleton to rejoin his forces retreating toward South Carolina. Thus Tarleton never did give chase to the Ghost Legion.

One of the ironic chapters of this campaign was the two retreating forces, each thinking the other was advancing to attack them. Cornwallis, having heard an exaggerated report of the number of Whig troops, thought that thousands of barbarian mountaineers would be on the march against him. He had practically been unaware of the settlements across the mountains.

Preparations were made for an early march Sunday morning, October 15th. Unencumbered with the wounded, the mountaineer army moved with greater

Catawba River

speed in spite of the rain. The prisoners were prodded with threats and bayonet points to speed the march. The continuous rain made walking tough over muddy roads. The grumbles from the men, both Whig and Tory, were loud and constant, but the leaders would not stop. If the rain continued, which it did, they might get caught this side of the Catawba River. Unable to cross, they would be sitting ducks for Tarleton and his men. On and on they marched, over the muddy road, without food or rest. They reached the river late at night and crossed at Island Ford in waist-deep water. Thirty-two miles had been covered during the day's march. Camp was made on the west bank of the Catawba River on the McDowell farm. These gracious men gave willingly of their seasoned fence rails for fire; more hidden beeves had been brought in to furnish meat; and from somewhere corn meal was provided for bread. For the first time in many

Robertson Creek at Bickerstaff Farm where the Patriots found water for man and beast.

days, with fire to warm and dry their bodies, and food to eat, the men felt safe and relaxed. It was almost a victory celebration, with fires dotting the countryside and a rain-swollen stream between them and Tarleton.

Some of the Tory officers were quartered in the McDowell home. It was just weeks ago that some of these same men had ransacked the house and told Mrs. McDowell, mother of Charles and Joseph, that a rebel's death awaited her sons. It took some persuasion on the part of Joseph to gain Mrs. McDowell's consent for the Tory officers to stay in the house.

During the day, Monday, October 16, the General Staff made plans for dismissing the various companies and disposing of the prisoners. Feeling safe, dry, warm and with a little food in their stomachs, the Patriots were in fine mettle.

Back at Bickerstaff's farm a grim scene, of a different nature, was taking place. As day dawned, the nine dangling bodies could be seen. Mrs. Martha Bickerstaff, with the aid of an old man who helped on the farm, cut the bodies down. Some of the neighbors came and helped dig a trench two feet deep where Colonel Ambrose Mills, Captain Grimes, Captain Walter Gilkey, Captain Wilson, Lieutenant Lafferty, John McFall, John Bebby, and Augustine Hobbs were buried. Friends of Captain Chitwood took his body on a plank to a graveyard at Benjamin Bickerstaff's for burial. Captain Aaron Bickerstaff, husband of Martha, was mortally wounded at King's Mountain. He commanded a Tory Company.

By mutual arrangement, various companies began leaving for their own settlements. Their mission for the moment had been accomplished. Colonels Lacey, Hill, Hawthorn, and the Sumpter forces left for South Carolina. Colonel John Sevier, his men, part of Shelby's force, and the footsoldiers of Colonel Campbell departed for the mountain crossing in the early afternoon of Monday, October 16. With Sevier were the Georgians, under Candler and Johnston, whose families had crossed the mountains with Colonel Clarke. Some of Sevier's and Shelby's men had chosen to remain in the services of McDowell and Cleveland as plans were made for other campaigns.

The mounted men of Campbell's company, troops of Cleveland, Winston and some of McDowell's, formed an escort for the prisoners. They traveled toward the head of the Yadkin River and followed down the valley of that stream toward the headquarters of General Gates.

On their arrival at Bethabara, a Moravian town, Colonels Campbell, Shelby, and Cleveland wrote out their official report and signed it. Here Colonel Campbell issued his final order of the campaign. He appointed Colonel Benjamin Cleveland as Commander of the troops and Official Escort of the prisoners. It was here that Campbell and Shelby took their leave and turned toward home.

Many contributing reasons were responsible for the dwindling number of prisoners. Lieutenant Allaire says that approximately one hundred escaped during one day's march. From all obtainable estimates, only three hundred reached Salem. When the prisoners were delivered to General Gates, it is said, there were less than two hundred.

So, like the Ghost Legion that it was, the victorious army that defeated Ferguson at King's Mountain on October 7, 1780, faded into the mountain fastness and partisan sections from whence it came.

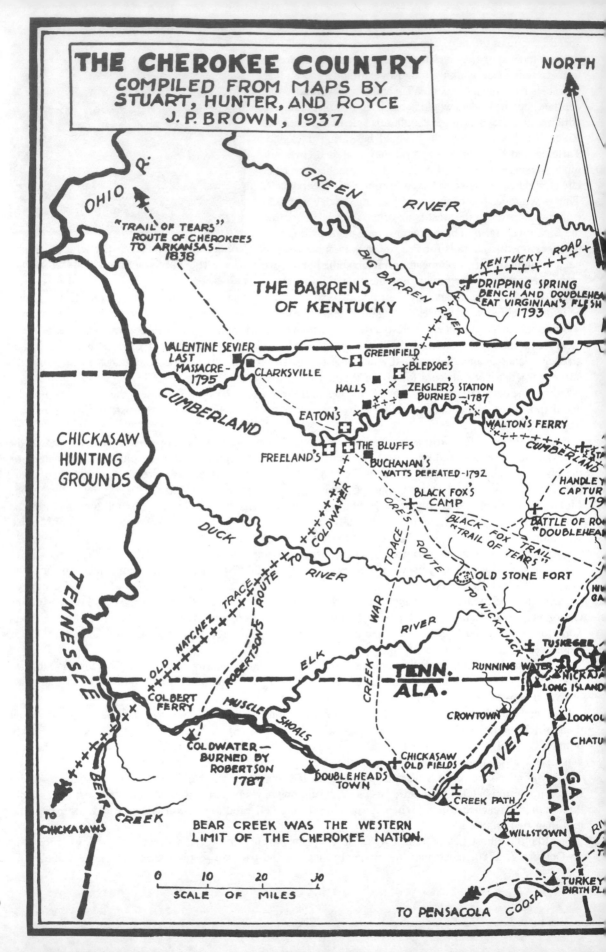

THE CHEROKEE COUNTRY

COMPILED FROM MAPS BY
STUART, HUNTER, AND ROYCE
J. P. BROWN, 1937

NORTH

OHIO R.

GREEN RIVER

BIG BARREN RIVER

"TRAIL OF TEARS"
ROUTE OF CHEROKEES
TO ARKANSAS—
1838

THE BARRENS
OF KENTUCKY

KENTUCKY ROAD

DRIPPING SPRING
BENCH AND DOUBLEHEAD
"EAT VIRGINIAN'S FLESH"
1793

VALENTINE SEVIER
LAST
MASSACRE—
1795

CLARKSVILLE

GREENFIELD

BLEDSOE'S

HALLS

ZEIGLER'S STATION
BURNED—1787

EATON'S

WALTON'S FERRY

CUMBERLAND

CHICKASAW
HUNTING
GROUNDS

CUMBERLAND

FREELAND'S

THE BLUFFS

BUCHANAN'S
WATTS DEFEATED—1792

HANDLEY
CAPTUR
179

BLACK FOX'S
CAMP

BATTLE OF RO
"DOUBLEHEA

DUCK

COLDWATER

BLACK FOX TRAIL
"TRAIL OF TEARS"

OLD STONE FORT

NI
GA

RIVER

OLD NATCHEZ TRACE

ROBERTSON'S ROUTE TO

WAR TRACE

ORE'S ROUTE

ROUTE TO NICKAJACK

TUSKEGEE

TENNESSEE

ELK

CREEK

RIVER

TENN.
ALA.

RUNNING WATER

NICKAJA
LONG ISLAND

COLBERT
FERRY

MUSCLE SHOALS

CROWTOWN

LOOKOU

CHATU

COLDWATER—
BURNED BY
ROBERTSON
1787

DOUBLEHEAD'S
TOWN

CHICKASAW
OLD FIELDS

RIVER

GA.
ALA.

TO
CHICKASAWS

BEAR CREEK

CREEK PATH

WILLSTOWN

RI
T

BEAR CREEK WAS THE WESTERN
LIMIT OF THE CHEROKEE NATION.

TURKEY
BIRTH PLA

TO PENSACOLA   COOSA

0   10   20   30
SCALE   OF   MILES

110

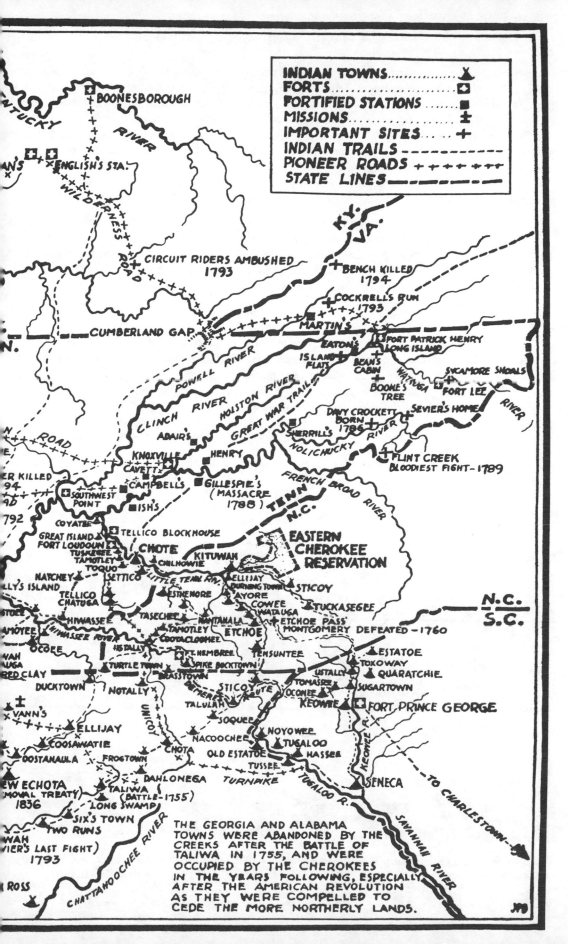

THE GEORGIA AND ALABAMA
TOWNS WERE ABANDONED BY THE
CREEKS AFTER THE BATTLE OF
TALIWA IN 1755, AND WERE
OCCUPIED BY THE CHEROKEES
IN THE YEARS FOLLOWING, ESPECIALLY
AFTER THE AMERICAN REVOLUTION
AS THEY WERE COMPELLED TO
CEDE THE MORE NORTHERLY LANDS.

A Tragic Alliance

The Indian's alliance with England had an imposing influence in forming the frontiersman's attitude toward the red man. The pioneers were prone to believe that English Agents were inciting all the bloody raids on scattered homes and settlements. In some situations it was only rumor, but the Agent was blamed nevertheless. This type of warfare — the surprise attack, kill, scalp and disappear — was adopted by War Chieftains like Dragging Canoe as the only way they could battle the white man. The atrocities, committed over the country by such tactics, created a permanent hostility in the hearts and minds of the Americans. Such incidents as the massacres in Wyoming Valley of Pennsylvania, the atrocities at Augusta, Georgia, and the killing of the Crockett family at Rogersville, Tennessee, only drew the Patriots closer together and widened the gap between white men and red men.

The Alliance between the Cherokees and the English dates back to 1721. Governor Nicholson of South Carolina invited the Cherokees to a council in Charleston. He wanted to woo the Indian fur trade away from the French traders plying the Mississippi Valley. At the conclusion of the Treaty, the Indians had ceded a fifty square mile tract of land between the Santee, Saluda, and Edisto Rivers. The Treaty also secured a trade agreement with the Cherokees for most of their furs.

Some nine years later Sir Alexander Cuming, taking advantage of the red man's ignorance, pulled off an amazing stunt. This feat influenced the Cherokee Nation for many decades. Cuming, standing outside a Council Hall where some three hundred Indians were meeting, prepared a cunning coup. Concealing guns and a sword under his long coat, he entered the Council Hall. With eloquent words, veiled in threats, he had all the headmen present kneel and swear allegiance to the King of England. To make this stunt creditable he practically forced all the white traders present to sign their names as witnesses. Messengers were then sent into all the towns of the Overhill Country, the Middle Towns, and the Lower Towns. All the Chiefs and headmen were told to meet at Nequassee so many days hence. Cuming planned to have these leaders swear allegiance to the English Crown. (Nequassee was located near present site of Franklin, North Carolina.)

Sir Alexander Cuming had no authority for this performance. He merely seized this course to gain prominence for himself. He dreamed of becoming important as the great benefactor of the red man. He made the grand tour of the Cherokee Nation in his attempt to set up his Kingdom. At Tellico he maneuvered to have Maytoy made Emperor.

From left to right are Ounaconoa, Prince Skalilosken, Kollanna, Oukah Ulah, Tathtowe, Clogoittah, and Ukwaneequa, who became the great Chief Attakullakulla. (From the British Museum.)

Cuming's exploit reached its climax at Nequassee, April 3, 1730. Determined to make all England conscious of his great achievement, he worked out a plan to take several of the young chiefs to London to personally meet the King. The Indians were hesitant about making such an unknown dangerous journey. Finally, seven were persuaded to undertake the long voyage. The Chiefs sailing were Kitagista, Oukahulah, Tiftowe, Clogoitah, Kilonah, Onokanowin, and Oukounaco. The party set sail on His Majesty's Ship, Fox, from Charleston, May 4, 1730.

The arrival of the young Chiefs in London caused quite a commotion. They were wined and dined by the royalty. King George II invited them as guests in the Palace where they were permitted to kiss his hands and those of his two sons. The Chiefs presented to the King their Indian Crown, made of possum fur dyed red, and decorated with scalps and eagle tails. The King paid the expenses of the Indians during their extended trip. Mutual pledges were given by the two nations. The Cherokees promised that no other white people would be allowed to settle in their country, and that they would trade with no one else but King George's representatives. They also promised to aid Great Britain in time of war.

Oukahulah, spokesman for the group, made the following speech as taken from Brown's *Old Frontiers*: "We are come hither from a dark and mountainous country, but we are now in a place of light. The crown of our nation is different from that which our Father, King George, wears, but it is all one. The chain of friendship shall be carried to our people. We look upon King George as the sun, and our Father, and upon ourselves as his children; for though you are white and we are red, our hands and hearts are joined together. When we have acquainted our people with what we have seen, our children from generation to generation will remember it. In war we shall always be as one with you. The great King's enemies shall be our enemies. His people and ours shall always be as one, and we shall die together."

Loaded with presents and honors, the Chiefs returned to their homeland May 11, 1731. The trip and visit consumed an entire year. Sir Alexander Cuming did not return with them because of financial difficulties. The Cherokees had gained a Great White Father but had lost their freedom. The Indian was used by the English, and in the end it was the red man who had to pay.

The Indians watching, as the settlements spread to the northwest and to the southwest, grew more disgruntled. More and more families were moving on his land and building cabins. This land he had won by battle and barter, the land that held the graves of his ancestors. The wilderness, being cut up and destroyed by the whites, furnished his way of life as it would that of his children. He would sign a treaty for so much land, and before he could adjust, another clearing and cabin was springing up on ungranted land. The encroachment moved nearer and nearer to his towns. The Indian could not understand the white man's wanton waste of forests and useless killing of wild animals. His worship of all the elements of nature and its products bordered on the fetish. The varying colors of the four winds governed his life. Every rock, tree, bush, animal, bird and hill contained a spirit that had an influence on his days.

It has been said that the Indian's childlike reasoning and response was indicative of a people emerging from the Stone Age of mind and experince. His desires were immature, his reasoning instinctive rather than the result of thinking. But all races and nationalities have gone, or are going, through various stages of mental development likened to the Stone Age. Thus the white man found the Indian when he landed on the American shores. The big problem was the Indian, an adult in body, could strike back and kill. This made the white man angry.

Then came the fight for freedom and the confusing conflict between people of the same race. The Indians, British allies, fought the Frontiersman from this viewpoint. On the other hand the Settlers, knowing that the Indians were English allies, were confronted with a difficult situation. The international law of having and holding spurred some to argue: "we beat the British; the red men were their allies; to the victor goes the spoils."

The approaching departure of the Overmountain men to battle Ferguson furnished the spark, needed by Agent Cameron, to incite the Cherokees to invade the Nolichucky and Watauga Settlements. While the men were away there would be no one left but the old men, women and children who could easily be captured, killed or driven off their land. "Now is the time," Cameron told the Cherokee-Chickamauga braves. The Agent also told the indian that Ferguson, with his trained British soldiers, would easily defeat the untrained mountaineers. The Indians, believing their White Father, began making plans for a great campaign to regain their lands. They expected little opposition.

The Battle across the mountains was over sooner than Cameron expected and with an entirely different outcome. The British were badly defeated and the Overmountain men back home before the Cherokee-Chickamauga campaign was fully started. The Indians were met at Boyd's Creek and badly defeated. The angry frontiersmen continued on to the Indian towns and burned many of them to the ground. The King's Mountain victory was the beginning of a very bad period for the Cherokee. The land grabbers and territory encroachers really took over. For the Indians it was the beginning of the end.

ROBERT SEVIER

Captain Robert Sevier was mortally wounded at King's Mountain during that final charge up the hill. This was the attack when Sevier's men gained the crest of the ridge and held, giving Shelby and Campbell the flanking support they needed to advance. Robert had stooped to pick up his ramrod from the ground, when a bullet struck him near the kidney. His brother James carried him down the slope to the spring, where he washed and dressed the wound as best he could.

After the Battle, Dr. Uzal Johnson, Tory doctor, tried to extract the bullet but was unable to do so. He treated the wound and advised Robert to lie and rest a few days until the bullet could be taken out safely. Robert insisted upon going home. His reputation as a Tory hater, and the expectation of an attack by Tarleton's forces, did not make King's Mountain a safe place to rest.

With his nephew and other men of his company, he spent the night in the home of John Finley, a Patriot who lived nearby. Joseph Sevier, oldest son of John Sevier, later married Mary Finley of this family.

The four men, James Sevier, Harmon Perryman, William Robertson, and Robert Sevier, left the next day for the Overmountain country and home. Nine days after the battle, at Bright's Place, Captain Robert Sevier became very sick while the men were preparing their meal. He died within an hour.

Robert was wrapped in a blanket and buried in Bright's Cemetery beneath an oak tree. His death occurred the day after the Overmountain men left Quaker Meadows on their return trip across the mountains. The D.A.R. erected a stone in Robert Sevier's honor September 9, 1951. The grave is near Spruce Pine, North Carolina.

TEN WHIGS

Colonel John Moore and some two hundred fifty Tories were camped in a church yard some twenty-five miles from King's Mountain. They were attacked by ten Whigs and completely routed. This event took place either the night before or the night after Ferguson's defeat. Moore's men were a part of Ferguson's returning furloughed soldiers.

The ten Whigs were hiding in the woods, watching the Tories as they were taking what supplies they could find from the Patriot homes along the way. By chance they were able to capture one Tory, and from him learned the location of the planned campsite that night. The Whigs then proceeded to plan a surprise party for the unsuspecting Loyalists.

After dark, the ten Whigs took their posts around the Tory camp. At a given signal they stood up in sight of the Tory guards and gave forth with loud bloodcurdling shouts. The surprised sentries challenged and fired at the attacking force. The Patriots, meanwhile, dropped to the ground and the shots went harmlessly over their heads. Then with loud Indian yells they jumped up, firing their guns as they ran toward the camp. The peaceful evening, the congenial meal, with song and happy campfire atmosphere, were exploded by a desperate fear. Confusion and fright were in complete command. These scared men thought the demons from across the mountains were breathing death and destruction down their backs. Guns, food, clothing and everything else were forgotten in their hurry to escape into the safety of darkness. The entire force, officers and privates, fled in terrified haste and from all reports kept traveling.

The ten Whigs cautiously entered the camp-site. Not one Tory was present. With the extra captured guns loaded and by their side, they stood guard all night, expecting a Loyalist attack every moment. When dawn arrived, they packed the supplies into wagons, hitched the fifteen captured horses up and carried the food and other needed items back home. It is said they divided with their needy neighbors.

CAPTAINS JOHN WEIR and ROBERT SHANNON, living in the vicinity of King's Mountain, had heard of the Patriot force marching to do battle with the Tories. They had summoned their men and moved forth to join them in the fight. They might have arrived too late to join in the actual battle, but it can be assumed that they assisted in every way possible in attending wounded, guarding prisoners and other chores that would give the tired fighters some relief.

Pictured are suits of clothing worn by Greer. They hang in the Tennessee State Museum, Nashville, Tennessee. Pictures of Greer's clothing and Sevier's Sword and Gun by courtesy Fred Estes, director of the state museum.

The King's Mountain Messenger

Soon after the King's Mountain victory Joseph Greer was dispatched, by Colonel John Sevier, to carry news of the Battle to Congress assembled in Philadelphia.

Young Greer, twenty years old and over seven feet tall, was armed with a musket and compass for the long dangerous trip. Many reasons can be conjectured as to why Sevier selected Greer for this particular mission. The important one was Greer's knowledge of the Indians. For years Joseph had traveled with his father among the Indian towns. Andrew Greer, a Scotsman, had traded with the red men from the moment he arrived in the new country. Another good reason, it would take an experienced woodsman to plot his way through the forests and Tory settlements. All this experience proved valuable to young Greer as he journeyed north.

Joseph Greer had one or more horses shot from under him by the Indians. Much of the trip had to be covered on foot. He had to swim several streams, some covered by ice. One night was spent in a big hollow log, hiding from a party of braves who had been following him all day. From his concealment in the log, he could hear them talking as they tried to pick up his trail. It is said that they actually sat on the log for a spell.

On Greer's arrival in Philadelphia, he made his way to Congressional Headquarters. The doorkeeper tried to bar his entrance. The giant messenger pushed him aside, stalked down the aisle, and delivered his message to a surprised body of men. It is said that General Washington commented: "With soldiers like him, no wonder the frontiersmen won."

Joseph Greer was given a grant of three thousand acres for this service and other participation during the fight for independence. The tract was located in what is now Lincoln County, Tennessee. Greer acquired several bordering tracts until his holdings covered some ten thousand acres. It is said that you could ride a straight line all day and not get off Greer land. The Greer Clan has many descendants living in Cane Creek Valley.

SWORD AND PISTOL PRESENTED TO COLONEL JOHN SEVIER

The General Assembly of North Carolina, during the first session after the King's Mountain victory, passed a resolution that a sword and pistol should be presented to both Colonel John Sevier and Colonel Isaac Shelby for the great service they had given their country. This session of the Assembly met in Halifax, January 18, 1781.

On one side of the sword handle, presented to Colonel Sevier, is engraved "State of North Carolina to Colonel John Sevier," and on the other side, "King's Mountain, October 7, 1780." The sword and pistol, in photograph on preceding page, were inherited by Colonel George Washington Sevier and given by him to the State of Tennessee.

Though this resolution was adopted in 1781, the swords and pistols were not delivered until 1813. North Carolina Governor William Hawkins wrote a letter to Sevier with apologies for the oversight. These historic reminders of King's Mountain are in the State Museum at Nashville, Tennessee. Swords and pistols were also presented to other commanding officers.

COLONEL PATRICK FERGUSON

(This list of officers very limited. Space and time did not allow a fuller roster.)
Killed (k)   Hanged (h)   Wounded (w)

Captain Abraham De Peyster
  (Second in command)
Captain Alexander Chesney *(Left Diary)*
Colonel Ambrose Mills (h)
Major _____ Lee
Major Daniel Plummer (k)
Major William Mills
Captain Samuel Ryerson (w)
Captain John McGinnis
Captain Aron Bickerstaff
  (Mortally wounded. Trial and hanging took place on his farm.)
Colonel Vesey Husbands (k)
Captain William Gist
Captain William Green

Captain _____ Wilson (h)
Captain James Chittwood (h)
Captain _____ Grimes (h)
Captain _____ Towsend
Captain Walter Gilkey (h)

Aid-de-Camp Elias Powell
Lieutenant William Langum
Lieutenant John Taylor
Lieutenant Anthony Allaire
  (Wrote diary)
Lieutenant William Stevenson
Lieutenant Duncan Fletcher
Lieutenant John McGinnis (k)
Lieutenant _____ Lafferty (h)

Privates: John McFall (h), John Bebby (h), Augustine Hobbs (h).

Major Patrick Ferguson was born in Aberdeen, Scotland. His father, Lord Pitfour, had restored the family fortune to the extent that he was able to afford a good family background for his children. Young Patrick began an early education, but hunting and soldiering appealed more than the academic. His family purchased a commission for him at the age of fifteen. He entered active service with the Royal North Dragoons, July 12, 1759. Although of small body frame, young Ferguson was serious-minded and had sound judgment and abundant energy.

After years of experience, excepting six of sickness, Captain Ferguson was sent to America in 1777. He soon had a reputation as one of the best marksmen in the country. During the first three years he saw action in the New England battles. He was sent to South Carolina when the invasion started at Charleston. Here he was given the temporary rank of Lieutenant-Colonel. Ferguson had received a wound in his right arm during the Battle of Brandywine, making it almost useless the rest of his life.

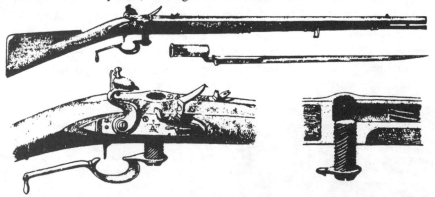

Pictured here is the first successful breech loading rifle which was developed by Patrick Ferguson. One of these guns hangs in the Museum at King's Mountain. Pictures by courtesy of King's Mountain National Military Park personnel.

KING'S MOUNTAIN SOLDIERS

An incomplete listing of the officers and men that participated in the King's Mountain Campaign

Rank listed is at time of battle. (k) killed, (w) wounded, (?) no proof

Allen, Richard, Captain
  (stayed with footsoldiers)
Anderson, Gerorge, Major
Anderson, John Jr., Lieutenant
Andrews, John, Lieutenant
Arbunkle, Mathew, Captain

Barnes, Alexander, Captain
Bartlett, William, Lieutenant
Barnett, Alexander, Captain
Barton, John, Captain
Barry, Andrew, Captain
Beattie, John, Lieutenant (k)
Beattie, William, Captain
Beattie, David, Captain
Bean, Jesse, Captain
Bean, William, Captain
Beverly, John, Captain
Blacock, Samuel G., Major
Blackburn, William, Lieutenant (k)
Blackmore, William, Lieutenant
Bishop, Levi, Lieutenant
Boyd, John, Lieutenant
Bowen, William, Captain
Bowen, Arthur, Captain
Bowen, Reese, Lieutenant
Brandon, Thomas, Colonel
Brandon, John, Captain
Boran, Baile, Lieutenant
Bradshear, Samuel, Captain
Bradshear, Robert, Captain
Breckenridge, Alexander, Captain
Breckenridge, Robert, Captain
Brown, Jacob, Captain
Brown, John, Captain
Brown, Andrew, Captain
Buckner, Joshua, Lieutenant
Black, Joseph, Lieutenant

Caldwell, Samuel, Captain
Caldwell, Thomas, Captain
Callahan, John, Captain
Callahan, Joel, Lieutenant
Campbell, William, Colonel
  (Commander-in-Chief)
Campbell, John, Captain
Campbell, Robert, Lieutenant
Campbell, Patrick, Lieutenant
Campbell, Hugh, Lieutenant
Caruthers, Andrew, Lieutenant
Candler, William, Major
Carr, Paddy, Captain
Carter, Landon, Lieutenant
Carson, John, Captain
Christian, Gilbert, Major
Chronicle, William, Major (k)
Clark, John, Captain
Cleveland, Benjamin, Colonel
Cleveland, John, Lieutenant
Cleveland, Larkin, Lieutenant
  (wounded enroute to King's Mountain)

Cloud, Joseph, Captain
Cowan, Andrew, Captain
Cowan, William, Captain
Corry, James, Lieutenant (k)
Condley, John, Captain
Colville, Andrew, Captain
Coulter, John, Captain
Cox, William, Captain
Craig, David, Captain
Craig, Robert, Captain
Crabtree, James, Captain
Crockett, Joseph, Captain
Crockett, Walter, Major
Crockett, William, Lieutenant
Crockett, Joseph, Captain
Crow, John, Captain

Davenport, William, Colonel
Davis, John, Captain
Davis, Andrew, Lieutenant
Davison, William, Lieutenant
Davison, Daniel, Lieutenant
Daugherty, George, Captain
Dickson, Joseph, Major
Dillard, James, Captain
Dryden, Nathaniel, Lieutenant (k)
Dysart, James, Captain (w)
Duff, William, Captain

Edmondson, William, Major
Edmondson, William, Captain (k)
Edmondson, Robert Sr., Captain (k)
Edmondson, Robert Jr., Lieutenant (w)
Edmondson, Andrew, Captain (k)
Elliot, James, Captain
Espey, Samuel, Captain (w)
Ewing, Alexander, Captain

Fapolson, Andrew, Captain
Fear, Edmond, Captain
Franklin, John, Captain
Franklin, Jesse, Captain
Forney, Peter, Captain
Fulkerson, James, Captain

Gilliespie, Thomas, Captain
Gilliespie, William, Captain
Gillilland, James, Lieutenant
Gilreath, William, Captain
Gist, Benjamin, Captain
Goff, Andrew, Lieutenant
Gordan, Charles, Major
Gray, William, Lieutenant

Hadley, Joshua, Captain
Hampton, Andrew, Colonel
Hambright, Frederick, Lieutenant-Colonel
Hambright, John, Lieutenant
Hannah, Robin, Captain
Hammond, Samuel, Major

KING'S MOUNTAIN SOLDIERS

Harvey, John, Captain
Hawthorne, James, Lieutenant-Colonel
Hayes, Joseph, Colonel
(succeeded to Gen. Williams' command)
Handley, Samuel, Captain
Hemphill, Thomas, Captain
Herndon, Benjamin, Lieutenant-Colonel
Herndon, Joseph, Major
(remained with footsoldiers)
Hickman, James, Captain
Hill, William, Colonel
(in command of Sumpter's force)
Hollis, John, Captain
Houston, James, Ensign
Houston, John, Ensign
Hughes, Joseph, Lieutenant

Isbell, Godfrey, Captain
Isbell, Zachery, Lieutenant

Jack, James, Captain
Jackson, William, Captain
Jamison, John, Lieutenant
Jernigan, George, Lieutenant
Johnson, James, Major
Johnson, John, Captain
Johnson, Samuel, Captain
Johnson, James, Captain
Johnson, Samuel, Lieutenant (w)
Johnston, William, Captain

Kennedy, Robert, Captain

Lacey, Edward, Colonel
(commanded the Sumpter force during battle)
Lenoir, William, Captain (w)
Leeper, James, Lieutenant
Lewis, James Martin, Lieutenant (w)
Lewis, Joel, Captain (w)
Lewis, Aron, Captain
Lewis, Micajah, Major (w)
Lewis, Joel, Lieutenant (w)
Litton, Solomon, Lieutenant
Looney, David, Captain
Looney, Moses, Lieutenant
Lowery, John, Lieutenant
Love, Andrew, Colonel
Love, William, Lieutenant
Lucas, Isaac, Captain
Lucas, Joseph, Captain
Lucas, Robert, Captain
Lusk, Joseph, Captain
Lytte, Thomas, Captain
Lyon, Huberson, Lieutenant (k)
Lane, Isaac, Lieutenant
Ledbetter, George, Captain

McDowell, Charles, Colonel
McDowell, Joseph, Major
(commanded his brother Charles' force during battle)
McDowell, Joseph, Captain
(cousin)

McCullock, Thomas, Lieutenant (k)
McCutchan, Samuel, Captain
McFarland, Robert, Lieutenant
McFerrin, John, Ensign
McKissick, David, Captain
McNabb, David, Captain
Mattox, Charles, Lieutenant
Mattox, John, Captain (k)
Martin, George, Lieutenant
Martin, Samuel, Captain
Maxwell, George, Captain
Meek, Adam, Lieutenant
Meredith, William, Captain
Miller, James, Captain
Moffett, John, Captain
Montgomery, James, Captain

Neal, William, Captain
(stayed with footsoldiers)
Newell, Samuel, Lieutenant (w)
Nixon, John, Captain

Oglesby, William, Captain

Pemberton, John, Captain
Phillips, James, Lieutenant (k)
Pittman, William, Lieutenant
Porter, James, Major
Preston, Thomas, Captain

Rabb, William, Lieutenant
Rains, John, Captain
Reynolds, Elisha, Lieutenant
Riggs, Bethial
Robinson, William, Lieutenant
Robinson, John, Lieutenant
Roseborough, William, Captain
Russell, George, Lieutenant
Russell, Andrew, Captain
Russell, William, Lieutenant

Sample, Samuel, Captain
Sawyers, John, Captain
Sevier, John, Colonel
Sevier, Valentine, Major
Sevier, Robert, Captain
(mortally wounded)
Sevier, Valentine, Captain
Scott, Joseph Sr., Lieutenant
Shannon, Robert, Captain
Sharp, Thomas, Lieutenant
Shelby, Isaac, Colonel
Shelby, John, Captain
Shelby, Evan Jr., Major
Shelby, Moses, Captain
Sigmon, John, Captain
Singleton, Andrew, Captain
Singleton, Richard, Major
Smith, Henry, Captain
Smith, William, Captain
Smith, Henry, Captain
Smith, Miner, Captain (w)
Smith, Daniel, Captain
Smith, J.M., Lieutenant

KING'S MOUNTAIN SOLDIERS

Snoddy, John, Captain
Steen, James, Colonel (k)
Steele, John, Lieutenant
Stinson, James, Captain
Syles, James, Captain

Taylor, Christopher, Captain
Tate, Samuel, Major
Thompson, John, Captain
Thompson, James, Captain
Tipton, Jonathan, Major
Tipton, William, Lieutenant
Trimble, Robert, Captain
Trimble, William, Captain
Topp, Roger, Captain

Vance, David, Captain
Vance, John, Lieutenant
Vanhook, Samuel, Lieutenant

Wallace, Andrew, Captain
Walker, Felix, Lieutenant-Colonel
Walton, Jesse, Major
Watson, Patrick, Major
   (stayed with footsoldiers)
Webb, David, Captain
Weir, John, Captain
Weir, Samuel, Captain
White, Thomas, Lieutenant
White, Isaac, Captain
White, Richard, Lieutenant
White, Joseph, Captain
Witherspoon, David, Lieutenant
Wilson, Zacheus, Captain
Withrow, James, Captain
Williams, James, Colonel (k)
Williams, Joseph, Captain
Williams, Samuel, Captain
Wilson, Joseph, Captain
Wiley, Alexander, Lieutenant
Willoughby, William, Lieutenant
Wood, Samuel, Captain
Womach, Jacob, Captain

Abernathy, Robert
Adams, John
Adams, William
Alexander, Daniel
Alexander, Elias
Alexander, James
Alexander, Jerimiah
Alexander, John
Alexander, Oliver
Allen, Moses
Allen, Richard
Allen, Vincent
Allison, John (w)
Alston, William
Anderson, Jacob
Anderson, James
Anderson, John
Anderson, William
Applegate, Thomas
Arbuckle, Thomas
Arbuckle, Mathew
Armstrong, Robert
Armstrong, James
Armstrong, Isaac
Armstrong, Mathew
Armstrong, William
Avender, Andrew
Axer, Sam

Blackwell, David
Bacon, Michael
Baker, John
Bakly, Charles
Balch, Amos
Ballew, Richard
Banning, Benoni (w)
Barker, Charles
Barker, Edmond
Barker, Edward

Barker, Enoch
Barker, Joel
Barker, Henry
Barnes, Alexander
Barnes, Benjamin (?)
Barnes, Shadrack (?)
Barnett, Alexander
Bartlett, William
Barton, Benjamin
Barton, John
Barton, Joshua
Barton, Isaac
Barry, Andrew
Bean, George
Bean, Jesse
Bean, John
Bean, Robert
Beard, Robert
Bearden, Jeremiah
Bearden, John
Beattie, David
Beattie, John (k)
Beattie, Francis
Beattie, William
Beeler, Jacob
Beeler, Joseph
Bell, Samuel
Bell, Thomas
Bell, William
Bennedict, John
Bentley, John
Berry, Bradley
Berry, James
Berry, Thomas
Berry, Andrew
Berry, Robert
Besall, John
Bickley, Summers
Bickley, Charles

Bicknell, James
Bicknell, Thomas (k)
Bingham, Benjamin
Biffle, Jacob
Bishop, Levi
Black, Joseph
Blackburn, Arthur
Blackburn, George
Blackburn, Joseph
Blackburn, Robert
Blackburn, John
Blackburn, William (k)
Blackmore, John
Blackmore, William
Blalock, Samuel
Blassingham, John
Blair, James
Blair, John
Blevin, Henry
Blevin, Daniel
Blyth, Thomas
Bolling, Jerry
Boran, Bazi
Boren, John
Bowen, Charles
Bowen, John
Bowen, Henry
Bowers, Leonard
Bowman, Esaius
Bowman, Sparkling
Box, Samuel
Boyer, Thomas (k)
Boyd, William
Boyd, John (k)
Boyce, John
Bradley, William (w)
Bradley, Richard
Brandon, Mathew
Brazelton, William

KING'S MOUNTAIN SOLDIERS

Brakshears, Mattis
Breckenridge, Alexander
Breckenridge, George
Breckenridge, John
Breden, John
Britt, Obediah
Briggs, John
Brimer, William
Brigham, James
Brooks, George
Brooks, Thomas
Brooks, John
Brooks, William
Brooks, David
Brooks, Moses
Broom, W. M.
Brown, John (k)
Brown, James
Brown, Low
Brown, John S. C.
Brown, Thomas
Brown, Stephen
Brown, Isaiah
Brown, Peter
Brown, George
Brown, Joseph
Brown, Michael
Browning, Enos
Bruster, E. (?)
Brush, Enoch
Buchanan, Samuel
Buchanan, Robert
Buchanan, Alexander
Budvine, Francis
Bullen, William (w)
Bullen, Isaac
Bullen, Luke
Burney, William
Burney, Simon
Burns, Laird
Burns, William

Caldwell, Samuel
Caldwell, William
Callahan, Joel
Callahan, John
Callaway, Elijah
Callaway, Richard
Callaway, William
Camp, Thomas
Camp, Nathan
Camp, Thomas
Camp, John
Camp, Benjamin
Camp, Edmund
Campbell, Joseph
Campbell, David
Campbell, William Jr.
Campbell, Robert (w)
Campbell, Hugh
Campbell, James
Campbell, Jeremiah
Campbell, Patrick
Candler, Henry
Cantrell, Stephen

Carmichal, John
Carmack, Cornelius
Carmack, John
Carpenter, John
Carr, Patrick
Carrol, William
Carson, Andrew
Carson, David
Carson, John
Carson, William
Carwell, Alexander
Carswell, John
Cartwright, Joseph
Carathurs, James
Cardwell, Perrin
Carter, Charles
Casewell, Zadrack
Casey, Benjamin
Casey, Levi
Casey, Randolph
Casey, William
Cash, David
Cathcart, Joseph
Castillo, John
Caunice, Nicholas
Chambers, Robert
Chapman, John
Chapman, Benjamin
Cheney, Thomas
Childers, John (w)
Childress, Mitchell
Childress, Thomas
Chisholm, John
Childress, Mitchell
Childress, William
Childress, John
Chittim, John (w)
Chitwood, James
Christian, George (?)
Clark, George
Clark, Michael
Clark, William
Clark, James
Clay, William
Clayborn, John
Clem, William
Cleveland, Ezekiel
Cleveland, Robert
Clon, William
Clowney, Samuel
Cloa, Willis
Cobb, Arthur
Cobb, Jerry
Cobb, Pharoh
Cobb, William Sr.
Cobb, William Jr.
Cockrell, John (?)
Cole, Joseph
Cole, Thomas
Cole, William
Colley, Daniel
Colley, Thomas
Collins, James
Collins, Samuel
Coleman, Spense

Collinworth, John
Colvill, Joseph
Colville, Samuel (w)
Compton, Jeremiah
Cook, William
Cook, Charles
Cook, Edward
Cook, Robert
Cook, Elisha
Coop, Horatia
Cope, John
Copeland, Zacheus
Corry, James (k)
Cosby, James
Costner, Thomas
Coulter, Martin
Coultrie, Robert
Covey, Samuel
Cowan, David
Cowan, James
Cowan, Andrew
Cowan, William
Cowan, Samuel
Cowan, Nathaniel
Cowan, Thomas
Cox, Charles
Cox, James
Cox, Curd
Cox, William (w)
Craig, Robert
Craig, David
Craig, James
Craig, John
Crawford, Charles
Crawford, John
Crawford, John
Crenshaw, John
Creswell, Andrew
Crock, William
Crockett, William
Crockett, Samuel
Crockett, John
Cross, Joseph
Cross, Elijah
Cross, Zachrack (?)
Crow, James
Crow, John
Crumbless, Thomas
Crunk, William
Culbertson, Josiah
Culbertson, Robert
Cummings, Andrew
Cunningham, Jonathan
Curry, James
Cusick, John
Cusick, George
Cutbirth, Andrew

Dalton, John
Dameron, George
Darnell, David (w)
Darnell, Cornelius
Darnell, Lawrence
David, Azariah

KING'S MOUNTAIN MEN

Dave, Thomas
Davidson, Benjamin
Davidson, William
Davidson, Samuel
Davidson, Daniel
Davis, John
Davis, Nathaniel
Davis, Robert
Davis, Samuel
Davis, William
Davis, Joel
Davis, Nathan
Dawson, Elias
Deatheridge, John
Delaney, William
Dennison, Robert
Depew, Isaac
Desha, Robert
Detgaoorett, John
Dickinson, Henry
Dickey, Andrew
Dickey, David
Dillard, Benjamin
Dillard, James
Dixon, Joseph
Dixon, John
Dixon, Joel
Doaling, Robert
Doherty, George Sr.
Dobkins, Jacob
Dobson, Robert
Dodd, William
Dobson, Joseph
Donald, James
Dolberry, Lytton
Doran, Alexander
Doran, James
Doran, Terence
Dorton, Moses
Dorton, William Jr,
Douglas, James
Douglas, Johnathan (w)
Douglas, Robert
Douglas, Edward
Dryden, James
Dryden, Nathaniel (k)
Dryden, William
Duck, Samuel
Duckworth, John
Duff, David (k)
Duff, Samuel
Dunn, Samuel
Dunn, William
Duncan, Jesse
Duncan, Joseph
Duncan, John
Duncan, Thomas
Dunlop, James
Dysart, John

Eaken, William
Earnest, Earnest
Earnest, Rev. Felix
Eddleman, Peter
Edgman, William

Edmiston, Samuel
Edmiston, John
Edmiston, Thomas
Edmiston, Robert
Edmiston, William
Elder, Robert
Elmore, William
Ely, William
Enlow, Potter
England, John
England, Joseph
Estill, Benjamin
Evans, Andrew
Evans, Ardin
Evans, David
Evans, Evan
Evans, Samuel
Evans, Phillip
Everett, William
Ewart, James
Ewart, Robert
Ewing, George
Ewin, Hugh
Fagan, John (w)
Fain, Samuel
Fain, Nicholas
Farewell, James
Farewell, John
Faris, Thomas
Faris, Isaac
Faris, John
Faris, Larkin
Faris, Martin
Faris, Richard
Farrow, Landon
Farrow, Samuel
Farrow, Thomas
Farrow, John
Fear, Thomas
Fear, Edmond
Feimster, William
Findley, John
Findley, George
Fisher, Frederick (w)
Fitch, John
Fleenor, Charles
Fleenor, Michael
Fleenor, Joel
Flemming, John
Fletcher, Thomas
Floyd, Andrew
Floyd, John
Flower, William (w)
Folson, Andrew
Ford, John
Fork, William
Fork, Peter
Forney, Abraham
Forrister, Robert
Fowler, William (k)
Fowler, John
Fowler, James
Fox, John
Francis, Thomas
Frazer, David

Frazer, Daniel
Frazer, John
Frazier, Samuel
Freeman, William
Freeland, James
Frierson, Robert
Frierson, William
Frierson, Thomas
Frierson, James
Frierson, John
Frigge, John
Frigge, J. C.
Frigge, Robert
Frost, Micajah
Fulkerson, Richard
Fulkerson, John
Fulkerson, James
Fulkner, David
Furgason, James

Gaines, James Sr.
Gaines, James
Gaines, Ambrose
Galbreath, Arthur
Galbreath, Robert (?)
Galbreath, John (?)
Galliher, John
Galliher, Joel
Galloway, Alexander
Gamble, Robert
Gamble, Choat
Gamble, Josiah
Gammon, Harris
Gann, Thomas
Garner, John
Gaspenson, John
Gass, John
Gaston, William
Geren, Solomon
Gervis, James
Gibson, John
Gibson, Thomas
Gibbs, Nicholas
Giles, William (w)
Gilleland, John (w)
Gillespie, James
Gillespie, Jacob
Gillespie, Thomas
Gillespie, George
Gilliam, Devereux
Gilmer, Enoch
Gilmer, William (w)
Gist, Joseph
Gist, Joshua
Gist, Nathaniel (k)
Gist, Richard
Gist, Thomas
Given, James
Given, John
Glenn, John
Godwin, Joseph
Godwin, Robinson
Godwin, Samuel
Goforth, Preston (k)
Goff, Andrew

KING'S MOUNTAIN SOLDIERS

Goff, William
Goodman, Henry
Gordon, Charles (w)
Gordon, Chapman
Gordon, George
Gorsage, John
Gourley, Thomas
Graham, James
Graham, William
Graves, Boston
Gray, James
Gray, Jessee
Grantham, Richard
Green, Jesse
Greenlee, James
Greever, Phillip
Greer, Alexander
Greer, Andrew
Greer, William
Greer, Andrew Jr.
Greer, Joseph
Gregory, John
Grier, John
Grier, James
Griffith, Joseph
Grimes, George
Grimes, James
Guest, Moses
Gwaltney, Nathan

Hackett, John
Hadden, George
Hager, Simon
Haile, John
Hale, William
Hale, Lewis
Hall, David
Hall, John
Hall, Thomas
Hall, Jesse
Hambright, John Hardin
Hamby, William
Hamer, James
Hamilton, Alexander
Hamilton, Joshua
Hamilton, Thomas
Hamilton, John
Hamilton, Robert
Hammond, Charles
Hampton, Edward
Hampton, Jonathan
Hampton, Andrew
Hampton, John
Hampton, Joel
Handly, Robert
Handly, Samuel
Hanna, Robert
Hanna, Andrew
Hancock, Stephen
Hancock, Joseph
Hank, Michael
Hankins, Abraham
Hansley, Robert
Handy, Thomas
Hardeman, Thomas

Hardin, Abraham
Hardin, Joseph Jr.
Hardin, John
Harkleroad, Henry
Harlison, Herndon
Harrell, Reuben
Harrell, John (?)
Harrell, Joseph (?)
Harrell, Kidder
Harris, James
Harrison, Gideon
Harrison, Nathaniel
Harmison, John
Harper, Richard
Hart, Leonard
Harwood, William
Hays, Samuel
Hayter, Israel (w)
Hedrick, William
Helms, John
Helm, Meredith (?)
Helton, Abraham
Hemphill, Charles
Henderson, John
Henderson, Daniel
Henderson, Joseph
Henderson, Robert
Henderson, William
Henderson, John
Hendrick, David
Hendrick, Solomon
Hendrick, Moses
Henegar, Henry (k)
Henegar, Jacob
Henegar, John
Henniger, Conrad
Henry, Henry
Henry, James
Henery, Moses (k)
Henry, John (k)
Henry, Joseph
Henry, Henry
Henry, Robert (w)
Henry, Samuel
Henry, Hugh
Henry, William
Hensley, Samuel
Hereden, James
Hereden, Edward
Hickman, James
Hickman, Joel
Hickman, Thomas
Higgins, John
Higgenbottom, Robert
Hill, James
Hillian, James
Hillian, John
Hobbs, Thomas
Hoffman, Jacob
Hoffman, John
Hotchkiss, Jared
Holloway, Charles
Holloway, John
Holloway, Benjamin
Hollingsworth, Benjamin

Holdway, Timothy
Holland, Isaac Jr.
Hood, John
Hortenstine, Abraham
Horton, Daniel (?)
Horton, Henry
Horton, Joshua (?)
Horton, John
Horton, Zephaniah (?)
Houston, William
Houston, John
Houston, James
Housley, Robert
Houghton, Thomas
Howard, William
Hubbard, James
Hudson, John
Hufacre, George
Hughes, David
Hughes, Peter
Hughes, Francis
Hughes, Thomas
Hundley, Samuel
Hunter, Thomas
Hyce, Leonard (w)
Hyden, William
Hyder, Michael

Ingle, John
Inglis, Michael
Ingram, Jeremiah
Inman, Abednego (w)
Ireland, Hans
Isaac, Samuel
Isbell, James
Isbell, Francis
Isbell, Livington
Isbell, Thomas
Isbell, Zackary
Isbell, Henry (?)
Ivy, Henry

Jack, James
Jack, Jerimiah
Jack, Patrick (?)
Jackson, Churchwell
James, John
James, Rolling
James, Marlin
Jamison, Samuel
Jamison, John
Jamison, Thomas
Jamison, Robert
Jarnigan, George
Jefferies, John
Jefferies, Nathaniel
Jefferies, Jean
Jefferies, Phillip
Jefferies, Nathan
Jenkins, Jacob
Jenkins, Thomas
Jenkins, William
Jenkins, James
Jennings, David
Jernigan, Thomas

KING'S MOUNTAIN SOLDIERS

Jernigan, William
Johnson, James S.
Johnson, Barnett
Johnson, John
Johnson, Robert
Johnson, Peter
Johnson, Samuel (w)
Jones, Daniel
Jones, David
Jones, James
Jones, John
Jones, Joseph
Jones, Joshua (w)
Judd, John
Judd, Rowland

Karr, Robert
Karr, Mathew
Keeps, James
Keele, Richard S.
Kelly, John
Kelley, William
Kendrick, Benjamin
Kendrick, Samuel
Kendrick, John
Kendricks, Solomon
Kennedy, Daniel
Kennedy, John
Kennedy, Thomas
Kennedy, Moses
Kennedy, William
Kennedy, Robert
Kendred, Thomas
Kerby, Henry
Kerr, Adam
Kerr, Joseph
Keys, James
Keys, Mathew
Kidd, John
Kilgore, Charles (w)
Kilgore, William
Kilgore, Hiram
Kilgore, James
Kilgore, Robert (w)
King, Robert
King, John
King, William
King, Andrew
Kincannon, Andrew
Kincannon, James
Kincannon, Mathew
Kindle, William
Kinkead, John
Kitchen, John
Knox, Robert
Knox, Benjamin (?)
Knox, Samuel
Knox, James (?)
Kuykendall, Mathew
Kuykendall, Benjamin
Kuykendall, Joseph

Laird, David
Laird, James (k)
Laird, John (k)
Lane, Isaac

Lane, Richard
Lane, Tidence
Lane, Aquilla
Lane, William
Lane, Jesse
Lane, Charles
Lane, James
Lane, John
Lane, Samuel
Landrum, James
Landrum, Thomas
Langston, John
Langston, Robert
Lankford, John
Lankford, Benjamin
Lannim, Joseph
Large, Joseph
Larrimore, Hugh
Lathan, John
Latman, Joseph
Lawson, William
Lay, Thomas
Lawson, John
Lee, James
Leeper, Samuel
Leeper, James
Leffy, Shadrack
Lengley, William
Leonard, George
Leonard, Frederick
Leonard, Henry
Leonard, Robert (?)
Lenoir, William
Lesley, Thomas
Lewallen, Michael
Lewis, James
Lewis, John
Lewis, Aron
Lewis, William Terrill
Lewis, Charles
Lindsay, James
Lindsay, John
Linn, Andrew
Linn, Daniel
Linn, William
Limonton, Robert
Litton, Catel
Litton, John
Liles, David
Liture, Harmon
Livingston, David
Logan, Joseph
Logan, William
Logan, James
Long, John
Long, William
Long, Richard
Long, Robert
Long, Nicholas
Love, Robert
Love, John
Love, Hezekiah
Looney, Robert
Looney, John
Lowery, John

Lowery, William
Loyd, John
Lyle, Henry
Lyle, Samuel
Lynn, David
Lynn, Adam
Lyon, Humberson
Lyon, William
Lytle, Archibald
Lytle, Micajah
Lytle, William
Lyman, Jacob
Lusk, William (k)
Lusk, Joseph
Lusk, Hugh

McAden, William
McAdoo, John
McBee, Silas
McBee, Israel
McCarthy, William
McCallister, William
McCallon, James
McCampbell, Solomon
McClelland, Abraham
McClelland, John
McClough, James
McClure, John
McConnell, Abram
McCormick, Thomas
McCormick, Joseph
McCormick, Robert
McCorkle, Francis
McCoy, Robert
McCroy, Mathew
McCroskey, John
McCulloch, John
McCutcheon, William
McCutcheon, Samuel
McCutcheon, John
McCulloch, Robert (w)
McCulloch, Thomas (k)
McDonald, Magnus
McElwee, James
McElwee, John
McElwee, William
McFarland, Robert
McFerrin, John
McFerrin, Martin
McGaughey, Samuel
McHenry, John
McJucken, Joseph
McKamey, James
McGrill, James
McGill, John
McKee, James
McKisnick, Thomas
McLain, Thomas
McLain, Alexander
McMaster, William
McLemore, John
McMillan, Alexander
McMillan, William
McMillan, Joseph
McNabb, John

KING'S MOUNTAIN SOLDIERS

McNelly, John
McNutt, Alexander
McNutt, George
McPeters, Joseph
McQueen, James
McShaney, William
McSpadden, William
McWheeler, Andrew
Madonough, Andrew
Mahannas, Taploy
Mahoney, Nichael (k)
Main, Tobias
Main, Henry
Malaby, John
Manley, Amos
Manor, Josiah
Manor, Thomas
Mason, William
Maples, Marmaduke
Martin, Samuel
Martin, Salathiel
Martin, John
Martin, Robert
Martin, William
Martin, Mathew
Marshall, Marcum
Marney, Amos
Mason, Patrick
Mason, James
Mason, Thomas
Mason, Edward
Massingale, Henry
Massingale, Michael
Massingale, James
Mathews, James
Mattox, Charles
Maxwell, John
Maxwell, James
Maxwell, Thomas
May, Cassimore
May, Humphrey
May, John
Mayes, Samuel
Mayes, William
Meaden, Andrew
Meaden, John
Meek, John
Meek, Adam
Meek, Moses
Meek, James
Mendenhall, Nathan
Metcalf, William
Miller, John
Miller, Robert (w)
Miller, John H.
Miller, Martin
Millen, John
Millon, Anthony
Miliken, James
Mitchel, James
Mitchel, Elijah
Mitchel, Edward
Moffett, John
Monroe, William
Montgomery, Alexander
Montgomery, James

Montgomery, Richard
Montgomery, Robert
Montgomery, Thomas
Mooney, Martin
Mooney, Richard
Moore, Alexander
Moore, Thomas
Moore, John
Moore, Alexander
Moore, James
Moore, William (w)
Moore, Samuel
Moore, William
Moorehead, John
Morgan, Isaac
Morrison, Peter
Morrison, William
Mosier, Francis
Moser, Abraham
Murdoch, John
Munday, Jeremiah
Murphy, Patrick (w)
Murphy, William
Murphy, Joseph
Murphee, Henry
Murphee, John
Musick, Lewis

Nave, Abraham
Nave, Conrad
Nave, Henry
Nave, Teeler
Neal, John
Neal, Zephaniah
Neally, B.
Neally, William
Nelson, John
Nelson, Sutney
Nelson, William
Newell, Samuel Sr.
Newell, Samuel Jr.
Newman, Isaac
Newman, Jacob
Newman, John
Newland, Lewis
Newland, Abram
Newland, Isaac
Newton, Benjamin
Nicholas, Flayl
Nicholas, James
Norton, Alexander
Norman, William
Nuanly, Henry

O'Brien, William
Oglesby, Elisha
O'Gullion, Barney
O'Gullion, Hugh
Oliver, Dionysius
Oliphant, John
Outlaw, Alexander
Overton, Eli
Owen, John
Owen, Robert

Palmer, John

Palmer, Peter
Palmer, Thomas
Panter, Adam
Parke, Ezekial
Parke, George
Parke, Henry
Parke, George
Parker, Humphrey
Patterson, Arthur (k)
Patterson, Arthur Jr.
Patterson, Thomas
Patterson, Robert
Patterson, John
Patterson, William
Patterson, William (k)
Parry, John
Patton, Robert
Patton, Jacob
Pearce, Joshua
Peck, Adam
Peeber, Silas
Peek, Able
Peek, Adam
Peden, John
Pendergast, Garrett
Pendergrass, Alexander
Penland, Robert
Pemberton, John
Pepper, Elisha (k)
Perkins, Elisha
Perrin, Joseph
Perry, Richard
Perry, Solomon
Perry, Jesse
Perryman, Harmon
Pertle, George
Peters, William
Phillips, James
Phillips, Samuel
Phillips, Joseph
Pierce, Joseph
Pilcher, Robert
Piper, James
Pippin, Robert
Pittman, William
Pitts, Louis
Plunk, Jacob
Polk, Ezekial
Pollard, Chattam
Polson, Andrew
Porter, William
Porter, Mitchell
Porter, John
Portwood, Page
Poston, Richard
Potter, William
Prather, Charles
Prather, Thomas
Preston, Robert
Preston, Walter
Price, James
Price, Jonathan
Price, Thomas
Price John
Price, Samuel
Pruitt, Martin

KING'S MOUNTAIN SOLDIERS

Purviance, James
Purviance, William
Purviance, Richard
Pryor, Mathew

Quarles, Francis
Quarles, John

Rabb, William (k)
Rankin, William
Rankin, David
Rawlings, Asahl (?)
Reagan, Jeremiah (?)
Reamy, Daniel
Reazer, Peter
Reed, John
Reed, Benjamin
Reed, James
Reed, Thomas
Reed, William
Reed, Joseph
Reed, Samuel
Reed, David
Reed, Lovett
Reed, Abraham
Reep, Adam
Reep, Michael (?)
Regan, Charles
Remfeldt, Henry (?)
Reese, James
Reese, David
Reeves, Asher
Reeves, William
Reynolds, Asher
Reynolds, Elisha
Reynolds, Henry
Reynolds, Nathaniel
Rhea, John
Rhea, Joseph
Rice, John
Richardson, Amos
Richardson, James
Riggins, James
Ritchie, Alexander
Ritchie, Samuel
Ritchie, William
Robertson, Joseph
Robertson, William (w)
Robertson, Thomas
Robertson, William
Robertson, John
Roberts, David
Roberts, James
Roberts, Joshua
Roberts, Edward
Robinson, William
Robinson, Thomas
Roddy, James
Rogers, William
Rogers, Benjamin
Roler, James
Roler, Martin
Roper, Roger

Roper, Drury
Ross, John
Ross, Isaac
Rudd, Burlington
Russell, Robert
Russell, Moses
Rutherford, Absolm
Rutherford, William

Sample, Samuel
Sawyers, John
Sarrett, Allen
Scott, Samuel
Scott, Alexander
Scott, Robert
Scott, Joseph
Scott, Joseph Jr.
Scott, Thomas
Scott, Walter
Scott, William
Scott, Samuel Sr.
Scott, John
Scott, Arthur
Scott, James
Self, Thomas
Selman, Jeremiah
Sevier, Joseph
Sevier, James
Sevier, Abraham
Sevier, Joseph II
Sellers, James
Sharp, Benjamin
Sharp, Robert
Sharp, John
Sharp, Samuel
Sharp, Edward
Sharp, James
Sharp, Richard
Sharp, Thomas E.
Sharp, William
Shannon, Thomas
Shaver, Michael
Shaver, Paul
Shaver, Frederick
Shelby, Moses (w)
Shelby, John
Shelby, David
Shelby, Thomas
Sherrill, Samuel Sr.
Sherrill, Adam
Sherrill, George
Sherrill, Samuel Jr.
Shipp, Thomas
Shirley, John
Shote, Thomas
Shook, Greenbury
Singleton, Richard
Simms, James
Simms, John
Siske, Daniel (k)
Siske, Bartlett
Skaggs, John (w)
Skaggs, Henry

Sloan, Alexander
Sloan, William
Sloan, John
Smart, John (k)
Smallwood, William
Smith, David
Smith, Edward
Smith, John
Smith, William
Smith, Henry
Smith, James
Smith, Obediah
Smith, Ransom
Smith, Eaton
Smith, Edward
Smith, George
Smith, Harnett
Smith, Phillip
Smith, Edward
Smith, Leighton
Snodgrass, William
Snodgrass, James
Snoddy, John
Somers, John
Sorter, William
Speltz, John
Stamey, John
Starnes, Nicholas
Steed, Thomas
Steele, William (k)
Steele, John
Steele, Samuel
Steele, Joseph
Steen, James (k)
Stellars, James
Stephens, Jacob
Stephens, Mashack
Stencipher, Joseph
Sterling, Robert
Stevenson, John
Stewart, James
Stewart, William
Stockton, John
Stockton, George
Stockton, William
Stone, William
Stone, Conway
Stone, Ezekial
Stone, Solomon
Stovall, Bartholemew
Stribling, Clayton
Street, Anthony Waddy
Sufferet, John
Sutherland, David
Swadley, Mark
Sweet, Benjamin
Sweeney, Moses
Sword, Michael

KING'S MOUNTAIN SOLDIERS

Tabor, William
Taff, George
Talbert, Charles
Talbot, Mathew Jr.
Talbot, James (?)
Talbot, Thomas (?)
Tate, John
Tate, Robert
Tate, David
Tate, Samuel
Tatum, James
Tatum, Andrew
Taylor, Andrew
Taylor, Andrew Jr.
Taylor, Isaac
Taylor, James
Taylor, James
Taylor, Leroy
Taylor, Parmenus
Temple, Major
Templeton, John
Terrell, Richmond
Terrell, Micajah
Terrell, William
Thatcher, Benjamin
Thomas, John
Thompson, William
Thompson, Alexander
Thompson, John
Thompson, Samuel
Thurman, Phillip
Tillman, Phillip
Tinsley, Golden
Todd, James
Topp, William
Topp, Tom
Tubb, John (w)
Tucker, John
Turnley, George
Turnley, Peter
Trail, James
Trice, James
Turney, Peter (?)
Twitty, William
Twitty, Anthony

Utterly, William

Vance, James
Vance, John
Vance, Samuel

Waddell, Martin
Waddell, John
Waldrin, Peter
Walker, William
Walker, John
Wallace, Thomas

Wallace, John
Walling, William
Walton, William
Walton, Martin
Ward, David
Ward, William
Watkins, George
Watson, David
Watson, Samuel
Watson, William (k)
Weakly, Robert
Wear, John
Weaver, John
Webb, George
Weir, John
Wells, Joseph
Wells, Joseph
Welchel, John
Welchel, Francis
Welchel, David
Welchel, William
Welchcl, John
White, William
White, Benjamin
White, Gordon
White, Isaac
Whitesides, John
Whit, Charles
Whitten, Solomon
Wilfong, John (w)
Williams, Benjamin
Williams, James
Williams, Phillip
Williams, Charles
Williams, John
Williams, Shadrack
Williams, Daniel
Williams, Samuel

Williams, Robert
Williams, Mathew
Willis, Smith
Williamson, John
Willoughby, William
Willoughby, Mathew
Williford, Jacob
Wilson, Robert
Wilson, Joseph
Winstead, Francis (?)
Withers, John
Withers, Elisha
Witherspoon, John
Withrow, James
Wood, Obediah
Woods, Michael
Woods, Jonathan
Woods, John
Woolsey, Thomas
Word, Charles (k)
Word, Thomas
Word, Peter
Word, John
Word, Cuthbert
Wynn, William
Wyley, John
Wyley, James
Wyley, Alexander
Yancey, Ambrose
Yates, Samuel (?)
Yeary, Henry
Yontz, George
Young, Robert
Young, Thomas
Young, William
Young, James
Young, Isham (?)
Young, Samuel

Painting by Valosio, depicting Greer as he barged in on Congress to announce the King's Mountain victory. Painting hangs in Tennessee State Museum. Courtesy Tennessee Conservationist.

ADDITIONAL NAMES

OFFICERS

Allison, Robert, Capt.
Buchanan, William, Capt.
Bryan, John, Capt.
Boys, William, Capt.
Chisolm, Elijah, Capt.
Carnes, John, Capt.
Cavett, Moses, Capt.
Christie, Colonel
Donelson, John, Capt.
Evans, Nathaniel, Capt.
Fain, John, Captain
Gibson, James, Capt.
Gillespie, George, Col.
Gambrel, Captain
Harrison, Michael, Capt.
Hicks, William, Capt.
Hoskins, Ninnam, Capt.
Keys, John, Captain
Kyle, Robert, Capt.
Mall, Peter, Capt.
Morgan, Charles, Capt.
McNabb, John, Capt.
Robertson, Elijah
Roddye, James, Capt.
Ridley, George, Capt.
Sherrill, William, Capt.
Shelby, James, Capt.
Smith, Ezekial, Capt.
Stewart, Thomas, Major
Wilfong, George, Major
Warren, Captain

Adair, John
Alexander, William
Arney, Christian
Ayers, Elihu
Burus, David
Billings, Jasper
Brotherton, Thomas
Bryan, Robert
Ballard, Devereau
Barker, Hezekiah
Bickley, William
Brooks, Littleton
Beattie, Joseph
Bolick, Caspar
Bowles, Benjamin
Cavett, Richard
Condry, William
Cooper, James (k)
Cross, William
Cross, Abraham
Callaway, Joseph
Chapman, Joseph
Church, Amos
Cline, Michael
Cole, Jobe
Chandler, Bailey
Dunsmore, James
Denman, John
Dickenson, Isham
Dobson, John
Fry, Phillip
Ferguson, Joseph
Foster, Anthony

Gabriel, James
Gilbreath, Alexander
Goodlett, William
Gregory, William
Henry, David
Haas, John
Haas, Simon
Hahn, Joshua
Hahn, Benedict
Hammons, Benjamin
Hammons, John
Harris, William
Hofner, Nicholas
Hunt, Abraham
Hunt, John
Hardmark, Charles
Johnson, George Sr.
Johnson, William
King, Thomas
Keeton, Hezekiah
Kuykendall, Simon
Leeper, Mathew
Laws, David
Lutz, Jacob
Mitchell, David
Montgomery, John
Morgan, Benjamin
Proffit, Pleasant
Parks, John
Powell, William
Simms, Littlepage
Simpson, William
Stevenson, James

Setzer, John
Shell, Michael
Sherrill, Uriah
Sigmon, Palsor
Simpson, William
Rose, Sterling
Rumfeld, Henry
Scurlock, James
Schultz, Martin
Smith, Jones
Smool, James
Sparks, John
Spicer, William
Stamper, Joel
Summerlin, William
Swanson, John
Smithers, Gabriel
Starnes, Peter
Toliver, Jesse
Toliver, Moses
Treadway, Robert
Tippong, Conrad
Turbyfill, John
Vickers, Elijah
Weaver, Frederick
Wall, Jacob
Wilson, Andrew
Wilson, John
Waters, Moses
Whitaker, John
Whitner, Abraham
Whitner, Daniel
White, Solomon
Yoder, Conrad

Pemberton Oak: Colonel John Pemberton mustered his men under this oak in 1780 enroute to King's Mountain. Oak still stands and Pemberton descendants still own the property. Soldiers of five wars have camped under this tree.

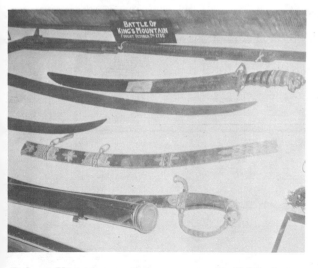

Robert Young gun; Ferguson sword, field glasses and sash, Tennessee State Museum, Nashville.

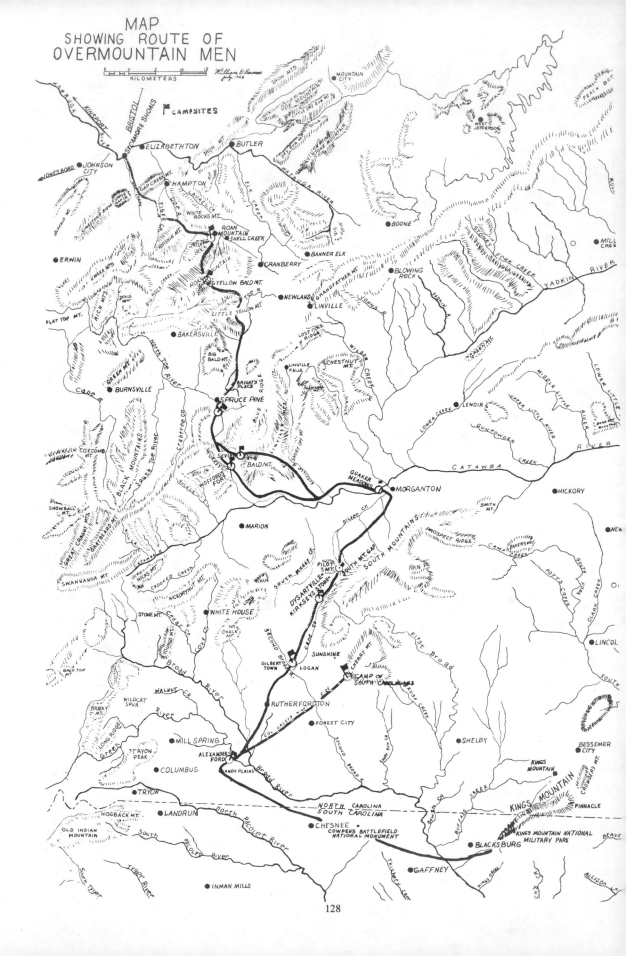

MAP
SHOWING ROUTE OF
OVERMOUNTAIN MEN

KILOMETERS

William D. Bowman
July 1968

⚑ CAMPSITES

FROM KING'S MOUNTAIN TO PARIS PEACE TREATY

The King's Mountain victory was an important link in the chain of events that brought the British to the Paris Peace Table. During the rough winter of 1780-1781, General Washington's army of 3,500 men were encamped outside New York. Heavy snows, little food, no pay or clothing gave poor incentive for the dispirited army to attack a well-fed British force of over 10,000, housed comfortably in the New York Barracks. The salvation of Washington's force was the concentrated effort being undertaken by Cornwallis in the South. This took the pressure off the northern army.

The treason of Benedict Arnold cast a curtain of gloom over the cause of Liberty. General Washington was greatly upset over this betrayal by one of his officers. American affairs and hopes looked anything but bright as the year 1781 dawned. Continental money was worthless and troop mutinies were commonplace. The two men responsible for changing the course of events were Robert Morris and John Laurens. Morris managed to raise money to aid Washington in supplying his men, and John Laurens was sent to seek more aid from France. The slowness of the French Ministry, in responding to America's request for help, irked young Laurens. He managed to obtain an interview with the French King, who agreed to supply desperately needed backing. Without the aid secured by these men, General Washington could not have continued the war effort. News that the French Fleet was sailing to American waters, and other promised help, charged the air with new hope. Fresh plans and actions were contemplated and enlistments increased.

John Laurens was 28 years old when Congress sent him to France in an effort to secure money in 1780. Young Laurens served with Washington from Brandywine to York Town; was killed in a South Carolina skirmish, August 27, 1782.

Robert Morris raised money with his own private credit, on several occasions, to aid General Washington in clothing and feeding the American Army. Final victory would have been impossible without his help. Morris served time in a debtor's prison, after the war, because of financial failures.

General William Lee Davidson experienced the desperate winter of 1777-78 at Valley Forge. Davidson County, North Carolina and Davidson College were named in his honor.

Shortly after the King's Mountain Battle, General William Lee Davidson and Captain W. R. Davie began to assemble a force in New Providence. They had hopes of raising a formidable army with which to confront Cornwallis. Because of the inactivity in the North, General Washington had sent Generals Daniel Morgan and Smallwood, with a detachment of Maryland recruits, to aid in the southern cause. General Gates had been able to assemble about 1,200 men from his defeated Camden army. General Stephens was sent to North Carolina with a force of newly enlisted Virginia Militia.

General Davidson, in charge of the Salisbury District, thought the time and conditions were right to organize a strong campaign. Messages were sent across the mountains, seeking assistance from the Overmountain riflemen. In response, Colonel John Sevier called a meeting of his officers at Jonesborough, November 20, 1780, to discuss the situation. Captains James Stinson, James Gibson and Luke Bower were directed to cross the mountains with 130 men to join Davidson. A similar request had been sent to Colonel Isaac Shelby, but he was already with General Morgan in an advisory capacity. This projected campaign was cancelled before it actually started.

Congress, having lost faith in Gates, asked General Washington to appoint a replacement. Washington's choice was Major-General Nathaniel Greene. General Greene had recently resigned his position as Quarter-master-General of the Continental Army. Congress, tired of the big commissions made by quartermasters, had placed them all on salary. This move caused much resentment and created problems in the supply depart-ment. Greene, not liking the situation, resigned and thus became available for active duty in the field. He

proved a good commander during the last years of the war. No great victories are recorded to his credit, but his type of warfare proved destructive to the British strength. Greene would often say after a battle, "We fight, get beaten and fight again."

General Greene arrived in Charlotte, North Carolina, December 1780, and with a very brief ceremony assumed the com-mand of the southern branch of the Continental Army. This was to herald a year of much blood-shed in the Carolinas, Georgia and Virginia, the final battlefields of the Revolutionary War.

Partisan conflicts, between the

General Greene takes over the southern command from General Gates at Charlotte, North Carolina. King's Moun-tain National Military Park.

Tories and Whigs, were continuing in many southern sections. We cite one such incident that took place on the Yadkin River eight days after the King's Mountain victory. A company of 300 Surry County Tories had been recruited to join the Loyalist cause. They had enlisted under Colonel Gideon Wright and his brother Captain Hezikiah Wright. They probably had not learned of the King's Mountain Battle, as they were march-ing to join General Cornwallis at Charlotte. They plundered, killed and burned on their march toward the British force. Colonel Joseph Williams, living near Shallow Ford on the Yadkin, called together some 200 riflemen from the area. They set up an ambush at the ford and awaited the Tory party. The 300 loyalists prepared to cross the river, not suspecting any opposition. The conflict was short, hard and decisive. The Tories, badly beaten, fled and scattered.

Now, back to the Overmountain men on the frontier, September 1780. They were preparing for the mountain crossing to meet Colonel Ferguson. When the British agents learned that this big force of riflemen would be absent from the settlements, they planned to use this opportunity to their advantage. They told the Cherokee Chiefs that only young boys and old men would be left to defend the settlements. Now was the time to attack, when they were weak. Pack horse loads of supplies were brought in from the Augusta depot. War councils were under way in most of the towns.

The old chiefs of the Overhill towns tried to dissuade the younger chiefs from this course of action, but their voices were not heeded. Attakullakulla, known as "The Little Carpenter," died during 1780. His son, Dragging Canoe, did not agree with his diplomatic father in treating with the whites. At-takullakulla had been the controlling spirit in the political and peace keeping councils of the Cherokee. Now he was gone. Oconostota, War Chief of many years, was getting old and his words were not heard. The disregard of Indian rights by many white settlers, in building cabins on Indian land, gave the English agents receptive ears among the young resentful warriors. The atmosphere was right for an all out war on the white settlements.

Attakullakulla, Cherokee Peace Chief often called "The Little Carpenter."

Oconostota resigned as War Chief in 1782. The Chota Treaty with Sevier that year was his last public appearance at a White-Indian council. Old and nearly blind, Oconostota, along with Nancy Ward and other members of the family, spent the winter of 1782-83 in the home of Joseph Martin on Long Island (Kingsport). In the spring, feeling the end near, he asked Martin to take him back to his beloved Chota. Oconostota was buried with Christian rites in a canoe coffin.

BOYD'S CREEK BATTLE

Major Joseph Martin, Virginia's Agent to the Cherokees, had been in the Overhill towns in an attempt to restrain the Indians from going on the warpath. He was unsuccessful in his mission. John McDonald, British Agent, tried to imprison Martin; but Chiefs Oconostota and Hanging Maw had sufficient influence to prevent this act. The Agents were able to persuade the younger chiefs to take Dragging Canoe by the arm and join in the war against the settlers. The Indians, unable to obtain supplies from the Americans, had turned to the British. The English agents used the Augusta depot to their advantage. They told the chiefs that any Indian towns that stayed friendly and peaceful toward the Americans would get no supplies. The Indians were urged to speed their war preparations; and a large force of several hundred warriors was assembled. This new alliance, with the British, was to prove a disastrous move for the Cherokee.

Nancy Ward, friend of the white and red people, operated an Inn on Womankiller Ford of the Ocoee River near Benton, Tennessee. Died 1824.

Nancy Ward again moved to befriend the whites. This Cherokee Chieftainess, anxious to save her people from utter destruction, was trying to carry on the role of her Uncle Attakullakulla in smoothing over the difficulties that were constantly arising. Knowing that she could not stop the warriors from taking the warpath, she sent warning of the impending attacks by Isaac Thomas, Ellis Hardin and William Springstone. These white traders slipped out of the Indian towns and carried word to the white settlements.

Many people have tried to call Nancy Ward a traitor to her people. Nothing is further from the truth. She realized that the Indians were unable to cope with the white man's superior know-how, strength and numbers. She struggled desperately to save her people from the very tragedy that finally came to their homes, towns and nation. Nancy Ward was held in respect by the red people and the white settlers. Her constant expression had been, *"The white men are our brothers; the same house shelters us, the same sky covers us all."*

Isaac Thomas and Ellis Hardin delivered the warning to the Nolichucky and Watauga people. William Springstone went on to Virginia and delivered a like message to Colonel Arthur Campbell. Campbell and Joseph Martin called a meeting of the officials and militia heads at Martin's Trading Post on Long Island (Kingsport). It was decided that a request to General Davidson, for a Commanding Officer, would make the campaign official. While all this was taking place, the Indians were raiding exposed cabins.

Colonel John Sevier, busy with other problems and troop requests from General Davidson, did not attend the Long Island meeting. He had been expecting this Indian attack, even before leaving for the King's Mountain campaign. He had dispatched Captain George Russell and his company, soon after the battle, on a forced march home in case hostile Indians approached the Nolichucky settlements.

Sevier, receiving the warning from Nancy Ward of the impending attack, moved immediately to raise a force to confront the invaders. Sevier believed that offense was the best defense. His riders called the men to muster at once, as the exposed Nolichucky frontier could not wait for the long drawn-out planning of the Martin-Campbell campaign. It is assumed that he sent word of his action.

The rendezvous was set at Swann Pond on Lick Creek in Greene County, December 15, 1780. Leading 200 men, Sevier started toward Indian territory. The second night out they camped on Long Island of the Nolichucky River. Captain Gist, on a scouting tour, sighted one party of warriors. Firing from horseback, the party returned to camp without attempting to fight the Indians. Sevier prepared for a possible night attack by placing his men in battle arrangement. After stationing guards in all quarters, the men slept on their arms. During the night Captain Pruett arrived with his men, and by daybreak other companies had caught up with the main force.

Early next morning Colonel Sevier pushed across the French Broad River at Big Island Ford. His force now numbered 300 men. As the riflemen moved nearer the Overhill country, signs indicated that a large force lay ahead; but Sevier led his men deeper into the Indian territory. The third night they camped near Boyd's Creek in the present Sevier County. Before daybreak next morning, Captain Stinson, in charge of the scouting patrol, discovered the main Indian camp about three miles from that of the white force. The

Braves, hoping to draw Sevier's force into an ambush, had left their campfires burning. Colonel Sevier seldom rushed into a situation until he looked it over. His acquaintance with the red man's tactics had saved him many times. Catching up to his advance scouts, he carefully studied the landscape in an effort to locate the positions of the large bands of warriors. He soon discovered the Indians arranged in a half-moon shape, ready to pounce on the pioneer riflemen should they charge the blazing campfires.

Clarke-Martin Fight

The following description of the battle is taken from Ramsey's **Annals of Tennessee**. *A reinforcement was immediately ordered to the front, and the guard was directed, if it came up with the Indians, to fire upon them and retreat, and thus draw them on. Three quarters of a mile from their camp, the enemy fired upon the advance guard from their ambuscade. The whites returned the fire and retreated, and, as had been anticipated, was pursued by the enemy till it joined the main body. This was formed into three divisions; the center commanded by Colonel Sevier, the right wing by Major Walton, and the left by Major Jonathan Tipton. Orders were given that as soon as the enemy should approach the front, the right wing should wheel to the left, and the left wing to the right, and thus enclose them. In this order were the troops arranged when they met the Indians at Cedar Springs, who rushed forward after the guard with great rapidity, till checked by the opposition of the main body. Major Walton with the right wing wheeled briskly to the left, and performed the order which he was to execute with precise accuracy. But the left wing moved to the right with less celerity, and when the center fired upon the Indians, doing immense execution, the latter retreated through the unoccupied space left open between the extremes of the right and left wings, and running into a swamp escaped the destruction which otherwise seemed ready to involve them. The victory was decisive. The loss of the enemy amounted to twenty-eight killed on the ground and very many wounded, who got off without being taken. On the side of Sevier's troops not a man was wounded. The victorious little army then returned to Big Island and waited there for the arrival of the reinforcements that promised to follow.*

The Indians had not expected to meet this large well-organized force. They had been led to believe that all the fighting men were across the mountain battling Ferguson. They had also been told, by these agents, that the well-trained British forces would soon defeat the untrained backwoodsmen. Their plans to retake their land by running the settlers back across the mountains had again gone amiss.

Quoting another descriptive narrative from Ramsey: *The Indians had formed in a half moon, and lay concealed in the grass. Had their stratagem not been discovered, their position and shape of the ground, would have enabled them to enclose and overcome the horsemen. Lieutenant Lane and John Ward had dismounted for the fight, when Sevier, having noticed the semicircular position of the Indians, ordered a halt, with the purpose of engaging the top extremes of the Indian line, and keeping up the action until the other part of his troops could come up. Lane and his comrade, Ward, remounted and fell back upon Sevier without being hurt, though fired at by several warriors near them. A brief fire was, for a short time, kept up by Sevier's party and the nearest Indians. The troops behind, hearing the first fire, had quickened their pace and were coming in sight. James Roddy, with about twenty men, quickly came up, and soon after the main body of the troops. The Indians*

THIS SHAFT MARKS THE SITE OF THE BATTLE OF BOYD'S CREEK DEC. 16, 1780

GEN. JOHN SEVIER AND HIS COMMAND OF EAST TENNESSEE PIONEERS, DEFEATED WITH HEAVY LOSS TO THE ENEMY, A LARGE FORCE OF CHEROKEE INDIANS WHO HAD ATTACKED THE SETTLERS WHILE HE AND HIS SOLDIERS WERE AWAY ENGAGED IN THE KINGS MOUNTAIN CAMPAIGN

noticed the reinforcements and closed their lines. *Sevier immediately ordered the charge, which would have been still more fatal, but that the pursuit led through a swampy branch, which impeded the progress of the horsemen.*

In the charge Sevier was in close pursuit of a warrior, who finding that he would be overtaken, turned and fired at him. The bullet cut the hair of his temple without doing further injury. Sevier then spurred his horse forward and attempted to kill the Indian with his sword, having emptied his pistols in the first moments of the charge. The warrior parried the licks from the sword with his empty gun. The conflict was becoming doubtful between the combatants thus engaged, when one of the soldiers, rather ungallantly, came up, shot the warrior, and decided the combat in favor of his Commander.

The horse of Adam Sherrill (John Sevier's brother-in-law) threw his rider, and in the fall some of his ribs were broken. An Indian sprang upon him with his tomahawk drawn. When in the act of striking, a ball from a comrade's rifle brought him to the ground, and Sherrill escaped. After a short pursuit, the Indians dispersed into the adjoining highlands and knolls, where the calvary could not pursue them. Of the whites not one was killed but three seriously wounded.

The Boyd's Creek battle is one of the few Indian fights, led by Colonel John Sevier, of which we have a detailed description. This was the first offensive campaign in which he was in command. All told, during his career, Sevier fought thirty-five Indian battles and never lost one. Very few of his men were killed or wounded. He is ranked first, by many writers, of all the Indian fighters. The red men feared and respected him. He led his men rather than sending them into battle.

Ramsey lists the following officers as participating in the Boyd's Creek Battle: Landon Carter, James Sevier, Abraham Sevier, Thomas Gist, Abel Pearson, James Hubbard, Ben Sharpe, Samuel Hadley, Jacob Brown, Jeremiah Jack, Nathan Gaun, Isaac Taylor, George Doherty, and George Russell. There were other officers not listed.

After the battle, Sevier and his men pulled back to Big Island to wait the arrival of Colonel Arthur Campbell.

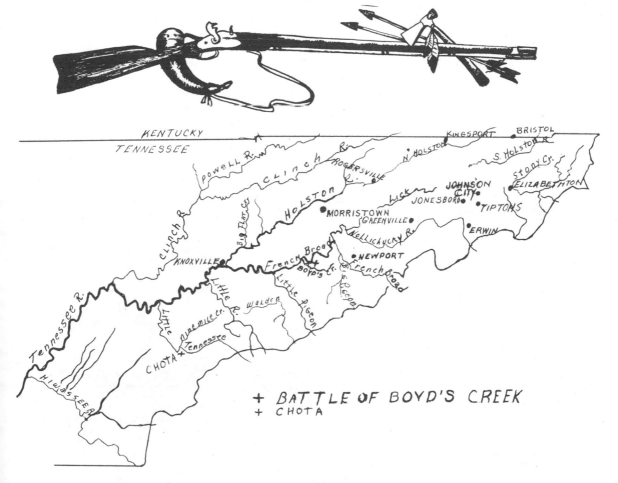

A messenger from Campbell stated that he would be there within the week, and requested Sevier to delay advancing on the Indian towns until the forces were joined. Campbell did not arrive on schedule. Game was scarce on the Island, and Sevier decided to move back to the Boyd's Creek area. Seasoned hunters, like Isaac Thomas and William Bean, were unable to find food. The men had to rely on parched acorns, corn, nuts and haws. A stray cow and calf found in the woods helped. This campsite was known for many years as "Hungry Camp." The stay here was short, as Colonel Arthur Campbell, with his Virginia Regiment, and Major Joseph Martin, with the Sullivan riflemen, soon joined the Sevier force. The troops now numbered about 700 mounted men. Colonel Arthur Campbell shared his limited food supply with Sevier's men.

On December 23rd, they marched to the Tennessee River. Scouts reported that the main crossing at Maliquo was heavily guarded. The Pioneer force moved upstream opposite Tommotley and forded the Tennessee River at this point December 24th. This maneuver upset the Indian plan of attack.

The march was continued to Chota, arriving there December 25th. Large bodies of Indian warriors were seen along the hills overlooking the route of march. The large body of riflemen discouraged any attack. A few scattered shots were exchanged between the two forces. Camp was made near Chota. Sentries and guards were posted in every direction. Food to feed the hungry men was obtained from the Indians. Nancy Ward sent a small herd of cattle to the white soldier's camp. Much of Christmas night was spent cooking and eating the fresh meat.

Colonel Elijah Clarke, who had accompanied Sevier with his Georgia riflemen, had a fight with Major Martin over the meat. Colonel Clarke, seeing the cattle being driven into camp, ordered his men to kill and dress the beef. Major Martin, who had married Betsy the daughter of Nancy Ward, felt that he was responsible for the gift. He resented Clarke taking over without his consent. Martin and a company of his men forcibly took the dressed and quartered beefs, hanging from tree limbs. When Colonel Clarke returned and learned what had happened, he confronted Martin. Angry words were exchanged between the two six-foot stalwarts. A man to man fight ensued.

Joseph Martin and Arthur Campbell were resentful because of Sevier's early march and victory at Boyd's Creek. Angry words were spoken and a rift, between the Sullivan and Washington County men, was opened. From Draper comes the following quote of Joseph Martin.

"Colonel Sevier, of Washington County, went on his own, in his own behalf with three or four hundred men several days before the army, met a party of Indians, had a little fight, killed a few, and retired some distance, waiting for the main army. This was complained of at the time not only as an unauthorized move, but as apprizing the Indians of our approach before the army was in position to act efficiently. It was thought that the motive of Sevier was to get glory for himself."

The towns of Chota, Tellico and Little Tuskegee were burned December 28th. The force moved on to Hiwassee and Chestuee and destroyed these two towns from which the Indians had fled.

The officers and men of this expedition started the return trip January 1, 1781. Seventeen Indian women and children were taken along as hostage prisoners. Twenty-nine Indian warriors had been killed and many wounded. The damaging results of this expedition greatly weakened the power and the spirit of the Overhill segment of the Cherokee. Their resistance to the increasing flow of the white man's encroachment on their lands was to grow more feeble each year. Colonel Arthur Campbell instructed the Chiefs to attend a Treaty at Long Island during July of the coming summer. Joseph Martin took Nancy Ward and members of her family back to Long Island. This was done for their protection.

BATTLE OF COWPENS

Shortly after taking over the southern command from General Gates, General Greene established his camp on the Pee Dee River in South Carolina. He sent General Daniel Morgan with a detachment to the western part of the country near the boundary of the two Carolinas. Cornwallis ordered Colonel Banastre Tarleton to attack the Morgan force and crush it, while he would move his army to Morgan's rear to cut off any retreat.

General Morgan had been sent into this region, where food and forage were scarce, and situated in a spot between the Tarleton and Cornwallis forces. General Morgan's detachment numbered about 900 men, including experienced militia and a company of cavalry under Colonel William Washington. Colonel Tarleton commanded a force of 1200 men including his own corps of cavalry. General Morgan had made camp near Cowpens, about five miles south of the North Carolina border. This was the site where the mountaineer army had made a conjunction with the South Carolinians enroute to King's Mountain three months earlier.

Before dawn, January 17th, Morgan had his men fed before arranging them in their battle positions. There was little underbrush in the terrain he selected for the engagement. His main lines were posted on a small ridge between two brooks. His best-trained soldiers were located in the center, the Virginia riflemen on the right and left wings. Colonel Washington and his cavalry unit were located in the rear as reserves. Pickens was in a skirmish position up front, with volunteer riflemen posted on each side of the expected route of Tarleton's approach.

Colonel Banastre Tarleton, British Officer, served with Cornwallis in the Southern Campaign.

Colonel Tarleton moved forward to the attack about eight o'clock in the morning. Two regiments, one regular and the other artillery, were lined up in front. Tarleton brought up the rear with his Cavalry Legion. The initial attack was met with a strong fire from Pickens' men flanking each side. These men retired a short distance, formed lines and fired again. Soon the riflemen posted on the wings were in range and opened fire. These expert marksmen were taking a heavy toll on the British and caused the front lines to give way. They began to retreat when Morgan's militia charged with bayonets. Both wings moved forward as the bayonet charge caused the Tory line to break and run. The Loyalists threw down their guns and everything else that hindered their running. Tarleton was never able to check their chaotic, scared flight. By this time Washington's cavalry charged Tarleton's Dragoons. They also broke and fled. The pursuit was continued for 20 miles before the American units were ordered back. It was a complete victory for the Patriots.

British losses in the battle were 300 or more killed and wounded, over 500 privates taken as prisoners, 29 officers captured. In addition, 800 guns, 100 horses, 35 wagons and two field pieces were taken. The cumbersome wagons and other baggage were destroyed. General Morgan knew that General Cornwallis would move fast, in an effort to cut him off and free the prisoners. He did not want to be burdened with the baggage and wagons.

The American losses were 12 killed and 60 wounded. Taking his wounded and forming his prisoners into a line of march, General Morgan moved into North Carolina and set his course toward the Virginia border. Heavy rains filled the streams and made progress slow. Parties of Tories caught up to the rear, and every creek and river crossing had to be defended. The large body of prisoners caused the march to move slower than it would ordinarily. It was at Cowan's Ford on the Catawba River that General Davidson, in charge of a rear guard action, was killed by Tories. General Greene had left his command and joined Morgan to aid in this great escape with 500 prisoners. Cornwallis nearly caught the Morgan force on one or two occasions, but high water delayed him, especially at the Yadkin. He pursued the Americans to the Dan River where he turned back. Generals Greene and Morgan continued on into Virginia.

Generals Greene and Morgan took time to rest their united forces, dispose of their prisoners and recruit more men. One of the requests for help went to the Overmountain leaders, Colonels Shelby and Sevier. Colonel Sevier, busy planning a campaign against the Middle Towns of the Cherokee, delegated Major Charles Robertson to lead a battalion to Greene's assistance. Robertson chose three Captains and their companies, numbering about 130 men. They left on the long march across the mountains the latter part of February, 1781. They reached Greene's Camp, near the site of the battle of Alamance, March 6th. Colonel Shelby did not lead a detachment to join Greene at this time. Colonel William Campbell arrived from Virginia with 60 men. Major Robertson's men were placed under Campbell's command.

GUILFORD COURTHOUSE BATTLE

General Cornwallis had issued a call to the Tories of North Carolina to join the King's cause. The response was not very satisfactory. General Pickens and his men were inflicting such heavy losses on Tory groups assembling to join Cornwallis, that this had a discouraging effect on others. Colonel Tarleton, the supporting arm of General Cornwallis, did not measure up to his vaulted reputation after King's Mountain and Cowpens. On several occasions he flinched at meeting the Patriots on equal terms.

General Greene avoided a direct encounter with Cornwallis until he felt that his force was in favorable number to match the British. Another blow to Greene was losing General Morgan. Cowpens was the last battle for this valiant General. Troubled with rheumatism and fever, he was unable to continue active duty.

The Americans moved into position sometime during the day of March 14th. Cornwallis learned this the same day, so early morning, March 15th, he marched his forces toward Greene's position. This was an encounter that the British General had been trying to maneuver Greene into making for several weeks.

General Greene's force was larger in number than the British, but his Militia were inexperienced fighters and had very little military training. The first line of the Patriot defense was made up of raw recruits of the North Carolina Militia. The Virginia Militia, almost as inexperienced,

Major-General Nathaniel Greene, American Commander in the South during 1780-1781.

Americans withdrawing from battlefield after Guilford Courthouse Battle. Guilford Courthouse National Military Park.

formed the second line. Continental troops made up the third line. Colonel Henry Lee and Colonel William Campbell's riflemen formed on the left wing, and Colonel William Washington, with cavalry and other continental troops, were placed on the right flank.

The British force was well organized, experienced and disciplined. It was a bloody battle. The first line of the Americans broke at the first attack. The second line held for a while, but they also broke and fell back. The right and left wings had become engaged in separate fights, almost removed from the main battle. The riflemen on both wings were causing the British heavy losses; but in spite of this, the Loyalists had reached a position from which they could hit the American positions with grape and canister. General Greene, not knowing that he held the advantage, was unwilling to risk his men in a final, desperate and costly charge. Wanting to save his force for other battles, he sounded orders to retreat. Thus, General Cornwallis gained the field of battle but his heavy loss made it a doubtful victory. The British loss, after the two and one-half hour bloody struggle, was over 600 casualties.

The Guilford Courthouse Battle climaxed a winter campaign that was very damaging to the British cause: the King's Mountain catastrophe, the defeat at Cowpens and now the Guilford debacle. Actually, for the British, all reports indicate that it was one of the severest engagements of the southern campaign.

General Cornwallis left the field of battle almost immediately and marched toward the seacoast, to be nearer his source of supply. He stopped at Cross Creek (Fayetteville, North Carolina), thinking this Tory country a safe haven but was disappointed in two ways. The Scots settled in the area did not flock to join the British force. Another reason why the British Commander did not stop long was that he was too far from a good port. Ships and boats could not navigate the Cape Fear River to bring supplies. The British were in great need of medical, camping and food sources. Headquarters was established in Wilmington.

General Greene had followed the British, hoping to force another encounter; but Cornwallis, unwilling to risk another engagement until better prepared, destroyed bridges, slowing Greene's efforts to catch up with the main force. General Greene changed his direction and marched into South Carolina to his former camp on Pee Dee River.

The Tory-infested country of North Carolina, between the Yadkin River and the Cape Fear, broke into a turmoil that was to leave communities torn asunder for several generations. Under the umbrella of the Cornwallis army they plundered, robbed, killed, burned and harassed Whig homes. David "Scaldhead" Fanning was one of the worst of the Tory leaders. He seemed to have a fatal attraction and quality that enlisted bloodthirsty men to his small army. They raided and killed in the name of the Crown but somehow evaded the regular British-American battles. Raiding courts was one of Fanning's special accomplishments. On one occasion they captured the Court of Chatham County at Pittsboro, and later raided the Hillsborough Court where they captured Governor Thomas Burke and other prominent Whigs. These prisoners were taken to Wilmington, North Carolina, and thrown into Major Craig's bull-pen prison. The Whigs, on the other hand, were equally cruel in their reprisal on Tory families.

Another hated Tory leader was Bloody Bill Cunningham. He had no regard for promises made or guarantees of safe conduct to surrendered prisoners. On many occasions Cunningham promised Whigs that they would be granted life and freedom, if they would throw down their arms and march out the doors of their fortification with their arms raised. As soon as they were outside, Bloody Bill's men would murder them in cold blood.

GREASY COVE MUSTER

In February, 1781, Governor Abner Nash commissioned John Sevier as a full Colonel, replacing Colonel John Carter who died during 1780. Before news of the appointment reached the West, Sevier was off on another Indian campaign. Some of the raids on the Nolichucky Settlements were blamed on the Middle Towns of the Cherokee Nation, located in the Western North Carolina area. Colonel Sevier had summoned his men to muster in Greasy Cove (Unicoi County, Tennessee) early March, 1781. Three companies, commanded by Captains Valentine Sevier, James Stinson, and David McNabb, assembled. Jonathan Tipton served as Major during this expedition.

They crossed Red Bank Ford off the Nolichucky River, followed the trail through Coxe's Cove Gap (now known as Spivey's Gap), rode on to Cane River which they followed some distance, crossed to Ivey Creek and continued on to an old Indian warpath which they followed to the Tuckasegee River. They made a surprise attack on the town of Tuckasegee, killing 50 or more warriors. Several women and children were taken as hostages. More than twelve Indian Towns were destroyed. The return march of Sevier's force was made through Indian Gap of the Smoky Mountains, down to the crossing of French Broad near the present town of Newport and on home. Two casualties were suffered on this trip.

Rendering Bear Grease in Greasy Cove from a painting by Edyth Price.

During an attack on Cowee, Nathaniel Davis was seriously wounded and John Bond killed. Sevier sent Davis, accompanied by a member of the force, back home by way of the trail they had traveled going down. Nathaniel Davis did not reach home, as he died in Greasy Cove and was buried there.

An earlier plan to send a force against the Middle Towns had been attempted during August, 1780. About 100 men mustered in Greasy Cove near Red Bank Ford on the Nolichucky River. A small skirmish at the ford, the shooting at one of the troop out hunting and the finding of a dead Indian, discouraged the undertaking. They feared that raiding parties were in the area and would use their absence as a good opportunity to attack their settlements. The men returned to their homes.

Red Bank Ford on the Nolichucky River, where crossings were made before bridge was built (Near Erwin, Tennessee).

YORK TOWN

General Cornwallis remained in Wilmington long enough to reorganize his army, replenish his supplies and restore the morale of his men. As he speculated on the progress of the war, he returned to the premise that Virginia was the key to overcoming the southern states. Ignoring General Clinton's advice, he marched toward Virginia the last of April or the first of May. There was friction between the two Generals. Cornwallis aspired to the Commander-in-Chief position held by Clinton. The British force reached Petersburg, Virginia, May 20, 1781. Here junction was made with Generals William Phillips and Benedict Arnold, both commanding sizeable forces.

Benedict Arnold's first exploit, after assuming a British Command, was the burning and plundering of Richmond. Cornwallis did not want the traitor Arnold in his command, so he instructed him to join Clinton in New York. Clinton, likewise reluctant to have him near, sent Arnold to a command in his home state, Connecticut.

General Greene had ordered General Lafayette, with his 3500 men, to remain in Virginia. General Washington meanwhile had

General Benjamin Lincoln surrendered his sword to Cornwallis at Charleston, South Carolina. The Cornwallis sword was surrendered to Lincoln at York Town.

sent General Anthony Wayne to assist Lafayette in the Virginia operation. Both sides moved and countermoved without any significant confrontation. Actions at Hot Water Plantation and Green Springs were the two outstanding engagements preceding York Town.

Clinton had ordered Cornwallis to secure a base for the English Fleet. This was done. Meanwhile, instead of attacking Clinton in New York, General Washington decided to make a campaign against Cornwallis in Virginia. Assembling all the forces, including those of Count Rochambeau, General Von Steuben, General Lincoln, General Henry Knox, Colonel Stephen Moylan, General Lafayette, General Wayne, Duke de Lauzun, Colonel d'Aboville, Colonel Desandrouins and Colonel Querenet, Washington surrounded York Town. Count DeGrasse, Admiral of the French Fleet, blockaded the British on the waterside. The combined American forces numbered about 16,000. Closer and closer Washington's forces drew their lines around the Cornwallis fortifications. They battered with cannon and took the redoubts by assault. With no avenue left for escape, General Cornwallis surrendered October 19, 1781. This was the climatic battle of the Revolutionary War. Nevertheless, hostilities continued for more than a year in several areas of the country.

After the Guilford Courthouse Battle, General Greene followed Cornwallis as far as Ramsey's Mill near the junction of Haw and Deep River. Finding this pursuit impracticable, Greene turned toward South Carolina with plans to attack Lord Rawdon at Camden. Rawdon surprised the Greene forces at Hobkirk's and defeated the Americans, April 25th. The loss on each side has been estimated at 300. General Francis Marion captured a British post at Santee, just a short while before the conflict on Hobkirk Hill. This made Camden an

American Battery No. 2 at National Military Park, York Town, Virginia. York Town National Military Park.

untenable post, so Rawdon pulled out May 10th. About the same time, General Sumpter defeated a British post at Orangeburg and Marion captured Fort Motte. This left the two strongholds of Augusta and Ninety-Six as the only strong points outside Charleston.

Many of the Overmountain men had volunteered to go with Colonel Elijah Clarke into Georgia. They left Colonel Sevier's force after the final phases of the Cherokee Indian Campaign, January 1781. Clarke, his Georgians and the Overmountain men arrived in Georgia in time to assist in clearing the British from that state. They participated

Fort Ninety-Six: Picture shows some of the breastworks of the English stronghold in South Carolina. King's Mountain National Military Park.

Night watchman in Philadelphia conducted express rider sent by Washington, with news of the York Town Victory, to door of the President of Congress. Thus, the Government officials learned of the defeat of Cornwallis. The German night watchman continued his rounds crying, "Three o'clock and Cornwallis is taken."

in the recapture of Augusta and most likely took part in the battles of Long Cane and Beattie's Mill.

General Greene attempted to take Ninety-Six during May, but the well-fortified fort withstood the siege. The Americans were unable to breech the outer walls. The report that Rawdon was coming to its relief rushed Greene's final attempt, which also proved fruitless. He pulled his force back further north. It is ironic that the position was evacuated not long after Greene's departure.

Lord Rawdon, unable to maintain the fortified posts covering his supply lines, pulled his various regiments into Charleston. Fugitive Tory families cluttered his march and hampered his campaign tactics. Arriving in Charleston, he boarded a ship, intending to return to England. This vessel was captured by the French and Rawdon was made a prisoner. He left behind a stained career and a dishonorable reputation.

LONG ISLAND TREATY

General Greene appealed to the Overmountain men for help. At the time they received this message, they were in the midst of a Treaty with the Cherokee at Long Island. Colonels Shelby and Sevier were both attending the Council with the Indians. The Treaty-Meet had been scheduled for July 20, 1781 but was a week late in getting started. General Greene had appointed a Commission composed of William Christian, William Preston, Arthur Campbell, Joseph Martin, Robert Sevier (Greene did not know of his death), Evan Shelby, Joseph Williams and John Sevier. This commission was empowered to work out peace agreements with the Cherokee and arrange for an exchange of prisoners.

During the meet, The Tassel, principal speaker for the Cherokee, addressed these remarks to Colonel Sevier. *"I know that you are a man and a warrior. I have heard different talks by different people quite different from what I expected. I fear you must have been angry and that it was caused by some evil persons.....You have risen up from a warrior to be a Beloved Man. I hope your speech will be good."* Colonel Sevier in replying to The Tassel said, *"I have never hated the Cherokee, but have had to fight them for the safety of my people."*

Nancy Ward, Chieftainess of the Cherokee Nation, arose at this point and made a talk. *"You know that women are always looked upon as nothing; but we are your mothers; and you are our sons. Our cry is all for peace; let it continue. This peace must last forever. Let your women's sons be ours; our sons be yours. Let your women hear our words.''*

The words moved the assembled group. Nancy Ward's friendship for the whites and her constant efforts to keep peace between the two races had their effect. Colonel William Christian made the reply.

"Mothers: we have listened well to your talk; it is humane...No man can hear it without being moved by it. Such words and thoughts show the world that human nature is the same everywhere. Our women shall hear your words, and we know how they will feel and think of them. We all are descendants of the same women. We will not quarrel with you, because you are our mothers. We will not meddle with your people if they will be still and quiet at home and let us live in peace.'' (These quotes and records have been taken from Williams' **Tennessee During The Revolution**). This is one of the very few Treaties where no request was made, by the whites, for more Indian land. Nancy Ward has often been characterized as the ''Pocahontas of the West.'' She was no ordinary woman.

During September General Greene made a push against Colonel Stuart, encamped at Eutaw Springs. The British were driven from the field with considerable loss. Much plunder was taken, including an abundance of food. For a period the Americans were able to eat well. The Stuart force moved back to Charleston, leaving that area to the Patriots.

OVERMOUNTAIN MEN VOLUNTEER

More letters and requests from Greene induced Colonels Shelby and Sevier to enlist a force and go to Greene's assistance. The Overmountain men were promised that this enlistment would be for sixty days only. Shelby raised 400; but Sevier, because of the Chickamauga raids, was unwilling to take more than 200 men away from the settlements. As they marched through North Carolina they heard rumors of the Cornwallis surrender at York Town. The men insisted on continuing the march. Sevier and Shelby were assigned to General Francis Marion. This was not very much to the liking of either. From Williams' **Tennessee During The Revolution**, we quote from Shelby's autobiography as used in the Greene papers and Henderson's ''Isaac Shelby''.

First, General Greene's letter to Shelby after Eutaw Springs Battle. It was after the September letter that Shelby and Sevier arranged to join Greene.

Head Quarters,
High Hills of Santee
Sept. 16, 1781.

Dear Sir:

I have the pleasure to inform you that we had an action with the British Army on the 8th in which we were victorious. We took 500 prisoners in and killed and wounded a much greater number. We also took nearly 1000 stand of arms, and have driven the enemy near the gates of Charleston. I have also the pleasure to inform you that a large French fleet of nearly thirty sail of the line, has arrived in the Chesepeak bay, with a considerable number of land forces; all of which are to be employed against Lord Cornwallis, who it is suspected will endeavor to make good his retreat through North Carolina to Charleston. To prevent which I beg you to bring out as many riflemen as you can, and as soon as possible. You will march them to Charlotte, and inform me the moment you set out, and of your arrival.

If we can intercept his lordship it will put a finishing stroke to the war on the Southern states.

Should I get any intelligence which may change the face of matters I will advise you. I am with esteem and regard, your most obedient and humble servant.

Shelby gives this account of the South Carolina Campaign in his Autobiography.

I made great exertions, and collected the men in a few days thereafter, many of them had not received more than 24 hours notice and lived more than 100 miles from the place of rendezvous - but were willing to go as the call was made for a special purpose - to wit, to intercept Lord Cornwallis who it was suspected would endeavor to make good his retreat through North Carolina to Charleston and Gen. Greene thought and so did I that if we could intercept him, it would put an end to the War in the Southern states. To effect this important object, the people on the western waters were induced to volunteer their services - it was for this purpose that they were prevailed upon to leave their homes 500 miles from the scene of operations to defend a Maritime district of country surrounded with a dense population and in comparative quiet while their own fire-sides were daily menaced by the Chickamauga Indians, who as you know had declared perpetual war against the whites and could never be induced to make peace. I was far advanced on my road when I received vague information of the surrender of Cornwallis in Virginia and hesitated whether to proceed. But as the men appeared to be willing to serve out a tour of duty which at the time of entering the service I repeatedly assured them should not exceed 60 days absence from their homes, I proceeded on more leisurely to Greene, who observed to me that such a body of horse could not remain in the vicinity of his camp on account of the scarcity of forage and requested me to serve out the tour with Marion, to which I consented, however, with some reluctance as the men would be drawn 70 or 80 miles further from their homes.

Despite the news of the Cornwallis surrender, Colonels Shelby and Sevier continued their march to join Greene. The following account comes from Shelby's Autobiography.

The enemies main Southern army, it was said, lay at that time near a place called Ferguson's Swamp on the great road bearing directly to Charleston. General Marion received information several weeks after our arrival at his camp that several hundred Hessians, at a British Post near Monk's Corner, eight or ten miles below the enemies main army, were in a state of mutiny, and would surrender to any considerable American force that might appear before it; and consulted his principal officers on the propriety of surprising it, which was soon determined on and Shelby and Sevier solicited a command in it. Marion accordingly moved down eight or ten miles, and crossed over to the South side of the Santee River, from whence he made a detachment of five or six hundred men to surprise the post, the command of which was given to Colonel Mayham. The detachment consisted of Shelby's mounted riflemen with Mayham's Dragoons, about one hundred and eighty, and about twenty or thirty lowland mounted militia, the command of the whole was given to Colonel Mayham. They took up their march early in the morning, and traveled fast through the woods until late in the evening of the second day, when they struck the great road leading to Charleston, about two miles below the enemies post, which they intended to surprise. They lay upon their arms all night across the road with a design to intercept the Hessians in case the enemy had got notice of our approach and had ordered them down to Charleston before morning. In the course of the night which was dark as pitch an orderly Sergeant rode into the line amongst us, and was taken prisoner. No material papers were found upon him before he made his escape except a pocket book which contained the strength of the enemy's main army and their number then on the sick list, which was very great.

As soon as daylight appeared, we advanced to the British Post; and arrived there before sunrise. Colonel Mayham sent in one of his confidential officers with peremptory demand for a surrender of the garrison, who in a few minutes returned and reported that the officer commanding was determined to defend the post to the last extremity. Colonel Shelby then proposed that he would go in himself and make another effort to obtain a surrender, which Mayham readily consented to. Upon his approach he discovered a gap in the Abbaties, through which he rode up close to the building, when an officer opened one leaf of a long folding door. Colonel Shelby addressed him in these words: "Will you be so mad as to suffer us to storm your works; if you do, rest assured that every soul of you will be put to the sword, for there was several hundred men at hand that would soon be in with their tomahawks upon them"; he then inquired if they had any artillery. Shelby replied, "that they had guns that would blow them to pieces in a minute." Upon which the officer replied, "I suppose I must give up." Mayham seeing the door thrown wide open, and Shelby ascending the high steps to the door, immediately advanced with his dragoons and formed on the right. It was not until this moment we discovered another strong British Fort that stood five or six hundred yards to the East, and this is the first knowledge we had of that post, the garrison of which immediately marched out, about one hundred infantry and forty or fifty cavalry came around the North Angle of the fort all apparently with a design to attack us; they however soon halted as we stood firm and prepared to meet them. We took a hundred and fifty prisoners, all of them able to have fought from the window of the house, or from behind Abbaties. Ninety of them were able to stand a march to Marion's camp that day which was near sixty miles; and we paroled the remainder most of whom appeared to have been sick and unable to stand so hard a march. Information soon reached Marion's camp that the Post had been burnt down immediately on our leaving it; but it was always the opinion of Colonel Shelby that the enemy had abandoned it, and burnt it themselves, for Mayham and Shelby were the two last men that left the place, and at that time there was not the least sign of fire or smoke about it. This it is most probable they would do, as they had previously destroyed and burned down almost every building in that part of the country. This post was an immense brick building, calculated to hold a thousand men and said to have been built by Sir John Colleton a century before that period as well for defense as comfort; and was well enclosed by a strong Abbaties. In it were found, besides the prisoners, three or four hundred stand of arms, and as many new blankets. The American detachment left this post between nine and ten o'clock of the same day, and arrived at Marion's camp the night following at three o'clock. General Stewart who commanded the Enemy's main army, eight or ten miles above, made great efforts to intercept us on our return. And it was announced to Marion about sunrise next morning that the whole British army was in the old field about three miles off at the outer end of the causeway that led into his camp. Shelby was immediately ordered out with the mountain men to meet him at the edge of the swamp, to attack the enemy if he attempted to advance, and retreat at his own discretion, to where Marion would have his whole force drawn up to sustain him at an old field. Shortly after his arrival at the edge of the open plain, he observed two British officers ride up to a house equidistance between the lines; after they retired he rode to the house to know what inquiries they had made; a man told him that they had asked him when the Americans detachment had got in, what was their force, and of what troops it was composed; he replied that the detachment had come in just before day, that he had supposed as they went out they were six or eight hundred strong, and were composed chiefly of Shelby's and Sevier's mounted men, with Mayham's mounted Dragoons. The enemy, then being in the edge of the woods, slightly withdrawn out of sight, retreated back in the utmost disorder and confusion. A small party, sent out to reconnoiter the enemy, reported that many of them had thrown away their napsacks, guns and canteens. A few days afterwards General Marion received intelligence that the British commander had retreated with his whole force to Charleston. Marion's sole design in moving from the camp when the mountain men first joined them, and crossing the Santee River below; was to get within striking distance of the before mentioned post, to make (safe) the said detachment, and be able to protect and support them on their retreat if hard pushed by the enemy. After this the enemy kept so within their lines that little or no blood was spilt; and all active movements appearing to be at end, Shelby made application to General Marion for leave of absence to go the the Assembly of North Carolina, of which he was a member, and which was to meet about that time at Salem, and where he had private business of his own of the first importance. The mountain men had then but a day or two to stay, to complete their tour of duty, of sixty days, and he verily believes that they did serve it out, as he never heard to the contrary.

The Overmountain men served their sixty day enlistment. It was January, 1782 when they arrived back home. Shelby, commenting on the men, had this to say:

These mountaineers were poor men who lived by keeping stock on the range beyond the mountains; they were volunteers and neither expected or received any compensation except liquidated certificates worth two shillings in the pound. General Greene had no right nor ought to have expected to command their services. For myself, for the whole services of 1780 and 1781, both in camp and in the General Assembly, I received a liquidation certificate which my good agent in that county (Sullivan), after my removal to Kentucky, sold for six yards of middling broadcloth, and gave one coat made of it to the person who brought it out to me. Indeed I was proud of receiving that.

LAST OVERMOUNTAIN BATTLE OF REVOLUTIONARY WAR

The last Battle of the Revolutionary War, west of the Appalachian Mountains, was fought on Lookout Mountain. Bands of the Chickamauga Indians were making daily raids on frontier cabins. The Chiefs of these lower Cherokee Towns, split off from the Overhill Cherokee, had neither signed treaties nor agreed to any peace terms.

The North Carolina Legislature had authorized a campaign against this troublesome group during its 1782 July Session. Colonel Charles McDowell and Colonel John Sevier had been delegated to raise a thousand troops with which to squelch the Chickamaugas. Colonel McDowell never got around to raising a force from Burke County. Virginia, Washington County, and Sullivan County were asked to take part, but the enmity created during the Boyd's Creek Campaign, December 1780, still existed. Sevier's hurried march and battle, the Clarke-Martin fight over the cattle provided at Chote, were still resented by the Virginia and Sullivan County groups.

The final result of all this planning and conferring was a campaign led by Colonel Sevier with 250 of his Nolichucky riflemen. They left the settlements September, 1782. At Chota they were greeted by several of the leading chiefs. Two Dragging Canoe followers, John Watts and Butler, volunteered to pilot the force to the Chickamauga towns. John Watts had been stationed in the Overhill towns by Dragging Canoe, to keep him informed of the various meetings, messages and arrangements between the Overhill Chiefs and the American officials. These two guides hoped to lead Sevier and his men away from the Chickamauga Towns.

Colonel Sevier had his own ideas regarding where he planned to go. He led his force to the Middle Towns in spite of the advice of the two guides. The abandoned cabins of Bull Town, Settico, Vann's and Chickamauga were destroyed. A battle took place on Lookout Mountain. This band of Indians was outnumbered and could not match the firepower of the pioneer riflemen. The conflict was of short duration. The Chiefs of this battle are thought to have been Bloody Fellow, Wyada and Little Owl.

Colonel Sevier led his men as far south as the Coosa River. He had the vacated towns of Spring Frog, Ustinaula, Ellijay and Coosawatie destroyed. John Watts had been able to steer the troops away from the new towns of Chickamauga. Jane Iredell, a white girl held captive in the lower Towns, was brought back to her people in present Johnson County, Tennessee.

Sevier and his men returned to Chota where a

Moccasin Bend and town of Lookout Mountain as seen from the top of the mountain. Battle site of two wars.

friendly conference was held with Oconostota, The Tassel, Hanging Maw and other Headmen. Thirty captives, taken during the campaign, were released to return to their homes. Majors Valentine Sevier and James Hubbard; Captains William Bean, Samuel Wear, Alexander Moore, George Russell, Neely (Cornelius) McGuire, William Smith and James Sevier were on this march, as were the Bean brothers William Jr., Robert, John, Jesse, and Edmund.

The party reached their homes in November. This expedition stopped the raids for a short while. The Chickamaugas did not molest the Washington and Sullivan County residents so much after this experience. They were learning to fear and respect the firepower of these experienced frontiersmen. This campaign did not stop the Chickamauga attacks against the Cumberland settlements.

The partisan warfare in the three most southern states continued for more than a year after Cornwallis surrendered at York Town. Most of the skirmishes were petty, but barbaric. General Washington had sent General Anthony Wayne to assist General Greene in clearing these bothersome areas. Wayne was assigned to the Georgia theatre. He drove the British-Tory groups from post to post. They were finally forced to evacuate Savannah, Georgia in July, 1782.

Charleston, South Carolina, was the last southern point to be cleared. The final skirmish took place on James Island late in 1782. It is said an American officer named Wilmont, killed there during this skirmish, was the last casualty of the Revolutionary War.

The British did not leave New York until November 25, 1783. They were placed on Staten Island and Long Island while waiting for vessels to take them away. General Henry Knox, with an American force, occupied the Bowery and Fort George on this same date. General George Washington joined them during this occupation.

A preliminary Treaty had been signed in Paris on November 30, 1782. The final Treaty was not signed until September 3, 1783. This was eight years after the first gun was fired in Lexington. Cornwallis surrendered in York Town one year and twelve days after the King's Mountain victory. It has been said that England's defeat by the Americans was her greatest victory. And for America, it can be said that her victory over England made it possible for her to conquer the whole world with her idealism of liberty for mankind. History will record how this new form of Government used its opportunity.

Council Oak, near Morganton, North Carolina, where Overmountain Men, Wilkes, Surry and Burke County Patriots discussed the Ferguson campaign that ended at King's Mountain. King's Mountain National Military Park.

Liberty Oak, at Guilford Courthouse Battle Ground. General Greene and his men camped around tree. Guilford Courthouse National Military Park.

THE CUMBERLAND DECADE

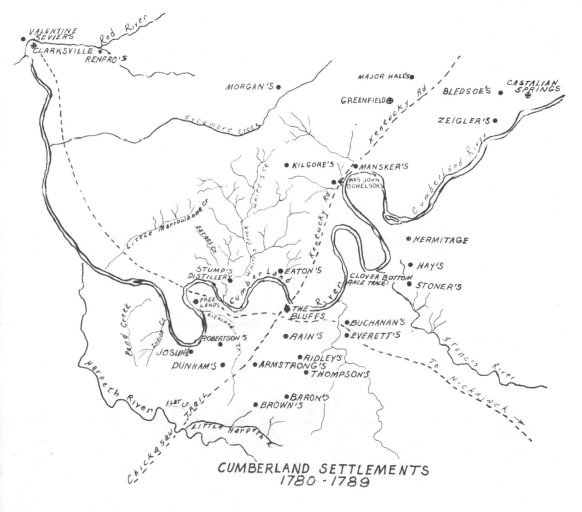

CUMBERLAND SETTLEMENTS
1780-1789

DEMONBREUN'S CAVE: Legend says that Jacques-Timothe Demonbreun visited French Licks earlier than history so records. It is said that this French-Canadian fur trader stored his supplies of iron tomahawks and other trinkets in cave and that on occasions was able to escape Indian attacks by hiding there. Demonbreun served as Lieut-Governor of the Illinois Country. Died in Nashville 1826.

SUNNYSIDE: These old log cabins were built by early French traders near the Bluffs. The two story cabin was the home of the post factor and the priest who always followed the traders into new country. Nashville was first called "French Licks."

CUMBERLAND SETTLEMENTS
1780

Richard Henderson exerted a strong influence in starting the Blue Grass Settlements in Kentucky. When Virginia refused to recognize the validity of the Transylvania Treaty purchase at Sycamore Shoals, (Elizabethton, Tenn.) this made his land speculation in Kentucky a hazardous undertaking. He began to cast a speculative eye toward the valleys of the Cumberland, which he felt were included in the 1775 Treaty with the Cherokees.

Encouraged by the willingness of James Robertson and John Donelson to lead the Cumberland expedition, Henderson pushed plans for starting a settlement around the French Lick (Nashville) territory. During the winter of 1778-1779 James Robertson, with eight men, began an explorative trip in that direction.

The nine men followed the Wilderness Trail through the Cumberland Gap to the Cumberland River as it meanders through Kentucky. Arriving at the river, they made crude canoes and continued the trip down that stream. A few miles above the Lick at a big bend, later named "Jones Bend," they saw a man named Jones that Robertson had talked with earlier in the Holston community. Jones had lived on the Cumberland for about nine months in a crude cabin. He had been frightened by Indian signs near his clearing. Taking his few possessions, he went upriver in his canoe, finally arriving in the Holston settlement. Talks with Jones may have influenced Robertson in making the trip down the river in canoes. Jones had evidently returned to his claim.

Many white settlers had erected cabins in the Cumberland Territory before arrival of the Robertson party. Timothy Demunbreum was at French Lick trapping and trading as early as 1777, according to legend several years earlier. He found six white men and one white woman living in the vicinity of the present town of Palmyra. Some 30 Tory families that had been driven from settlements in western North Carolina had made an attempt to establish a community on the Cumberland. Indian hostilities in the area had caused most of them to leave and seek sites nearer British posts.

Casper Mansker and Michael Stoner had arrived and cleared some land before the Holston party arrived. Michael Stoner had staked a claim on Stone River in the section now known as Clover Bottom. Henderson wanted this particular land. A trade arrangement was worked out with the German, who moved to Kentucky. This transaction caused much litigation in the Kentucky Courts during later years.

In the fall of 1779, Robertson led a large body of men with their loaded pack horses, brood mares, cows, hogs and sheep over the Wilderness Trail through Kentucky and down to the French Lick. Many other groups joined the caravan as they made their laborious way along the trail. Colonel Donelson followed later with the families of the men on a flotilla of boats. Robertson and his party reached the Cumberland across from the French Lick around Christmas of 1779. They drove the horses and stock across the river covered with an ice crust thick enough to support the men and animals. Some historians place the crossing as December 25th, others January 1st, 1780.

Isaac Bledsoe, Shelby Blackman, Morgan Hall and Ephraim Peyton were among a group that settled in present Sumner County late in 1779. Another group from South Carolina, including

RICHARD HENDERSON at Nashborough 1780. (Artist illustration.)

John Buchanan, Alexander Buchanan, Daniel Williams, Sampson Williams, James Mulherrin and Thomas Thompson built cabins near French Lick about the same time as the Robertson frontiersmen.

It is estimated that some 300 people were living in the Cumberland Basin by May, 1780. Under Henderson's influence they named the central point Nashborough, later changed to Nashville. Thus was started the furthermost frontier of young America.

Even though this new settlement was part of Washington County, it was isolated by some 300 miles of Wilderness from Jonesborough, the official County Seat. Civil and legal functions, law and order standards were needed. Following the general plan of the Watauga Association, organized in 1772, they put together the Cumberland Association. "The Cumberland Compact," written symbol of the new Association, was composed by Richard Henderson. The Settlers adopted the document and 256 signatures were affixed. The Compact was adopted May 1st, 1780. Additional provisions were added May 13th. This document was in part a declaration of the rights, terms and conditions of the Transylvania Company for selling parcels of land to the settlers. Otherwise the Pact's political structure was similar to that of the Watauga Association which James Robertson helped write. The pact can be read in many historical publications. Putnam is responsible for it being available.

For a period, this written code served as a guiding influence in the civil, legal and moral conduct of the community. The authority of the Association was vested in 12 Judges, or tryers, elected by the people. Each of the main stations could elect number of judges according to population: Nashborough, 3; Mansker's Lick, 2; Bledsoe, 1; Asher, 1; Freeland, 1; Eaton, 2; Fort Union, 1. James Robertson was elected to serve as Chairman. Ordinary cases, disputes, marriages, registering legal papers, could be handled by the individual Judges. A stronger court was to be convened for more serious cases involving crimes carrying penalties. These people were determined to handle their own affairs rather than refer them to the far distant court at Jonesborough. 16 year old males could own land, must serve in the militia, but could not vote until they were 21.

The early settlers on the Cumberland felt that as they were not near Indian towns, nor positively claimed territory, they would be safe from Indian harassment. This feeling of security would soon be dispelled. Henderson wrongly assumed that the Cumberland Territory had been purchased from the Cherokees in 1775. The Cherokees and Chickasaws had driven the Shawnees from this part of the country several years previous. In 1769, the Cherokees invaded the Cumberland Basin with their best warriors. They were badly defeated by the Chickasaws and the flower of their race was destroyed. The Chickasaws claimed this territory by right of conquest. At the Sycamore Shoals Land Treaty, Cherokee War Chief Oconostota, made this talk to Henderson, as recorded in "William Tatham" by Williams.

NASHVILLE'S FIRST MARRIAGE was performed by James Robertson. The couple, Captain James Leiper and Susan Drake.

"Why you know you are telling lies. We always told you those lands were not ours; that our claim extended not beyond the Cumberland mountain; that all the land beyond the Cumberland River belonged to our brothers, the Chickasaws. It is true you gave us some goods for which we promised you our friendship in the affair, and our good will. These you have had according to bargain, and more we never promised you; but you have deceived your people."

Another factor that was to prove bad for the Cumberland people was Fort Jefferson, built by George Rogers Clark under orders of Thomas Jefferson, Governor of Virginia. This Fort was erected a few miles south of the mouth of the Ohio River on land claimed by the Chickasaws. They were not asked, consulted or treated concerning this trespass.

Jefferson, thinking the land belonged to the Cherokees, ordered construction of the Fort during the early part of 1780. The Fort was garrisoned and commanded by Captain Robert George. The Chickasaws, under the leadership of Chief James Colbert, laid siege to the fortification during the spring of 1780. The series of harassing attacks lasted about a week. The small force within the stockade, with their families, sustained these numerous assaults. The final attack was repelled by the use of a swivel gun. The big load of small scatter shot proved too costly in number of Indians killed and wounded. Chief Colbert himself was wounded during this final battle. Nevertheless, the Garrison was doomed. Cut off from supplies and help, they were evacuated under the direction of Colonel John Montgomery. With canoes and guards, the survivors were taken up the river to the Falls of the Ohio (Louisville, Ky.).

This incident was one of the many that ignited a period of killing, scalping, stealing, burning and harassment that lasted nearly 15 years. The new settlements were ordained to withstand a bloodbath of death, trouble and desolation that nearly destroyed them morally, spiritually and physically. Many times these people would have left, but there were no horses to ride. They could not get into the woods to cut timber for boats. The Cumberland Basin had been used by many tribes and nations as a common hunting ground, thus it was to become a prime target for raids by the Chickasaws, Creeks, Choctaws, Shawnees and Chickamaugas. They raided separately and at times joined forces.

The first strong attack was directed toward the small Renfroe Settlement. Moses Renfroe, his sons James and Joseph with their families, the Johns family, Nathan and Solomon Turpin and families, some 40 in all settled here. They left the Donelson flotilla when they reached the mouth of the Red River. They built their cabins and began clearing land in the vicinity of the present town of Clarksville, Tennessee.

During June many Indians were seen in the neighborhood. Nathan Turpin was killed and scalped. Other killings reported nearby frightened the Red River settlers into moving nearer the larger Station at Freeland's. The Turpins were related to the Freelands. They collected what possessions they could carry and departed. The journey had to be made through dense, unchartered wilderness. At the first night's camp, the women were fussing at the men for leaving behind some of their most needed property. After some discussion, some of the men and women decided to return and get the items left behind. They made the trip back that night, recovered the property and made their way back to where they had made camp the night before. Many of the group had continued the journey that day and made the Freeland Station in safety. When the travelers rejoined those who had waited their return, they continued a ways and made camp that night on the banks of a small stream that emptied into Sycamore Creek. During the night, or at daybreak, the Indians attacked the camp. Every person was killed except Mrs. Johns, who escaped during the confusion of the slaughter. She fled, stumbling through the rough woods with little direction. She was finally rescued by a hunter named Henry Ramsey and taken to Eaton's Station. She was in an almost incoherent state, bruised, tattered and frightened. The story she told gave the people at Eaton's enough direction that a party of men left for the scene of the massacre to look for survivors and bury the dead. The creek was later named "Battle Creek."

This unexpected attack by the Chickasaws caused panic and fear throughout the settlements. Death and harassment by the Indians became a way of life. Men working in the fields had to keep a constant guard on watch at all times. Two men working in a field would work back to back. When one was stooping down, the other would be standing watch. Hunters had to fetch game in groups instead of singly. Hunting trips became longer as game became scarcer. The pioneers thought that the deer and buffalo were gone, but the Indians had contrived to drive the game away from the settlements. They hoped to lure the men further from the forts, where they would be easier to kill. Most of the Indian bands were not of force sufficient to attack a station; they preferred to watch for small groups that could be wiped out without too much risk.

THE BUFFALO has been called the trail-maker or engineer because of his habit of finding the route of least resistance between salt licks and cane brakes. His trail some 4 or 5 feet wide was hard packed by many hoofs. Indians adopted and followed his traces later called war paths. The white man followed with a road.

CLOVER BOTTOM

No documented records of the many fights between the settlers and the Indians are complete. A fragment here and there has been pieced together to give some accounts that tell part of the story. We relate an account of the Clover Bottom episode as condensed from Putnam's "History of Middle Tennessee." It is typical of such events during the first decade of the Cumberland Settlements.

Colonel Donelson had planted corn and cotton on his property along Stone River, now known as "Clover Bottom." Most of the fields were near the mouth of the River. Because of the Indian depredations, Donelson had moved his family to Mansker Station. The Indian scare had postponed the regular harvest. Donelson offered any group that would help him house the crop a half share. The Nashborough people needed the corn; their crop had been ruined by high water. In November, Captain Abel Gower and a crew of eight men poled his boat up the river to the mouth of Stone River, where he was met by Captain John Donelson, son of the Colonel. Young Donelson had come down the River from Manskers with a crew of eight, and a horse, on his boat. They spent several days gathering the corn. It was carried down to the boats on a pole drag pulled by horse. Donelson also planned to use the horse to help pull the loaded boat back upstream. They camped in the half-faced cabins built by Donelson in the spring. They had a pack of hunting dogs along to help them secure wild game for food. During the last night's camp the dogs kept up a vicious bark and howl. They would chase from one side of the camp to the other. The men thought it

was wolves and other animals fighting over the leavings where they had dressed the deer and buffalo. It is assumed the men, accustomed to the nightly barking, paid little heed.

Early morning, breakfast cooked and eaten, Captain Donelson and his crew poled their boat across the river to start picking cotton, expecting the Gower boat and crew to follow. Nobody had taken the trouble to scout for Indian signs, as they expected no hostiles in the area. The Gower crew meanwhile had pushed off from shore and were headed downstream. Donelson was surprised when he saw them leaving without helping with the cotton. He went to the bank and hallooed, with a loud shout, asking why they were leaving and not helping finish with the cotton picking. Captain Gower replied, *"We are not coming over; it's getting late in the day, we wish to reach the Bluffs before night. I think there is no danger."* While yet yelling across the water to each other, the Gower boat drifted on the banks of a narrow island in midstream. A party of Indians, lying in ambush on the south banks, opened heavy fire on the boat. Donelson saw this while standing on the bank. He raced to his boat to get his gun and ammunition. The Indians were out of gun range so he was helpless to aid. He saw some of the men leap out of the boat into shallow water in an attempt to reach safety on the shore. Some were caught and tomahawked before reaching the bank. Captain Abel Gower, his son Abel Junior, and James Randolph Robertson were among the five killed. One white man and one negro managed to escape into the woods and, after wandering 20 hours, finally found their way to the Bluff Fort. Jack Civil, a free negro, surrendered and went with the Indians to Chickamauga, where he bacame one of them. The town of Nick-a-Jack is said to have been named for him, but this is doubtful. The Gower boat with its grain and some of the dead bodies floated down the river to the Bluffs, where it was rescued.

Meanwhile Captain John Donelson, seeing a band of warriors coming upstream opposite his boat, fired on them. They fled into the woods. Donelson, realizing that leaving by boat was impossible, went in search of his crew. After much searching he found them hiding in the tall cane, where they had fled when the firing began. Putting the older Cartwright on the horse, they started a roundabout trip upstream. They spent a cold, wet night huddled in the top of a fallen tree. They finally reached the Cumberland River several miles above the mouth of Stone River. After a futile attempt to build a raft, Somerset, Colonel Donelson's faithful black servant, volunteered to swim the horse across the river and go for help. This he did, finally reaching the station. When he had told the story, some of the men at the station went to the bank across from the crew. They built a crude raft and were able to bring the Donelson crew across. The Bluffs lost five men, but were able to save the grain. The Donelson crew lost their boat, but saved their lives.

During the year 1780, at least 37 men were killed by the Indians. A partial list is given, but as records were sparsely kept, many names, dates and places are impossible to obtain.

Keywood and Miliken were fired on at Richland Creek, Miliken was killed, Keywood managed to escape. Captain Rains moved his family to the Fort where they lived four years. Joseph Hay was killed on Lick Branch, Bernard was slain and beheaded at Denton's Lick. Joseph and William Dunkam, two small boys with Bernard, escaped. In May, D. Lariman was killed near Freeland's, shortly after Isaac LeFevre was shot near the Bluffs. Solomon Phillips was mortally wounded and died after reaching the fort. Samuel Murray, working with Phillips in the field, was killed outright. Bartlett Renfroe was killed, John Kendrick and John Maxwell taken prisoner. During July and August, Jonathan Jennings was shot. Ned Carver was killed, his wife and two children escaped to Nashborough. William Neely and a crew were experimenting with salt making at the Lick by his name. He was sitting near the fire resting. His daughter was preparing the evening meal. He was killed and the girl taken prisoner. Near Eaton's, James Mayfield was killed from ambush.

At Mansker's Lick, Jesse Balestine and John Shockley, David Goin and Patrick Quigley were shot. At Bledsoe's Station, W. Johnston and Daniel Mungle were attacked. Johnston was killed, Mungle escaped. Frederick and Jacob Stump were staking out a claim on White's Creek. Jacob was killed, Frederick managed to outrun the Indians to the Fort.

Thomas Sharpe Spencer, with several horses loaded with fresh meat and hides, was attacked. Spencer escaped, but the Indians captured his horses and the meat. At Asher's Station (near present town of Gallatin), some white hunters were shot while sleeping, killed and scalped. One Phillips in charge of the horses was wounded, horses stolen. The two different bands of Indians who had committed several of these attacks had united and were traveling toward Bledsoe's Lick. They were suddenly confronted by several hunters returning toward the Bluffs. Among them were Alexander Buchanan, James Manifee, William Ellis and Alexander Thompson. These hunters had been keeping a sharp watch and were ready when they met the Indians. They fired a heavy blast at the warriors, killing one and wounding others. The Indians fled leaving the stolen horses and meat they had taken from Spencer and Phillips.

The only person that died a natural death in the Cumberland Settlements during the year 1780 was Robert Gilkey. A natural death caused more comment and interest than one by the redskins.

Many of the settlers, disillusioned with the situation, moved to Kentucky. Colonel Donelson with his family moved to sanctuary in the Blue Grass country. Some went south to Natchez, where there were British holdings. Mansker's Station was abandoned, shortly after the Indians destroyed it.

During the winter of 1780-1781, most of the settlers moved into the three strongest stations: Nashborough, Freeland's and Eaton's. The winter's provisions were stored in these three compounds. As much of the corn crop planted in the river lowlands had been destroyed by floodwaters, there was very little grain. Walnuts and hickory nuts were gathered in large quantities and put inside the forts. Sometime before winter set in, a party of 20 hunters had been able to go up Caney Fork after meat. It is said they killed 105 bear, 75 buffalo and about 90 deer. They brought the meat and hides back to the fort in canoes. They had plenty of meat, but little bread, for winter.

CHICKASAWS
1781

FELIX ROBERTSON

During the early part of the winter of 1780, James Robertson went to Kentucky. A shortage of powder and lead and a request for help were two of the pressing reasons for the trip. The Settlement was also anxious to find out the progress of the war. They felt that the Indians, as British allies, were fighting on the frontiers under the influence and advice of English Agents.

Robertson made the trip both ways without encountering Indians. He came across many campfires and other signs indicating Indians were recently there. He arrived back at the Bluffs January 15th, 1781. The people were relieved by his return and gave him a happy welcome. After being ferried across the River, he learned that his family was at Freeland's Station. Knowing the supplies were now safe, he continued on to Freeland's. News of his arrival had preceded him. Another warm welcome awaited him there.

He spent most of the evening telling the people what news he had learned. He had to report that the Kentuckians could send them no relief, as they were fully occupied protecting their own borders. Another surprise was to see his new son, born January 11th. Felix Robertson is said to be the first white child born in the environs of the present city of Nashville. Robertson was up late talking to the people and his wife. Perhaps as he thought of his new son, he also was thinking of James so recently killed at Clover Bottom.

Restless, and still unable to sleep, he was alerted by suspicious noises at the gate. He grabbed his gun and gave the warning shout, "Indians." In a fast moment every person in the Station was alert. The men grabbed their guns and made ready to resist. Fortunately, Robertson had given each of the men a charge from his own powder horn. The supply, brought from Kentucky, was back at the Bluffs.

A large band of Chickasaw Indians had managed to unfasten the chain that held the main gate and had made their entrance into the stockade. They were shooting at every porthole from close range. The men stood back from the vulnerable openings and watched the doors. The fire of the Indians killed Major Robert Lucas and one Negro. Several were wounded. From Goodpasture in "Tennessee Historical Magazine," we quote:

A large party of Chickasaws, having found means to unfasten the gate, were now entering the stockade. In an instant every man in the fort--eleven in number--was in motion. Major Robert Lucas, who occupied a house that was untenantable because the cracks between the logs had not yet been chinked and daubed, rushed out into the open, and was shot down, mortally wounded. A negro man of Colonel Robertson's, who was in the house with Major Lucas, was also killed. These were the only fatalities, though the death of Major Lucas alone was a serious loss to the colony. He had been a leading pioneer on the Watauga, as he was on the Cumberland. He was a party to the treaty on Sycamore Shoals, and in connection with Colonel John Carter, had received from the Cherokees a deed to part of Carter's Valley. On his removal to Cumberland, he was elected Major in the first military organization of the district.

Hundreds of shots had been fired into the houses; and so great was the uproar from the firing, and the whooping and yelling of the Indians, that the stationers at Eton's and the Bluffs (Fort Nashborough) were aroused and the sound of the small cannon at the latter place gave notice that relief was at hand. The Indians then withdrew. They had lost one killed, whose body was found, and the traces of blood indicated that others had been wounded.

One woman later said it sounded like a thousand devils. Shortly after dawn, Captain Rains arrived from the Bluffs with men and ammunition. This was the last attack on the settlements by the Chickasaws. James Robertson was able to arrange talks with Chief Piomingo. A pact was agreed between them. The Chickasaws and Cumberland people maintained a friendly relationship from then on.

But much damage was done. The Chickasaws, joined by a band of Cherokees, went through the country burning fences, cabins, barns and generally destroying everything they could. As the people were all crowded into three forts, there was no resistance. Several days after the Freeland attack, a few reckless people ventured to their cabin sites to check on the damage. Several lost their lives as small bands of Indians remained on watch for just such an opportunity to get white scalps.

The Dunhams had settled a claim near the Bluffs. Dunham had started his cabin and cleared some land, leaving the brush heaps piled around the area. One day Mrs. Dunham asked her small girl to fetch her a turn of sticks and chips to put on the fire. They had moved to the stockade for safety. The young girl, remembering the cut wood lying around the cabin some 300 yards away, went there after her turn of firewood. Indians, hidden behind the brush piles from the felled trees, grabbed her and were in the act of scalping the screaming child. Her terrified cries brought the mother rushing to her aid. Some of the men eating dinner hurried out to help. Mrs. Dunham was shot and seriously wounded as she was running toward the girl. The little girl was scalped but recovered. Captain Rains and Castlemen, with a body of pioneers, pursued the Indians for a distance. They reported killing one. After this, the cabin builders were careful to burn all of the brush piles around a new clearing.

David Hood, who was nicknamed "Possum," did much to comfort the young lady who was trying to recover from the loss of her scalp. Hood, a unique, droll quibbing personality did much to keep up the morale of the community. He was a great misquoter of the Scripture. People were never sure if he was irreverent, ignorant, or merely speaking in jest. His ability to play possum saved his life on one occasion. The women and children all liked him. He was ever ready to fetch a pail of water, tote a turn of wood, or look for a boy or girl that was out of place.

BATTLE OF THE BLUFFS

The campaign against the Cherokees, December 1780, by the Overmountain Men of the Holston, Watauga and Nolichucky settlements, was led by Colonel John Sevier, Major Joseph Martin and Colonel Arthur Campbell. Even though many towns were burned and treaty terms agreed on, this left untouched the main source of the Cumberland Indian troubles. The Chickamauga Nation was made up of dissident Cherokees who broke away from the Overhill Tribes and formed a Nation of their own. Many Creeks from north Georgia and Alabama territory joined the renegade warriors. Dragging Canoe, leader of the exodus, walked out of the Sycamore Shoals treaty 1775, in protest. He was against selling the Henderson Company the land and promised a bloody settling. Many of the young Chiefs followed him in this move. Among them were Willenawah, Bloody Fellow, Hanging Maw, Kitegiska, Young Tassel (later known as John Watts), Lying Fish, Tsaladihi, the Buck and others. When the migration took place the Overhill towns of Settico, Great Island, Tellico, Toque, and Chilhowie were practically abandoned.

Dragging Canoe settled his people from Great Island at an old Creek Town site called Chickamauga (dwelling place of the War Chief). The new Nation, and the small creek along which the towns were built, took its name from Dragging Canoe's town and these people became known as the Chickamaugas.

Unable to do much against the stronger settlements of the Holston, Watauga and Nolichucky, Dragging Canoe decided to move against the young, weak settlements in the Cumberland basin. He wanted to wipe them out before they had time to grow strong. So, in March of 1781, he left Chickamauga leading a strong force of several hundred. His first attack was to be against Nashborough at French Lick. When he had overcome and destroyed the main stronghold of the whites, the others would fall easily. Plans and details for the attack were worked out carefully. The various bands of warriors were able to move into the settlements without any problem. As the settlers had not anticipated an attack of this magnitude, Dragging Canoe's plan was working better than he had hoped.

During the night of April 1st, Dragging Canoe arranged his forces in the pre-battle positions. They moved into strategic places for an all-out assault. James Menefee, standing watch, fired a shot during the night at an Indian scout. This was not an unusual occurrence, so the hemmed and herded people asleep inside the stockade were not alarmed. They had little inkling of what was taking place outside the fort.

Early dawn April 2nd, the sentry cry of "Indians" aroused the people. Three braves had approached the fort, fired their guns, and run back out of gun range. They stopped, reloaded and went through a lot of motion to attract attention.

The men in the fort somehow felt that this was a ruse to draw them outside. But the decision was made to go after them. Robertson left the fort with a force of 20 men planning to run them down. At full gallop they took off after the warriors. The Indians ran away from the fort and were soon joined by another group. They stopped to make a stand. Arriving within firing distance, Robertson and his men dismounted and prepared to fight. About this time, a large band of Indians concealed in the bed of a creek rushed out behind the whites and began firing on the frontiersmen from the rear. The 20 guns returned the fire with good effect. This crossfire and the loud whoops of the redskins so frightened the horses that they stampeded back towards the fort. Now another large body of Indians, that had been concealed in the cedars, ran out to join in the fray. Their lines extended back toward the fort. The frantic horses broke through both lines in their mad panic. The sight of those 20 beautiful horses caused many of the Indians to forget the battle in progress and chase the animals. Horses were prized about as much as scalps. By this time the large force stationed beyond the fort sallied out to come between the men and the fort gate. This band of Indians were the ones designated to enter the Stockade.

The horses breaking through the Indian lines made an opening, through which the 20 men were trying to fight their way toward the gate. This advantage was greatly strengthened by so many of the warriors chasing after the horses, which had swerved away from the fort in their mad effort to escape this new menace of whooping, banging redskins.

All of the fighting and commotion of the battle raging outside was being watched by the people inside. Mrs. James Robertson and the others were doing what they could. The women, with loaded guns and axes in hand, were determined to sell their lives dearly. Mrs. Robertson had gone to the wall overlooking the area where the 20 men were fighting. She saw the horses break through the Indian lines followed by a host of warriors. She watched her husband and his men desperately fighting their way toward the fort through the broken Indian lines. The wailing whines and cries of the Indian-hating dogs, penned in the fort, gave her the great inspiration. She went to the guard at the gate and told him to open it and let the dogs out. With savage fury this reserve army of Nashborough rushed into the fray. The Indians became so excited with this unexpected attack, they almost forgot the pioneers. The Red Warriors were kept busy defending themselves from the vicious attacks of the more than 50 dogs. They did not want to waste shots on the animals. Also, it was next to impossible to hit the whirling, snarling, biting beasts.

The confusion caused by part of the Indians chasing horses, others fighting off the vicious dogs, gave the pioneers a chance to gain the fort gate. Five men were killed: Alexander Buchanan, George Kennedy, Zachariah White, Peter Gill and Captain Leiper. James Manifee, Joseph Moonshaw and Isaac Lucas were wounded. During the last part in the desperate run for the fort, Isaac Lucas was shot and his hip broken. Lying on the ground, he reloaded his gun and shot the front Indian of the pursuing group. Lucas was rescued. Another struggle took place within yards of the fort wall. Edward Swanson was overtaken by a big Buck. The Indian hit Swanson with the butt of his gun, causing Swanson to drop his own rifle. Swanson turned and grabbed the Indian's gun in an effort to wrest it away from the redman. It was a life and death

BATTLE OF THE BLUFFS by Bernie Andrews, used by courtesy Mary U. Rothrock.

struggle in which the Indian was winning. Getting complete possession of his gun, the big Buck knocked Swanson to his knees and was in the act of finishing him off when his own gun refused to fire. At this point John Buchanan, who had nearly reached the gate, shot the Indian and helped Swanson to safety.

As the men reached the protection of the fort walls, they were able to give the Indians some deadly fire. About ten o'clock the Indians withdrew out of gun range. The Battle of the Bluffs was really the Battle of the Horses and Dogs. The Indians' lack of discipline, at the critical moment, lost the victory already won. One of the mothers in the fort (this statement has been credited to Mrs. James Robertson) remarked, "Thanks be to God, that He gave the Indians a fear of dogs and a love of horses."

The demoralized Indians continued to chase after the horses. They caught some of the animals with the saddles and gear still intact. Many of the horses eluded the warriors and returned to the fort gates, which were opened for them to pass inside.

A close watch was kept throughout the day. The Indians had pulled back out of gun range to plan their next move. That night they began firing at the fort. This continued for some time. Very little damage was done. The lookouts noticed a band of several hundred Indians assembled in an area beyond rifle range. It was decided to fire the small swivel cannon at this body of warriors. They collected scraps of iron and broken stones to use in place of regular cannonballs. The men each gave a charge from their own powder horn to supply the load. Many protested this because of the scarcity of powder. The gun was placed in position and aimed at this large group. Its boom was worse than its bite, but the loud bang of the explosion frightened the Indians. These warriors also knew that men from the other stations would be coming to the aid of the besieged fort. The Indian force left.

Sometime after the cannon was fired, a shout was heard from across the river. The boats used for ferrying service were kept on the Nashborough side under guard. Two boatmen went across the river and brought over men from Eaton's who had rushed to their aid when they heard the cannon. The Eaton men shared the watch through the rest of the night with the Bluff defenders. A searching party went out early the morning of April 3rd, looking for bodies of their fallen comrades and signs of the Indians. They reported that the Indians had passed beyond Richland Creek. This was the last major attack on the Settlements. Hit and run tactics and guerrilla warfare were to be a constant menace for several years. From Putnam, we take the following quote:

"Mrs. James Robertson said she stood by the sentry gate as the horsemen passed out and dashed down the hill through the cedars and bushes. She had glimpses of the Indians upon whom the whites made their attack, heard the crack of every gun, saw some of the movements of the Indians who were in ambush"; and "her heart began to fail, for fear that every man that had gone out would be killed, and the station probably fall into the hands of the murderers."

One of the stories that comes from this event is that Mrs. Robertson stood by the gate as the dogs returned inside and patted each dog's head as it passed by.

All during the remainder of 1781, tragic events followed each other. To go outside the station meant possible death. The men had to learn Indian ways and outdo the redman. The white hunter had to aim, fire and hide quicker in order to survive. It is said that the hunters could recognize each pioneer's individual gun when fired. Indians' gunfire was easy to know because they used smaller loads.

One of the big losses was milk cows. The women and children depended on this source of food. The cows were almost as important to the families as the humans. The Indians took great delight in killing the white man's buffalo whenever they could. They resented the use of cows by their squaws.

THE PEOPLE – DAVID HOOD – WATER MILLS
1782

HOAR-FROST, RHYME, FROZEN FOG

Things were relatively quiet during the winter 1781-1782. The settlers were still crowded into the three stations and exposed themselves only when necessary. Indians were in the vicinity most of the time, but in small bands. They watched for any opportunity to steal a horse or take a single scalp without too much risk to themselves. The heavier-loaded gun of the white man was a thing to fear. Tension, fear and dread of the warning cry of "Indian" was ever present. More of the faint-hearted deserted the settlements with hopes of reaching a safe sanctuary. Some were able to slip through the redman's menace, others were killed on the trail.

They fared well if not sumptuously. Black and white walnuts, chestnuts and hickory nuts provided a change from jerkin. The cattle and horses within the enclosures were fed on cane that had been cut, cured and stored. There were no doctors in the community, but every person knew the art of preparing nature's herbs, roots and barks for remedies. They could set broken arms and legs that mended well; knew how to remove bullets, tend wounds and birth babies. Thus this rough, tough, blunt settler man and woman had learned through naked experience the requirements needed to face the rugged frontier life.

During the winter of 1781-1782, there came one of those rare occasions when the world was transformed into a fairyland. A time of low temperature when the rain and fog froze on every bush, vine, limb and tree. This silver coating twinkled like a multitude of diamonds. The trees, clothed with their sparkling coat, were bowed toward the earth with their load of beauty. The cedars of the Bluffs were a wondrous sight. It was the first time some of these people had ever seen the earth's vegetation covered with this miracle of nature. For a brief day, the worries and fears of human conflict were forgotten.

Then came the beating rains, turning this jeweled forest back into a wilderness of desolation. The work of survival continued. When hunters brought their kill of buffalo, deer, coon and bear into the compounds, the hides were one of the important parts of the animals. Careful attention was given to the curing of animal skins because of vital need. They were made into clothing, blankets, moccasins, shot bags and saddle bags. The hunting shirt and leggings were the chief dress of the men. They preferred moccasins made of buffalo hides rather than deer. Many of the women wore deerskin skirts and jackets. The shoemaker's

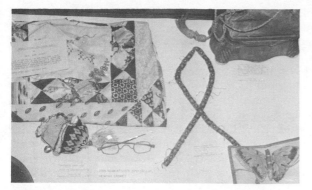

SEWING BASKET, GLASSES AND QUILT that belonged to Anne Robertson Cockrill. Displayed at Tennessee State Museum.

awl was the most used needle of the settlements. In addition to cooking meals and raising babies, the women learned to handle a gun along side of their men during an Indian attack. They doctored and stayed with the wounded men. When a cabin was to be raised, they would lend a hand at cooking, gossiping or helping raise a log. Even though ministers of the Gospel had not yet arrived for permanent congregations, they remembered the Sabbath and read the Scripture.

During February, a few people ventured short distances from the forts. The winter had been relatively quiet from Indian trouble. They hoped against hope that the Indians were gone. The redmen were still there. John Tucker and Joseph Hendricks were fired on between Freeland's and the Bluffs. They both suffered broken arms, but were able to outrun the Indians back to the stockade. A party made a search for the warriors without success. Ten days later David Hood was shot and scalped. He had gone out with two others when they were attacked. Here is a descriptive quote from Haywood:

They shot him down, scalped him; then ran in pursuit of the others toward the fort, but did not capture them. Hood, supposing the Indians were gone, got up softly and began walking toward the Bluffs, when, to his horror or mortification, he saw the same Indians. They began to make sport of such a dead man, blind and bloody, attempting to walk. They fell on him again, and having given him several new wounds, apparently mortal, they keeled him over and left him. He fell into a brushheap in the snow, and next morning he was tracked and found by his blood. He was taken to the fort and placed as a dead man in one of the outhouses and left alone. After some time he recovered, and lived many years.

The facts of this case have been well authenticated. After David Hood was placed in the outhouse (the reason he was placed there was to keep his body protected until his burial could be arranged), some of the women, who were very fond of Hood asked to see his body. When they examined Hood, they insisted that signs of life were there and had him carried into one of the cabins. With wounds dressed and some whiskey to warm his innards, he was before long able to speak. The women took turns nursing Hood. By summer he was back at his coopering.

Hood had the ready quip for any occasion. Always willing to show his scalped skull he would say, *"They got it, but still I hoodwinked them by playing 'possum' and saved my life."* I think my life is worth more than my crown-piece, the savages can't jerk me by the hair and get another trophy." *Another remark by Hood, "I am better dressed than that man who, 'cried in the wilderness before me'; he had but a leathern girdle, I am doubly skinned all over."* Hood wore animal skins made double for his coat.

DAVID HOOD

They said Hood remarked one day to some fellows in the fort who were complaining that they had nothing to eat, "How unlike they were to Jeshurum, who didn't kick until he was full and waxed fat." Hood's answer to an oft-repeated question, "Are we strong enough to stay?" was, "Better able to stay than to depart. Our strength is to sit still."

Early one morning, after the Hood event took place, many guns were heard blasting. It was turkeys; droves and droves of turkeys had come in. You could shoot them from the stockades and stations as they came within 50 yards of the fort walls. As the guns frightened the turkeys into the woods, hunters with their dogs hunted a stort distance in the forest. This change of diet gave the people a fresh outlook on life.

The Mauldins and Kilgores had erected a fort near the site of Cross Plains (Robertson County), thinking that the isolation of the spot would protect them from Indian trouble. When signs of new cabins showed, the redmen were soon there. Two Mason boys, watching for meat at a clay lick, shot two Indians and brought their scalps to Kilgore's fort. John and Ephraim Peyton, enroute to Kentucky, had stopped there for the night.

The people slept and the Indians moved. They stole all the horses including those belonging to the Peytons. This band was joined by another band that had been on a similar horse-stealing mission. At daybreak, the men, discovering their loss, began to follow the tracks on foot. They caught up with the Indians that night camped on the banks of a small creek. The whites fired on the culprits, killing one; the others fled. The horses and other loot were recovered. The men, tired after their day's march on foot, decided to make camp by the stream. This creek was later named Peyton's Creek.

While the men slept and rested, the Indians circled around them and set up an ambush along the trail that the men must follow on their return to the station. As the white party came in range, the redmen fired, mortally wounding Josiah Hawkins and one of the Mason boys. The men were able to reach the fort. After they had buried the two men, it was decided to abandon the station and move to Nashborough.

Reports of the increasing number of Indian killings in the vicinity, and the sounds of guns that might mean another death, brought the settlers to the point where all hope seemed lost. They began to pressure Robertson to lead them away. Some wanted to make boats and go to Illinois; others wanted to go to Kentucky. The harsh facts were that the Indians had stolen so many horses there was no transportation left. There were not enough horses in the Nashborough settlements to tend crops, much less to travel. But the people wanted to leave. They didn't want to stay and be picked off, one at a time, when they ventured outside the protection of the stations and forts.

Robertson resisted all the arguments for leaving with the following statements, *"With Indians watching all the trails, you would be killed." "We cannot stay in the woods long enough to secure trees to make boats." "Everyone must decide for themselves. My mind is made up; I have never thought of leaving. We have reason to believe that the war with England will not last much longer. Others will be arriving looking for land. The government is giving land grants to the soldiers who fought in the war; they will be coming." "We will have to fight it out here, or fight our way out from here."* Thus the die was cast; it was fight and hold on.

There was not much recorded documentation of events during these first three years. Most of the records are from remarks related in after years by people who were there: basically accurate, but colored with many years of telling.

HOMINY POUNDER

Sometime during the fall of 1782, Daniel Smith, William McMurray and other personalities came into the Cumberlands to take up grants obtained from North Carolina. Daniel Smith had been commissioned to make an experimental survey for grants being given Revolutionary War Soldiers by North Carolina. Daniel Smith married a daughter of Colonel John Donelson.

James Robertson somehow managed to attend the North Carolina Assembly this same year. He was responsible for getting an act passed to grant the Cumberland settlers rights of preemption. Each head of family that settled in the Cumberland Basin before June 1st, 1780, was granted 640 acres of land free of fee. Single men were also granted, free of the file fee, tracts with their improvements.

Salt Licks and Springs were reserved for public use. An act was also passed to establish a Court of Equity.

Heydon and James Wells, under guard, set up a corn mill and hominy pounder near Eaton's Station. It was slow, but an improvement over the hand pounder. Other mills were soon built in the vicinity of stations and forts.

THE NOTABLES
1783

News that the war had ended on the Atlantic Seaboard reached the Cumberlands by way of new immigrants. The people rejoiced. They felt that the peace treaty signed by the British would lessen the Indian problems. Freedom from the English King and the promising outlook of a country of their own were the topics of much fireside talk during the winter nights. There was a Fourth of July spirit in the air: some of the more jubilant men used their precious powder to noise up the celebration. New hopes brightened the hearts of the settlers.

PRIVATE PAPER BOX that belonged to James Robertson. Was carried to Nashville on "The Adventure" the Donelson boat on which Mrs. Robertson made the journey.

Judicial, political and civil functions had been performed rarely during the preceding years owing to the Indian presence. Few records were kept after the Cumberland Compact had been adopted and signed. There had been no official meetings of the elected court. The people had been too preoccupied with the business of survival. The family heads had been reduced to 70. One authority states that at the beginning of 1783 there were less than 200 men able to bear arms, but through Robertson's influence the valiant held on.

Preserved records show that new life began to infuse the leaders in early 1783. A call was given to the Stations to elect their judges, as per the Cumberland Compact, and the first assembly of the elected Notables is described in the following document:

NORTH CAROLINA, CUMBERLAND RIVER, JANUARY 7TH, 1783

The manifold sufferings and distresses that the settlers here have from time to time undergone, even almost from our first settling, with the desertion of the greater number of the first adventurers, being so discouraging to the remaining few, that all administration of justice seemed to cease from amongst us; which, however weak, whether in Constitution, administration, or execution, yet has been construed in our favor, against those whose malice or interest would insinuate us as people fled to a hiding place from justice, and the revival of them again earnestly recommended; and now, having a little respite granted, and numbers returning to us; it appears highly necessary that, for the common weal of the whole, the security of peace, the performance of contract between man and man, together with the suppression of vice, again to revive our former manner of proceedings, pursuant to the plan agreed upon at our first settling here; and to proceed accordingly, until such times as it shall please the Legislature to grant us the salutary benefit of the law duly administered amongst (us) by their authority.

To this end, previous notice having been given to the several stationers to elect 12 men of their several stations, whom they thought most proper for the business and being elected to meet at Nashborough on the 7th of January, 1783.

Accordingly, there met at the time and place aforesaid,

Colonel James Robertson	*Heydon Wells*
Captain George Freeland	*James Maulding*
Thomas Molloy	*Ebenezer Titus*
Isaac Linsey	*Samuel Barton*
David Rounsevall	*Andrew Ewin*

constituting themselves into a Committee for the purpose aforesaid, by voluntarily taking the following oath, viz.:

"I, A. B., do solemnly swear that, as a member of Committee, I will do equal right and justice, according to the best of my skill and judgment, in the decisions of all causes that shall be said before me, without fear, favor, or partiality. So help me God."

The Committee so constituted proceeded to elect Andrew Ewin as their Clerk, John Montgomery to be Sheriff of the district, and Colonel James Robertson to be their Chairman. And to fix the Clerk's fees.

As the year progressed, records indicate that the Notables convened fairly regularly. They tried cases and handled the civil functions in a well-regulated manner: almost an independent government that functioned with neither support nor much interference from the North Carolina Legislative body. Each Station was enjoined to set up its own military organization for better defense and security.

At Nashborough, William Pruett was made Captain; Samuel Martin, 1st Lieutenant; John Buchanan, 2nd Lieutenant; and William Overall, Ensign. Freeland's people selected Joshua Howard, Captain; James Donelson, Lieutenant; and John Dunham, Ensign. Heatensburg (Eaton's) chose Josiah Ramsey, Captain; James Hollis, Lieutenant; Joshua Thomas, Ensign. At Manskers (the Station was rebuilt that year about a mile from where the first structure stood), Isaac Bledsoe, Captain; Gasper Mansker, Lieutenant; and James Linn, Ensign. At Maulding's, Francis Prince, Captain; Ambrose Maulding, Lieutenant.

The Notables, in session April 1st, passed an act against persons bringing in liquors from foreign parts and selling it at exhorbitant prices. A heavy bond was to be given before such a sale could be made. If bond was not given or all requirements not met, the beverage could be seized.

A partial list of the killed and wounded this year includes Roger Top, Ireson and Barnett killed, and Roger Glass badly wounded. William, Joseph and Daniel Dunham, Betsy Williams, Joseph Nolan, and his father Thomas, were victims of Indian bullets. William Mulherrin, Samuel Buchanan and three others were slain while doing guard duty at Buchanan's. William Overall and Joshua Thomas were downed by red men

THE NOTABLES: the elected government officials of Nashborough, Davidson County, and Mero District during the 1780 decade.

The Indians made no big attacks and tried to avoid face-to-face fights. They preferred to pick the settlers off one at a time while remaining concealed.

The whites suffered a bad defeat during 1783. Captain Pruett with 20 men went after a party of Indians that had stolen several horses and fled. The horsemen caught up with the party and, after a fierce attack, the braves fled. Taking the recovered horses, the men started back toward the Bluffs, camping that night on Duck River. As daylight came, the Indians surrounded their camp in the canebrakes and began firing. Most of the whites escaped to more open ground, where they made a stand. The Indians, with a force much larger than the whites, advanced and the battle started. The whites had to abandon their recovered horses, and those of their fallen comrades, and beat a fast retreat toward the Fort. Moses Brown, Daniel Pruett and Daniel Johnson were killed; Morris Shine and several others were wounded. The victory was a great event for the Indians.

The Notables, in the May session, sent a letter to the Spanish Governor and leaders in other sections disavowing that any citizens of the Cumberlands were mixed up with, or participants in, the piracy activities on the Mississippi River. Another bill stated that no person or inhabitant of the settlements could trade with the Indians beyond certain boundaries, without special permission from the Governing Body.

CHICKASAW TREATY

During the early months of the settlement after the Renfro Massacre, and attack on Freeland's, Robertson had conferred with Piomingo, Chief of the Chickasaws, and they had reached an agreement. In Kentucky, Colonel John Donelson had written Governor Benjamin Harrison urging that a treaty with the Chickasaws at French Lick was necessary to secure rights to certain lands that were needed. The Virginia Governor appointed Colonel Donelson, Colonel Joseph Martin and Colonel Isaac Shelby to arrange treaties not only with the Chickasaws, but with all of the Southern Tribes.

Goods, presents and grain were shipped from Richmond to Long Island (Kingsport), on the Holston River, and from there on to French Lick (Nashborough). The Virginia and Kentucky interest was a big tract of land between the Tennessee Ohio and Mississippi Rivers.

Major John Reid was sent to the Cumberland Territory to make arrangements for the treaty. Colonel Robertson was opposed to having the Virginia Treaty held at Nashborough. He felt, as did others, that assembling so many Indians at the Fort, where so much fighting had occurred, was a bad idea. He insisted that a vote of the people be taken, a sort of pioneer poll. Here we quote from Williams the minutes of the June 3rd meeting of the Notables:

STATE OF NORTH CAROLINA
CUMBERLAND DISTRICT
June 3, 1783

The Committee met according to adjournment; members present, Colonel James Robertson, George

CHICKASAW TREATY OAK, where Virginia Commissioners met with Chickasaw Chiefs and Cumberland people June 1783. Tree is gone but marker designates the site. Tennessee State Library

Freeland, Thomas Malloy, Ebenezer Titus, Samuel Barton, James Shaw, Isaac Bledsoe, David Rounsevall Heydon Wells.

When on motion made by Major John Reid, relative to assembling of the Southern Tribes of Indians at the French Lick, on Cumberland River, for holding a treaty with the commissioners appointed by the State of Virginia; when the committee, considering how difficult it will be for a handful of people reduced to poverty and distress by a continued scene of Indian barbarity, to furnish any large body of Indians with provisions and how prejudicial it may be to our infant settlement should they not be furnished with provisions, or otherwise disaffected with the terms of the treaty; on which considerations the committee refer it to suffrages of the people of this settlement whether the treaty shall be held here with their consent or no and that the suffrages of the several stations be delivered to the Clerk of the Committee by Thursday evening June 5th inst., at which time the suffrages of Freeland's Station, Heatonsburg, and Nashborough were given in, and are as follows: Freeland's Station, no treaty here, votes 32; Heatonsburg (Eaton's), treaty here, votes 54; no treaty, 1; Nashborough, no treaty here, votes 26; for a treaty here, votes 30.

For the treaty the votes total 84 ayes, against the treaty 59 nays. Mansker and Maulings did not return their vote.

The Chickasaws set the time of the meeting in June, 1783. The site selected was Sulpher Springs, about four miles from Fort Nashborough. A large body of Chickasaws attended. Piomingo, The Mountain Leader and Mingo-Homa, The Red King, were among the many Chiefs present.

The Chiefs ceded a large segment of land on the south side of the Cumberland River. Most of the ceded lands were in the Cumberland Basin and the present-day Tennessee. The affair created a lasting friendship between the Cumberland people and the Chickasaws. This was to prove useful on future occasions. The irony was that Virginia footed the bill and the Cumberland Settlers reaped the benefit. It is said that this is one of the few times that James Robertson erred in his judgment; thanks to the Eaton vote, the treaty was held.

DAVIDSON COUNTY

The Cumberland Settlements were legislated into a civil body October 6th, 1783, by the North Carolina Government. The bill reads:

Be it enacted by the General Assembly of the State of North Carolina, and it is hereby enacted by the authority of the same, That all that part of the State lying west of the Cumberland Mountains where the Virginia line crosses, extending westward along the said line to the Tennessee River, thense up said River to the mouth of Duck Creek, thence up Duck Creek to where the line of marked trees, run by the Commissioners for laying off land granted the Continental Line of this State, intersects said river (which said line is supposed to be in thirty-five degrees, fifty minutes north latitude), thence east along said line to the top of Cumberland Mountain, thence northwardly along said mountain to the beginning, shall after the passage of this act be, and is hereby declared to be a district County by the name of Davidson.

This boundary included nearly 12,000 square miles and covered more than three-fourths of the present Middle Tennessee Area.

The County was named Davidson in honor of General William Lee Davidson of Mecklenburg County, North Carolina. For a period during the Revolutionary War, until his death at Cowan's Ford on the Catawba River, he was in command of the Salisbury District Militia, which included all of Tennessee. He was aiding General Daniel Morgan escape with prisoners taken at Cowpens when he was shot by Tories at the crossing.

The Notables, who made up the court, selected a site and drew up plans for a courthouse at Nashborough. The building was to be 18 feet square and built out of hewed logs. A lean-to, or shed, 12 feet wide was to be added to one end. Benches, a bar and a table were to be constructed for the use of the court. The prison was to be of hewed logs one foot square, with a floor and the loft boarded. The same was to be built on rock. The erection of these buildings was let out on bid, to the lowest bidder, on October 14th, 1783.

One important sign of the Cumberland progress during this year was the big increase in population. New settlers were arriving in sizable numbers, some coming from unexpected sources. In the final treaty between the Spanish and English in the South, all claims of the British were relinquished. Many grants had been given as service payments to soldiers serving in the French-Canadian War. Most of these grants were in the Natchez Country.

Putnam, Schuyler and Lyman were among those locating around Natchez. Many Cumberland, Tory-inclined settlers had moved south and taken up claims. Lyman thought they were strong enough to run the Spanish out of that vicinity. Enlisting all the Tories and non-Tories into a good-sized force, an attack was made against Fort Panmure, on the Bluffs of Natchez. Lyman's force soon overran the small garrison, but their victory was short-lived. News was received that a large Spanish force was coming upriver to retake the settlement. Dire threats were made against those responsible for the uprising. All the English leaders and Tories fled. Among the group reaching the Cumberlands were Philip Alston, John Turnbull, James Drumgold, James Cole, John Turner, Thomas Hines, Thomas James and Philip Mulkey, a sometime preacher and father of Jonathan Mulkey, one of the early Baptist preachers of Tennessee.

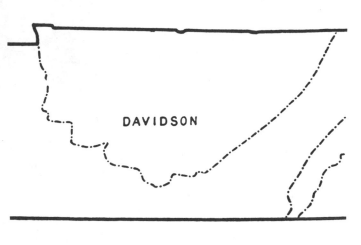

News that a Commission from North Carolina was coming out to survey land grants for the military caused much hope. The Commission was to be accompanied by a force of 100 soldiers, who would escort a large number of families coming west to take up grants. This militia proved to afford the Cumberland people very little relief from the Indians.

Other outstanding personalities, whose family names are well known, arrived about the same time as the Commission. Colonel William Polk had been appointed by North Carolina as surveyor-general for the Cumberland Basin, that territory now known as Middle Tennessee. He arrived December, 1783, accompanied by Henry Rutherford and Ezekial Polk. Polk had a batch of hand warrants for soldiers and many others that he acquired for himself and his father, Thomas Polk. Ezekial was the grandfather of President Polk.

WILLIAM POLK

NASHBOROUGH TO NASHVILLE
1784

The North Carolina Commissioners began their surveys January, February and March of 1784. During these months the foliage was off the trees, making the job easier. The North Carolina Legislative Act of 1782 had awarded Revolutionary Soldiers grants in this military reservation. Following is a classification of grants.

Privates 640 acres; Non-Commissioned officers 1,000 acres; Subalterns 2,560 acres; Captains, 3,840 acres; Lieutenant Colonels, 7,200 acres; Brigadier-Generals 12,000 acres. The three Commissioners, Absolom Tatom, Isaac Shelby and Anthony Bledsoe, were to receive 5,000 acres each for their services. Surveyors, chainbearers and guards were awarded grants for their work.

One of the unusual parts of this survey was for grant to General Nathanael Greene for 25,000 acres. These lands were laid off on Duck River in the present County of Maury. The deed was the first deed registered in Greene County. Greene County was cut off from Washington in 1783, and for a short period encompassed all of present Tennessee except Washington, Sullivan and Davidson Counties.

The Court of Pleas and Quarter Sessions was convened in January of 1784. Justices Isaac Bledsoe, Samuel Barton, Francis Prince, Isaac Linsey, James Robertson, Thomas Malloy, Anthony Bledsoe and Daniel Smith sat during this session. They went through the agenda of civil and legal needs as indicated on the memoranda. One of the items discussed at length was the "Colbert Pirate Gang" operating on the Mississippi.

James Colbert was a Chickasaw half-breed Chief. After the British defeat at Pensacola, by the Spanish, Colbert decided to prey on every Spanish boat that plied the Mississippi. John Turner, a Tory that had fled the Natchez threat to the Cumberlands, left Nashborough with other Tories not wanted and joined Colbert and his gang. They captured several well-stocked Spanish boats. Some French and American boats were

ROCK CASTLE, home of General Daniel Smith is located in Hendersonville. The foundation was laid 1784 on land granted to Smith for Revolutionary War service. It was seven years in building. Several workers were killed by Indians. Daniel Smith was Secretary of Southwest Territorial Government. It was Smith who suggested TENNESSEE as the state name.

boarded. They became a menace to most any and every boat plying the river.

John Montgomery had been elected Sheriff of Davidson County when the County Court was organized. More interested in exploration of the country than the job of Sheriff, he paid little attention to his duties. He was in high respect in the community. His campaign with George Rogers Clarke gave him the rank of Colonel. It was rumored that Montgomery was connected with the Colbert Gang and charges had been preferred against him. He was ordered to appear at the next term of Court to answer charges. Elijah Robertson and Stephen Ray signed his bond to the amount of 150 pounds. Montgomery never did appear in court. The rumor was never proved. The charge eventually was dropped and Montgomery's name seems to have been exonerated.

Previous legislation had given the first permanent Cumberland settlers their grants of land.They asked that the State Commission give them legal certificates. No copies have been found. Sixty-four families deprived of their head by Indian killings were awarded land titles. Some of the first families to settle, who left and then returned, paid their fee and resettled.

During the July, 1784, session of the Davidson County Court, the name Nashborough was changed to Nashville. The name of Nash had been suggested by Richard Henderson when the Cumberland Pact was written. Francis Nash had served as a Clerk in the North Carolina Court presided over by Judge Henderson. Nash was killed in the war against the British during the Germantown Battle, September, 1777. The Court merely shortened the name by changing "borough" to "ville."

The town was laid off in lots. Samuel Barton, Thomas Mulloy, James Shaw, Daniel Smith and Isaac Linsey were named as trustees. Samuel Barton was named treasurer. The first deeds to Nashville lots bear dates of April 8th, 1785. A purchaser was supposed to build within three years. The building was to be well framed, log, brick or stone, 16 feet square with eight foot pitch. This was one of the earliest zoning laws.

The "White's Creek Battle" or the "Battle for the Doe" happened during 1784. Nicholas Trammel and Philip Mason had killed a doe and were in the act of skinning it when attacked by Indians. Trammel went back to the fort for help. Mason hid to keep watch. Arriving back at the scene with more ammunition and some men who volunteered to help, they found Mason still able to fight. They went to where the deer had been hanging, but the skinned doe was gone.

They were determined to follow the Indians and put them to route. The plain trail gave evidence of a large party. The whites were so eager to catch the Indians that no notice was taken that the tracks became fewer as more distance was covered. An occasional brave would peal from the main group and hide away from the trail until the whites had passed, then he would take up the trail behind them. Thus the settlers were led into an ambush. The riders finally catching up with the main body dismounted to give battle. Meanwhile, the Indians in the rear closed in to wipe the white hunters out. The rear band of Indians captured the horses immediately--the whites were far enough away. The whites had no alternative but to

BATTLE OF THE DOE   **BATTLE OF THE KEGS**

run for their lives. They scattered through the forest, every man for himself. The braves, meanwhile, happy with capturing the horses and the fresh meat, didn't make too much effort to pursue.

Trammel had not gone far before he met another group who had come to help. He persuaded five of them to go with him to Mason's aid. Mason had been mortally wounded during the first battle. Josiah Haskins proved a bold, though foolhardy, partner in the undertaking. The battle turned out to be a draw, but Trammel and Haskins, thinking they were winning, fell for another Indian ruse and paid with their lives.

Another fight not far distant took place shortly after this. We quote from Putnam:

Aspie, together with Andrew Lucas, Thomas Sharp Spencer, and one Johnson, had left the Bluff on horseback, to go on a hunting tour to the headwaters of Drake's Creek. In crossing the creek their horses stopped to drink; that was when the Indians opened fire. Lucas was shot through the neck and mouth. He dismounted, but in attempting to fire, the blood gushed out of his mouth and wet his priming. Perceiving this, he crawled into a bunch of briers. Aspie (Espie), as he alighted from his horse received a wound which broke his thigh, but still he fought heroically. Johnston and Spencer acquitted themselves with imcomparable gallantry, but were obliged to give way, and leave Aspie to his fate, though he entreated them earnestly not to forsake him. The Indians killed and scalped Aspie, but did not find Lucas, who shortly after returned to his friends. The whole family of the Aspies were superlatively brave.

Cornelius Riddle had killed two turkeys and hung them in a tree while hunting for others. The Indians waited in ambush, killed him when he returned for his turkeys. His companions fled.

During 1784, Colonel Isaac Bledsoe built a fort at the Lick by his name. Colonel Anthony Bledsoe built a station some two or three miles away at Greenfield.

Many cases, involving fights, collecting debts, false entries and Tories were heard by the Notables during this year. One such case was "A Cask of Red Wine." Since imported spirits had been banned by the courts, a cask of red wine shipped from Cas-kas-kia, Illinois, had been slipped into Nashville. We quote from Putnam:

"Everybody wished to taste it." Many feared the Mississippi River had faded its redness and reduced its quality; they were, however, perfectly willing "to taste it, free, gratis, for nothing." "Some offered a deer skin for a quart or pint of it." "The Honorable Lardner Clarke, Sam Martin of course, Mr. Wycuff, Mr. Truckey (both proper men), John East and John Sigvault were prominent litigants, or consarned." "The Batteau" in which the cask was conveyed from port to port is an object of interest. "The Battle of The Kegs" was fought again here. No record tells who finally got the keg of red wine in the fight for ownership.

DOCTORS – SCHOOLS – IDOLS
1785

Indian attacks and harassments, in all sections of the Cumberland Community, continued to be a source of worry and trouble to the people as 1785 became part of their calendar. Even so, new arrivals were adding to the growth of the population. Some Spanish authorities reported that by the end of 1785 there were upwards of 4000 people settled in the valley.

New stations were being built. One by William Hall, James Harrison and William Gibson was just above Bledsoe's Lick. Another west of Bledsoe's at the mouth of Dry Fork by Charles Morgan. Moses Brown built a cabin with very poor palisades near Richland Creek, just a short distance from Nashborough. Brown was killed and scalped soon after getting settled. Near the same area, William Stewart was slain. Edmund Hickman, a surveyor, was killed on Piney River.

These killings by the Indians were a sharp reminder that constant watch and caution were needed. Rumors were also spread through the settlement that the Spanish Authorities were planning to restrict all navigation on the Mississippi River. The River Route was about the only way the Kentucky and Cumberland people could get their hides and farm produce to market. Robertson and the Notables carried on some correspondence with the Spanish officials. This started the rumor, which persisted many years, that they were forming an alliance with Spain. This did not receive a very popular reception. Many of the settlers, who had fought through one war to get rid of the British yoke, didn't want to have another King saddled on their freedom. James Robertson was constantly asking the people to have caution and patience. Favors would be needed from the Spaniards, so diplomacy was better than abuse. Robertson also told them that adherence to their country would bring prosperity. Robertson told the people, "a favor and protection which wolves give lambs."

One of the big events of the year was the arrival of Doctor John Sappington in Nashborough. He had the courtly airs and conduct of a fine man from the East. His bedside manner and vigilance, during sick hours, won him a great welcome with the settlers. His sugar-coated pills were much easier to take than the bitter homemade remedies of the pioneers. His practice attracted support and much following. His popularity lasted until he unwittingly revealed the formula of his concoctions. The people found out that they had been using the same herbs, roots and nature remedies for years without having to pay the Doctor's fee.

James Robertson left the first of November, accompanied by Col. Isaac Bledsoe, to attend the 1785 session of the North Carolina Legislature. He and Bledsoe were the Davidson County Representatives. They had to make the long, hazardous journey on horseback. When they arrived in Hillsborough, where the session was to be held, they naturally learned of the treaty being held with the Cherokee at Hopewell, South Carolina, on the Keowee River. Congress had directed that this treaty be arranged. They had not bothered to consult the Overmountain people who were most concerned with the results. The Treaty began November 18th and lasted until November 28th. It started one day before the opening of the Assembly.

It is possible that the results of the Treaty or its contents became known before the Assembly adjourned. Robertson, along with most of the North Carolina leaders, was strongly opposed to its contents. Benjamin Hawkins and Joseph Martin of North Carolina, Andrew Pickens of South Carolina, and Lachlan McIntosh of Georgia were the Commissioners selected by Congress to hold the Treaty. The Indians were granted nearly the same legislative and judicial right as American citizens and promised the boundaries set up in the Treaty, which would move many whites from their cabin sites. A map drawn by The Tassel of the Cherokees was used during the Treaty.

FIRST DOCTOR HANGS SHINGLE

BELOW — Illustration of early school building.

North Carolina leaders so opposed the make-up of the agreement that it was not passed at the 1786 Assembly. Even though the Treaty was ratified by Congress it was never effective.

DAVIDSON ACADEMY

In spite of the menace of Indian harassment the settlers, realizing the need of formal education for their children, made plans for schools. During the early years of the Cumberland and other frontier settlements, some of the communities would set a day and gather at a chosen site for the purpose of erecting a building to be used for schooling. Trees would be selected and cut, logs shaped and cut in proper lengths and size. Often, as the walls were going up, one log would be left out on one side of the building to permit the room to be lighted. Hewed logs with peg legs would serve as benches. Another long log would be shaped and placed along one wall to be used as a writing desk. The school would last three months each year. Some man with good character and religious morals would be selected as teacher. His qualifications should be ability to read, write and do arithmetic sums as far as the double rule of three. He would teach five days each week, 12 hours each day. His fee must be reasonable.

Robertson, citing the needs for a State-chartered school in Davidson County, was able to get an act passed the last day of the Legislative session for the establishment of an Institution of Learning. The school was to be named Davidson Academy, which was later changed to Cumberland College, and then to The University of Nashville. The school did not get into active operation until the next year.

CASTALIAN SPRINGS

The original description of Bledsoe's Lick, or Castalian Springs, as it is known today, is hereby given as Haywood wrote it in his "Natural and Aboriginal History of Tennessee," published 1823, and reprinted 1959 by Mary U. Rothrock.

In the County of Sumner at Bledsoe's Lick eight miles northeast from Gallatin, about 200 yards from the lick, in a circular enclosure between Bledsoe's Lick Creek and Bledsoe's Spring Branch, upon level ground, is a wall 15 or 18 inches in height, with projecting angular elevations of the same height as the wall: and within it are about 16 acres of land. In the interior is a raised platform from 13 to 15 feet above the common surface, about 200 yards from the wall to the south, and about 50 yards from the northern part of it. This platform is 60 yards in length and breadth and is level on the top. And to the east of a mound to which it joins, of 7 or 8 feet higher elevation, or 18 feet from the common surface to the summit, about 20 feet square. On the eastern side of the latter mound is a small cavity, indicating that steps were once there, for the purpose of ascending from the platform to the top of the mound. In the year 1785 there grew on top of the mound a black oak three feet through. There is no water within the circular enclosure or court. Upon top of the mound was ploughed up some years ago, an image made of sandstone. On one cheek was a mark resembling a wrinkle, passing perpendicularly up and down the cheek. On the other cheek were two similar marks. The breast was that of a female, and prominent. The face was turned obliquely up towards the heavens. The palms of the hands were turned upwards before the face, and at some distance from it, in the same direction that the face was. The knees were drawn near together; and the feet, with the toes towards the ground, were separated wide enough to admit of the body being seated between them. The attitude seemed to be that of adoration. The head and upper part of the forehead was represented as covered with a cap, or mitre, or bonnet, from the lower part of which came horizontally a brim, from the extremities of which the cap extended conically. The color of the image was that of a dark infusion of coffee. If the front of the image were placed in the east, and the countenance obliquely elevated, and the uplifted hands in the same direction, would be towards the meridian sun. Near to this mound is a cave, which contained at the time of the first settlements by the whites a great number of human skulls, without any other appearance of human bones near them.

SPENCER TREE: Hollow tree in which Thomas Spencer lived for a period was near Castalian Springs formerly known as Bledsoe's Lick.

THE OLD TAVERN, now renovated, was erected by Colonel Anthony Wynne 1812 a short distance from Castalian Springs.

New settlers continued to arrive and locate claims in the new frontier. Many of the newcomers were Revolutionary War soldiers taking up their Land Grants awarded by the Government in payment for services. New stations and cabins were being raised in all sections of Davidson County. A letter written from the Cumberlands stated that during 1785 over a thousand families from across the mountains and the Watuaga country had moved to Cumberland and Kentucky Country.

The Cumberland militia, commanded by Captains Rains, Gordon and Castleman, were on constant patrol. The marauding Indian parties on constant watch could avoid these patrols. The redmen knew hidden trails through the dense canebrakes and wide stretches of wilderness unknown to the whites.

Indian killings were still reported from the stations. Peter Barnet and David Steele were ambushed by the Indians near the present site of Clarksville. William Crutchen was wounded, but managed to make one of the forts.

Colonel John Donelson had moved his family to Kentucky late in 1780. Many other families made the migration at the same time. Colonel Donelson settled near Davis Station in the vicinity of Harrod's. During the five years residence in Kentucky, he was active in locating and surveying land claims, many of them for himself. Earlier he had helped in running the boundary line between North Carolina and Virginia. Kentucky did not prove a safe sanctuary for John Donelson as he was killed by the Indians during the early part of 1786.

This episode is paraphrased from Putnam. John Peyton, surveyor, his brothers Ephraim and Thomas Peyton, Thomas Pugh, John Frazer and Esquire Grant were surveying grants during February, 1786. Tired from the rugged work of the day, they made camp on a small island above the mouth of a creek that feeds into the Cumberland River. They had finished eating and were lying around the campfire, which had been chunked for the night. One report says that they had played cards for awhile. The horses were tethered close by and the dogs, used for hunting, were near the fire. The dogs showed signs of unwanted presence in the area. The men seemed to think that the leavings from the fresh game killed that evening had attracted wolves and other wild animals to the vicinity.

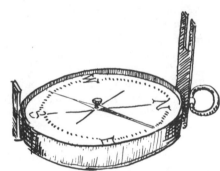

No watch was set and no special scout had been made to check on possible presence of Indians. They had all lain down, ready for sleep, expecting no trouble.

A band of some 60 Cherokee Indians, led by Chief Hanging Maw, had approached within firing range without disturbing their quiet. The dogs made known the foreign presence, but the men paid no heed. When the guns blasted at the men around the campfire, four were wounded. John Peyton had presence of mind to throw his blanket over the fire, making escapé possible in the darkness. All six men managed to make their way through the Indian lines and get away. Each man went his own way, bareheaded and barefooted. They managed to travel some 70 miles in this condition over snow-covered ground to Bledsoe's Station. As each man struggled into the station, separately, he reported that the others had been killed. Ephraim Peyton and Thomas Pugh were not wounded, but Peyton sprained his ankle badly and had to crawl a piece before he could find a stout tree limb to help him limp along. The excitement over easy capture of horses, meat and other plunder must have retarded any pursuit by the Indians. All of the men recovered and continued their activities.

John Peyton, in a message to the Indian Chief, told him that he could have the horses and gear, but to please return his compass. Hanging Maw replied, "You ran like cowards, as for your land stealer (compass) I have broken it against a tree." The stream where the attack took place has been named "Defeated Creek."

Sometime during 1786, two gentlemen with their green saddle bags arrived from the East with their families. Their names were Edward Douglas and Thomas Mulloy. They announced to one and all that they would practice law in Davidson County. They had no formal legal training, but being glib of tongue and smart thinkers they soon had clients. Their law library consisted of some pamphlets listing the North Carolina laws. This was the first Cumberland law shingle hung up. Their wives were well received because they brought fresh news and gossip from the seaboard. They enlivened the social life of Nashville with their talk and entertainment.

The Notables, and Colonel Robertson in particular, continued to express in strong terms their disapproval of the Hopewell Treaty. It has been reported nevertheless, that Indian depredations were somewhat less during 1786, but the wise were still cautious and careful.

North Carolina looked on the Overmountain Settlements as distant and almost foreign countries. Because of the Franklin controversy, they granted the Davidson County people almost any request in legislative acts, provided the State Treasury didn't have to foot the bill. They wanted the land and jurisdiction without the responsibility. Thus the Notables were practically the legislative, judicial and military authorities in this faraway American province.

Putnam has taken this act of the Quarter Sessions Court from the records. We quote:

Whereas, the frequent acts of hostility committed by the Indians upon the inhabitants of this county for a considerable time past, render it necessary that measures should be taken for their protection:
1. *Be it resolved, that 210 men shall be enlisted and formed into a military body, for the protection of said inhabitants, to rendezvous at the lower end of Clinch Mountain.*
2. *Every able-bodied man shall enlist and furnish himself with a good rifle or smooth-bored gun, one good picker, shot-bag, powder-horn, twelve good flints, 1 lb. good powder, 2 lbs. lead-bullets or suitable shot, shall be entitled to receive each year, for his services, one blanket, one good woolen or fur hat of middle size, one pair of buckskin breeches and waistcoat lined.*

A tax was levied, payable in specie: corn, pork, beef or other provisions. This was for the use of the troops. Officers were allowed the same clothing as the Privates. The Paymaster could draw on the Sheriff of Davidson for money to buy powder and lead for the soldiers.

The State of Franklin was talked of in the community. Many sympathized with the Franks in their effort to establish a separate state. Cumberland did not participate in this struggle, but most likely would have become part of Franklin if the movement had succeeded. Robertson and Sevier were very close friends. Colonel Robertson had hinted of this idea in some of his letters to Sevier. More is said of Franklin in another section.

When James Robertson returned to the Cumberlands, he immediately started getting things organized for the school chartered by the North Carolina Assembly. Having secured a Schoolhead in the person of Rev. Thomas B. Craighead, he proceeded to make plans for financing the school. Trustees named were Thomas B. Craighead, Hugh Williamson, Daniel Smith, William Polk, Anthony Bledsoe, Lardner Clarke, Ephraim McClean, Robert Hays and James Robertson.

Various plans were promoted to raise money to finance the academy. Many families donated land, tax free for 99 years. A ferry was built and the toll receipts put in the Academy fund. Craighead had built a small church building some six miles from Nashborough Fort. It was called "Spring Hill Meeting House." The school met here for 15 years. Finally a suitable building was erected in Nashville. This academy was to grow into The University of Nashville.

The first merchant in Nashville set up his emporium of business in 1786. Lardner Clark, with ten pack horses, brought his stock of needles, thimble, thread, pins, pans, calico, pewter plates, iron pots, etc. and started his store. Lardner Clark, Merchant and Ordinary Keeper and Provender for Horses, served the community about six years. He accepted skins and pelts in exchange for good.

An act of the North Carolina Assembly of this year divided Davidson County. The new County was to be named Sumner. Many soldiers settled in this area of The Cumberlands had served under Brigadier-General Jethro Sumner of the North Carolina line. It seemed only natural that they honor their Country with his name.

SUMNER COUNTY
1787

One big event of the year 1787 was the erection of Sumner County. The map indicates its first general size and shape. Principal streams were Goose, Bledsoe, Station Camp, Drake and Mansker. Springs were Tyree and Bledsoe's Lick, now known as Castalian Springs.

Magistrates of the new County were General Daniel Smith, Major David Wilson, Major George Winchester, Isaac Lindsey, William Hall, John Hardin and Joseph Keykendall. The first meeting was held in the home of

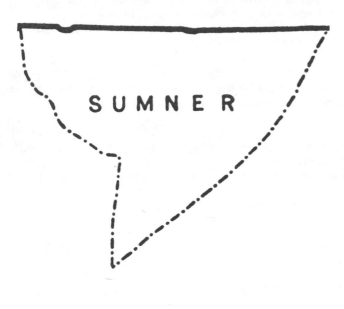

John Hamilton the second Monday of April, 1787. David Shelby was elected Clerk. Colonel Isaac Bledsoe and Edward Douglas were later added as Magistrates. These men were responsible for the civil and military administration of Sumner County.

Newcomers during this year took up claims along the Red River. They were told of the many Indian atrocities in that area. They thought the isolation and seclusion of their cabin sites would protect them. The roving bands of warriors soon located these clearings and the people were soon exposed to killings and scalping. Constant rumors spread through the settlement that the Indians, backed by the Spanish officials, were forming an army to wipe out the Cumberland frontiersmen. "We want horses and Nashville is the place to get them. Let us show the the white men that we can fight in armies as well as they."

During 1787, David Hays was elected to serve with James Robertson as Representative to the North Carolina Legislature. The Assembly met in Tarborough this year. A paper was prepared describing the conditions of the people in this distant province of the State. We quote from Putnam:

The Inhabitants of the western country are greatly distressed by a constant war that is carried on against them by parties of Creeks, Cherokees and some of the western Indians; that some of their horses were daily carried off secretly or by force, and that their own lives are in danger whenever they lose sight of a station of stockade; that in the course of the present year thirty-three of their fellow citizens had been killed by the Indians, [a list of names was annexed] and as many more were wounded; that by original letters or talks from the Chickasaw Nation, which they submitted to the Assembly, it appeared that they were uneasy or jealous lest encroachments should be made on their hunting grounds; and that unless some assurances were given them that their lands should not be located, there was reason to apprehend that they shortly would be as hostile as the Creeks and Cherokees (Chickamaugas); that these counties have been settled at great expense and personal danger to the memorialists and their constituents, and that by such settlements the adjacent lands were increased in value, by which means the public has been enabled to sink a considerable part of its domestic debt.

They and their constituents [say these worthy representatives] have cheerfully endured the almost unconquerable difficulties in settling the western country, in full confidence that they should be enabled to send their produce to market through the rivers which water the country; but now we have the mortification not only to be excluded from that channel of commerce by a foreign nation, but the Indians are rendered more hostile, through the influence of that very nation [Spain] with a view to drive them from the country, as they claim the whole of the soil.

We call upon the humanity and justice of the State to prevent any further massacres and depredations of ourselves and our constituents; and we claim from the Legislature that protection of life and property which is due to every citizen, and recommend, as the most safe and convenient means of relief, the adoption of the Resolves of Congress, of the 26th October last; [that the States which owned western lands cede them to the U. S.].

William Blount assisted Robertson and Hays in preparing this paper. It told of Spanish influence with the Indians and their encouragement of the attacks while North Carolina officials seemingly ignored these facts in their talks and communications with the Dons.

COLDWATER

Many of the Indian bands harassing the settlements came from Dragging Canoe's people, the Chickamaugas. Robertson, after a council with his leaders, made plans to raise a force and invade the town of Coldwater in the vicinity of Muscle Shoals. He had been told by government officials to defend, but not to make offensive campaigns. Thus the offensive became the defensive. The Coldwater Expedition was made soon after Mark Robertson, brother of James, was killed by the Indians May, 1787.

Two friendly Chickasaws agreed to pilot the force of 120 men to the Shoals. Colonel James Robertson was Commander in Chief of the campaign. Supporting officers were Colonel Robert Hays and Lieutenant Colonel James Ford.

A fortilla of three boats under command of David Hays was going the river route. Captain Rains referred to Hays as Admiral Hays, and Shelby as Commodore Shelby. These boats carried extra supplies and were to be used to carry the troops across the river when the Shoals was reached. It was thought that the boats would arrive before the armed force. Another purpose of the boats was to bring the wounded back if so needed.

Moses Shelby was in charge of one boat. The 20 men going by boat used poles and paddles to propel the canoe-like vessel. They had proceeded along the Tennessee as far as the mouth of Duck Creek. Shelby, seeing a canoe near the bank of the river, pulled his boat over to investigate. A body of Indians, concealed on the banks, fired on the Shelby boat. Josiah Renfroe was killed, John Top, Hugh Roquering and Edward Hogan were wounded. Shelby was able to move his boat back to midstream to hold a consultation with the others. They decided to return to the settlements to better doctor the wounded. At Eaton's, the supplies from the boats were stored, until the return of the land army.

Meanwhile the land force, with a big farewell from the families that had gathered, set forth on their rough, hazardous journey. The hard, twisting march took them by the mouth of Little Harpeth, up Turnbull's Creek and on to Lick Creek. They turned across country to Swan Creek, then to Blue Water Creek which empties into Tennessee River near Muscle Shoals.

Coldwater, inhabited mostly by Creeks, was on the other side of the river. Many French traders living there furnished much of the guns, whiskey and other goods to the Indians in exchange for their animal

skins. Wishing to keep this trade, they encouraged the constant attacks against the Cumberland people.

The scouts report, that the expected flotilla of boats had not arrived, posed a difficult problem of getting the soldiers and ammunition across the river. This was eventually accomplished. Several of the men swam across with their horses. A leather boat carried ammunition and some of the men by making several trips. A heavy rain caused the men to take refuge in some deserted cabins found across the river. Here they ate breakfast and partially dried their clothing before marching orders were given. Scouts had, and were, keeping a sharp lookout ahead.

They followed a worn path some six miles before coming to some patches of corn near Coldwater. Robertson sent Captain Rains and a body of men to the mouth of the creek, on which the town was located, to prevent possible escape by boat. Allowing Rains and his men time to get near their position, Robertson led his men in a charge across the creek and into the Indian town. The warriors, learning of the white army's approach, fled to their boats in an effort to escape. They were in the act of pushing loaded boats into the water when the Rains company arrived and began firing. 26 Indians were killed, as were three French Traders and one white woman. Six half-breed traders, and the number one French Trader, were taken prisoners. Most of the Indian women and children had fled into the safety of the canebrakes. They were not pursued and hunted down.

Much French goods, such as rum, sugar, coffee, clothing, blankets, beads, paints, knives, tomahawks, powder, lead, guns and ammunition were captured. The personal property of the Indians was placed outside in a safe place, where they could find it. The cabins were burned. Robertson did not pursue the campaign further. He had demonstrated the ability of the Cumberland Militia to attack the Indian towns.

Early next morning, the captured boats were loaded with the captured property and the captives. This flotilla was placed in charge of Jonathan Denton, Benjamin Drake, John and Moses Eskridge. When the boats had reached Colbert's Ferry, the French Traders were given one of the lighter boats with sufficient provisions and allowed to continue down the river toward the Wabash, where their homes were located. The captured Indian boats loaded with the supplies continued on to the mouth of the Cumberland River

and back up that stream toward Nashville. En route, they met other French traders with boats loaded with goods intended for the Indians. They captured this bounty and took the supplies along.

Toka and the other Chickasaw guide were given one horse each, with full equipment and all the goods they could pack on the two horses. This is said to have pleased them greatly.

Robertson's men came through the battle without loss. The goods obtained were distributed among the men after their return home. For many days after this campaign, the settlements were not bothered. However, too much confidence was placed in the results of the battle. The lull lasted about a month, then small bands began raiding the Cumberlands with more hostility than ever. Militia groups chased the warriors after many such raids.

One one such occasion, Captain Shannon and a company chased after a raiding party. When the Indians were contacted, a hand-to-hand fight ensued. The Indians were led by "Big Foot" Oo-la-se-la-na. His

172

footprints were said to be as large as those of Thomas Sharp Spencer. Chief "Big Foot" was killed and the leaderless band of redmen fled into the woods.

In July, Robertson received the report that a force of 200 Creeks were headed towards the Cumberland country. It was also rumored that this force was backed by the Spanish. This large body of warriors did not attack in force. They broke up into several small parties that harassed, stole and killed in many sections of Davidson and Sumner Counties.

HELP COMES SLOWLY

Major John Evans was commissioned by the North Carolina Authorities to enlist 300 troops and march to the Cumberlands. He was also instructed to open a road from the Clinch River to Nashville. This company of militia were to make headquarters in Davidson County and aid in the defense of the settlements. North Carolina was to pay for this service out of tax money received from the Overmountain counties. Colonel Bledsoe traveled to Sullivan County to meet Colonel Evans and escort him west. Evans and his men were due to arrive at the Clinch River in April. Colonel Bledsoe waited a month without seeing troops or receiving any word. He left for home mad and disgusted. Correspondence indicates that he passed through Kentucky June 1st on his return trip.

This might have had a great influence on the Cumberland officials in their request to become part of the Kentucky settlement. They were too far distant to participate in the Franklin movement. Jefferson had designated them as a separate commonwealth in his plan for western states. From Draper's Ms. Samuel McDowell to Arthur Campbell Sept. 23, 1787:

"The Cumberland People have sent two gentlemen to wait on our State Convention to try if Kentucky will allow them to join with it in government; and, if so, on what terms, they first obtaining leave from North Carolina. What may be done I cannot tell at this time."

Colonel Evans and his men did not arrive in Nashville until October 16th, 1787. Virginians and Franks had enlisted in the company as they passed through their country. They were in destitute circumstance on arrival at the Bluffs. No equipment, clothing worn out and in shreds, very little food and dispirited. It is assumed they were aided by the Cumberland people in getting outfitted as they are later reported escorting groups from the Clinch to the vicinity of Nashville.

Several patrol groups were organized to act as scouts and watchouts in all sections of the country. They played hide-and-seek with the Indians. Scouts, with their dogs, played an important role in this type of protection. The white men had learned from the Indians to use the wild animal sounds and bird calls to lure their prey into shooting range. Sometimes the Indians would prove the best imitators and the white hunter would be "gobbled up." Close listening was necessary to distinguish between the real call and the imitation.

Hendricks Station was assaulted, the Price home broken into, the parents killed, children wounded. A Baird boy was slain; William Hall, his son Richard, and another man were killed near Bledsoe's Lick. William Montgomery was killed on Drakes Creek, his son scalped.

In spite of all the harassment and perils of the country, the settlers would get together in one of the well-protected cabins or stations for a festive occasion. The pants might be patched or of animal skins, the shoes mocassins made of buffalo hide, but they would do the jig and other types of dances common to the period. Some of the best entertainment was furnished by the men retelling stories of their narrow escapes from the Indians and how they had outwitted the redmen at their own game.

The constant requests to the North Carolina Officials for military help received the same negative answers. They would have to defend themselves at their own expense. Therefore, this is really the story of a struggle for survival, in a country that belonged to a sovereign state, but was unable to furnish protection for their own. Even so, the settlers of Cumberland received more considerate treatment than the Franks.

Preachers of the Methodist faith began to travel their circuits by this time. Some Presbyterians and Baptists were beginning to hold services at scattered meeting houses. It is usually said that preachers blaze the way and people follow. But in the case of the Overmountain Settlements, the pioneers were there before the preachers.

MERO DISTRICT
1788

1788 continued to usher migrations from the East toward the Cumberland Country. The arrival of new stock, which included cattle, stallions, brood mares and sheep, aroused the people somewhat from their everyday routine. These new arrivals settled mostly in the Sumner County territory. Farmers back East were drawn to the settlements by the reports of good cotton and tobacco land. All of this was happening despite the ever-pervading presence of the Indian menace.

This constant worry and problem of safety continued to be a big factor in all the official discussions and plans. They tried to figure how they could best defend themselves and the constant flow of new settlers from the marauding bands of Indians. They felt that the "Confederacy Of States" was inadequate for the task. They had received no special help or benefit from the mother state of North Carolina. They knew that the established communities and states along the Atlantic Seaboard considered the frontier settlers as uncouth mountain barbarians. Thus, they planned their own defenses and ran their own government as best they could.

The trustees of the Town of Nashville, Samuel Barton, Thomas Molloy and James Shaw, continued to execute deeds to those who purchased lots for 4 lbs. Each lot contained approximately one acre. A fence had been erected around the seven or eight log cabins and the few half-face buildings in the Nashville Settlement.

The watchword was caution as the people worked in the field or passed from one station to another. Even so, the killings continued. During early March, another son of James Robertson was killed. Peyton Robertson, John Johnson and several other boys were out gathering maple sap to be used in making syrup and sugar. Peyton was killed on the spot; John Johnson was taken captive. At Bledsoe's, George Hamilton was wounded. Jesse Maxey was shot and wounded near Asher's. Three sons of William Montgomery were

killed near their station on Drake's Creek. Robert Jones was killed near David Wilson's home; Ben Williams was slain near the Head of Station Camp Creek. The Widow Neely, whose husband was killed several years earlier, and her daughter taken captive, was killed near Neely's Lick. In October, two men named Dunham and Astill were killed near Nashville. They were scalped and chopped, as had become the practice of the Indians. At Southerland Mayfield's Station, the Indians were able to get between the men and their guns. A watchout had left his post. Mayfield and a son were killed on the spot. Another son named George was taken to the Creek towns and was held captive there 12 years. Brown's Station was attacked and several lost their lives.

One of the heavy blows that befelll the settlement was the killing of Colonel Anthony Bledsoe at his Greenfield home. Colonel Bledsoe was awakened by his dogs and the sound of cattle running past his house. He stepped out of a door, into a passageway between his double loghouse. The Indians fired on him and mortally wounded the Colonel. The Indians often used this ruse of running cattle to bring the men into the open and range of their guns. A young man, Campbell, was also killed during the attack.

TENNESSEE COUNTY

The North Carolina Assembly passed an act, during the 1788 Session, that again divided Davidson County. The new County was named Tennessee. Very little was done in the way of organization until 1791. According to records written during 1791 and 1792, the Tennessee Court was organized either in 1789 or 1790, as a Sheriff was mentioned and several other actions noted.

In 1784, Colonel John Montgomery and Col. Martin Armstrong laid off a town site on the North bank of the Cumberland River, near the Mouth of Red River. Montgomery gave it the name Clarksville, in honor of his Commander, George Rodgers Clark. Not much was accomplished until several years later.

One of the major problems the Cumberland people faced was finding a way to get their hides and produce to market. Their prosperity depended on using the Mississippi River as a gateway for trade. The Spaniards were rattling swords and saying that any boat from Kentucky or the Cumberland frontier would be seized. Folk, like Colonel James Wilkinson, were going about the settlements causing some dissent with their talk. He was running down the American Government and advising an alliance with the Spanish. Much talk was made by the Overmountain people concerning separation from the seaboard states.

The protests of James Robertson and Bledsoe to the North Carolina Government, that the Indians were being furnished arms and encouraged by the Spanish Officials, were strongly denied by the Spanish Minister.

James Robertson sent a direct message to the Creek Chief McGilivray, asking that the Johnson boy be returned to his people. He also asked that the Creek Indian attacks on the Cumberland people be stopped. Chief McGilvray talked with the Spanish Governor of Pensacola, Arturo O'Neill, about the Cumberland negotiations. He said that the distress of these people had brought them to the point that they were willing to submit to any conditions to obtain peace and were willing to become subjects of Spain. He said he had granted the Cumberland people a peace truce until his people had their assembly and decided on the course they would take.

The raids continued despite said truce. Letters were exchanged between the Spaniards and Cumberland people. A move had to be made. Robertson would not consider becoming a Spanish subject, contrary to all reports and rumors, but peace and the navigation of the Mississippi River were goals that had to be achieved.

Robertson presented a proposal to the Notables and to the Magistrates of Sumner to name their settlements, for diplomatic reasons, "Miro District" in honor of the Spanish Governor, Don Estevan Miro. At the November Assembly of the North Carolina Legislature, he presented the plan which was adopted. The name was misspelled on the records so instead of "Miro" it became "Mero." Thus the Cumberland settlements became the "Mero District" of the state.

James Robertson wrote a letter to Governor Miro, January 25, 1789. The letter informed the Governor that the Country had been named in his honor and that he was happy that some restriction on the trade measure had been eased. He asked Miro if he could use his influence to stop the Indians from the frequent harassment in his country. Many more letters passed between the Cumberland leaders and the Spanish authorities. This so-called Spanish intrigue has been kicked around in many ways. The real objectives being sought were somewhat concealed in the phrasing. The goal was finally accomplished without the frontiersmen ever having to bow to the Spanish King. Trade was allowed down the Mississippi for a price, but that was better than no trade at all.

ANDREW JACKSON ARRIVES IN NASHVILLE
1789

The year 1789 was to prove a turning point for all the Overmountain settlers: perhaps not in the expected, and hoped for, manner or just the way they would have planned it. It was to usher in new personalities who would create a new era and the settlements would become a Territory.

For the Cumberland people, Indian hostilities would continue. The Spanish problems regarding the use of the Mississippi would become more complex. English Agents were moving among the Indian towns trying to create friction. Haywood says that only 30 known persons were killed this year. Many were wounded and some taken captive to the Indian towns.

Putnam says that it was in early 1789 that Andrew Jackson arrived on the Nashville Scene. Other authorities say it was early 1790 that he arrived in Nashville. He was granted a license to practice law in Davidson County, January 12, 1789, and he soon was appointed Prosecuting Attorney for the County. Although uneducated, crude and fond of fighting, he had the qualities of honesty, self-confidence and straight-forwardness that won him high esteem in this distant American frontier.

Young Jackson was indifferent to books and resented anyone trying to teach him. He never learned to write English correctly. One critic said that his letters, with their crudities in spelling, would make the Angels weep. On some of his Davidson County Court records he would give his approval by writing "Oll Korrect" on the paper. This became laborious, so he soon began putting the initials O. K. instead of writing it out. Today this signature of approval is almost universal. This O. K. is found on a record dated *"Wednesday, 6th October, 1790: Court met according to adjournment. Andrew Jackson, Esq., proved a bill of sale from Hugh McGary to Gasper Mansker for a negro man, which was O. K."*

ANDREW JACKSON, Seventh President of the United States. Andrew Jackson received his license to practice law in Washington, Sullivan and Greene Counties 1777-78. Was first Governor of Florida Territory.

RACHEL DONELSON JACKSON, wife of Andrew, was daughter of John Donelson. Rachel made trip to Nashborough on boat Adventure with her family. Was sister of Mrs. Daniel Smith. Stockley Donelson, surveyor-speculator was her brother.

The news that General George Washington had been elected President of the United States and inaugurated April 30, 1789, was the cause of happy rejoicing among the Overmountain people, and especially the Cumberlands. They felt that he would "defend them from all assaults of our enemies." They had great confidence in the new President and felt that at last they could get some protection from the Indians and that a way would be opened to ship their produce to a market down the River. Their hopes were higher and their expectations greater than could be accomplished at this time.

Meanwhile the killing continued. Captain Hunter was killed at Johnson's Station and Hugh F. Bell was wounded. A party of white men pursued the band of Indians. After an hour's chase they rode into an ambush. Major Kirkpatrick was killed; Foster and Brown were wounded.

In May, Judge John McNairy, friends and a group of families were traveling toward Nashville when they were attacked. They had crossed the Clinch River and had continued on their way till dark. They made camp and spent the night. At daybreak, as they were preparing to continue their journey, they were fired on by a large body of warriors. The whites fled down the road toward the river. The Indians, satisfied with the horses and plunder, didn't bother to pursue. Those members of the party still alive reached the River and swam across to safety. Three persons were killed: Stanley and a Chickasaw Chief and his son. Judge McNairy had been appointed to serve as Judge in the Mero District. He later arrived in Nashville and began his duties in the Courts of the Cumberland. He became very wealthy. Miss McGaugh was killed this year at Hickman's Station. Hugh Webb, Jane Hendrick's husband and Henry Ramsey were slain.

General James Robertson had several hands working in a field not far from his house. A guard, or lookout, was stationed to watch for Indians. About eleven o'clock the guard thought he detected some movements in the nearby woods. He moved to place himself between the woods and the field workers. Robertson saw this maneuver and went towards the woods to have a look. Several guns were fired at Robertson, the guard and workers. Robertson was shot in the foot, but no bones were broken. The group returned to Robertson's home. The Colonel issued an order to call the militia together to pursue the Indians. Andrew Jackson was one of the 60 reporting for duty. Captain Sampson Williams was in command. Early light the next morning, the men picked up the trail which led up West Harpeth to the Ridge at Duck River. Here Captain Williams selected 20 men to continue the hunt. After discussing the situation the men decided they would have a better chance to surprise the hostiles on foot. Leaving their horses with the 40 that remained, they set off at a jog-trot along the Indians' trail. Crossing the River at night, they turned downstream and went as far as they could through the canebrakes in the darkness. They lay on their arms until dawn and then continued their march. Williams and his men were surprised when they saw the Indian camp so nearby, just a few hundred yards from where they had stopped. Captain Williams, in front, saw the redskins first.

The warriors were preparing their morning meal. The 30 Indians had not yet discovered the presence of the white men. Williams and his men crept within 50 yards of the group before they fired on the camp. The Indians fled leaving all behind them. One was killed instantly, several were wounded and were helped by their brothers as they fled.

The Indians crossed the River and disappeared into the woods before the white men could reload and pursue. The pioneers captured 16 guns, 19 shot pouches and all their blankets, moccasins, leggings and skins. The Indians did not fire a shot at the white soldiers. Captain Williams and his men collected the plunder and retraced their trail to the force left behind with the horses. This is one of the successful battles. Sampson Williams and Andrew Jackson became close friends after this incident.

JUDGE JOHN McNARY

The pioneer has been considered a reckless person, prone to waste time, drink and loaf when not clearing land, raising a cabin or hunting. Many writers have tried to wrap these early American Frontiersmen in a philosophical, unethical, conniving, barbarous style of personality and character. They imply that killing was a way of life and a most enjoyable pastime. They have tried to insinuate other motives when pioneers acted purely for self-preservation. Pioneers have been criticized for scalping Indians and doing many of the same things the redmen did. They retaliated in language and action the Indian could understand. The Indian practiced an eye for an eye, tooth for a tooth no matter whose eye or tooth they got. So to survive in the land of the redmen, the pioneers had to learn to out-do the Indian at his own game and with his own tricks.

Putnam relates that these hardy people would dance even while the war whoops could be heard outside the station. Some would dance and some would keep on firing through the portholes the while. They were always on the alert to answer the call to arms to defend the settlements or chase a band of marauding Indians. There were, and are, a few slack-twisted men who would shirk and "could not come it," in every community.

As the settlements continued to grow and increase in number, doctors with their pack saddles, lawyers with their green bags, and Ministers of the Gospel with saddle bags filled with books made their appearance in greater numbers. Remarks from Captain Rains are quoted from Putnam: *"We used to think we had the devil to pay (and a heavy debt, too, running on long installments) before the doctors and the lawyers came; but the doctors introduced diseases, and the lawyers instituted suits, and now we all have to pay. Good health and harmony prevailed until they came."*

One of the big questions discussed and argued in the Overmountain Settlements as well as back East was the adoption or rejection of the Constitution. The Overmountain people were strong in their opposition. North Carolina did ratify November 13, 1789.

They were in the Union and the North Carolina Legislature was making plans to cede the Territory, now Tennessee, to the Federal Government. Each of the two frontier settlements had experienced their day of almost independent statehood. The Watauga and Nolichucky people had their State of Franklin; Cumberland had their Government of The Notables. Both governments had arisen from necessity and were an expression of a people willing to fight for their freedom and independence.

General Joseph Martin had gone on a fruitless campaign against the Chickamaugas. The Indians defeated Martin's force. Washington District, as per usual, had to pay the bill. The Indians had pulled their forces and families into more secluded areas. This campaign again left them unscarred. The warrior bands were to continue their Cumberland raids for some five or six years.

North Carolina established a provision store in Hawkins County at the home of John Adair where flour, corn, pork and beef were stored here for use by the guards escorting families through the wilderness to Cumberland. A road from Campbell Station to Nashville had been opened Sept. 25th, 1788.

Colonel Isaac Tittsworth and his brother John were taking up their claims near the mouth of Sulphur Fork on Red River. They, their wives and children were all killed. Colonel Tenen, Evan Shelby, Jr., Abednego Lewellen and Hugh F. Bell ran into an Indian ambush while on a hunting trip in the Cumberlands. Shelby and Lewellen were killed, Tenen and Bell escaped.

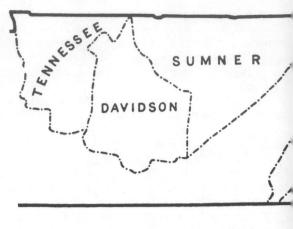

MERO DISTRICT was created by N. C. Legislative Act October 1788. Named for Don Estevan Miro, Governor of Orleans. Name misspelled on records and thus continued.

Major Joseph McElrath and Captain John Hickerson were killed while out scouting.

A tobacco inspection was provided for Clarksville in Tennessee County. Later an inspection was provided at Cairo in Sumner County. Another act was to provide care for those wounded by the Indians. The Mero District was to pay the doctors out of the treasury. Doctors were exempt from militia duty.

During the past ten years the loss of life and property was heavy. The number of horses stolen from the settlers has been estimated at 1000. General James Robertson and his brother Elijah lost 93. A near neighbor is said to have lost 75. Nevertheless, 1789 was considered a good year.

On the 25th of February, 1790, Samuel Johnson and Benjamin Hawkins executed a deed that made Washington and Mero Districts (now Tennessee) the Territory of the United States South of the River Ohio.

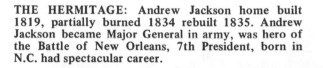

THE HERMITAGE: Andrew Jackson home built 1819, partially burned 1834 rebuilt 1835. Andrew Jackson became Major General in army, was hero of the Battle of New Orleans, 7th President, born in N.C. had spectacular career.

GLEN ECHO: Home of Thomas Brown Craighead, founder and head of Davidson Academy. The school was started in the "Springhill Meeting House" a 24 by 30 foot stone building erected for church services. The Glen Echo house was built on an Indian Mound 1794, burned and later rebuilt on same location.

GENERAL JAMES ROBERTSON

CHARLOTTE REEVES ROBERTSON

RICHLAND: Home of the James Robertsons was first called "Traveler's Rest" later changed to "Richland". It is said to be the first brick house built in Cumberland Territory. Legend says that friendly Indians molded and baked brick used in the walls and helped with the handcarved woodwork.

Artist conception of Robertson greeting wife Charlotte on her arrival at the Bluffs.

ROBERTSON'S HAND SAW, taken to Cumberlands 1779-1780. Can be seen in Tennessee State Museum.

TRAVELER'S REST: House built by Judge John Overton; N.C. revenue collector in the Mero District; developed west Tennessee; founded and gave name to Memphis.

SPENCER'S CHOICE: Site was bought by Colonel David Shelby from the Spencer family after Thomas, "Big Foot" Spencer was killed by Indians 1794. House built 1798 had walls two feet thick. David Shelby married Sarah, daughter of Colonel Anthony Bledsoe. The Bledsoes had lived near the Shelbys before moving west.

CRAGFONT: This imposing stone structure, built by General James Winchester, is located near Gallatin. Winchester arrived in the Cumberland Settlements 1785. He and his wife Susan Black settled near Bledsoe's Lick. James Winchester was active in the Cumberland development and was associated with John Overton in opening up west Tennessee.

THE STATE OF FRANKLIN

It has been in purpose to treat of the State of Franklin not merely as a local movement, but to give it a broader setting: to discuss the effort to establish a new State, as the fourteenth in the Union, as a part of the movement for separation that was at that time rife on all frontiers, eastern as well as western. Franklin was without doubt the most pronounced and significant manifestation of the spirit of separation which gave deep concern to the national leaders. No other movement for separate statehood reached, even approximately, the stage attained by Franklin — that of a de facto *government, waging war, negotiating treaties and functioning for a term of years in the three great departments that mark an American State, the legislative, executive, and judicial.* This quote, by Samuel Cole Williams, is from his **History of The Lost State of Franklin.**

THE STATE OF FRANKLIN

THE NOLICHUCKY RIVER NAME begins where the Toe and Cane rivers merge near Huntdale, N. C. It flows westward through the Unaka Mountains to join the French Broad and Holston Rivers. The Nolichucky flows through one of the most beautiful gorges in eastern America. The name Nolichucky comes from the Cherokee word Nula-tsu' gu-yi meaning *Spruce Tree Place.* Another literal name applied was "Rushing Waters."

FRANKLIN PROLOGUE

The Declaration of Independence was not a declaration of Union. All thirteen states had to learn by experience that there can be such a thing as too much independence. The process of learning this lesson nearly cost them their freedom. The change from rule by a King to self-rule was sudden. The inexperience and immaturity of the new leaders was frightful. Their judgment, not yet seasoned to this new concept of a democratic government, was uncertain in those tumultous years.

Each state had gone deeply in debt in financing the war. Congress had contracted heavy obligations both at home and abroad to the extent of $140 million dollars. The $236 million dollars in paper, issued by the Congress, was worthless as it had no backing. Eight million dollars had been borrowed abroad and when the creditors began demanding their pay it had a sobering effect on the American leaders. Peace had not brought prosperity.

The elected leaders in Congress began taking inventory of the situation and canvassing possible remedies. They soon found that the solution must come from the people. The Citizens, realizing that liberty and freedom without restraint was dangerous, also began clamoring for a reform in their projected government.

FACSIMILE of Continental Currency 1776.

Those early patriots were introduced to a problem during the infancy of their new nation that was to have an eroding effect on democracy 200 years later. Latter day patriots were to learn that the words "liberty and freedom" are misused and misrepresented; that liberty is construed as a license for licentiousness; that commercialization of community, state and national peril is a constitutional right; and freedom of worship is practicing unshackled proselytism, producing political wealth.

The selfish prejudices of states and individuals nearly destroyed the union of states. Some in high places did not hesitate to stick their knife into the vitals of government, if, in so doing they could destroy the objects of their personal envy or animosity. As each state was practically a law unto itself, Congress was hampered by a lack of power granted to it by the individual states. This was caused mainly by each local concept of liberty. The people of young America faced newness and inexperience. They were afraid to concede to Congress the authority they had willingly surrendered to the King. They wanted liberty in general but had not come to the particular points of their concept. It was a fight between instinct and reason.

THE LIBERTY BELL, Independence Hall, Philadelphia, Penn.

Americans had inherited the concepts of individual liberties but were not adjusted to the idea of community and individual liberties being part of the whole. The absolute sovereignty of one state they could understand but the sovereignty of several states combined was a matter of suspicion. Thus, as the thirteen states were moving individually toward strong governments, the United States Government was growing weaker and less effective. As General George Washington said; "One state will comply with the request of Congress, another neglects it, a third executes it by halves and all differ in either manner, matter or in point of time to the extent that we are always working uphill. Thus we are unable to use our strength or resources to good advantage. I see in our present course instead of one government head, thirteen heads; instead of one army thirteen disunited armies."

Another big spectre that was rearing its head in the congressional discussions was the controlling rule by the coastal states. Some leaders felt that the cultural East must dominate the political and cultural policies of the new country. Outspoken leaders said that the West was being settled by people of low culture with little concept of the elite of society. They argued that these uncouth pioneers, opening up the western frontiers, should have little voice in government circles. They proposed, "Let's keep their states small and their representation ineffective."

Thomas Jefferson had advocated that those states having western territory cede it to the Federal

Government to help defray the war expenses. Jefferson also projected the plan of erecting several new states in the territory, setting up military reservations and giving the soldiers land grants in payment for their service.

At the end of The Revolutionary War, the men who did the actual fighting, had empty pockets and hungry stomachs. General McDougall and a committee of soldiers appeared before Congress January 1783 to state their grievances. This was their argument: "The citizens murmur at the greatness of their taxes—yet no part reaches the army—shadows are offered us to pay for our services while the substance has been gained by others. We ask that Congress convince the army and the world that the independence of America shall not be placed on the ruin of any particular class of her citizens. The liberties, freedoms and rights of the minority groups must have their separate voice in the government. The majority rules but must not tyrannize, because the majority is made up of numerous minorities."

The Minister of finance declared to the Committee that he had no money and other demands were pressing. Members of Congress had voted to pay themselves and other civil employees—while the army was left unpaid. Mutiny and dissension were about to break out into a civil war. The country really faced a desperate situation. The old cliche, that the enemy in the field is less dangerous than the enemy in your own house, was being felt.

General Washington, learning the situation, was able to change the picture and avoid a civil conflict. England, Spain and France, watching developments and waiting to see the failure of the noble experiment, were ready to move in and pick up the pieces. General Washington talked his officers and men into accepting delayed payments in the form of land grants. Washington's "Legacy", written in the form of a letter, is one of our most effective documents on American stability and peace. He advocated Union and Fidelity.

As political tension and taxation increased, individual sections began to assert their desire for statehood. The northern segment of

BENJAMIN FRANKLIN

New England wanted their own state of Maine. Vermont, was destined to become the 14th state in 1791 as a result of disputed boundaries between New York and New Hampshire. Colonel Arthur Campbell was sounding the cry for a state made up of South West Virginia and part of the present East Tennessee. Kentucky was asking to be cut off from the Virginia Commonwealth. So why not the Overmountain Country of the Holston, Watauga and Nolichucky valleys become a state named Franklin.

NEW STATE MOVEMENT

Congressional effort to establish control or claim to western lands was started sometime in 1780 when Joseph Jones introduced a bill in that Body *"that in case the recommendations in the states of Virginia, North Carolina and Georgia, to cede to the United States a portion of their unappropriated western territory, so ceded shall be laid out in separate states at such times and in such manner as Congress shall hereafter direct."* A later resolution stated that *"such states be republican in form and members of the Federal Union and would have same rights of sovereignty, freedom and independence as other states."*

Colonel Arthur Campbell, with a dream of a great western state, started such a movement in 1782. He circulated a document with the intent of organizing a state whose boundaries would encompass southwest Virginia and much of the upper portion of present east Tennessee.

His projected plan of statehood stirred up a hornet's nest in the Legislative circles of Virginia. For several years Colonels Arthur and William Campbell had dominated the political forces of southwest Virginia. Colonel Arthur lost a strong supporting arm when Colonel William Campbell died. The opposing were able to muster enough strength to take control. The proposal of the new state gave them the needed issue along with some tax collecting records they tried to use against Campbell. Mrs. William Campbell, a sister of Patrick Henry, soon married General William Russell. Russell didn't like Arthur Campbell so he lined up with the opposing faction. All of this had a dampening effect on Colonel Arthur Campbell's immediate plans for a new state.

This controversy and rift in the political structure of southwest Virginia frightened the North Carolina Officials into action. They saw the possibility of losing control over their western territory.

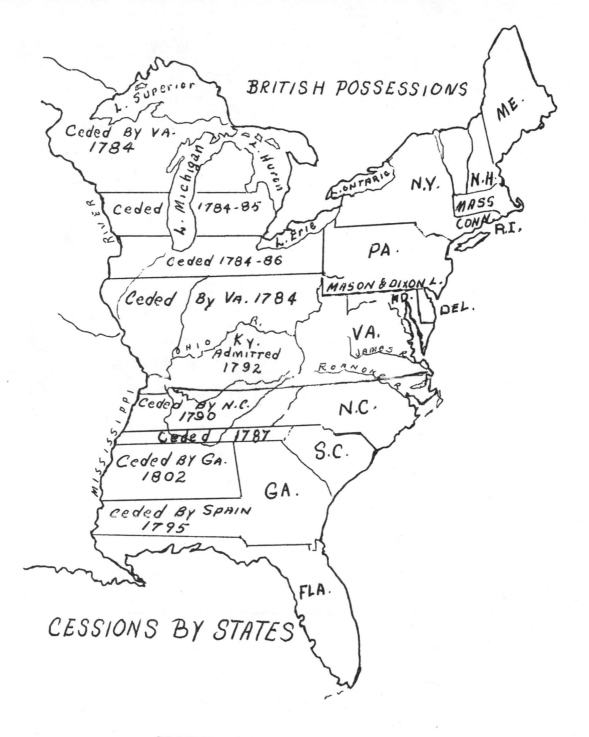

Ceded By VA. 1784

Ceded 1784-85

Ceded 1784-86

Ceded By VA. 1784

KY. Admitted 1792

Ceded By N.C. 1790

Ceded 1787

Ceded By GA. 1802

Ceded By Spain 1795

BRITISH POSSESSIONS

CESSIONS BY STATES

GREENE COUNTY ERECTED 1783

The North Carolina Legislature divided Washington to form another County during the 1783 Assembly session. The new County was named Greene in honor of General Nathaniel Greene. For some months the boundaries of Greene county extended over a large portion of the present Tennessee. The first deed recorded in Greene County was for 25,000 acres of land awarded to General Greene for Revolutionary War service. This grant was laid off on Duck River in the present county of Maury.

Another act of this session divided Salisbury into two separate Districts. The new District, named Morgan, included Burke, Wilkes, Rutherford, Lincoln, Washington, Sullivan and Greene. A district court to serve the Overmountain Counties of Washington and Sullivan had been set up in 1782 at Jonesborough.

Spruce McCay was its first Judge, Waighstill Avery, State Attorney and John Sevier, Clerk. William Cocke was admitted to the practice of law during the February term. In the 1783 session F. A. Ramsey was qualified as surveyor.

The first Greene County Court met in the home of Robert Carr in Greeneville. This was near the site of the First Baptist Church. Magistrates present for this session, third Monday of August 1783, were Joseph Hardin, John Newman, George Doherty, James Houston, Amos Bird and Ashel Rawlings. Daniel Kennedy was appointed Clerk; James Wilson, Sheriff; William Cocke, Attorney; Joseph Hardin, Entry Taker; Isaac Taylor, Surveyor; Richard Wood, Registrar.

A tax was levied for the purpose of erecting public buildings. (The 1783 Greene Tax list is on Appendix 1 of this section.) Settlers were already raising cabins in the areas now known as Jefferson and Sevier Counties. Alexander Outlaw, Thomas Jarnigan, Robert McFarland, James Hill, Wesley White, James Randolph, Joseph Copeland, Robert Gentry, James Hubbard and Thomas Stockton are some of the known persons settled in these lower reaches by 1783.

During August of 1783 Colonel James White, Colonel Robert Love and Colonel F. A. Ramsey made an explorative trip as far south as the junction of the Holston and Tennessee Rivers. All three held land warrants and were searching for

SEVIER-LOWRY-JOHNSON-O'KEEFE-JONES HOUSE, located in Greeneville, Tennessee, has an unusual history. The original house, built of logs during 1780's is said to be the oldest building in Greeneville. Once owned by Valentine Sevier and Andrew Johnson, President of the United States. Now owned and occupied by John M. Jones.

desirable locations. It was during this trip that James White first saw the land on which he would later locate and establish the town of Knoxville. F. A. Ramsey selected the land on which he would later live and build.

It was October 20, 1783 that the John Armstrong land office was opened at Hillsborough, North Carolina, for the sale of land not included in the military reservations. The prospect of large tracts of cheap land brought a flood of emigrants across the mountains. Fields were cleared and cabins built as far down as the banks of Little and Big Pigeon Rivers. Neither the land office nor the settlers paid much heed to Indian boundaries. The big land grab was under way.

BIG LAND GRAB

North Carolina paid little attention to the first requests of Congress for the cession of her western lands. They were practically shamed into action by stories in the news print of the northern states who insinuated that North Carolina and Georgia were backward states and viewed in an unfavorable light.

North Carolina's two representatives, Hugh Williamson and William Blount were in close contact with Governor Alexander Martin during this period and the general text of the cession act, later passed, was worked out before the Assembly had much opportunity to study the situation. Blount and Williamson insisted that the following conditions should be imposed.

a - The whole expense of the State's Indian expeditions should pass to her account in the quota of the Continental expenses.

b - Actual valuation of all lands and improvements claimed by any state should be made before the cession should be confirmed.

c - If any separate State should ever be erected on any of those lands, part of the public debt should be transferred to such State according to the value of the lands therein.

Many political leaders in North Carolina were opposed to any cession and by postponement and delays in legislative action let the matter drag as long as possible. In January 1783 Governor Martin wrote the delegates in Congress. *"It will not be to our interest or policy to make a cession of our western lands on any terms yet proposed by Congress. . . .To insist that the State should cede her vacant lands which are daily settling up with numerous inhabitants and from which she expects to derive considerable advantage. . . .is the same as to urge an individual to give up to a stranger without compensation part of his land he is daily improving with husbandmen and husbandry to his own enrichment and that of his family. This is, in short endeavoring to carry into effect, a vile agrarian law the Romans anciently made in vain respecting their conquered lands."*

Actions behind the delay and what was actually taking place is somewhat explained in the following letter to the representatives in congress. Following is letter from Governor Martin to these delegates, dated December 8, 1783:

Perhaps Congress may be dissatisfied with the mode of our land office being opened, as we have made no cession of any part of our western lands. We have made provision for our continental line, on the Cumberland, and a territory reserved for the purpose is erected into a county by the name of Davidson; the residue of the lands to the southward and westward is opened for entry of any citizen of this or the United States, who will pay to the entry taker ten pounds per hundred in specie, specie certificate of this State, or currency at 800 for one, restricted however to 5,000 acres. . .No doubt we are railed at for want of generosity, but I know not for what reason. . .I can venture to say there will be no cession of any land worthy of acceptance, as the principal lands will be entered before this reaches you."

Herein was being perpetrated one of the biggest land grabs by speculators in the history of the United States. Vast acreages of land in the territory, now Tennessee, was to be obtained by a small North Carolina clique. The citizens of that state including, the Overmountain settlers and the Indians were being victimized.

Partisan fights between Tories and Whigs, in central and eastern parts of North Carolina during the closing years of the War, had caused much property loss. Very little economic exchange had been possible. This left the people of North Carolina destitute and in desperate financial straits. Members of the 1782 Assembly were paid in corn. Every one was in debt to somebody else. Valueless paper money was issued. Some leading citizens and political officials planned to retrieve their fortunes by exploiting the western lands. This they did, and somehow large grants of land fell into the hands of a very few. The speculations were set up during the seven months operation of the Armstrong Land Office in Hillsborough, North Carolina. During surveys, larger sections were laid off than those paid for or authorized. Speculators obtained by one means or another many of the grants given soldiers. All told more than four million acres of land were issued through the Armstrong Office during that short seven month period. A total of more than 8 million acres of Tennessee territory was taken up by private and military claims during the turmoil of the 1780's.

More consideration was accorded the Cumberland settlers, than was given the Watauga and Nolichucky people in land rights. This was partly due to the fact that North Carolina officials needed the cooperation of the Cumberland leaders in carrying out their plans. Many Franklin as well as Cumberland personalities were deeply involved in the western land speculations. The blame cannot all be placed on the shoulders of the North Carolina group. One writer has suggested that this was one of the reasons behind the Tipton-Sevier feud.

Many of the deals transacted during this period, both military and civil, caused much court litigation in later years. Bitter feelings were kindled between sections and states that would last for generations. The political aristocracy of the coastal communities were constantly casting slurs at the frontiersmen. This was especially true as regards the Franklin citizens. They were called the "offscourings of the earth and fugitives from justice."

THE FIRST CESSION ACT, APRIL 1784

Pressured by Congress, and influenced by Virginia's vote to cede her western land, North Carolina finally passed the first cession act during the April, 1784, Assembly, convening at Hillsborough. Opposition to the act was led by W. R. Davie and Gen. Thomas Person. Many capable leaders were members of this Legislature. Samuel Johnston, William Hooper, William Blount, Nathaniel Macon, Alexander McClaine, Alexander Mebane, William Lenoir, John Hay, John Ashe, Stephen Caburrus, Richard Caswell and others.

The bill to cede the land was introduced by William Blount. The watershed of the mountains was fixed as the boundary between North Carolina and the western Territory. The act was passed by a vote of 52 ayes, and 43 nays. The Representatives from the western counties were equally divided. Voting for cession were Charles Robertson, Washington County, Joshua Gist, Greene County, and David Looney, Sullivan County. Voting against cession were Landon Carter, Washington William Cage, Sullivan and Elijah Robertson, Davidson. James White, founder of Knoxville, Tennessee, voted against cession.

GOVERNOR ALEXANDER MARTIN

Among the several conditions and stipulations included in the wording of the act were:

(a) After the cession should be accepted, neither the lands nor the inhabitants of the ceded territory should be estimated in ascertaining North Carolina's proportion of the expenses of the late war.

(b) The lands provided for North Carolina officers and soldiers should inure to their benefit.

(c) The ceded lands should be deemed a common fund, for the benefit of all existing and future States of the Union.

(d) "The territory so ceded shall be laid out and formed into a State or States, containing a suitable and convenient extent of territory; and that the State or States so formed shall be a distinct State or States and admitted as members of the Federal Union, having the same right of sovereignty as other States; and that the State or States which shall thereafter be erected in the territory now ceded shall have the most full and absolute right to establish and enjoy, in the fullest latitude, the same constitution and the same bill of rights which are now established in the State of North Carolina, subject to such alterations as may be made by the inhabitants at large or a majority of them, not inconsistent with the Confederation of the United States. Provided always, that no regulation made or to be made by Congress shall tend to emancipate slaves, otherwise than shall be directed by the Assembly or legislature of such State or States."

(e) If Congress should not accept the cession and give due notice within twelve months, the act should be of no force and the lands should revert to the State.

At a later date, during the same session, they passed another act, declaring:

"That the sovereignty and jurisdiction of this State in and over the territory aforesaid, and all and every inhabitant thereof, shall be and remain the same in all respects, until the United States in Congress shall accept the cession, as if the act aforesaid had never been passed."

The North Carolinians maintained that they had given aid to South Carolina and Georgia, when they were hard pressed during the War with England, and that North Carolina should have credit for this aid. The Legislature also insisted that the expense of the various Indian campaigns should pass to the credit of North Carolina along with the Continental expense. Moreover, they stated that the western territory was solemnly pledged by legislative action, as security for the domestic creditors of the State; that debt, due in large part to her own citizens, which should be paid first.

Governor Martin notified the North Carolina Representative in Congress of the passage of the act; and had this to say: *"Whether the cession will be accepted is with some doubt, as our land office hath been open for some time for entries of these lands, and large quantities have been taken up; but still there remain great tracts undisposed of beyond the Tennessee to the Mississippi claimed by the Chickasaws."*

BIRTH OF FRANKLIN

News of the cession reached the Overmountain People with the return of their representatives from Hillsborough. The action of the Assembly almost caught them unprepared. They had been aware of Colonel Arthur Campbell's efforts toward creating a new state, and had heard rumors of Kentucky's efforts for self government but this had little to do with their remote life. They wanted statehood, but their natural instinct was to have as little government as possible.

Details of the cession spread from settlement to isolated cabin by word of mouth. The movement was spontaneous without need of prodding or urging. Their incentive was self preservation. Their motive, the same as prompted the organization of the Watauga Association 1772. They followed the plan of selecting delegates, as had been advocated earlier by Colonel Arthur Campbell. Two men from each captain's company were chosen as representatives.

The meeting was set at Jonesborough August 23, 1784. Many people assembled around the small log court house. They were part of this movement so they wanted to be present to see and hear. A member of the Assembly reported to them, from the doorway, what was being said and done inside.

Delegates had been given power and authority to adopt whatever plans or measures advisable. Haywood gives the following list of delegates:

WASHINGTON COUNTY - John Sevier, Charles Robertson, William Murphey, Joseph Wilson, John Irvin, Samuel Houston, William Trimble, William Cox, Landon Carter, Hugh Henry, Christopher Taylor, John Chisolm, Samuel Doak, William Campbell, Benjamin Holland, John Bean, Samuel Williams and Richard White.

SULLIVAN COUNTY - Joseph Martin, Gilbert Christian, William Cocke, John Manifee, William Wallace, John Hall, Saml. Wilson, Stockley Donelson, and William Evans.

GREENE COUNTY - Daniel Kennedy, Alexander Outlaw, Joseph Gist, Samuel Weir, Asahel Rawlings, Joseph Ballard, John Maughon, John Murphey, David Campbell, Archibald Stone, Abraham Denton, Charles Robinson, and Elisha Baker.

The assembled delegates elected John Sevier, President of the Convention, and Landon Carter, Secretary. A Committee was appointed to study the situation and make a report to the body. Committee members were Cocke, Outlaw, Carter, Campbell, Manifee, Martin, Robinson, Christian, Kennedy, Houston and Wilson.

The Committee went into session and prepared the following report for the body proper. As discussions among the members were under way, definite action was started as follows:

"A member rose and made some remarks on the variety of opinions offered, for and against a separation, and taking from his pocket a volume containing the Declaration of Independence by the colonies in 1776, commented upon the reasons which induced their separation from England, on account of their local situation, etc. and attempted to show that a number of the reasons they had for declaring independence, applied to the counties here represented by their deputies."

"After this member had taken his seat, another arose and moved to declare the three western counties independent of North Carolina, which was unanimously adopted."

REPORT

"Your Committee are of opinion and judge it expedient, that the Counties of Washington, Sullivan and Greene, which the Cession Bill particularly respects, form themselves into an Association and combine themselves together, in order to support the present laws of North Carolina, which may not be incompatible with the modes and forms of laying off a new state. It is the opinion of your committee, that we have a just and undeniable right to petition to Congress to accept the cession made by North Carolina, and for that body to countenance us in forming ourselves into a separate government, and either to frame a permanent or temporary constitution, agreeable to a resolve of Congress, in such case made and provided, as nearly as circumstances will admit. We have a right to keep and hold a Convention from time to time, by meeting and convening at such place or places as the said Convention shall adjourn to. When any contiguous part of Virginia shall make application to join this Association, after they are legally permitted, either by the State of Virginia, or other power having cognizance thereof, it is our opinion that they be received and enjoy the same privileges that we do, may or shall enjoy. This Convention has a right to adopt and prescribe such regulations as the particular exigencies of the time and the public good may require; that one or more persons ought to be sent to represent our situation in the Congress of the United States, and this Convention has just right and authority to prescribe a regular mode for his support."

These people were not unaware of governmental affairs but acted slowly in their plans for statehood. Not too much was accomplished in the August meeting. About the only information available concerning these sessions came from Samuel Houston's notes.

NORTH CAROLINA REPEALS CESSION ACT

Seaboard Representatives, opposed to the cession act, used this as their main issue during the summer political campaign of 1784. Their talks, discussions and criticisms created more opposition among the people. When the Assembly met in Newbern, for the October Session, several new members of the opposition had been elected. When the cession act was brought up for vote it was repealed by a count of 37 nays to 22 ayes in the house and 19 nays to 11 ayes in the senate. Congress had not yet met to consider the cession act of April.

This action called forth a vigorous protest from seven senators led by Colonel Allen Jones. They wrote and signed the following document.

(a) "The act of the former Assembly evidently vested an optional right in Congress, and the repeal is attempted before that body could accede."

(b) "Political and moral honesty are unvariable and immutable. We cannot agree in a political capacity to do that which would dishonor us in a private action."

TRYON PALACE, Newbern, North Carolina.
Seat of North Carolina Government 1777-1790's.

In the house a similar protest was presented by Hay and Mclaine and signed by twenty members.

(a)   "The grant by the act of cession is irrecovable on the part of the State, and therefore the repeal is disgraceful."
(b)   "We prove ourselves unworthy to receive for North Carolina any benefits resulting from the liberal cessions by other individual States."
(c)   "During the confusion which must naturally spring from such situation, the numerous inhabitants resident in the country contended for may from necessity erect themselves into a distinct government" and the repeal "may produce confusion and distress to our brethren westward of the Alleghany mountain."

The stage was being set for a bitter struggle that was to last many years. The unethical action of the Assembly was not in the best legal procedure as indicated in many later decisions. The following is a quote from foot note by Judge Williams in "History Of The Lost State Of Franklin."

(Ante, page 25.) The soundness of this view has been demonstrated by many later judicial decisions. If it be premised that the offer of North Carolina to Congress was either under seal or based upon a valuable consideration (and that there was a concurrence of both seems certain) then it was not within the power of the offerer to withdraw within the period of one year allowed to Congress for consideration and acceptance. The offer was irrevocable within that period. Nor was the right of Congress lost by reason of the fact that North Carolina repealed the cession act or refused to perform before Congress could accept and demand performance. If there had been in existence a court with jurisdiction to pass upon the rights of the two sovereigns involved, a specific performance would have been grantable on the prayer of the National Government.

Alexander Outlaw, representative from Greene County, arrived late for this Session. When he learned of the repeal action, he proposed the creation of a small state called "West Carolina." This move was an effort to stop developments that were creating a chaotic situation. Outlaw was voted down and his proposal hardly noticed.

The New Bern Assembly, in an effort to pacify the people, divided the Morgan District and established Greene, Washington and Sullivan Counties into Washington District. David Campbell was appointed Judge of the Superior Court and John Sevier was appointed Brigadier General of Washington District. This move was barely noticed as revolutions once started are hard to stop. The North Carolina Officials didn't understand the situation and conditions across the mountains. The Overmountain people, removed by distance from the political and economic problems of the costal states, were not in a mood to turn back. They wanted a change.

DECEMBER CONVENTION 1784

The elected delegates met in Jonesborough December, 1784 to set up a form of government. News of the repeal action, by the North Carolina Assembly, had not reached the western counties when the convention assembled. John Sevier, President and F. A. Ramsey, Secretary called the convention to order. Joseph Hardin and William Cocke presented the following report:

To remove the doubts of the scrupulous; to encourage the timid, and to induce all, harmoniously and speedily, to enter into a firm association, let the following particulars be maturely considered. If we should be so happy as to have a separate government, vast numbers from different quarters, with a little encouragement from the public, would fill up our frontier, which would strengthen us, improve agriculture, perfect manufactures, encourage literature and every thing truly laudable. The seat of government being among ourselves, would evidently tend, not only to keep a circulating medium in gold and silver among us, but draw it from many individuals living in other states, who claim large quantities of lands that would lie in the bounds of the new state. Add to the foregoing reasons, the many schemes as a body, we could execute to draw it among us, and the sums which many travellers out of curiosity, and men in public business, would expend among us. But all these advantages, acquired and accidental, together with many more that might be mentioned, whilst we are connected with the old counties, may not only be nearly useless to us, but many of them prove injurious; and this will always be the case during a connexion with them, because they are the most numerous, and consequently will always be able to make us subservient to them; that our interest must be generally neglected, and sometimes sacrificed, to promote theirs as was instanced in a late taxation act, in which, notwithstanding our local situation and improvement being so evidently inferior, that it is unjust to tax our lands equally, yet they have expressly done it; and our lands, at the same time, not of one fourth of the same value. And to make it still more apparent that we should associate the whole councils of the state, the Continental Congress, by their resolves, invite us to it. The assembly of North Carolina by their late cession bill, opened the door, and by their prudent measure invite to it; and as a closing reason to induce to a speedy association, our late convention chosen to consider public affairs, and concert measure, as appears from their resolves, have unanimously agreed that we should do it, by signing the following articles:

"First. That we agree to entrust the consideration of public affairs, and the prescribing rules necessary to a convention, to be chosen by each company as follows: That if any company should not exceed thirty, there be one representative; and where it contains fifty, there be two; and so in proportion, as near as may be, and that their regulations be reviewed by the association."

"Secondly. As the welfare of our common country depends much on the friendly disposition of Congress, and their rightly understanding our situation, we do therefore unanimously agree, speedily to furnish a person with a reasonable support, to present our memorial, and negotiate our business in Congress.

"Thirdly. As the welfare of the community also depends much on public spirit, benevolence and regard to virtue, we therefore unanimously agree to improve and cultivate these, and to discountenance everything of a contradictory and repugnant nature."

"Fourthly. We unanimously agree to protect this association with our lives and fortunes, to which we pledge our faith and reputation."

After a prayer by Samuel Houston a motion for separation was presented to the delegates. From Ramsey and Williams we quote the motion and the vote.

"On motion of Mr. Cocke, whether for or against forming ourselves into a separate and distinct state, independent of the State of North Carolina, at this time, it was carried in the affirmative.

"On motion of Mr. Kennedy, the yeas and nays were taken on the above question.

"Yeas, - Mr. Tirril, Samms, North, Taylor, Anderson, Houston, Cox, Talbot, Joseph Wilson, Trimble, Reese, John Anderson, Manifee, Christian, Carnes, A. Taylor, Fitzgerald, Cavit, Looney, Cocke, B. Gist, Rawlings, Bullard, Joshua Gist, Valentine Sevier, Robinson, Evans and Maughan. (28)

"Nays. - John Tipton, Joseph Tipton, Stuart, Maxwell, D. Looney, Vincent, Cage, Provincer, Gammon, Davis, Kennedy, Newman, Wear, James Wilson and Campbell." (15)

It was also at this convention that a temporary constitution was presented and adopted. It was modeled after the North Carolina document of 1776. It was recommended to the Convention that the instrument be studied by the people for a period of six months or more and before the expiration of a year another constitutional convention would be called to adopt a permanent form. (copy of constitution Appendix II)

Shortly after the December Convention Colonel Sevier received the following letter from Joseph Martin.

December 31, 1784,

"I left Governor Martin's the 19th instant. He informed me that Outlaw was sent forward nearly four weeks ago with some dispatches to you. enclosing your general's commission with a number of other papers. He likewise charged me with a letter to you with many others to the different gentlemen in the District. He informed me the first business that the Assembly did was to repeal the cession bill before Congress could meet to accept it. David Campbell is appointed one of the circuit judges. But as Mr. Outlaw has been so long on his way home, I have no doubt but that you have the particulars; and as you have formed a government here, I must beg that you will inform me whether you will persist or let it lay over until you can be better informed, as the governor has sent me on to purchase a large quantity of beef, pork, and corn, for the use of a treaty to be held with the Cherokees in April next, which treaty he

CHESTER INN, Jonesboro, Tenn. Reproduced from a picture taken in 1891 as shown in "Dropped Stitches" by John Allison.

is to attend in person; also many gentlemen from below, in particular General Caswell, who is to succeed the present governor, and Colo. Blount. But if you are determined to oppose the measure, I shall not proceed to purchase. The letters from the governor to the other gentlemen, together with all my own, I left in Mr. Hardin's wagon as I landed with him two nights and when I pushed on forgot them, but expect him down by Monday. Thus shall forward on your letter."

Colonel Sevier had received word of his appointment as Brigadier-General of Washington District. He also felt that some of the problems brought about by the cession act had been relieved, and urged the people not to take further action. During the first Monday in January, while Court was in session at Jonesborough, he made public the contents of Joseph Martin's letter. It was after or during the November session of the North Carolina Legislature that Martin decided to pull away from the Franklin movement. He did not want to jeopardize his position as Indian Agent by opposing the North Carolina Officials.

Sevier clearly states his position at the beginning of 1785 in a letter to Colonel Daniel Kennedy.

2nd JANUARY, 1785

Dear Colonel: - I have just received certain information from Col. Martin, that the first thing the Assembly of North Carolina did was to repeal the Cession Bill, and to form this part of the country into a separate District, by name of Washington District, which I have the honour to command, as general. I conclude this step will satisfy the people with the old state, and we shall pursue no further measures as to a new state. David Campbell, Esqr., is appointed one of our judges I would write to you officially, but my commission is not yet come to hand.

I am, dr. Colo., with esteem, yr. mt. obdt.

Colo. Kennedy.   **JOHN SEVIER.**

This created a period of uncertainty among the westerners. Their leader was advising against separation while the people wanted to move forward with the formation of the new state. One historian suggests that Cocke's persuasive arguments along with the urging of many followers pushed Sevier into the leadership. William Cocke, who had spent much time on this project, was making every effort toward its success. Leaders on both sides of the mountains were watching to see which way Sevier turned. The March Assembly had been postponed until Colonel John Sevier made up his mind.

MOUNT PLEASANT: Home of the John Sevier family during period of the State of Franklin. Picture courtesy Tennessee State Library.

FRANKLIN'S FIRST LEGISLATIVE ASSEMBLY

Jonesborough, March 1785

The first Franklin Assembly, elected by the citizens, met in Jonesborough's log Court House early March 1785. John Sevier was elected Governor and sworn into office; Landon Carter, Speaker of the Senate; Thomas Talbot, Clerk; The House elected William Cage, Speaker; Thomas Chapman, Clerk; David Campbell was appointed or elected Judge of the Superior Court. Joshua Gist and John Anderson assistant Judges. Many resolutions were passed and laws incorporated in the actions of this Assembly but copies of the journal have been lost. Titles and acts passed, were sent to North Carolina Officials and these give some clues of actions and future plans.

The following acts were ratified March 31st, 1785:

1. An act to establish the legal claims of persons claiming any property under the laws of North Carolina, in the same manner as if the State of Franklin had never formed itself into a distinct and separate State.

2. An act to appoint commissioners, and vest them with full powers to make deeds of conveyance to such persons as have purchased lots in the town of Jonesboro.

3. An act for the promotion of learning in the County of Washington. This was the foundation of Martin Academy later Washington College Academy.

4. An act to establish Militia in the State.

5. An act to divide Sullivan County and part of Greene into two distinct counties, and erecting a county by the name of Spencer. (Spencer County would cover same territory as present Hawkins County.)

6. An act for procuring a great seal for the State. (This was never accomplished.)

7. An act directing the method of electing members of the General Assembly.

8. An act to divide Greene County into three separate counties, and to erect two new counties by the name of Caswell and Sevier. (Caswell would be the present Jefferson County. The other county would still be the present Sevier County.)

9. An act to ascertain the value of gold and silver foreign coin, and the paper currency now in circulation in the State of North Carolina, and to declare the same to be lawful tender in this state.

10. An act for the levying a tax for the support of the government.

11. An act to ascertain salaries allowed the Governor, Attorney General, Judges of the Superior Courts, Assistant Judges, Secretary of State, Treasurer and members of the Council of State.

12. An act to ascertaining what property in this state shall be deemed taxable, the method of assessing the same, and collecting public tax.

13. An act to ascertain the powers and authorities of the Judges of the Superior Courts, The Assistant Judges and Justices of the Peace, and of the County Courts of Pleas and Quarter sessions, and directing the time and place holding the same.

14. An act for erecting a part of Washington County and that part of Wilkes lying west of the extreme heights of the Appalachian or Alleghany Mountains, into a separate and distinct county by the name of Wayne. (This county was named in honor of General Anthony Wayne and covered area in present Carter and Johnson Counties.)

This act, to create Wayne County, brought into the State seven distinct Counties; Sullivan, Washington, Wayne, Spencer, Greene, Caswell, and Sevier. The boundaries of the State of Franklin are very loosely defined and each authority has indicated different boundaries. Loosely the lines would include parts of some eighteen upper east Tennessee Counties: Johnson, Carter, Sullivan, Hawkins, Washington, Unicoi, Greene, Hancock, Claiborne, Grainger, Hamblin, Jefferson, Cocke, Sevier, Knox, Blount, Anderson and Union.

State Officials elected during this Assembly were Landon Carter, Secretary of State; William Cage, State Treas.; Stockley Donelson, Surveyor-General; Daniel Kennedy and William Cocke, Brigadier-General.

over the Franklin armed forces. Members of the State Council included William Cocke, Landon Carter, Francis A. Ramsey, David Campbell, Daniel Kennedy and Andrew Taylor.

Under the act to establish a State Militia the following field officers were appointed: Sullivan County; Gilbert Christian, Colonel; John Anderson, Lieutenant-Colonel; George Maxwell, First Major: Caswell County; Alexander Outlaw, Colonel; James Roddy, Lieutenant-Colonel; John McNabb, first major; Nathaniel Evans, second major. Greene County; Daniel Kennedy, Colonel; George Doherty, Lieutenant-Colonel; James Houston, first major; Alexander Kelly, second major. Washington County: Charles Robertson, colonel; Valentine Sevier, lieutenant-colonel; Landon Carter first major; Jacob Brown, second major.

FRANKLIN'S ECONOMY

The salaries of the State officials were fixed at the following rate. Governor - 200 pounds annually; Attorney-General 25 pounds for each court; Secretary of

FIRE PLACE, MANTLE AND MURAL from the Landon Carter home in Elizabethton, Tenn. built 1780. It is called "The Mansion".

State 25 pounds annually; Judges of Superior Court 150 pounds annually; Assistant Judges 25 pounds each court; Treasurer 40 pounds annually; Council Members 6 shillings per day service. The levy to pay these salaries was made as follows.

"Be it enacted, That it shall and may be lawful for the aforesaid land tax, and all free polls, to be paid in the following manner: Good flax linen, ten hundred, at three shillings and six pence per yard; nine hundred at three shillings; eight hundred, two shillings and nine pence; seven hundred, two shillings and six pence; six hundred, two shillings, tow linen, one shilling and nine pence; linsey, three shillings, and woollen and cotton linsey, three shillings and six pence per yard; good, clean beaver skin, six shillings; cased otter skins, six shillings; uncased ditto, five shillings; rackoon and fox skins, one shilling and three pence; woollen cloth, at ten shillings per yard; bacon, well cured, six pence per pound; good, clean tallow, six pence per pound; good clean beeswax, one shilling per pound; good distilled rye whiskey at two shillings and six pence per gallon; good peach or apple brandy, at three shillings per gallon; good country made sugar, at one shilling

per pound; deer skins, the pattern, six shillings; good, neat and well managed tobacco, fit to be prized, that may pass inspection, the hundred fifteen shillings, and so on in proportion for a greater or less quantity."

"And all the salaries and allowances hereby made, shall be paid by any treasurer, sheriff, or collector of public taxes, to any person entitled to the same, to be paid to specific articles as collected, and at the rates allowed by the state for the same; of in current money of the State of Franklin. In specifying the skins, which might be received as a commutation for money, the risibility of the unthinking was sometimes excited at the enumeration. The rapidity of wit, which never stops to be informed, and which delights by its oddities, established it as an axiom, that the salaries of the governor, judges, and other officers were to be paid in skins absolutely; and to add to their merriment, had them payable in mink skins."

Wealth standards have varied during the history of America. Money, paper and minted coins were scarce during the early years of the young country. For instance Virginia placed the value or price of a wife at 150 pounds of tobacco. In 1688 Virginia paid her preachers with tobacco. Maryland used tobacco as a standard of value. North Carolina used hides and tallow to pay debts as late as 1722. South Carolina used corn. Musket balls and milk pails were used in some northern states as legal tender. The provisions of the Franklin Government were laughed at in some quarters but most states were tainted with similar standards somewhere along their road to statehood.

GOVERNOR MARTIN SENDS EMISSARY TO FRANKLIN

Governor Alexander Martin, in an effort to find out the true conditions in the Overmountain Country, sent a representative with a letter to Colonel Sevier.

From North Carolina State Records Martin's letter of instructions to Major Samuel Henderson is reproduced:

"You will please to repair with despatch to General Sevier and deliver him the letters herewith handed you, and request his answer. You will make yourself acquainted with the transaction of the people in the Western Country, such as holding a convention; and learn whether the same be temporary, to be exercised only during the time of the late cession act, and that since repeal thereof they mean to consider themselves citizens of North Carolina; or whether they intend the same to perpetual; and what measures they have taken to support such government. They you procure a copy of the constitution and the names of such officers at present exercising the powers of the new government. That you be informed whether a faction of a few leading men be at the head of this business, or whether it be the sense of a large majority of the people that the State be dismembered at this crisis of affairs, and what laws and resolutions are formed for their future government; also, where the bounds of their new State are to extend, and whether Cumberland or Kentucky, or both, are to be included therein, and whether the people of these places have taken part in these transactions. You will learn the temper and disposition of the Indians, and what is done in Hubbard's case, and how his conduct is approved or disapproved in general. Lastly, every other information you think necessary to procure, you will communicate to me as soon as possible; at the same time you will conduct yourself with that prudence you are master of, in not throwing our menances, or making use of any language that may serve to irritate persons concerned in the above measures."

The Franklin Assembly was in session when Henderson arrived in Jonesborough. Governor John Sevier, sworn in as Governor, March 1st, 1785, read Martin's letter to the assembled legislators. Even though the letter was addressed to Brigadier-General John Sevier, both Sevier and the Assembly replied:

TO GOV. ALEXANDER MARTIN

Washington Courthouse, March 22, 1785

Sir: Yours by Maj. (Samuel) Henderson of 27th February came safe to hand, wherein you express your concern in regard to the measures taken in our western counties.

I had the honor to lay your Excellency's letter before the Assembly who have undertaken to answer the same, and hope they will give you full and ample satisfaction in regard to the proceedings of this Country and the reasons for so doing.

The People of this Country consider themselves illy treated, first being ceded without their consents, secondly by repealing the act in the same manner.

Your Excellency well knew in what manner the lands was taken from the Indians. You also know that there was a quantity of goods to be given them as compensation; but as soon as the cession act passed, the goods was refused; and no sooner than the melancholy news reached our country, the Indians were murdering on the Kentucky road and in some of our own counties, and have lately killed and taken several prisoners. I am sensible an Indian War will ensue this summer, and it is the Western people alone that must suffer and undergo all the hardships and cruelties that usually attend a savage and bloody war.

You cannot be insensible that North Carolina in opening her land office tolerated all the lands on the north side of the Tennessee as far up as the mouth of Holston River to be entered. Have (you) been informed that within this limits that there is several Indian towns, and the greater part of all the corn plantations belonging to Chickamaugo lie on the north side of Tennessee (River), together with all the principal part of their hunting grounds? If not, I can assure your Excellency it is the case, and this alone I have sufficient reasons to believe in the principal reason why the Indians commit hostilities.

As to the lands on the south of Broad River, where some few people are settled, I cannot believe the Indians care anything about (it) and have expressed themselves to me in that light. For they have no hunting in that quarter, and consequently care little about those lands, especially when the people are allowed by act of your Assembly to settle down to and in their towns, and are now settled and making great preparations for settling near one hundred miles below the upper settlements.

It gives me great pain to think there should arise any disputes between us and North Carolina, and I flatter myself that when Carolina states the matter in a fair light, she will be fully convinced that necessity and self-preservation have compelled us to the measures we have taken, and could the people (have) discovered that North Carolina would have protected and governed them, they would (have) remained where they were, but they perceived a neglect and coolness. And the language of many of your most leading members convinced them they were altogether disregarded.

I beg leave to assure your Excellency that we have always had a most perfect regard to your administration, and had you come to the treaty, I am satisfied all due deference would have been paid you, and further, no person here blamed you for any past measures, but on the contrary believed you to be a friend to the Western Country.

I am, Sir, your Excellency's most obedient, humble servant,

JOHN SEVIER

The Franklin Assembly formulated their reply:

Jonesborough, 22nd March, 1785.

Sir:

Your letter of the 27th of February, 1785, to his Excellency Governor Sevier, favored by Major Henderson, was laid before the General Assembly of the State of Franklin by the Governor.

We think it our duty to communicate to you the sense of the people of this State. We observe your Excellency's candor in informing us that the reason North Carolina repealed the cession act was because the sense of Congress was to allow the State of North Carolina nothing for the land ceded. The truth of that assertion we will not undertake to determine; but we humbly conceive the terms on which Congress was empowered to accept the cession were fully expressed in the cession act itself. Consequently every reason existed for not passing the cession act that could have existed for the repeal, except that of doing justice to the United States in general, who, upon every principle of natural justice, are equally entitled to the land that has been conquered by our own joint efforts.

We humbly thank North Carolina for every sentiment of regard she has for us; but we are sorry to observe that it is founded on principles of interest, as is apparent from the tenor of your Excellency's letter. We are therefore doubtful, when the cause ceases which is the basis of your affection, we shall consequently lose your esteem.

Sir, reflect upon the language of some of the most eminent members of the General Assembly of North Carolina at the last spring session, when the members from the Western Country were supplicating to be continued a part of your State. Were not these their epithets: "The inhabitants of the Western Country are the offscourings of the earth, fugitives from justice," and we will be rid of them at any rate." The members of the Western Country, upon hearing these unjust reproaches and being convinced it was the sense of the General Assembly to get rid of them, consulted each other and concluded it was best to appear reconciled with the masses in order to obtain the best terms they could, and were much astonished to see North Carolina, immediately on passing the act of cession, enter into a resolve to stop the goods that they, by the act of the General Assembly, had promised to give the Indians for the lands they had taken from them and sold for the use of the State. The inadequate allowance made the judges who were appointed to attend the courts of criminal justice, and who had to travel over the mountains, amounted to prohibition as to the administration of justice in this quarter, and altho' the judge appointed on this side the mountain might, from the regard he had to the administration of justice in the Cumberland Country, have held a court there, yet, as your Excellency failed to grant him a commission agreeable to the Act of Assembly, he could not have performed that service had he been ever so desirous of doing it. In short, the Western Country found themselves taxed to support government, while they were deprived of all the blessings of it - not to mention the injustice done them in taxing their lands, which lie five hundred miles from trade, equal to land of the same quality of the sea shore. The frequent murders committed by the Indians on our frontiers have compelled us to think on some plan for our defense. How far North Carolina has been accessory to these murders we will not pretend to say. We only know that she took the land the Indians claimed, promised to pay them for them and again resolved not to do it; and that in consequence of the resolve, the goods were stopped.

You say it has been suggested that the Indian goods are to be seized and the commissioners arrested when they arrive on the business of the treaty. We are happy to inform you that the suggestion is false, groundless and without the least foundation; and we are certain you cannot pretend to fault us that the goods are stopped by a resolve of the assembly of your State; and if your State are determined to evade their promise to the Indians, we entreat you not to lay blame upon us, who are entirely innocent and determined to remain so. It is true that we have declared ourselve a free and independent State, and pledged our honors, confirmed by a solemn oath, to support, maintain and defend the same. But we had not the most distant idea that we should have incurred the least displeasure from North Carolina, who compelled us to the measure; and to convince her that we still retain our affection for her, the first law we enacted was to secure and confirm all the rights granted under the laws of North Carolina in the same manner as if we had not declared ourselves an independent State; have patronized her Constitution and laws and hope for her assistance and influence in Congress to precipitate our reception into the Federal Union. Should our sanguine hopes be blasted, we are determined never to desert that independence which we are bound by every sacred tie of honor and religion to support. We are induced to think, that North Carolina will not blame us for endeavoring to promote our own interest and happiness, while we do not attempt to abridge hers; and appeal to the impartial world to determine whether we have deserted North Carolina or North Carolina deserted us.

You will please to lay these our sentiments before the General Assembly, whom we beg leave to assure, that, should they ever need our assistance, we shall always be ready to render them every service in our powers, and hope to find the the same sentiments prevailing in them towards us; and we hereunto annex the reasons that induced the convention to a Declaration of Independence, which are as follows:

1st.   That the Constitution of North Carolina declares that it shall be justifiable to erect new States westward whenever the consent of the Legislature shall countenance it; and this consent is implied, we conceive, in the cession act, which has thrown us into such a situation that the influence of the law in common cases became almost a nullity, and in criminal jurisdiction has entirely ceased; which reduced us to the verge of anarchy.

2nd.   The Assembly of North Carolina have detained a certain quantity of goods which was promised to satisfy the Indians for the lands we possess, which detenure we fully conceive has so exasperated them that they have actually committed hostilities upon us, and we are alone impelled to defend ourselves from their ravages.

3rd.   The resolutions of Congress held out from time to time encouraging the erection of new States have appeared to us ample encouragement.

4th.   Our local situation is such that we not only apprehend we should be separated from North Carolina, but most every sensible, disinterested traveler has declared it incompatible with our interest to belong in union with the eastern parts of North Carolina. For we are not only so far removed from the eastern parts of the State, but separated from them by high and almost impassable mountains, which naturally divide us from them. Have proved to us that our interest is also in many respects distinct from the inhabitants on the other side and much injured by a union with them.

5th.   We unanimously agree that our lives, liberty and property can be more secure and our happiness much better propagated by our separation; and consequently that it is our duty and inalienable right to form ourselves into a new independent State.

We beg leave to subscribe ourselves,

Your Excellency's Most Obedient Humbl. Servt's,

    William Cage, S. H. C.

    Landon Carter, S. S.

By order of the General Assembly.

    Thomas Talbot, C. S.

    Thomas Chapman, C. C.

When Major Henderson returned to Martin's headquarters, he carried not only Sevier's letter and the the Assembly document, but a vast amount of information picked up while on His mission. Governor Martin immediately summoned the State Council into an emergency meeting. Tempers flared, when they learned the full particulars of what was happening across the mountains. Some wanted to call out the militia, march across the Appalachia, arrest the leaders and quell the revolt. They went so far as to request military aid from Georgia, South Carolina, Virginia and Maryland. All the states, save one, refused. South Carolina reluctantly agreed to send troops.

After tempers had cooled, the Officials realized the folly of attempting to subdue the Overmountain Men with military force. Those King's Mountain Riflemen would put to route any coastal military force that could be mustered. And also such tactics would only serve to unite those uncouth frontiersmen more firmly in their purpose of separation.

The South Carolinians, in replying to Governor Martin's request for military aid said: "Colonel John Sevier might be a fool in his political ventures but his riflemen didn't shoot like fools." The battle of invasion became a battle of words with the mountaineers ready to use words or bullets. Sevier is supposed to have said: "We sleep with our rifles beside us in the best of times. If we are able to keep the hostile Indians at a distance I don't believe we have much to fear from an invading force from North Carolina."

After this flareup, a more diplomatic solution was adopted in an effort to halt the progress of the new State. About all that came out of the emergency meeting of the North Carolina State Council was a "Manifesto" printed and distributed to the citizens of Franklin.

STATE OF NORTH CAROLINA

By His Excellency ALEXANDER MARTIN, Esquire, Governor, Captain-General and Commander-in Chief of the State aforesaid---

To the Inhabitants of the Counties of Washington, Sullivan and Greene:

A MANIFESTO

Whereas, I have received letters from Brigadier-General Sevier, under the style and character of Governor, and from Messrs. Landon Carter and William Cage, as Speakers of the Senate and House of Commons of the State of Franklin, informing me that they, with you, the inhabitants of part of the territory lately ceded to Congress, had declared themselves under the sovereignty and jurisdiction of the same, stating their reason for their separation and revolt - among which it is alleged   that the western country was ceded to Congress without their consent, by an act of the legislature, and the same was repealed in the like manner.

It is evident, from the journals of that Assembly, how far that assertion is supported, which held up to public view the names of those who voted on the different sides of that important question, where is found a considerable number, if not a majority, of the members - some of whom are leaders in the present revolt - then representing the above counties, in support of that act they now deem impolitic and pretend to reprobate - which, in all probability, would not have passed but through their influence and assiduity - whose passage at length was effected but by a small majority, and by which a cession of the vacant territory was only made and obtained with a power to the delegates to complete the same by grants, but that government should still be supported, and that anarchy prevented - which is now suggested - the western people were ready to fall into. The sovereignty and jurisdiction of the state were, by another act passed by the same assembly, reserved and asserted over the ceded territory, with all the powers and authorities as full and ample as before, until Congress should accept the same.

The last Assembly having learned what uneasiness and discontent the Cession act had occasioned throughout the state, whose inhabitants had not been previously consulted on that measure, in whom, by the constitution, the soil and territorial rights of the state are particularly vested, judging the said act impolitic at this time, more especially as it would, for a small consideration, dismember the state of one half of her territory, and in the end tear from her a respectable body of her citizens, when no one state in the Union had parted with any of their citizens, or given anything like an equivalent to Congress but vacant lands of an equivocal and disputed title and distant situation; and also considering that the said act, by its tenor and purport, was revocable at any time before the cession should have been completed by the delegates, who repealed it by a great majority; at the same time, the Assembly, to convince the people of the western country of their affection and attention to their interest, attempted to render government as easy as possible to them, by removing the only general inconvenience and grievance they might labour under, for the want of a regular administration of criminal justice, and a proper and immediate command of the militia; a new district was erected, an assistant judge and a brigadier-general were appointed.

Another reason for the revolt is assigned, that the Assembly on the Cession act stopped a quantity of goods intended for the Cherokee Indians, as a compensation for their claim to the western lands; and that the Indians had committed hostilities, in consequence thereof. The journals of the Assembly evince the contrary; that the said goods were still to be given to the Indians, but under the regulations of Congress, should the cession take place; which occasioned the delay of not immediately sending them forward; of which the Indians were immediately notified, and I am well informed that no hostilities or mischiefs have been committed on this account; but, on the other hand, that provocations have been, and are daily given, their lands trespassed upon, and even one of their chiefs has been lately murdered, with impunity.

On the repeal of the Cession act, a treaty was ordered to be held with the Indians, and the goods distributed as soon as the season would permit; which, before this, would have been carried into effect, had not the face of affairs been changed.

Under what character, but truly disgraceful, could the State of North Carolina suffer treaties to be held with the Indians, and other business transacted in a country, where her authority and government were rejected and set at naught, her officers liable to insult, void of assistance or protection.

The particular attention the legislature have paid to the interest of the western citizens, though calculated to conciliate their affection and esteem, has not been satisfactory, it seems: but the same has been attributed to interest and lucrative designs. Whatever designs the legislature entertained in the repeal of the said act, they have made it appear that their wisdom considered that the situation of our public accounts was somewhat changed since that Assembly, and that the interest of the state should immediately be consulted and attended to, that every citizen should reap the advantage of the vacant territory, that the same should be reserved for the payment of the public debts of the state, under such regulations hereafter to be adopted; judging it ill-timed generosity at this crisis, to be too liberal of the means that would so greatly contribute to her honesty and justice.

But designs of a more dangerous nature and deeper die seem to blare in the western revolt. The power usurped over the the vacant territory, the Union deriving no emolument from the same, not even the proportional part intended the old states by the cession being reserved, her jurisdiction and sovereignty over that country (which, by the consent of its representatives, were still to remain and be exercised) rejected and deposed; her public revenue in that part of her government seized by the new authority, and not suffered to be paid to the lawful Treasurer, but appropriated to different purposes, as intended by the Legislature, - are all facts, evincing that a restless ambition and a lawless thirst of power, have inspired this enterprise, by which the persons concerned, therein, may be precipitated into measures that may, at last, bring down ruin, not only on themselves, but our country at large.

In order, therefore, to reclaim such citizens, who, by specious pretences and the acts of designing men, have been seduced from their allegiance, to restrain others from following their example who are wavering, and to confirm the attachment and affection of those who adhere to the old government, and whose fidelity hath not yet been shaken, I have thought proper to issue this Manifest, hereby warning all persons concerned in the said revolt, that they return to their duty and allegiance, and forbear paying any obedience to any selfcreated power and authority unknown to the constitution of the state, and not sanctified by the Legislature. That they and you consider the consequences that may attend such a dangerous and unwarrantable procedure; that far less causes have deluged states and kingdoms with blood, which, at length, have terminated their existence, either by subjecting them a prey to foreign conquerors, or erecting in their room a despotism that has biden defiance to time to shake off; - the lowest state of misery, human nature, under such a government, can be reduced to. That they reflect there is a national pride in all kingdoms and states, that inspires every subject and citizen with a degree of importance - the grand cement and support of every government - which must not be insulted. That the honour of this State has been particularly wounded, by seizing that by violence which, in time, no doubt would have been obtained by consent, when the terms of separation would have been explained and stipulated to be mutual satisfaction of the mother and new state. That Congress, by the confederation, cannot countenance such a separation, wherein the State of North Carolina hath not given her full consent; and if an implied or conditional one hath been given, the same hath been rescinded by a full Legislature. Of her reasons for so doing they consider themselves the only competent judges.

That by such rash and irregular conduct a precedent is formed for every district, and even every county of the state, to claim the right of separation and independency for any supposed grievance of the inhabitants, as caprice, pride and ambition shall dictate, at pleasure, thereby exhibiting to the world a melancholy instance of a feeble or pusillanimous government, that is either unable or dares not restrain the lawless designs of its citizens, which will give ample cause of exultation to our late enemies, and raise their hopes that they may hereafter gain by the division among ourselves, that dominion their tyranny and arms have lost, and could not maintain.

That you tarnish not the laurels you have so gloriously won at King's Mountain and elsewhere, in supporting the freedom and independence of the United States, and this state in particular, to be whose citizens were then your boast, in being concerned in a black and traitorous revolt from that government in whose defence you have so copiously bled, and which, by solemn oath, you are still bound to support. Let not Vermont be held up as an example on this occasion. Vermont, we are informed, had her claims for a separate government at the first existence of the American war, and, as such with the other states, although not in the Union, hath exerted her powers against the late common enemy.

That you be not insulted or led away with the pagentry of a mock government without the essentials - the shadow without the substance - which always dazzles weak minds, and which will, in its present form and manner of existance, not only subject you to the ridicule and contempt of the world, but rouse the indignation of the other states in the Union at your obtruding yourselves as a power among them without their consent. Consider what a number of men of different abilities will be wanting to fill the civil list of the State of Franklin, and the expense necessary to support them suitable to their various degrees of dignity, when the District of Washington, with its present officers, might answer all the purposes of a happy government until the period arrive when a separation might take place to mutual advantage and satisfaction on an honourable footing. The Legislature will shortly meet, before whom the transactions of your leaders will be laid. Let your representatives come forward and present every grievance in a constitutional manner, that they may be redressed; and let your terms of separation be proposed with decency, your proportion of the public debts ascertained, the vacant territory appropriated to the mutual benefit of both parties, in such manner and proportion as may be just and reasonable; let your proposals be consistent with the honour of the state to accede to, which, by your allegiance as good citizens you cannot violate, and I make no doubt but her generosity, in time, will meet your wishes.

But on the contrary, should you be hurried on by blind ambition to pursue your present unjustifiable measures, which may open afresh the wounds of this late bleeding country, and plunge it again into all the miseries of a civil war, which God avert; let the fatal consequences be charged upon the authors. It is only time which can reveal the event. I know with reluctance the state will be driven to arms; it will be the last alternative to imbrue her hand in the blood of her citizens; but if no other ways and means are found to save her honour, and reclaim her head-strong, refractory citizens, but this last sad expedient, her resources are not yet so exhausted or her spirits damped, but she may take satisfaction for this great injury received, regain her government over the revolted territory or render it not worth possessing. But all these effects may be prevented, at this time, by removing the causes, by those who have revolted returning to their duty, and those who have revolted returning to their duty, and those who have stood firm, still continue to support the government of this state, until the consent of the legislature be fully and constitutionally had for a separate sovereignty and jurisdiction. All which, by virtue of the powers and authorities which your representatives and others of the state at large have invested me with in General Assembly, I hereby will command and require, as you will be liable to answer all the pains and penalties that may ensue on the contrary.

Given under my hand and the Great Seal of the State, which I have caused to be hereunto affixed, at.Hillsborough, the twenty-fifty day of April, in the year of our Lord 1785, and ninth year of the Independence of the said State.

ALEXANDER MARTIN.

By His Excellency's command
   James Glasgow, Secretary.

Governor John Sevier responded to Martin's "Manifesto" with a "Proclamation" of his own.

State of Franklin.
A PROCLAMATION.

WHEREAS, a manifesto is sent in and circulating through this State, in order to create sedition and stir up insurrection among the good citizens of this STATE, thinking thereby to destroy that peace and tranquility that so greatly abounds amont the peaceful citizens of the new happy country.

And, notwithstanding that their own acts declare to the world that they first invited us to the separation, if in their power, would now bring down ruin and destruction on that part of their late citizens, that the the world well knows saved the State out of the hands of the enemy, and saved her from impending ruin.

Notwithstanding we have the fullest confidence in the true attachment and fidelity of the good citizens of this State, I have thought it proper to issue this my Proclamation, strictly enjoining and requiring all and every the good citizens of this State, as they will answer the same at peril, to be obedient and conformable to the laws thereof.

Witness, John Sevier, Esq., Governor, and Captain-General in and over the said State, under his hand and seal of arms, in Washington, this fifteenth day of May, one thousand seven hundred and eighty-five, and in the first year of our Independency.

JOHN SEVIER.

GOD SAVE THE STATE!

The Governor had now formally proclaimed, "The State of Franklin." Most authorities have agreed that if Martin had continued in the Governor's role, Franklin would have succeeded in gaining statehood. His contemptuous, unrelenting attitude toward the Franks, without militia or Federal aid to back him up, would have consolidated the people into a forceful move. It was Governor Richard Caswell, the understanding, clever politician who won the battle against separation with his program of conciliation. Following is transcribed letter from Governor John Sevier to Governor Richard Caswell of North Carolina.

STATE OF FRANKLIN,
Washington County, 14th May, 1785.

Sir: Governor Martin has lately sent up into our country a Manifesto, together with letters to private persons, in order to stir up sedition and insurrection, thinking, thereby, to destroy that peace and tranquility, which have so greatly subsisted among the peaceful citizens of this country.

First in the Manifesto, he charges us with a revolt from North Carolina, by declaring ourselves independent of that state. Secondly, that designs of a more dangerous nature and deeper die seem to glare in the western revolt, the power being usurped over the western vacant territory, the Union deriving no emolument from the same, not even the part intended for North Carolina by the cession, and that part of her revenue is seized by the new authority and appropriated to different purposes than those intended by your legislature.

His Excellency is pleased to mention that one reason we have assigned for the revolt, as he terms it, is that the goods were stopped from the Indians, that were to compensate them for the western lands, and that the Indians had committed murders in consequence thereof. He is also pleased to say that he is well informed to the contrary, and that no hostilities have been committed on that account but on the other hand, provocations are daily given the Indians, and one of their chiefs murdered with impunity. In answer to the charge relative to what His Excellency is pleased to call the revolt, I must beg leave to differ with him in sentiment on that occasion; for your own acts declare to the world that this country was ceded off to Congress, and one part of the express condition was, that the same should be erected into one or move states; and we believe that body was candid, and that they fully believe a new state would tend to the mutual advantage of all parties; that they were as well acquainted with our circumstances at that time, as Governor Martin can be since, and that they did not think a new government here would be led away by the pageantry of a mock government without the essentials, and leave nothing among us but a shadow, as represented by him.

But if Governor Martin is right in his suggestion, we can only say that the Assembly of North Carolina deceived us, and were urging us on into total ruin, and laying a plan to destroy that part of her citizens she so often frankly confessed saved the parent state from ruin. But the people here, neither at that time nor the present, having the most distant idea of any such intended deception, and at the same time well knowing how pressingly Congress had requested a cession to be made of the western territory ever since the 6th of September and 10th of October, in the year 1780 these several circumstances, together with a real necessity to prevent anarchy, promote our own happiness, and provide against the common enemy, that always infest this part of the world, induced and compelled the people have to act as they have done innocently: thinking, at the same time, your acts tolerated them in the separation. Therefore, we can by no means think it can be called a revolt or known by such a name. As to the second charge, it is entirely groundless. We have by no act, whatever, laid hold of one foot of the vacant land, neither have we appropriated any of the same to any of our use or uses, but intend everything of that nature for further deliberation, and to be mutually settled according to the right and claim of each party.

As to that part of seizing the public money, it is groundless as the former. For no authority among us, whatever, has laid hold of or appropriated one farthing of the same to our uses in any shape whatever, but the same is still in the hands of the sheriff and collectors. And on the other hand, we have passed such laws as will both compel and justify them in setting and paying up to the respective claimants of the same; all which will appear in our acts, which will be laid before you and fully evince to the reverse of Governor Martin's charge in the Manifesto.

Very true, we suggest that the Indians have committed murders in consequence of the delay of the goods. Nearly forty people have been murdered since the Cession Bill passed, some of which lived in our own counties, and the remainder on the Kentucky Path; and it is evidently known to the Cherokees, and their frequent talks prove, they are exasperated at getting nothing for their lands, and in all probability had their goods been furnished, no hostilities would have been committed.

The murder committed with impunity, alluding to Major Hubbard's killing a half-breed, which Governor Martin calls a chief (but who was never any such thing among the Indians.) We can't pretend to say what information His Excellency has received on this subject more than the others, or where from. This we know, that all the proof was had against Hubbard that ever can be had, which is, the Indian first struck, then discharged his gun at Hubbard, before the Indian was killed by Hubbard. As Governor Martin reprobates the measure in so great a degree, I can't pretend to say what he might have done, but must believe, that had any other person met with the same insult from one of those bloody savages, who have so frequently murdered the wives and children of the people of this country for many years past, I say had they been possessed of that manly and soldierly spirit that becomes an American, they must have acted like Hubbard.

I have now noticed to your Excellency the principal complaints in the Manifesto, and such as I think is worth observation, and have called forth such proofs as must evince fully the reverse of the charge and complaints set forth.

The menaces made use of in the Manifesto will by no means intimidate us. We mean to pursue our necessary measures, and with the fullest confidence believe that your legislature, when truly informed of our civil proceedings, will find no cause for resenting anything we have done.

Most certain it is, that nothing has been transacted here out of any disregard for the parent state, but we still entertain the same high opinion and have the same regard and affection for her that ever we had, and would be as ready to step forth in her defense as ever we did, should need require it.

Also our acts and resolutions will evince to the world, that we have paid all due respect to your state. First, in taking up and adopting her constitution and then her laws, together with naming several new counties and also an academy after some of the first men in your state.

The repeal of the Cession act we cannot take notice of, as we had declared our separation before the repeal. Therefore, we are bound to support it with that manly firmness that becomes freemen.

Our Assembly sits again in August, at which time it is expected commissioners will be appointed to adjust and consider on such matters of moment as will be consistent with the honour and interest of each party.

The disagreeable and sickly time of the year, together with the great distance from Newbern, as also the short notice, puts it out of the power of any person to attend from this quarter at this time.

Governor Caswell replied on June 17, 1785, to Governor Sevier:

KINGSTON, N.C., 17th June, 1785.

Sir: Your favour of the 14th of last month, I had the honour to receive by Colonel Avery.

In this, sir, you have stated the different charges mentioned in Governor Martin's Manifesto, and answered them by the sense of the people, and your own sentiments, with respect to each charge, as well as the reasons which governed in the measures he complained of.

I have not seen Governor Martin's Manifesto, nor have I derived so full and explicit information from any quarter as this you have been pleased to give me. As there was not an Assembly, owing to the members not attending at Governor Martin's request, and sense of the Legislature on this business, of course, could not be had, and as you give me assurances of the peaceable disposition of the people, and their wish to conduct themselves in the manner you mention, and also to send persons to adjust, consider and conciliate matters, I suppose, to the next Assembly, for the present, things must rest as they are with respect to the subject matter of your letter, which shall be laid before the next Assembly. In the meantime, let me entreat you not, by any means, to consider this as giving countenance, by the executive of the state, to any measures lately pursued by the people to the westward of the mountains.

With regard to the goods intended, by the state, for the Indians as a compensation for the lands, they, I believe, have been ready for many months at Washington, and if I can procure wagons to convey them to the place destined, (the Long Island,) I mean to send them there to be disposed of according to the original intention of the Assembly, and will either attend myself or appoint commissioners to treat with the Indians; but in this, you know, it is necessary that whoever attends should be protected by the militia, and, under the present situation of affairs, it is possible my orders may not be attended to in that particular; and however a man may submit to these things in a private character, he may be answerable to the people, at least they may judge it so, in a public situation. Therefore, without your assurances of the officers and men under your command being subject to my orders in this case, as matters stand, I think it would be imprudent in me to come over or send commissioners to treat with the Indians. Of this you will be pleased to write me the first favourable opportunity. It is my wish to come over myself, and if matters turn so that I can with convenience, it is probable I may.

Thus the matter rested for the time being, as The Franklinites went forward with the business of erecting a state.

CONGRESS AND FRANKLIN

William Cocke was delegated by the Franklin Assembly to present their cause before Congress. Cocke arrived in New York, May 15th, 1785, and was permitted to present his petition the next day, May 16th. The document, written by Cocke, is as follows:

GENERAL GEORGE WASHINGTON taking oath as President, April, 1789 in New York, seat of Federal Government.

To the HONORABLE CONTINENTAL CONGRESS:

This memorial of the freemen, by their representatives in General Assembly met, who were included within the limits ascertained by an act of the General Assembly of the State of North Carolina ceding certain vacant lands to Congress, Humbly sheweth,

That having in many instances discovered the friendly disposition of Congress, not only to guard the liberties of the State now in the Union, but also to encourage the erection of new States on the western side of the Appalachian Mountains; and finding the disposition of North Carolina to comply with the requisitions made by Congress requesting liberal cessions of vacant western territory, which requisitions being complied with by North Carolina, she immediately stopped the goods she had promised to give the Indians for the said land which so exasperated them that they began to commit hostilities on our frontiers; in this situation we were induced to a declaration of independence, not doubting but we should be excused by Congress when she came to hear the reasons that called for such a declaration and when she was assured that it was necessity rather than choice, as North Carolina seemed quite regardless of our interest; and the Indians were daily murdering our friends and relatives without distinction of age or sex. And we are sorry to inform Congress that notwithstanding the act of cession must have bound North Carolina at least in honor to have continued the act in force for the space of twelve months from the passing of the same, unless Congress should have refused to accept the cedure, yet North Carolina has repealed the cession act and claims a sovereignty over a country whose prayers she has rejected and whose interests she has forsaken. Impressed with every sentiment of our duty and respect, we earnestly request Congress to accept the offered cession and to receive us into the federal union that we may enjoy all the rights reserved to us in the cession act, and which freemen are entitled to. And we humbly pray that you be pleased to call upon our agent for such further information as you in your wisdom shall think proper, in whose integrity we confide, and earnestly pray that you will adopt such suitable measures as may promote the peace and prosperity of those who wish ever to be found a zealous and useful part of the people that form so dignified a union; and your memorialists shall ever pray.

> Landon Carter, S. W.
> Wm. Cage, S. C.
> By order
> Thomas Talbot, C. S.
> Tho. Chapman, C. C.
> State of Franklin, March 12th, 1785.

This is to certify that William Cocke, Esq., was chosen by the General Assembly of this State as an Agent to carry and introduce this Memorial to the Congress of the United States of America. And he is further invested with full power and authority to state and explain the local and political situation of this State, and to make such representation as he may find conducive to the interest and independence of this country.

> Landon Carter, S. W.
> Wm. Cage, S. C.
> By order
> Thomas Talbot, C. S.
> Tho. Chapman, C. C.

Congress appointed a committee to study the cession act of North Carolina and report their advice. The committee, consisting of King, Johnson, Grayson, and McHenry, brought their report back May 20th.

Report

"That the act of cession of the State of North Carolina, of the 2nd day of June, 1784, gives a right to the United States in Congress assembled, at any time within one year from the passing of the act, to accept the cession of Western territory therein described, subject to the conditions and reservations in said act contained; and that no subsequent act or law of the State of North Carolina could so repeal and make void the said act of cession as to annul the right of the United States in Congress assembled to accept the territory therein ceded within the period, and subject to the conditions and reservations aforesaid.

"That consistently with the objects of the resolution of Congress of the 6th of September and the 10th of October, 1780, and with the duty Congress owes to the federal union, they cannot decline an acceptance of the cession aforesaid; and therefore recommend:

"That the United States in Congress assembled, do accept the cession of western territory made by the State of North Carolina. . . "

William Cocke, learning the attitude of some representatives, tried to have the vote postponed until he could secure more support. On the other hand the North Carolina delegation pushed for a quick vote as this was to their advantage. Little debate was had before the vote was taken. States voting yes were: New Jersey, Rhode Island, Connecticut, New York, New Hampshire, Pennsylvania, and Georgia. Maryland and Virginia voted against the report. North Carolina, being involved did not vote. The South Carolina vote was divided, one for and one against. The damage was caused by Massachusetts and Delaware, though strong in their expressed sentiments for creating the new state, did not vote on the report to accept the North Carolina cession. The vote was close but not enough. The two thirds majority or yes vote of 9 states was ordinarily required. In this particular situation a yes vote by 8 states would have carried the motion in the affirmative as North Carolina could not vote. The State of Franklin was therefore defeated by a single vote. The vote was 7 states for – 2 states against – 1 split vote and 2 states not voting.

The only unanimous vote was on the following report:

"That it be recommended to the State of North Carolina to consider the principle of magnanimity and justice that induced the passage of said act of 2nd day of June, 1784, and evince the operation of the same good sentiments by repealing their act of 20th of November, 1784, and directing their delegates in Congress to furnish a proof of their liberality in the execution of a deed to the United States of the territory ceded by the act of 2nd of June aforesaid."

Thomas Jefferson believed in the statehood of the western territory. He stated that it was only a matter of time until Kentucky and Franklin would be admitted. He told the Virginia and North Carolina leaders that they were wrong in their opposition to pleas of these two territories for their own government.

When the Franklin people were told of Jefferson's statements and attitude, they were ready to change the name from Franklin to Jefferson. The leaders continued with the Franklin title. It has never been ascertained who suggested the name Franklin but the name was Franklin never Frankland.

William Cocke had made an eloquent plea before the assembled Congress. No mention was made in the document of the legislative action recinding the cession act. A North Carolina representative called attention to this omission. Cocke, citing an English common law, responded. *"Can pardon be granted a people with one hand and taken away with the other. This is not the liberty for which you and I fought."*

THOMAS JEFFERSON

England watched the conflict, between North Carolina and Franklin, with great interest. The English press stated that North Carolina was denying the same right to the new State that they had been fighting for.

DUMPLIN CREEK TREATY

The Franklin Officials moved forward with the business of establishing the new state. After the March Session the authority of the new Commonwealth was recognized in all the western counties except Davidson. Deeds, wills, writs and all legal transactions were handled in proper form. A commission had been appointed, during March session, to treat with the Indians. It suddenly dawned on the Franks that they were free to make their own treaties. They were not bound any longer by the North Carolina arrangements. This Commission was composed of Alexander Outlaw, Joseph Hardin, Luke Boyer, Joshua Gist, Ebenezer Alexander and John Sevier.

A meeting was arranged at Major Hugh Henry's Station near mouth of Dumplin Creek, June 10, 1785.

MAJOR HUGH HENRY STATION; Site of the Dumplin
Creek Treaty near French Broad River.

Not many Chiefs attended this treaty and only a portion of the written document has been preserved.

It is agreed by us, the warriors, chiefs and representatives of the Cherokee Nation, that all the lands lying and being on the south side of Holston and French Broad rivers, as far south as the ridge that divides the waters of Little river from the waters of Tennessee, may be peaceably inhabited and cultivated, resided on, enjoyed and inhabited by our elder brothers, the white people, from this time forward and always. And we do agree on our part and in behalf of our Nation, that the white people shall never be by us or any of our Nation, molested or interrupted, either in their persons or property, in no wise, or in any manner or form whatever, in consequence of their settling or inhabiting the said territory, tract of land and country aforesaid, or any part of the same whatever.

John Sevier, for and in behalf of the white people, and for and in behalf of the State or government, or the United States, as the case may hereafter be settled and concluded on with respect to the jurisdiction and sovereignty over the said tract or territory of land, agrees that there shall be a reasonable and liberal compensation made the Cherokees for the lands they have herein ceded and granted to the white people, and to the State or States that may hereafter legally possess and enjoy the country aforesaid, in good faith. That this bargain and engagement now made and entered into between us, the white people and the Cherokees, may never be broken, disannulled or dissolved, in consequence of any claim, right or sovereignty over the soil hereby mentioned and described, as aforesaid.

Done in open treaty, the 10th of June, 1785.

John Sevier,
The King
Anchoo, chief of Chota,
And chiefs of the different towns.

Witnessed:
Lew Boyer,
Alex. Outlaw,
Joshua Gist,
Ebenezer Alexander,
Jos. Hardin,
Charles Murphy, Ling't.

The Indians received clothing and other articles for the lands included in this transaction. Only part of the Cherokee Nation was represented. Those present felt that the Chiefs and towns not represented would repudiate their action. After the Treaty, The Tassel, in a talk sent to the North Carolina Governor said; "The Franklin Authorities only asked, liberty for those that were then living on the lands to remain there, till the headmen of their nation were consulted on it, which our young men agreed to. Since then we are told that they claimed all the lands on the waters of Little River, and call it their ground."

After the Dumplin Treaty, new settlers, flocked into the French Broad area. It has been said that whole communities in North Carolina were abandoned when the migration started. The Treaty was also the basis of a rumor that spread all the way to Congress. Three sources furnish what evidence is available for the report or rumor.

Colonel Arthur Campbell, writing to Governor Henry of Virginia, stated that the treaty *"was of a neighborly and friendly kind."* A Washington County resident wrote that *"The executives of the State of Franklin have concluded a Treaty of amity and perpetual friendship with Cherokee Indians and a negotiation was on foot to give that nation a representation in the new Legislature."* A letter from a Caswell County writer stated, *"a negotiation is on foot with the Cherokee and the aim will be to incorporate them and make them useful citizens. I dare say the project will startle your rigid secretaries -- but you, we expect, will be more liberal, when it manifestly appears that the interest of humanity and of our new society will be promoted."* This last letter is thought to have been written by either Balch or Houston. It was addressed to the Maryland Gazette, October 11, 1785.

Either the Indians didn't want any part of the new society or the Franklin Officials didn't push the idea. Some Federal Officials thought that the Franklin Leaders were merely trying to increase their population count in their fight for statehood.

FRENCH BROAD RIVER originates in North Carolina. The Davidson and Little Mills Rivers; Mud and Cane Creeks, Hominy and Swannanoa Rivers are all tributaries. Many other streams join its flow before it meanders into Tennessee. Pioneer Hunters, seeing this river for the first time, saw that it flowed toward French Territory. They called this broad stream the "French Broad." It became a natural boundary in the settlements.

TOMAHAWK WAR

The Hopewell Treaty promises, by the Federal Government, and Dragging Canoe's success in forcing the Valentine Sevier party to abandon the Muscle Shoals undertaking, encouraged the Indians, in making raids as far north as the Ohio River. Many settlers were being killed. Colonel John Logan and a party of 80 Kentuckians set out in pursuit of a party of Chickamaugans that had killed in that territory. They happened on a band of Indians and thinking this was the party they were after, opened fire, killing 7. They learned too late that this was a friendly tribe of Cherokee from the upper towns. One of the Chiefs killed was Fool Warrior's brother. After this incident, Logan and his party returned to Kentucky country.

Joseph Martin, greatly disturbed, went immediately to Chota in an effort to explain the mistake. Colonel Arthur Campbell sent a letter of explanation to Fool Warrior and Bloody Fellow hoping to prevent a full scale outbreak of war.

Bloody Fellow replied to Campbell; "Demanding satisfaction from the white man has been tried and produced little results; I will take my own satisfaction for my brother." The two Chiefs led a party of braves into the Dumplin Creek Settlements where they burned cabins, killed cattle, took horses and carried back 15 scalps. Bloody Fellow left a note for Governor Sevier by one of the bodies, "I have now taken satisfaction for my brother and friends who were murdered. I did not wish for war, but if the white people want war that is what they will get."

It was hard for the white man to accept the simple fact that the Indian lived by his own primitive code and methods of meting out justice. These early frontiersmen and politicians tried to force their laws, ways of life and courts of justice on the red man. This the Indian resented and rejected. These first native Americans owned the land by virtue of birth, heritage and conquest, so it was natural that they oppose the trespasser with their own style of warfare. The white man's better weapons, know-how and strength were to overcome, subdue, dominate and take the land from this race of people that claimed their own culture and civilization.

HOPEWELL TREATY

Congress was making a valiant effort to establish peaceful relations with the Indians. Conflicting claims of the Cherokee and the Frontiersmen, in the southern region, was one of the main trouble spots. Without consulting Franklin officials or Cumberland leaders, arrangements were made for talks with the Cherokee.

Hopewell, South Carolina, on the Keowee River was selected as the meeting place. Congress appointed Benjamin Hawkins, Joseph Martin, Andrew Pickens and Lachlan McIntosh as commissioners. William Blount, special representative from North Carolina, went early hoping to secure special concessions before the formal ceremonies began. He had no success. John King and Thomas Glasscock, sent from Georgia for the same purpose, met with the same results.

The meet began November 18, 1785 with most of the upper Cherokee towns represented. The Chiefs and headmen were hopeful of this meet. They felt that maybe the new government was going to give them justice and fair treatment in this first Federal-Indian conference. The Cherokee acknowledged the supremacy of the United States, for the first time, during this series of talks. The commission disavowed all previous treaties, such as Dumplin Creek, and promised the return of much of the disputed land. The agreed boundary lines left Greeneville outside the white man's domain as well as areas south and west of Greeneville. Here are excerpts of the talks as transcribed from Brown's "Old Frontiers." A Commissioner speaks:

"Congress is now sovereign of all our country, which we point out for you on the map. They want none of your lands, or anything else which belongs to you. As an earnest of their regard for you, we propose to enter into a treaty perfectly equal and conformable to what we now tell you. If you have any grievances, we will hear them, and will take such measures to correct them as may be proper."

Old Tassel replied:

"The land we are now on, is the land we were fighting for in the late war. The Great Man above made it for us to subsist upon. The red men are the aborigines on this country. It is but a few years since the white men found it. I am of the first stock, a native of this land. The white people are now living upon it as our friends. From the beginning of the friendship between white people and red, beads have been given as confirmation of friendship, as I now give you these beads." (Here he handed to the commissioners a string of white beads.)

"The people of North Carolina have taken our lands without consideration, and are now making their fortunes out of them. I know Richard Henderson says he purchased the lands at Kentucky, and as far as Cumberland, but he is a rogue and a liar, and if he was here I would tell him so. He requested us to sell him a little land on Kentucky River for his horses and cattle to feed on, and we consented; but told him at the same time he would be much exposed to the depredations of the Northern Indians, which he appeared not to regard, provided we gave our consent. If Attakullakulla signed his deed, we were not informed of it; but we know that Oconostota did not, yet we hear his name is to it. Henderson put it there, and he is a rogue."

Taking the map, offered by the Commissioner, Old Tassel marked the boundaries claimed by the Cherokee.

Later, one of the Commissioners replied to the chief:

"You know, Old Tassel, that Colonel Henderson, Oconostota, and the Little Carpenter are all dead. What you say may be true, but here is one of Henderson's deeds. Your memory may fail you, but this is of record, and will remain forever. The parties being dead, and so much time having elapsed, and the country being settled upon the faith of the deed, puts it out of our power to do anything respecting it; you must, therefore, be content with it, as if you had actually sold the land, and point out your claims exclusive of this land."

The Tassel replied:

" I know they are dead, and I am sorry for it, and I suppose it is now too late to recover it. If Henderson were living, I should have the pleasure of telling him that he was a liar. We will begin at Cumberland, and say nothing more about Kentucky, although it is justly ours." He then marked the boundaries on the map with which he said the Cherokees would be satisfied.

"In the forks of French Broad and Holston," Old Tassel continued, "are three thousand white people on

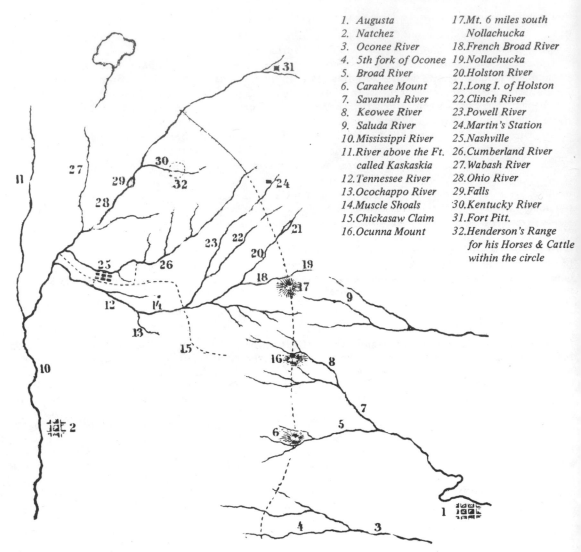

REFERENCES

1. Augusta
2. Natchez
3. Oconee River
4. 5th fork of Oconee
5. Broad River
6. Carahee Mount
7. Savannah River
8. Keowee River
9. Saluda River
10. Mississippi River
11. River above the Ft. called Kaskaskia
12. Tennessee River
13. Ocochappo River
14. Muscle Shoals
15. Chickasaw Claim
16. Ocunna Mount
17. Mt. 6 miles south Nollachucka
18. French Broad River
19. Nollachucka
20. Holston River
21. Long I. of Holston
22. Clinch River
23. Powell River
24. Martin's Station
25. Nashville
26. Cumberland River
27. Wabash River
28. Ohio River
29. Falls
30. Kentucky River
31. Fort Pitt.
32. Henderson's Range for his Horses & Cattle within the circle

This Map is copied from one drawn by the Tassel to describe Cherokee claims presented at treaty at Hopewell, November, 1785 at Hopewell on Keowee. The dotted lines show the reduced territory now agreed upon as a dividing ridge between the Cumberland River, Tennessee and forty miles above Nashville.

our lands. This is a favored spot, and we cannot give it up. It is within twenty-five miles of our towns These people must be removed."

"They are too numerous, and cannot be removed," replied the commissioners. "They settled there when the Cherokees were under the protection of the King of England. You should have asked the King to remove them."

"Is not Congress, which conquered the King of England, strong enough to remove these people?" asked the chief.

Old Tassel insisted that they would not give up the land but finally agreed to leave the matter to Congress. The final boundaries agreed on at Hopewell started on the Cumberland River 40 miles North of Nashville and ran to a point six miles South of the Nolichucky and southward of Oconee River. The town of Greeneville, now Capital of the State of Franklin, had been returned to the Cherokee.

Before signing the treaty, Old Tassel requested permission for the Woman of Chote, the famous Nancy Ward, to talk to the commissioners. She said,

"I am glad there is now a peace. I take you by the hand in real friendship. I look upon you and the red people as my children. I have a pipe and a little tobacco to give to the commissioners to smoke in friendship. I have seen much trouble in the late war. I have borne and raised up warriors. I am now old, but hope yet to bear children who will grow up and people our Nation, as we are now under the protection of Congress and shall have no more disturbance. The talk that I give you is from the young warriors, as well as from myself. They rejoice that we have peace, and hope that the chain of friendship will never be broken."

The last clause in the treaty stated: "Any settler who fails to remove within six months from the land guaranteed to the Indians shall forfeit the protection of the United States, and the Cherokee may punish him or not as they please." This Treaty brought protests from North Carolina, State of Franklin and the Cumberland Officials. Nobody liked it. This last clause was an open invitation to the Indians to harass the five thousand settlers below this boundary line. The State of Franklin completely disregarded any part of the Hopewell Treaty.

Joseph Martin's influence with the Franks was hurt by his participation in this Treaty and Benjamin Hawkins, another North Carolina commissioner, came in for his share of criticism. There is evidence that the North Carolina Commissioners used this Treaty as a punishment for the Franks. This is shown in that part of the Treaty where the Commissioners induced the Indians to give up their claims to lands within the bounds of Henderson's Sycamore Shoals Treaty. This left the Cumberland Settlements outside the Cherokee territory, and the southern counties of Franklin inside the Cherokee boundaries.

FRANKLIN LEADERSHIP DIVIDED
Greeneville Convention November 1785

History has recorded that nations, big and small, have fallen apart from internal conflict rather than outside influence. History has also written that church controlled states are weak and ineffective, and on the other hand state controlled churches have little spiritual voice.

The beginning of Franklin's dissolution started partly from a fight between the early leaders of the Presbyterian Church. This controversy was carried into the political Assembly of the New State. Several Franklin leaders had received their education at Liberty Hall College in Virginia (now Washington and Lee University). Reverend William Graham, head of the institution, exerted a strong influence over his students. Samuel Houston, chairman of the committee appointed to draft a constitution for study, was a close friend and confidant of his teacher William Graham. He sought Graham's assistance in preparing the document. It has been said that Colonel Arthur Campbell had a hand in the writing and wording of the instrument. Campbell was still hopeful that a greater State of Franklin would evolve taking in part of southwest Virginia.

Some of the items stipulated in the Houston document were: 1 - The changing of the name Franklin to Frankland. (This is where the confusion in names originated.) 2 - That the Governor should be chosen annually by popular election. 3 - One provision stipulated that there would be only one legislative body. 4 - A fourth measure included the suggestion that any new bill or law introduced in the legislature should be presented to the people for study before final passage. Section 42 of the Houston-Graham Draft stipulated that the Legislature should employ some person at public expense to draw the constitution out into a familiar catechetical form to be used in the schools. The draft also included a provision that each session of the Assembly was to be opened with a sermon by a minister of the Gospel.

Reverend Samuel Houston read this draft before the Constitutional Convention assembled in Greeneville November 14, 1785. After reading the entire document he then proposed its adoption. As he was reading those sections that declared '*only virtuous believers could hold office or take part in political functions*' and '*no person who is of an immoral character, or guilty of such flagrant enormities as drunkenness, gaming, profane swearing, lewdness, Sabbath-breaking, or such like could hold office.*" Then in somewhat contradictory terms stated; '*no minister of the gospel, lawyer, or doctor should be a member of the Assembly.*' The document also indicated that, '*every citizen of Franklin would have religious freedom, but to hold office he must hold to the orthodox belief.*' Special interest was given to the reading of these clauses.

Houston had barely finished when Reverend Hezekiah Balch, not a member of the Convention, asked permission to speak. (Balch organized Greeneville College, now Tusculum). Balch objected to several clauses in the document, especially to one that provided a levy for a state supported school. This con-

Artist Drawing of Franklin Capitol Building, Greeneville, Tennessee.

frontation on the Assembly floor was to start a controversy that would divide the leadership and the people of Franklin.

The Convention rejected the Houston-Graham document and voted to keep the same instrument, temporarily, adopted at the Jonesborough Convention December, 1784. Houston and his followers were able to get one statement in the records of adoption "That this Constitution would be used until the State was received into the Federal Union; or a majority of the freemen of the State of Franklin shall otherwise direct." The Houston sympathizers and followers were also given permission to enter their names in protest on the Convention journal. These dissenters became prominent in the story of Franklin and Tennessee. They were: David Campbell, Samuel Houston, John Tipton, John Ward, Robert Love, William Cox, David Craig, James White, Samuel Newell, John Gilliland, James Stuart, George Maxwell, Joseph Tipton, Peter Parkinson.

Samuel Houston was mad and upset because his Constitution was not accepted. Many of the people, siding with him, cared little about the religious issues involved but used this situation as an excuse for a fight. This was the beginning of the two state rule over the same people and a schism in the Presbyterian Church. Two factions emerged, the Franklin adherents, and the group that turned back to the North Carolina jurisdiction. It seems evident that here was the beginning of the end of Franklin.

Houston had his documents printed and circulated throughout all the communities of Franklin. A pamphlet titled "Principles of Republican Government by a Citizen of Frankland" was printed and distributed. Balch was just as active in his campaign against Houston. Arguments, debates, fights and dissension grew stronger as the weeks passed. The strife and bitterness created by this controversy was dividing friends, citizens and sections of the new state even before the Commonwealth was able to function properly. The strife was so intense that it reached the jurisdiction of the courts. Balch was burned in effigy. Graham's pamphlet lambasting Balch was brought to court. Ramsey gives us this bit of information on the dispute as taken from the Washington County Records. Greene County took similar action.

"On motion being made by the Attorney for the State, who at the same time exhibited a hand-bill containing an 'Address to the Inhabitants of Frankland State,' under a signature of a citizen of the same, the Court, upon the same being read publicly in open court, adjudged it to contain treasonable insinuations against the United States, and false and ungenerous reflections against persons of distinction in the ecclesiastical department, fraught with falsehood, calculated to aleniate the minds of their citizens from their government and overturn the same.

Upon mature deliberation, the Court condemned said hand-bill to be publicly burned by the High Sheriff, as a treasonable, wicked, false and seditious libel."

The western leaders, opposed to John Sevier and separation from North Carolina, now came out into the open in their fight against Franklin. They knew that they had the political backing of the North Carolina officials. Some writers say that John Tipton was jealous of John Sevier's position and leadership among the people and that he had coveted the Governor's role in the new state and that it was purely a personal attitude that motivated his fight. No matter what the reasons the fight was on in earnest and the people of the new state were fighting among themselves while trying to gain Federal recognition on the outside.

Fundamentally the Houston-Graham Constitution differed very little in its religious phraseology from the Constitution that was adopted by Franklin. But the controversy started by its leaders reached into the heart of Franklin. Governor John Sevier was caught in the middle. No previous experience had prepared him with the diplomatic tools needed to handle this situation. The structure was beginning to crumble and all the Governor's horses and all the Governor's men couldn't pull it up again.

THE GREAT BEND 1785

Many Franklin leaders, including Governor John Sevier, were planning toward the settlement, development and inclusion of the Great Bend or Muscle Shoals territory into the State of Franklin. An agreement had been reached with Georgia who claimed this particular desirable section of country. Some of the North Carolina officials also had promotional plans for this area and disliked seeing the prospect slipping out of their hands.

Valentine Sevier, with 90 settlers, undertook the settling of the Great Bend during the latter part of 1785. They made the trip down by boat. Stockley Donelson was in charge of the surveying and issuance of land grants. Erection of stockades and blockhouses for the central settlement was started immediately on arrival.

The Indians did not like this bold move on to lands that had been promised them for all time in the treaties they had signed. Dragging Canoe and his warriors surrounded the main encampment and placed the settlers in a state of seige. It was unsafe to attempt cabin raising or land clearing as the Indians would ambush the men who ventured away from the protection of the partially erected walls. Discouraged, the party left the Bend early 1786. Bands of warriors followed the group , harrassing and making the return trip perilous and difficult. The many Whites and Indians killed during this episode practically caused a state of war to develop between Franklin and the Cherokee.

One Headman, who lost two sons during the skirmishes with Valentine Sevier's returning party, paid warriors to get two white scalps in revenge. These scalps were taken in Greene County at the home of Ebenezer Birum. Archie Scott and four children were killed in Powell's Valley. Mrs. Scott was taken prisoner but managed to escape about the ninth day. She wandered some 30 days through the Cumberland Mountains, living on berries, roots and fish. She finally reached Martin's station not far from her former home. These are only two of many similar happenings on the frontier.

SPANISH INTRIGUE

The elements of the so-called Spanish Intrigue present an interesting study of the maneuvering and thinking of the frontier leaders. Spanish officials attempted to make a cloak and dagger affair of their participation in this intrigue. On the other hand, the Franks were quite open in their dealings as they used the controversy as a lever and weapon in their fight for statehood.

Spain wanted control of the Mississippi Valley. They feared the rapid spread of the frontiersmen toward their possessions. Having failed in their initial attempt, in having the boundary line set along the mountain range, the Spanish Officials began making exaggerated claims of their territory. They claimed all the southern land bounded by the Ohio, Tennessee, Hiwassee and Flint Rivers. They raised another barrier by closing the Mississippi River to all American navigation. They thought this would discourage and slow down western expansion. The Dons also claimed more influence with the southern Indians than they were able to exert. The Indians needed supplies and had nowhere else to secure them. As the redmen didn't like the Spanish goods, an English trading post, Panton-Leslie & Company, was allowed to operate on Spanish territory in order to keep the Indian fur trade. During the Controversy between the North Carolina officials and the Franklin people, Spanish representatives attempted to bring the Franks and Cumberland settlements into their political influence.

During the 1786 session, Congress had instructed John Jay, Secretary of Foreign Affairs, to hold talks with the Spanish Minister to America. Don Diego de Gardoqui was willing to open trade relations with America on one condition: America must grant Spain complete control of the Mississippi Basin. The New England shipowners and businessmen pressured Jay into proposing to Congress a deal that would permit Spain to close the Mississippi River to all American navigation for a period of 25 years. This proposal failed in the Congressional vote. Seven northern states voted for the measure. The southern states were able to muster enough strength to defeat the bill as nine votes were required for passage.

JOHN JAY in charge of American Foreign Affairs during negotiations with Gardoqui. Served as Chief Justice under President Washington.

This situation stirred up quite a hornet's nest among the Franklin, Cumberland, and Bluegrass citizens. Thomas Greene, with official backing from Georgia, had attempted to start a colony at Natchez named Bourbon. Governor Miro had quickly put a stop to this and Green fled to safer quarters. Green wrote many letters to various people in the western country. There was enough truth in his exaggerated statements to give the letters credence. These documents were passed from hand to hand through the territory and added fuel to the fires.

The antagonistic talk among the westerners was so strong against the seaboard officials, that England, France and Spain were led to believe that the western frontiersmen would leave the American Flag and become subjects of another country. Virginia's Grayson made a statement in a letter to Madison, "If the Federal Government remains much longer in its state of imbecility, we shall be one of the most contemptible nations on the face of the earth."

The western frontiersmen felt that the seaboard leaders of the New England states were willing to sell them out for their own gain. This attitude was to have its effect on these southern states for years to come. In the same manner the callous treatment by North Carolina officials of their western citizens would affect the relationship of Tennessee and North Carolina for generations.

These westerners were farmers and trappers. They needed the open navigation of the Mississippi River and its tributaries to get their products to market. Their economic survival depended on the southern ports for shipping. Spanish officials knowing this used their control of the lower Mississippi as a bargaining point in every discussion. The confusion and bitter feelings aroused by this controversy were fed by personalities like Wilkerson, who in the pay of the Spanish, advocated coming under their influence.

Dr. James White, congressman from North Carolina, now enters the western picture. (This James White is not to be confused with the James White that settled Knoxville.) Dr. White had gained possession of grants for large tracts of land in the Cumberland basin. Uneasy that closure of the Mississippi River would destroy the value of his holdings, Dr. White arranged talks with Don Gardoqui during 1786. It is said that Dr. White made the statement to the Spanish Minister that the westerners, angered at Jay's proposal would most likely cut themselves off from the seaboard countries and ally with either Spanish or English interests. These freedom loving men, having fought for liberty from one king would hardly accept the domination of another royal master but the Franks were willing at this point to become part of Kentucky or Georgia in order to get out from under the coastal domination of the North Carolina officials. They had learned that the only interest the political rulers of that state had in the western territory was land control.

COYATEE TREATY

Early August 1786, 250 men, under General William Cocke and Colonel Alexander Outlaw, were sent by the State of Franklin into the Cherokee country in an effort to subdue Indian attacks. Old Tassel and Hanging Maw protested this invasion and expressed their peaceful actions and intentions toward their white brothers. Outlaw and Cocke accused them of the murders of Colonel John Donelson, William Christian and the two Birums killed in Greene County.

Old Tassel insisted that it was not the Overhill Indians who were guilty of committing these deeds and that they should not be punished. Cocke and Outlaw marched their force to Coyatee and in the fray two of the braves responsible for some of the killings were caught.

The Cherokee Chiefs were called together and practically forced to sign a treaty permitting the white settlers to build cabins between French Broad and Little Tennessee Rivers. The treaty was signed under duress as a force of two hundred rifles, standing over the redmen, gave them little choice. They were told that the land would be settled with or without their permission or signature on the treaty.

A land office was opened shortly after this Treaty to sell titles to the constant stream of immigrants flocking in to take up claims. This was not a very creditable action on the part of Franklin and placed them in the same category of other groups who used force and the Indian's ignorance of the white man's barter system, to exploit the Red Man.

DAVY CROCKETT
Born In The State Of Franklin

Davy Crockett had no part in the State of Franklin's formation, but he became one of her most widely known citizens. His birthplace was between Jonesborough and Greeneville, the two capitol sites of that almost 14th State. The cabin of John and Rebecca Crockett was located near the mouth of Limestone Creek on the banks of the Nolichucky River.

Davy's experience in the wilderness and the world of combat began at an early age. His schooling was a four month session taught by the son of his Virginia employer. Davy served as an officer in the Creek war of 1813-1814. He was elected to the Tennessee Legislature two sessions. The world of politics lured him into a congressional race which he lost, ran again and won. He served in the United States Congress three sessions. Davy Crockett was in great demand as a speaker in the northern states. His tall, homespun tales of folk-lore, wilderness bear hunts, Indian fighting and frontier life attracted wide attention.

When President Andrew Jackson was pushing the Cherokee Removal Bill through Congress, Davy Crockett was the only Tennessee Representative that voted against the bill. This, and related events, caused a break between Davy and the Jackson crowd. Because of this stand, Davy was defeated in his last campaign for re-election.

Disgusted with politics, Davy and a group of friends decided to move. They crossed the Mississippi and headed toward Texas. He joined Colonel William Travis at the Alamo, February 1836. This valiant group held out against a greatly superior force for days. March 6, 1836, Santa Anna was able to take the fortified mission. All the men lost their lives. A few of the women were spared to tell about the tragic battle.

Davy Crockett was dedicated to liberty and individual freedom. Much of his adult life was spent in Middle and West Tennessee. 1811-13 he located on a site in present Moore County. From there he moved to Franklin County site. His last homesite before the Alamo was in Gibson County territory.

LIMESTONE MARKER placed at birth site during middle 1800s; said to have been door step to original cabin. David Crockett Birthplace Association developed site and presented to State of Tennessee 1958.

RESTORED CABIN, said to contain some of original logs, is located in upper Greene County, Tennessee.

CROCKETT TAVERN, located in Morristown, Tenn. was originally built on this site during 1790s by John Crockett. Davy spent boyhood years here.

DAVID CROCKETT

OCTOBER 1786 SESSION FRANKLIN ASSEMBLY

Governor Sevier called the Franklin Assembly together in October. Gilbert Christian was speaker of the senate and Joseph Conway, clerk. The house elected Henry Conway, speaker and Isaac Taylor, clerk. Two matters needed urgent attention. The joint campaign with Georgia against the Creeks needed official sanction. Another matter was selecting official representatives to the North Carolina Legislature to present the cause of Franklin to that body. It was also during 1786 that the County of Blount was made a part of the new State.

William Cocke and David Campbell were appointed to attend the Legislative session soon to meet in Fayetteville. Judge Campbell, unable to make the trip because of health, sent his message and discussion of the situation in the form of a letter. Cocke presented Franklin's cause in an eloquent, dramatic manner. Many of the members, listening to his pleas for consideration of the westerners,

HENRY CONWAY: settled on farm located on Little Chucky Creek 1783 where he had entered 600 acres on north side of Nolichucky River in Greene County. This house was built on Conway farm by Hugh Douglas Hale who married Sarah Hundley Sevier, granddaughter of both Henry Conway and John Sevier.

were moved emotionally. Some had served with Cocke during hard fought battles of the recent war for freedom. Haywood, the historian, was present as secretary of the Carolina senate and recorded an outline of Cocke's speech that lasted hours.

These astute politicians were not yet ready to turn loose their hold and control of the western territory. They turned deaf ears to the requests of Congress as well as the Overmountain inhabitants. General Griffith Rutherford introduced a bill that would relieve the situation but it was voted down after the first reading. Joseph Martin also added to the official opposition. As Indian Agent he reported that the Franks were encroaching on Indian land and that a state of war was in existence on the frontier.

Several reasons underlay the desire of the Overmountain people for their own government. One was a suspicious distrust of those in political power; another the high tax rate. The tax levy on the westerners was the same as that of eastern citizens and no benefit was derived in the overmountain country from these taxes. North Carolina wanted to control the land but didn't want to pay the bill for protection in the continous border wars. This same attitude was applied toward the Cumberlands. Another big problem was distance and the mountain barrier that lay between the frontier and the seat of government.

Colonel John Tipton, who was blamed for much of the bitterness and division of the western people, was hung in effigy with a will in his mouth. This feeling toward Tipton was partly due to the fact that he had appointed himself spokesman for the western people without their consent and approval. During the November session Tipton made an attempt to have the seat of government moved from Jonesborough to Davis' Store. After much talk and looking around it was continued where it was.

Earlier in the year during the regular session of the Franklin Superior Court their first murder case was scheduled. George Clarkson was tried, convicted and hung in Jonesborough April 13, 1786.

HAWKINS COUNTY ERECTED 1786

North Carolina disregarded all pleas in behalf of Franklin and continued to legislate for the westerners. They took the Franklin County of Spencer and established the county named Hawkins. The new county was named in honor of Benjamin Hawkins, member of the Continental Congress; U. S. Senator from North Carolina, member of the Hopewell Treaty Commission; signed deed of cession conveying territory, now

Tennessee, to the Federal Government. Civil and military officials for Hawkins County were appointed by the Legislature. For a period Hawkins County served under two governments as two different counties.

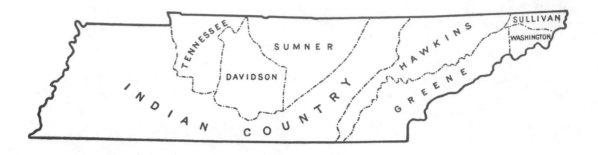

SEVIER AND SHELBY MEET

In an effort to prevent civil war between two factions of the Overmountain settlers, Colonel Sevier agreed to have a conference with General Evan Shelby. It was the 67 year old Shelby who introduced Sevier to the Watauga and Holston communities in the early 1770's. The families had retained close ties through the years. They met at Samuel Smith's in Sullivan County for the conference. Sevier's sincere regard for the venerable Shelby permitted that astute veteran to talk Sevier into signing the following agreement:

CONFERENCE AT SMITH'S

At a conference at the house of Samuel Smith Esquire, on the 20th day of March, 1787, between the Hon. Evan Shelby, Esquire, and sundry officers of the one part, and the Hon. John Sevier, Esquire, and sundry officers on the other part.

Whereas disputes have arisen concerning the propriety and legality of the State of Franklin, and the sovereignty and jurisdiction of the State of North Carolina over the said State and the people residing there.

The contending parties, from the regard they have for peace, tranquility and good decorum, in the Western Country, do agree and recommend as follows:

"First, that the courts of justice do not proceed to transact any business in their judicial departments, except the trial of criminals, the proving of wills, deeds, bills of sale, and such like conveyances; the issuing of attachments, writs, and legal process so as to procure bail, but not to enter into final determination of the suits except the parties are mutually agreed thereto.

"Secondly, that the inhabitants residing within the limits of the disputed territory are in full liberty and discretion to pay their public taxes to either the State of North Carolina or the State of Franklin.

MAPLEHURST: A portion of this house served as meeting place for the Sullivan County Court 1787-1788; owned by Joseph Cole. It is assumed that some records of these court sitting were lost during the Franklin-Carolina raids.

"Thirdly, that this agreement and recommendation continue until the next annual sitting of the General Assembly of North Carolina, to be held in November next, and not longer. It is further agreed that if any person, guilty of felony, be committed by any North Carolina justice of the peace, that such person or persons may and shall be received by the Franklin sheriff or jailer of Washington, and proceeded against in the same manner as if the same had been committed by and from any such authority from under the State of Franklin. It is also recommended that the aforesaid people do take such modes and regulations, and set forth their grievances, if any they have, and solicit North Carolina, at the meeting of the next general assembly, for to complete the separation, if thought necessary by the people of the Western Country, as to them may appear most expedient, and give their members and representatives such instructions as thought to be most conducive to the interest of our western world, by a majority of same, either to be separate from that of North Carolina, or be citizens of the State of North Carolina.

"Signed and agreed on behalf of each party, this day and year above written.

"Evans Shelby
"John Sevier."

This conference and the resulting agreement did not cool the situation, instead it caused even more violent expressions and actions. The word was spreading as far as the seaboard that an all-out conflict was in the making and bloodshed was imminent. Shelby fearful of a mortal clash suggested asking Virginia's help. He called a meeting of Colonels Tipton, Maxwell and Hutchings at his home. After the conference this message was sent to Governor Caswell:

"I have, therefore, thought it expedient to call upon you for your immediate assistance, having the faith and honor of the legislature of North Carolina pledged to us that we shall remain secure in our liberties and properties. The matter is truly alarming, and it is beyond a doubt with me that hostilities will in a short time commence, and without the interference of government without delay an effusion of blood must take place. I, therefore, think it highly necessary that one thousand troops, at least, be sent, as that number might have a good effect, for should we have that number, under the sanction of the government, it is no doubt with me they would immediately give way, and would not appear in so unprovoked an insurrection. On the contrary, should a faint and feeble resistance be made the consequences might be fatal, and would tend to devastation, ruin and distress. Should your Excellency think it convenient to call on the Common-wealth of Virginia, I have reason to believe it might meet their aid, as they have four counties nearly bordering on us, and would be the most speedy assistance we could come at in case your troops do not reach us in time to relieve us. I think it highly necessary that a quantity of ammunition be forwarded to us as it is very scarce in this country. . . Thus, sir, you have the result of my conference with the aforementioned Colonels. . . .

"Your Excellency will perceive that the people of Franklin have not assented to the agreement I entered into with their governor for the preservation of peace and good order in the country. Not many men here are engaged in vindicating the authority of North Carolina."

John Sevier, learning of Shelby's action, took a stronger stand as expressed in the following communication to Caswell:

I had the fullest hopes and confidence that the body would have either agreed to a separation on honorable principles and stipulations, or otherwise endeavored to have reunited us upon such terms as might have been lasting and friendly, but I find myself and country entirely deceived; and if your Assembly have thought their measures would answer such an end, they are equally disappointed. But I firmly believe had proper measures been adopted, a union, in some measure or perhaps fully, would have taken place. We shall continue to act as independent, and would rather suffer death in all its various and frightful shapes than conform to anything that is disgraceful.

Governor Caswell was greatly disturbed over the course events across the mountains had taken. He had no intention of a forceful subjugation of the Franks, mainly because the North Carolina forces were not strong enough. He presented the situation at an emergency meeting of the State Council. Here is his reply to Shelby:

It would be very imprudent to add to the dissatisfaction of the people there by showing a wish to encourage the shedding of blood, as thereby a civil war would eventually be brought on, which ought at all times to be avoided if possible, but more especially at the present as we have great reason to apprehend a general Indian war, in which case there is no doubt that they will meet with support from the subjects of foreign powers; or at least they will be furnished with arms and ammunition. And if the western and southern tribes should unite with your neighbors you will stand in need of all your force; and therefore recommend unanimity amongst you, if it can be by any means effected, as you will be thereby much more able to defend yourselves than you possibly can be when divided, but also save the circumstances of cutting each other's throats. Besides this, it would be impracticable to raise an armed force at this time, if we were ever so much disposed thereto, for the following reasons: the people in general are now engaged in their farming business, and if brought out would be very reluctant to march; there is no money in the treasury to defray the expenses of such as might be called out; nor in fact, have we arms or ammunition. Under such circumstances it would be madness to attempt it.

I must therefore recommend to you the using every means in your power to conciliate the minds of the people, as well those who call themselves Franklinites as the friends and supporters of government. The measures you took with Mr. Sevier and his party, of which you first acquainted me, if again they could be adopted, would be best under the situation that things now are. If things could lie dormant as it were till the next Assembly, and each man's mind be employed in considering your common defense against the savage enemy, I should suppose it best. And whenever unanimity prevails among your people and their strength and numbers will justify an application for a separation, if it is general, I have no doubt of its taking place upon reciprocal and friendly terms.

Governor Caswell also wrote an open letter to the Western People that was sent along with Shelby's letter:

Is there an individual in your country who does not look forward to such a day [of separation] arriving? If that is the case must not every thinking man believe that this separation will be soonest and most effectually obtained by unanimity? . . . 'Tis my opinion that it may be obtained at an earlier day than some imagine, if unanimity prevailed amongst you. Altho' this is an official letter, you will readily see that it is dictated by a friendly and pacific mind. . . I will conclude by once more entreating you to consider the dreadful calamities and consequences of a civil war. Humanity demanded this of me; your own good sense will point out the propriety of it. At least, let all animosities and disputes subside till the next Assembly; even let things remain as they are, without pursuing compulsory measures until then, and I flatter myself that honorable body will be disposed to do what is just and right and what sound policy may dictate.

Caswell was a very astute politician and he wrote Sevier a personal note that indicated close friendship.

"I cannot account for the conduct of our Assembly at this last session. I know that some of the gentlemen's sentiments did not coincide with my own, but still think if the people on your side the mountains had have been more unanimous, the measures of separation would have been pursued. . . You may only rely upon it that my sentiments are clearly in favor of a separation whenever the people to be separated think themselves of sufficient strength and abilities to support a government. My idea is, that nature, in the formation of the hills between us and directing the course of the waters so differently, had not in view the inhabitants on either side being longer subject to the same laws and government. . . I conclude by recommending unanimity among you as the only means by which your government can obtain energy even when the separation is effected by consent of North Carolina."

More and more people were drifting away from Franklin. Governor Caswell's policy of conciliation was showing a pronounced effect. Also the fact that Governor Sevier had signed the agreement with General Shelby showed a move in that direction, and many used this as an argument to adhere to the North Carolina Government.

EVENTFUL 1786

Reports indicate that the new State was moving ahead, during the first part of 1786, in a somewhat haphazard confused manner. Not much data is available except from letters which furnish parts of the story. Joseph Martin wrote Governor Caswell that Franklin had adopted a great seal and a coat of arms and that Charles Robertson had been authorized to mint $30,000 dollar specie. No evidence of a seal, coat of arms or coins has been found. The common wax wafer was being used two years later. One writer has given a description of three different coins supposed to have been minted. This writer describes the dollar as having the state seal on one side and the outline of the mountains engraved on the other. The fifty cent coin had the seal on one side and the engraving of a poplar tree on the other; the quarter was supposed to have had the seal and on the other side crossed rifles. No Franklin coins are in evidence. The only minted coins known to have been used in Franklin were either Spanish or

SPANISH COINS: These coins dated 1777 and 1795 are of the type used by the Franks. These particular pieces were found in Greene County by Reed Jennings.

other foreign mint. Congress did not authorize a coinage system or mint until 1786 and first Federal coins were minted in 1793.

The confused situation became more pronounced during the summer. Rival elections were attempted in the upper counties. The Franks showed more strength at the polls than the Tiptonites. The official conduct on both sides added to the bitterness between the two factions. Haywood gives this description:

Here was presented the strange spectacle of two empires exercised at one and the same time, over one and the same people. County courts were held in the same counties under both governments; the militia were called out by officers appointed by both; laws were passed by both Assemblies and taxes were laid by the authority of both States. The differences in opinion in the State of Franklin between those who adhered to the government of the North Carolina and those who were friends to the new government became more acrimonious every day. Every fresh provocation on the one side was surpassed in the way of retaliation by still greater provocation on the other. The judges commissioned by the State of Franklin held superior courts twice in each year, in Jonesborough. Colonel Tipton openly refused obedience in the new government. There arose a deadly hatred between him and Sevier, and each endeavored by all means in his power to strengthen his party against the other. Tipton held courts under the authority of North Carolina, ten miles above Jonesborough, which were conducted by her officers and agreeable to her laws. Courts were also held at Jonesborough in the same country under the authority of the State of Franklin.

As the process of these courts frequently required the sheriff to pass within the jurisdiction of each other to execute it, an encounter was sure to take place, hence it became necessary to appoint the stoutest men in county to the office of sheriff. This state of things produced the appointment of A. Caldwell, of Jonesborough, and Mr. [John] Puch, the sheriff in Tipton's court. Whilst a county court was sitting at Jonesborough in this year, for the county of Washington, Colonel John Tipton with a party of men entered the court house, took away the papers from the clerk and turned the justices out of doors. Not long after, Sevier's party came to a house where a county court was sitting for the county of Washington, under the authority of North Carolina, and took away the clerk's papers and turned the court out of doors. Thomas Gourley was the clerk of this court. The like acts were several times repeated during the existence of the Franklin government. . . In these removals, many valuable papers were lost, and at later periods for want of them, some estates of great value were lost, In the county of Greene, in 1786, Tipton broke up a court sitting at Greeneville, under the Franklin authority. The clerks in all the three old counties issued marriage licenses, and many persons were married by virtue of their authority. In the courts held under the authority of the State of Franklin, many letters of administration of interstate estates were issued, and probates of wills were taken. The members of the two factions became excessively incensed against each other, and at public meetings made frequent exhibitions of their strength and prowess in boxing matches. As an elucidation of the temper of the times, an incident may be mentioned which otherwise would be too trivial for the page of history. Shortly after the election of Sevier as governor of Franklin, under the permanent Constitution, he and Tipton met in Jonesborough, where as usual a violent verbal altercation was maintained between them for some time, when Sevier, no longer able to bear the provocations which were given him, struck Tipton with a cane. Instantly the latter began to annoy him with his hands clenched. Each exchanged blows for some time in the same way with great violence and in a convulsion of rage. Those who happened to be present interfered and parted them before victory had been declared for either. But some of those who saw the conflict believe that the governor was not so well pleased with his prospects of victory as he had been with the event of the battle of King's Mountain, in which his regiment and himself had so eminently distinguished themselves. . . To such excess was driven by civil discord a people who, in times of tranquility, is not exceeded by any on earth for all the virtues, good sense and genuine politeness that can make mankind happy and amiable.

GEORGIA AND FRANKLIN

Georgia was affected by the Hopewell Treaty nearly as much as Franklin. Governor Sevier was contacted by Governor Telfair concerning a combined campaign against the Creeks. Sevier was strong for his plan as Georgia was promising the Franks the Great Bend territory for their participation.

The congenial relationship existing between Sevier and the Georgia officials had many ties. Colonel Clarke, a Georgia hero, had fought with Sevier and had been a guest in his home. Governor Mathews, who succeeded Telfair, came from same section in Virginia as Sevier. Governor Sevier had formed a friendship with General George Elholm while in the South Carolina Campaign in 1781. Elholm, a Danish soldier, had joined the American cause and settled in Georgia after the war. That state made him Adjutant-General of her army.

Governor Telfair sent Elholm to Franklin as a sort of Ambassador. Elholm liked Franklin and the leaders to the extent that he remained and became a part of the new state movement. He was appointed drill master of the militia and was accepted a full member of the official staff. He remained with the Franks throughout the duration of that state.

JOHN SEVIER SPEAKS

Replica of the log building used by the State of Franklin at Greeneville, Tennessee 1785-1788. Greeneville was the official Capital of the lost state from 1785 until its demise.

Bitterness over the situation, with two taxes, two courts and two sets of state officials trying to run their affairs, caused some of the Franks in the upper counties to return to North Carolina allegiance. They figured that their land titles would be safer in that direction.

The May 1787 Franklin Convention meeting in Greeneville voted final acceptance of the Constitution. Few changes have been noted although it has been said that several amendments were adopted. It was during this session that William Cocke made the following motion:

"In view of the fact that Franklin's commissioners who waited on the Assembly of North Carolina last year were not attended to with that respect due to commissioners; and, notwithstanding the illegal manner in which the members from the western counties had been elected in the name of North Carolina, yet they were permitted to take their seats as legislators; and as those members were mortal enemies to our rising Republic, whose citizens the Assembly of North Carolina called their western inhabitants, a separation was thereby prevented. But as we find that some individuals of the said Assembly now warmly express themselves in favor of a separation, upon condition that Franklin would join North Carolina, and send from Franklin members to take seats in their Assembly to effect a separation, such separation would undoubtedly be granted. Therefore, the holding of an election on the same day appointed for the election for the State of North Carolina would enable us to send members to negotiate a separation, and thus we could easily obtain our wish without trouble or hazard."

This motion brought forth quite a long debate and discussion of the conditions and situation of the State of Franklin. The arguments pro and con on Cocke's motion have been preserved from newspaper reports transcribed in William's "Lost State of Franklin." One of the rarities during this session is a two part speech by John Sevier. The Assembly asked the Governor's opinion on the motion. Here is Sevier's reply:

Governor Sevier, who had been waited on by a committee for his opinion, observed that it was well known in general that North Carolina, in compliance with a requisition made by Congress in June, 1784, passed a cession act, which gave us the privileges which we now unhappily are obliged to contend for. He then cited the clauses that give those rights to the people of Franklin; and further observed that, on the fourteenth of July following, Mr. Spaight, from North Carolina, laid the act before the Committee of States under the great seal of North Carolina State; and, therefore, he was fully satisfied that, after being thus received, the virtue of the very act itself, deprived North Carolina of the right they presumed in repealing the said cession act on the 20th of November following. And that Congress is sensible that they have complied with the requisition of the said act is fully ascertained by their frequent demands on North Carolina to comply agreeable to the tenor of the same. This cession act, therefore, he said, cannot be compared to any common statute, made only for the regulation of their own internal police, which only respects her own citizens; but it was no sooner constitutionally passed than it became a sacred charter for three different powers, viz., the Congress, the people of the State of Franklin, and North Carolina. Of course it can never be lawfully repealed without the consent of the said three different powers. The people of the West had not released North Carolina from her sacred pledge of an independent separation; and, what was of more importance in regard to the benefit of the Union, neither had the United States relinquished their claim; and he was highly prompted to believe they never would; but, should such a thing happen, it would then be time enough for the people of Franklin to consult as to what measures to pursue. But as to the independency of Franklin, it existed in full force undeniably. He referred the Convention to take a view of the Constitution of North Carolina, where they would find a clause which mentions that there may be a State or States erected in the West, whenever the legislature gives consent to the same. Now for North Carolina to attempt to insinuate that the said cession act had not been constitutionally passed, and that another is still wanting for that purpose, can only serve to expose themselves in a disadvantageous way to a just and sensible world. He well perceived that tools were set at work among us, but he was sure that North Carolina would stop rather than run the risk of quarreling openly with the United States; that the people of this country have ever proved good, faithful and powerful citizens to the interests of the United States; and they only contended now for the sacred rights and privileges given them already. It was his opinion, however he might be for unanimity, that further application was unnecessary, and that the act of cession and the Constitution of North Carolina were plenary proof of his assertions.

Many of the representatives expressed their feeling either for or against Cocke's motion. It resolved into a lengthy debate. General Kennedy spoke against the motion and concluded his talk with the following remarks. But, laying aside all these objections, the measure proposed could never be excusably executed, but to save a government on the verge of destruction. But as this is not our situation at present then, as a citizen of a brave people who ever scorned duplicity, Kennedy utterly condemned the motion, and fully agreed with the gentlemen who would not enter into negotiations with North Carolina, on any other terms than with other Sister States of the Union.

His Excellency, the Governor, here taking the floor again, produced an act passed in the last General Assembly of Franklin, which directed the executive to make use of hostility, if nothing else would do, to prevent elections within the limits of the State of Franklin under the authority of North Carolina. Therefore, the tenor of the motion now before the House would bring the friends of independency under the rigor of that act. It is extraordinary that the conduct of the citizens who had sent members here should uniformly support the independency of Franklin, and that those members should also unanimously express themselves in favor of supporting the same, and yet at the same time blindly pursue a method which could not fail to bring about reunion with North Carolina. Let us suppose for a moment that the scheme now in agitation would answer the end supposed by some among us, which it certainly never would. It would in in fact only alter our condition from independency to dependency, and ourselves from freemen to servants, and the course would disqualify us from every privilege above mere favors. But let us suppose that it would bring about a second separation as apparently favorable to our Commonwealth as the cession act. The quota of our debt would then be laid proportionally to the number of citizens we have now, which is on a ratio as is four to one to what they were at the time of our separation. Of course in the midst of our frugality we would be obliged to bear part of the expense requisite to support the extravagance and luxury of North Carolina government, besides our proportion to Congress for discharge of the foreign Continental debt. Thus situated, we are equally interested in the character of the cession act with the honorable Congress; and thereby bound in honor to give it a mutual support. Therefore, were we now to revert, it would remove us from all confidence due to a spirited power, to wallow in disgrace forever. A concise narrative of the settling of Franklin would show that the first colony in the country was settled by Virginians, about fifteen years ago, and that a line afterward run by Virginia and North Carolina left a helpless number of industrious citizens destitute of any more protection than what their own inconsiderable strength afforded them against the outrageous warlike tribes of Indians. That, in this situation of that settlement, the British superintendents, Cameron and Stuart, offered them protection on condition that they would transplant themselves further down toward West Florida, which their abhorrence of British tyranny at that time made them refuse. Soon after, in the year 1776, they applied to a convention held at Halifax, North Carolina, to become citizens of that State, in order to prevent that they might be thought inimical to the Revolution, which would have added to their distress. Their petition underwent a high and long debate before it was favorably received by North Carolina; and in that convention the clause was inserted in the North Carolina Constitution which makes the cession act constitutional and just. The people of Franklin territory had paid

From Allison's "Dropped Stitches of Tennessee History" we quote: "On the old record books of the minutes of the proceedings of the Court of Pleas and Quarter Sessions kept at Jonesboro will be found the following entry: 'State of North Carolina, Washington County, Monday the Twelfth Day of May Anno Domini One Thousand Seven Hundred and Eighty Eight. Andrew Jackson Esq. came into Court and Produced a license as Attorney with a Certificate sufficiently Attested of his Taking the Oaths Necessary to said office and Was admitted to Practiss as an Attorney in this County Court.' The entry immediately

preceding recites that Archibald Roane, David Allison and Joseph Hamilton Esquires Produced sufficient Licenses to Practiss as Attorneys and were admitted. The entry immediately following recites, 'John McNairey Produced a license as an Attorney and was admitted to Practiss as an attorney.'"

large sums of money for the greatest part of their land before the Revolution of North America took place. Besides this, the settlers had held it by the sword, a mode that has confirmed the most powerful charters round the globe. Now going on ten years, the savages laid waste their buildings, carried off their stock and other movable property, killed and scalped several families and obliged the rest to fly to the safety of forts for the space of twelve months. In their helpless conditions, the Virginians had proved their warmest supporters. He was, therefore, fully satisfied that if the matter were thoroughly discussed no impartial judicial power would judge North Carolina entitled to govern that territory which nature had formed a castle for a Commonwealth. Our enemies would find to their sorrow that it is garrisoned by brave, independent people should they concern unjustly with the western citizens, and we adhere to our former virtue. But should this day involve an offspring into slavery, it would fall a heavy curse on our own heads.

Major Samuel Newell called for a vote on Cocke's motion. It was defeated and another plan substituted. The 'yes' votes on the motion came mainly from the upper counties where a big number had already taken the oath of allegiance. The 'no' vote came from the lower counties which gave a good indication of how the tide was running.

The Assembly divided the State into two districts. Not much data is available on this phase of the state organization. Most historians have figured the division as follows: Sullivan, Washington, Wayne (Carter and Johnson) and Greene were included in the Washington District. Spencer (Hawkins) Caswell (Jefferson), Sevier and Blount were organized into the Elholm District. Militia officers were appointed for each District.

Delegates were appointed to attend Congress in another effort toward gaining statehood. The delegates named for this mission were William Cocke, William Nelson and George Elholm.

Much debate was aired during this session of Congress. Much argument for and against creation of new states was presented but no definite action was taken. A final resolution, sealing the fate of Franklin, was passed before Congress adjourned. It left the creation of any new state, from the western territories, entirely within the jurisdiction of the claiming state. This left Franklin's fate at the mercy of the North Carolina Legislature.

Sevier's only hope now lay in the prospect of a campaign against the Creeks in conjunction with Georgia. A peace treaty doomed this move before it started.

Separation petitions were being circulated among the people in an effort to influence the North Carolina leaders. (See appendix 3) Many notable names are on the list of signers. These petitions were disregarded by the North Carolina Assembly. The August Assembly elected General Evan Shelby as the next Governor of Franklin to take office March 1, 1788. Shelby declined the honor and resigned his Brigadier-General commission. He recommended John Sevier for the position but the North Carolina officials appointed Joseph Martin instead.

The days of Franklin were drawing to a close. John Sevier faced a discouraging situation. The road toward statehood seemed blocked at every turn. Many of the people and friends who had encouraged and insisted on his taking the lead in the Franklin movement had deserted the cause. John Sevier for the first time and only time on record began to drink whisky in great quantities.

THE BATTLE OF FRANKLIN

Franklin Government was gradually falling apart. The division that began during the 1785 Constitutional Assembly, was becoming more pronounced. It is a strange parallel that in the very beginning of the Franklin movement it was John Tipton who was more assertive, and voiced loud support for the new state. On the other hand John Sevier counseled against separation and cautioned the people to move slowly and not be rash in their plans. Now the people who had talked loudest had left or were leaving. Members of the State Council veered back toward North Carolina allegiance; Franklin's Legislative sessions were poorly attended; Judge David Campbell had accepted a North Carolina appointment as Judge.

Court Raids started again in Washington, Greene and Spencer counties. Unarmed groups from each Government seemed to make a game of confiscating the records of the other side. Fist fights, brawls and an air of comedy were all part of these escapades. Little malice or hostile feelings were demonstrated as neighbors, separated in their state loyalty, seemed to retain their friendship with each other.

Colonel John Tipton returned home from the North Carolina Assembly mad at losing his Senate seat. He was more determined than ever to get at the man whom he felt was the cause of his problems. A court, sitting under North Carolina authority, ordered seizure of slaves and stock belonging to John Sevier for unpaid North Carolina taxes. Sheriff Jonathan Pugh had taken this property to John Tipton's for safe keeping.

Colonel Sevier was absent from home when this incident occurred. The Sheriff's action caused Sevier to fly into a rage and he resolved to put a stop to the illegal court raids by Tipton's men. He assembled 150 men from Greene, Sevier and Caswell counties and marched to the farm of Colonel Tipton on Sinking Creek. Other men from Washington County joined Sevier as he passed on his march.

The Franklin forces arrived in the vicinity of the Tipton house during the afternoon of February 27, 1788. Camp was set up about a quarter of a mile from the house. Colonel Sevier sent a letter to Tipton asking that he surrender unconditionally in thirty minutes. Tipton sent a verbal flag back "Fire and be damned." "That he asked no favors, and if Sevier would surrender himself and his leaders that all should have the benefit of North Carolina's laws." The number of men guarding Tipton's house has been estimated from 15 to 75. Tipton's son says there were 45.

TIPTON-HAYNES FARM. This historic house, erected by John Tipton during 1782, has traversed three centuries. Site of battle between State of Franklin troops and the North Carolina adherents. The bold spring near house was site of Daniel Boone's Camp in 1760, and has been part of history since 1673.

ATTEMPTED SEIGE OF TIPTON'S PLACE

Captain Peter Parkinson, from eastern Washington County (now Carter), arrived with a company of men to assist Tipton. Sevier's men opened fire on the new arrivals killing three horses and driving these reinforcements back temporarily. During darkness, two women going to the still house were fired on accidently. One was wounded in the shoulder.

STILL HOUSE, Tipton Farm.

All indications point to the fact that Sevier tried to cover all points of entrance and exit around the Tipton Farm. Guards were supposed to be posted but in spite of this Colonel Robert Love was able to slip away from the house during the dark and cloudy night. He was going to Greasy Cove (Unicoi County) to raise more men. Enroute he met his brother Thomas Love on the way to Tipton's with some 12 men. Because of the absence of guards this party was able to slip into the Tipton house unobserved.

Many battles have been won or lost because of weather conditions. This element played a major role in the Sevier-Tipton skirmish. It was an extremely cold period and the air was fogged with thick falling snow. The guards, that had been posted, had returned to the campfires. This permitted the Tiptonites to move to and from the house with little trouble.

Early next morning Sevier sent another flag (message under white flag) to Tipton. Colonel Tipton replied that if Sevier would acquiesce he would disband his troops and countermand the march of the troops from Sullivan County. This message was received by some of the officers and they answered it themselves. Pretending that the message was for Valentine Sevier rather than Governor John Sevier, they intimated that John Sevier was absent. They told Tipton that they could handle the troops on the ground as well as those on march from Sullivan.

Near night William Cox reported to the Sevier camp that a company of Sullivan County troops were marching to reinforce Tipton. He said that they would cross Watauga River at Dungan's Mill that night, (St. John's Mill at Watauga). Captain Joseph Harding and John Sevier Jr. did start for the ford, some ten miles distant, with 40 men. They traveled to within one half mile of the ford without any contact with the Sullivan force. The men, suffering from the bitter cold, returned to camp.

The Sullivan County men under Colonels George Maxwell and John Pemberton were able to reach the Tipton farm undetected. Shortly before their arrival, morning of the 29th, a party of Franks, under

James and John Sevier, went past the Tipton house at full gallop. They were fired on but no one was hit as they continued their scouting trip. They were barely out of sight when the Sullivan County force started a charge against the Sevier Camp. The Tiptonites joined in the battle as the Sullivan Troops passed near the house. The North Carolina troops captured the ordinance, on the hill above the spring house, and moved on against the main camp. The Franks, unable to determine the strength of the attacking force, withdrew to a higher hill. The Tiptonites captured all the camping equipment and several saddles.

Six of the North Carolina troops were wounded, John Webb was killed and Sheriff Jonathan Pugh, mortally wounded, died eight days later. On the Franklin side several were wounded including John Smith, Henry Polley and Casper Fent.

The Franklin force continued their retreat toward Jonesborough. Either side was capable of knocking the other out. The best marksmen in the country were facing each other during this skirmish. They had fired into the air purposely to avoid killing each other.

The scouting party under James and John Sevier, hearing the firing in the direction at the camp, turned back to investigate. When they arrived they did not suspect the true situation. A volley from the Tiptonites halted them and they were pulled from their horses. Colonel Tipton was ready to hold court, convict and hang the Sevier boys but was talked out of this action. He released his prisoners on parole and later returned the property confiscated from the Sevier home for taxes and that captured during the battle.

Thus weather and the unwillingness of the frontiersmen to kill each other ended the Battle of Franklin. Following are three papers related to this event.

The first paper is transcribed from the original as written by Colonel John Tipton in making a report of the battle to Brigadier-General Joseph Martin. This copy made available by Mrs. L. W. McCown, member of the State Historical Commission from Johnson City, Tennessee. Mrs. McCown also furnished a copy of letter to Colonel Arthur Campbell.

March 2, 1788

Dear Genl.

I recd. yours of this inst. and can inform you of my safe return without being interrupted but can inform you that Coln. Christian's treatment is more favorable than it has been represented to you. Coln. Christian has always acted inimical to the authority of North Carolina since this unhappy dispute commenced and ever since the ruling of the last General Assembly and for a man of such character to ride armed without being apprehended would betray too much diffidence in friends to government who had the opportunity of detecting him but more especially as he could produce nothing to show that he was on your business.

I am glad Sir to find that you are about to transmit to government the situation of our public affairs here but it is not in my power to transmit to you the whole of the flags you request Coln. Maxwell took the first to Sullivan but its purport was for me to surrender in thirty minutes at their discretion and submit to the laws of Franklin signed John Sevier Capt. Genl.

To this daring insult I sent no answer upon which hostilities commenced by their firing on Capt. Parkinsons Company and afterwards on two women one of which was wounded. Those preceedings happened on the evening of 27th of February.

Matters continued so only with several guns being on both sides when Sevier sent in another flag of a more mild nature insisting that if I should not discontinue firing he must take some means to prevent it with many other things but this flag is either mislaid or lost.

To this flag I sent an answer letting the men assembled there know that all I wanted was submission to the laws of North Carolina and if they would acquiesce with this proposal I would disband my troops and countermand the march of the troops from Sullivan and directed this flag to Coln. John Sevier.

To this flag some gentlemen in their camp sent in for answer letting me know that Col. Sevier was not there but they would answer me themselves which was to this import. Vis. That the troops here they were above and as for the troops on their march to join in they would countermand their march themselves without putting me to any trouble.

Several other circumstances occurred during that evening of small moment not worthy of long details. However on the morning of the 29th before daylight I rcd. information that Colonel Maxwell with his troops from Sullivan and a number from this county had collected into one body at Dungan's about ten miles from this place. From which place they marched and before sunup attacked them when as soon as the firing began I with the troops from the house sallied out and drove them from their ground without much resistance with the loss of four or five wounded one of which died a few hours after viz. M. Webb from Sullivan and Jonathan Pugh Esquire, Sheriff of Washington County who died eight days after the action.

However we followed up the pursuit when we met Robert Young with a verbal flag from Sevier that if we would spare his life he would submit to the laws upon which we discontinued the pursuit and Colonel Maxwell sent him a flag giving him and his party to the 11th of this instant to submit to the laws of North Carolina.

To which he sent me and answer with a private letter both of which I herewith transmit you. To which I sent Mr. Sevier a private letter letting him know my pacific intentions and that I had no intention of taking any advantage of them by force. A submission to the laws which they had violated was all I desired.

I should be happy to see you when convenient and can assure you that I should be happy that a reconciliation should take place on honorable principals. But still must insist that violaters of the laws should be brought to suffer especially those who have so flagrantly transgressed.

But Sir I can inform you that I suspect that there will be private inquires if not murders done in this quarter as numbers of small parties are going about armed in the night and has been about my house and James Stuarts Esq. and several other houses and certainly some measures ought to be taken to prevent such depredations. I am Sir with respect your most Obd. Hon. Servant.

JOHN TIPTON

Taken from the Drader MSS— 9 D D 47–

SULLIVAN CO. --- March 19, 1788---

Dear Sir: Our long threatening has at last come to blows betwixt us and the Franklinites. I suppose that you have heard that Sevier and his party surrounded Col. Tiptons house and requested him and his party to surrender to the discretion of the people of Franklin. Which terms he refused they fired on Capt. Parkinsons Company coming to Col. Tiptons assistance and wounded three horses - afterwards wounded a woman and sundry times fired at his house. Col. Tipton sent me a pressing letter for assistance. I raised some men and marched to his assistance and had a skirmish with the Franklinites, I have not time to write the particulars after it was over Sevier sent in a flag. Asking his life and his parties and they would submit to the laws of the State. We reced. the flag and sent him an answer. He has never come in to comply with the terms and the enclosed Deposition will satisfy you that he is trying to raise another party.

Sir, if you can feel a freedom to assist us with a few Volunteers to quell the insurrection it will be gratefully acknowledged for, if we contend with equal parties their will be a number of lives lost, but if we overpower it at once it will save further bloodshed.

We wish an answer as soon as possible.

We are, Sir - with esteem

Your most Obt-----

JOHN TIPTON

GEO. MAXWELL

To - Col. Arthur Campbell
  Washington County (Virginia)

DEPOSITION John Tipton and others Versus
John Sevier and others filed in office
Jonesborough August 1788

State of North Carolina

The Deposition of Colonel John Tipton esq., James Stuart, Esq. Alexander Muffit, Esq. Thomas Gourley Esq. and Joseph Culton taken before me the subscribers this 20th day of August 1788 in the court house of the County of Washington is as follows (to wit). That on the 27th of February last inst. John Sevier marched within sight of the house of the said John Tipton esq. with a party of men to the amount of one hundred and upwards with a drum beating colours flying in military force and in an hostile manner and thereupon immediately sent a flag to the said Coln. John Tipton demanding of him and the people in the house with him to surrender within the space of thirty minutes to him the said John Sevier at his discretion an submit themselves to the laws of Franklin he the said John Sevier stiling himself Captain General and Commander in Chief in and over the State of Franklin as far as these deponents can recount. Upon the refusal of the said Coln. Tipton to comply with the aforesaid requisition Henry Conway (who acted as Colonel under the said John Sevier) and with a detachment of men from the aforesaid party and took his station on an eminence near to the spring and still house of the said Coln. Tipton from which place he fired upon Captain Peter Parkinson and took five of his men prisoners and killed a horse upon the which of one said Parkinson's men was riding, the said Parkinson then a coming in to the assistance of said Coln. Tipton whose house was beseiged by said John Sevier and his said party.

Two young women passing by near to the still house before mentioned were fired upon from which firing one of them received a bullet through her shoulder. This firing was from the detachment of men that then were under the command of the before mentioned Henry Conway.

On the day following being the 28th day of February hostilities still continued by sundry guns being fired by said John Sevier party at the house of the said Coln. Tipton but no damage was thereby sustained the seige continuing until Friday morning being 29th February on which morning the said Sevier's party fired upon a party of men then coming to the assistance of the said Coln. Tipton and killed Jonathan Pugh Esq. Sheriff of the County of Washington and John Webb of Sullivan County and wounded Captain William

Delany and John Allison and that- - -
Hugh Beard and Joseph Hardin of the aforesaid party were aiding and abetting him the said John Sevier and others of this party to commit the hostilities aforesaid:

Sworn and subscribed before us the day above mentioned.

Signatures

SAMUEL SPENCER
        JSCSE

DAVID CAMPBELL
        AJWS

JOHN TIPTON

JAMES STUART

ALEXANDER MOFFITT

THOMAS GOURLEY

JOSEPH CULTON

Paul Fink, Jonesboro, Tenn. has original copy of Desposition.

JOHN KIRK MASSACRE

The John Kirk family was killed by Indians during May 1788. This family lived on Little River 12 miles south of White's Station (Knoxville). The Indian band was led by Slim Tom and Red Bird. The Kirk family had befriended Slim Tom on many occasions. On this particular day he came to the Kirk cabin and asked for food which was given him. After he left he met up with Chief Red Bird and a band of warriors. Slim Tom told this group about the cabin and its defenseless condition. They went to the cabin, killed all eleven and took their scalps.

Another episode that happened about this same period was the killing of Colonel James Brown, two of his sons and five other men. Mrs. Brown and five children were taken captive. The Browns were traveling toward the Cumberland country by river boat. Chief Vann had received word of the approaching party and prepared his ambush. This massacre and capture happened at Nickajack, one of Dragging Canoe's Chickamauga towns. Vann boarded the Brown boat under a false truce.

These two incidents gave rise to a rumor that a big Indian offensive was under way. General Joseph Martin, North Carolina Indian Agent and also General of Washington District Militia, was caught in the middle. Martin had been given the General's commission when Evan Shelby asked to be relieved. Martin hesitated in undertaking a campaign without specific orders from Governor Samuel Johnston.

General Martin had gone to Chota in an effort to quiet the unrest and learn who was responsible for the killings. Because of Martin's marriage to Betsy, daughter of Nancy Ward, many of the whites distrusted Martin and on the other hand the Indians felt that Martin looked after the white interest more than theirs. When Martin learned that Colonel John Sevier was marching toward the Indian Towns with 150 men he had his horses and slaves moved from Chota to a place of safety. General Martin then rode to Sevier's camp and made an effort to persuade Sevier to discontinue the march against the Cherokee. In this he was unsuccessful. General Martin, wrote

Governor Johnston severely criticizing the Sevier action. Colonel Hutchings of Hawkins also wrote a very angry letter lambasting Sevier's unofficial campaign.

Nevertheless, Colonel Sevier continued his march. He destroyed the town of Hiwassee and then turned back toward the Little Tennessee River. Events were now in the making that would give Sevier's record a blemish that was undeserved but rumor and circumstances burdened him with the blame.

Colonel Sevier had sent Major James Hubbard to Chilhowee to destroy that town. Slim Tom and Red Bird, who had massacred the Kirk family in May, were from Chilhowee. As Hubbard's force passed through Chota they requested Chief Old Tassel to accompany them to Chilhowee for talks. Not suspecting anything, the Old Chief and some of his men went along in good faith. The pioneer force was ferried across the river under a flag of truce.

On arrival in the town they summoned the Chiefs for talks at house of Old Abram. When the Chilhowee Chiefs and headmen had gathered and were seated for the council talks, Major Hubbard posted guards around the house and closed the door. Turning to John Kirk Jr. he handed him a tomahawk and told him to take vengeance for the massacre of his family. Young Kirk, still grieving over the loss of his people, needed no urging.

The Old Tassel, head Chief of the Overhill Towns, Abram and his son, Hanging Maw and his brother were slaughtered by Kirk. The Indians made no move to resist nor ask any mercy. They had come here under a flag of truce.

Colonel Sevier reached Hubbards Camp a short time later. He reprimanded both men for the act but Sevier was at a disadvantage as he held no official status on this campaign. Both Hubbard and Kirk defended their actions. Kirk wrote a letter exonerating Sevier from any knowledge or part in the deed.

The Chilhowee episode caused many of the upper Town warriors to join Dragging Canoe. John Watts, nephew of Old Tassel, now declared open warfare on the whites in his plans for revenge.

When Governor Johnston was told about the Chilhowee massacre he had a warrant issued for the arrest of John Sevier charging him with treason. He said, "I fear that we will have no peace in the western Counties until this robber and free booter is checked."

GENERAL MARTIN'S DEFEAT

Joseph Martin was practically forced into leading a force against the Chickamauga towns near Lookout Mountain. This campaign was against his wishes but a letter from George Maxwell caused him to return from North Carolina and organize a force to lead against Dragging Canoe and his lower town warriors.

In selecting officers General Martin ignored John Sevier. He did choose several leading Franks for his staff. Among them were: Alexander Outlaw, Daniel Kennedy, George Doherty, and Gilbert Christian. Colonel Robert Love, Major Thomas King and Captains Miller, Richardson and Hunter were named. A council to make plans and arrangements, was held in Jonesborough August 19, 1788. As Colonel Love was present in Greasy Cove later in August it seems doubtful that he actually went on the campaign.

About 500 men rendezvoused at White's Station (Knoxville). They made a fast march from here hoping to reach their objective before the Indians learned of the approaching force. They followed an old Indian War Trail, making the last 20 miles at night. The surprise element didn't work as they found the town of Lookout Mountain practically deserted . One officer suggested sending a force to secure a pass needed for the next day's march. The old experienced Indian fighters didn't like the plan neither did they volunteer. General Martin gave his consent and 50-100 men left on this mission.

They followed the narrow trail which led along a bench of the mountain. The trail was almost blocked by huge boulders causing the force to be strung out in a thin line of several hundred yards. The red warriors, hidden behind the boulders, opened up a heavy fire on the approaching whites. The men retreated in a chaotic scamper back toward the main camp. Fortunately there were no dead and only a few wounded. The men stayed in battle readiness all night with each man standing by his saddled horse.

Next morning Captain Beard led a company on a scouting mission toward the pass to check Indian presence. The reinforced warriors were waiting at about the same position and opened a heavy fire on Beard's men. General Martin, on hearing the intensive firing ordered the entire force to the attack. The men dismounted at the foot of the hill and began to advance toward the Indian position. The Indian attack, much heavier than the night before, caused the men to retreat. Carrying their dead and wounded the entire force returned to the main camp.

Many of the officers refused to follow Martin

into another battle. They took their men and departed. As the various commands broke up into independent groups, General Martin was left with only 60 of the original 500 men. With no other alternative General Martin returned to Long Island.

The victorious Chickamaugans were jubliant. They felt that the victory spirit was looking on them with favor. Dragging Canoe summoned the Chiefs for a council and plans were made for a general attack on the settlements. The large force of 1600 warriors planned to break up into small bands raiding isolated families and stations. They would drive the whites into their forts and starve them out.

When Colonel Sevier learned of Martin's defeat he collected a force and headed for the frontier. He knew that the Indian victory would signal a border war and many killings would result. On the night of September 21 a fire was spotted in the distance. The men headed in that direction, knowing that Indians were at work. Sevier and his men rode as fast as their horses could safely travel in the dark. It was soon determined that the fireglow was coming from the settlement of Samuel Sherrill's station. The Indians had set fire to one of the barns. The pioneer force made the charge in their usual manner with war whoops and loud yells. The redmen, hearing those eerie yells mixed with pounding hoof beats, fled into the darkness leaving their dead on the ground. The Sherrills, parents of John Sevier's wife, gave the force a happy welcome. Many similar attacks were taking place along the border.

John Sevier, Junior says (in quote from Draper) that 1788 was one of the bloodiest, hottest and hardest of all the years of Indian fighting. He gives some description of the Tellico Plains campaign in which he took part. Colonel Sevier had led a volunteer force of 172 men into this area with the idea of destroying the corn crop, essential to the Indian on the war path. Colonel Sevier thought that destruction of the crop would slow down the Indian attacks. John Watts, with over 500 warriors, tried to lure the Sevier force into an ambuscade. It was a game of hide and seek as the two leaders tried to out-maneuver each other. Watts was in close proximity to the white force all the time. Neither risked a face to face confrontation. One false move by Sevier would have been fatal. Many skirmishes took place but no major battle was fought during this episode. Young Sevier said that it was the most dangerous and perilous experience of his life.

The Indians halted their conquest for a short period when a Federal representative showed them a written promise signed by Congress saying 'that the settlers below the French Broad would be moved.' John Watts and Dragging Canoe didn't put too much faith in this promise so they continued to make plans of their own.

GREASY COVE RACE

One of the most famous horse races of all time was staged in Greasy Cove in late August, 1788. The track was located within the environs of the present town of Erwin. Part of the original tract is still open, as pictured on the next page.

The participants were Colonel Robert Love and Andrew Jackson, later President of the United States. Andrew Jackson had crossed the mountains to begin his law practice in the new country, riding one horse and leading another. Across one saddle was a brace of pistols and a holstered rifle. Along with Jackson came a pack of hounds. Jackson loved every kind of sport: horse racing, hunting, cock fighting, target shooting, etc.

In Greasy Cove resided Colonel Robert Love, who with his brothers had established a settlement in the present Love Station section of the county. Colonel Love was an ardent follower of horse racing and had his own private tract near his home. It was a half-circle, half-mile tract meandering along the lowland by the Nolichucky River. His horse was the champion of all the Western country. People in every community sang the praises of his famous horse, Victor of All. Jackson, jealous of Love's reputation and popularity in the realm of his favorite sport, challenged him to a race. Love quickly accepted the challenge. A date was set and word of the big event was soon spread over the countryside.

Both Jackson and Love put their horses through days of rigid training in preparation for the occasion. On the appointed day, the settlers and their families began to gather early in the morning. Barbecue pits that had been fired throughout the night gave forth their tangy smell of cooking beef and venison. Full demijohns hung from saddles and shoulder straps. Betting was fast and furious on every hand. Many guns, horses, furs, and homesteads were to change hands before the day was over.

Another favorite sport participated in, during one of the big festive occasions such as this, was fisticuffs. Two men spoiling for a fight would strip to the waist and square off. The men would exchange blows until one of them was down or would hollar. "Take him off". The two fighters would shake hands, go down to the river and wash up, and then empty a demijohn together.

ANDREW JACKSON   ROBERT LOVE

RACE TRACK

As the day grew older, the large assembled crowd began to show its impatience for the big event to get under way for such events were rare and looked forward to and talked about for a long time afterward. A big roar went up when the two groups of horsemen were seen approaching the starting point. Jackson was accompanied by a group of friends from around Jonesboro. Love had a crowd of followers from the Greasy Cove neighborhood.

Some days before the race Jackson's jockey had been taken sick with fever. Love agreed to let Jackson ride his mount. A group of judges selected with much finesse and agreement from both parties took their places, half at the starting point and half at the other end of the track. The riders maneuvered their horses into position. The air in the area was electrified with the excitement of the crowd as the moment arrived.

At the signal "GO", the horses, spurred by their riders, charged down the track. Neck and neck they raced down that first half mile. As they rounded the turn, they were still churning the turf side by side. This was the race of all time, exciting beyond the wildest imagination of the assembled settlers. Their frenzied shouts echoed from hill to hill, and even the racing horses seemed to realize the importance of the occasion. Urged by their riders, these two champion steeds put forth their utmost effort. As they neared the finish line, Colonel Love's horse began to inch ahead and crossed the rope just a length ahead. Pandemonium broke loose as the excited followers of Love's horse saw their champion cross the line a winner.

Andrew Jackson, a hard loser with a quick temper, immediately began to abuse Colonal Love with every invective word at his command. Among his statements Jackson called all of the Loves "a band of land pirates". Robert Love, Jackson's equal in word exchange, called Andy "a long, gangling, sorrel-topped soapstick". They were approaching each other in such a belligerent attitude that mutual friends forcibly led them from the area of the race track in separate directions.

Colonel Robert Love, who has many descendants in the vicinity of Unicoi County, moved later to western North Carolina and was largely responsible for starting the settlement that became the present town of Waynesville, North Carolina. The site of the original race track is now owned by the Clinchfield Railroad Company, whose general offices are located in Erwin, Tennessee.

1A 39
GREASY COVE
RACETRACK

In the valley 500 yards north were held many kinds of frontier diversions, including racing on a half-mile semicircular track. Here, in 1788, Andrew Jackson, then 21 years old, rode his horse in a match race against a horse belonging to Col. Robert Love, ridden by a professional jockey. Jackson lost.

SEVIER'S ARREST

Governor Samuel Johnston ordered the arrest of John Sevier on a charge of high treason. The warrant, issued July 29, 1788, was first sent to Judge David Campbell who refused to execute it. Campbell sent the warrant to a North Carolina Judge named Spencer who did process the warrant and sent it to John Tipton. By this delay it was October 10 before the warrant was served.

John Sevier, despondent and despressed over the situation of Franklin and the attitude of many of the upper county friends, was drinking heavily. October 9th he visited Jonesborough and in the course of a few hours managed to get into arguments with Captain David Craig and a merchant named David Deadrick. No doubt Sevier knew about the warrant Tipton held for his arrest.

After dark Colonel Sevier rode to the home of Mrs. Jacob Brown near the Nolichucky River. Ruth Brown, widow of his friend and comrade Jacob Brown, was also mother of Benjamin Brown, husband of Nancy Sevier. Mrs. Brown put Sevier up for the night.

Colonel Tipton, had left Jonesborough where he had attended a staff meeting of the militia officers. One of his supporters rode to his home some ten miles distant on Sinking Creek to apprise him of Sevier's presence. Colonel Tipton, with a force of ten men, went looking for his enemy. With the power of his warrant they first went to the home of Charles Robertson and searched the house and out buildings without success. After other fruitless attempts they reached the home of Widow Brown about sunrise.

SAMUEL JOHNSTON: Governor of North Carolina 1788; ordered Sevier's arrest; member of Congress when Greene County citizens urged him to recommend John Sevier as Gov. of S. W. Territory.

Mrs. Brown, knowing about the warrant, was on the lookout. With her loaded gun she took her seat in the front doorway to keep watch. She saw the Tipton party approaching. Colonel Tipton was going to make a forceful entrance into the house. Mrs. Brown barred the way with her gun. The loud voices and the scuffling at the door awakened Sevier. Seeing Robert Love from Greasy Cove, who had joined the group, Sevier managed to reach Colonel Love and make his surrender to him.

This maneuver made Colonel Tipton mad, he swore that he would hang the prisoner. They took Sevier to Jonesborough where Tipton ordered Sevier to be shackled with iron handcuffs. John Sevier asked Colonel Love to intercede in his behalf and prevent his being sent to North Carolina for trial. Love told Tipton that his extreme treatment and threats toward the prisoner would arouse the people to a conflict.

BROWN HOME was built 1800's by Byrd Brown. The log cabin where John Sevier was arrested was near this building site. Ruth Brown, widow of Jacob did not move to area until after accidental death of Jacob Brown June 1785.

Disregarding any advice, Colonel Tipton sent Sevier across the mountains to Morganton under a guard composed of Jacob Tipton, Thomas Gourley and George French. Colonel Love accompanied the party as far as his place in Greasy Cove. He talked the guards into removing the iron handcuffs. James Love, at the request of Sevier, had carried word of the arrest to the Sevier family and also the Colonel's request that Mrs. Sevier send him money and clothing.

Just outside Morganton the party passed the McDowell home at Quaker Meadows. Charles McDowell went with the party to the Court House and stood Sevier's surety until a relative could go his bond. The Sheriff, William Morrison, as well as the McDowells was with Sevier in the battle against the Ferguson forces at King's Mountain. Sevier was allowed his freedom.

A group of Sevier's family and friends made haste to follow Sevier the moment they learned of his arrest. Colonel Love observed them as they passed his place in Greasy Cove. The group included John Sevier, Jr., son, Joseph Sevier, brother, Nathaniel Evans, George North, James Cozby, Jesse Green, and William Neatlook. They rode into Morganton individually and not in a body. They found Colonel Sevier sitting in a tavern with Major Joseph McDowell. They told him their purpose and that they would take him away from Morganton by force if necessary. After an hour or so discussing the situation, Colonel Sevier secured his horse and they rode out of Morganton together. No pursuit was attempted and no effort made to take Colonel Sevier back into custody.

Soon after the party arrived back home on the Nolichucky, Sevier wrote a strong letter of protest to the North Carolina Assembly.

TO BOTH HOUSES OF THE GENERAL ASSEMBLY OF NORTH CAROLINA

Greene County, October 30, 1788

Sirs: It is with inexpressible concern I am constrained to make a few observations to your honorable body. However trifling and insignificant the author of this may appear in the eyes of your august House yet from the patriotic and paternal spirit that I hope do and ought to prevail in every legislature induces me to believe with a flattering expectation that some regard will be shown, at least so far as to suffer this to be read before your honorable body.

CATHERINE SHERRILL SEVIER lived through a very eventful period; climbed 10 foot fort wall to escape Indians 1776; married John Sevier 1780; First Lady of Franklin; Wife of First Overmountain Congressman; First Lady of Tennessee; called "Bonnie Kate."

In regard to the political divisions raging in this Country, I humbly request you will be pleased to have reference to your own records and journals, in which I presume you will readily find the foundation and original cause from whence all our troubles have arisen. A long detail of facts and transactions here would be too tedious and unnecessary, as I am confident the greater part of your House are fully acquainted with every particular circumstance.

The integrity, uprightness and good disposition of your Government is not doubted or questioned with the greater part of the inhabitants of our Western Country. Our peculiar situation and local circumstances is what induced the people to wish a separation, and are constrained to believe that such a thing would have tended much to the advantage of each party. You are sensible and sufficiently acquainted how recently we were all employed and deeply engaged to keep off the British yoke of slavery and tyranny, and in the days of your greatest extremity, the people who are now suffering for differing in political sentiments were those who gave you the first relief, at the expense of their blood and loss of their dearest relations.

Is it not obvious to you that the rigid prosecutions now carried on is more to gratify the ambition and malice of an obscure the worthless individual than to appease the Justice of the State?

Is it not contrary to your Constitution and all the laws made in pursuance hereof to not only deprive a man of his liberty, but treat him with wanton cruelty and savage insults before trial, or any evidence of the breach of the laws adduced, borne off, out of the District, at a distance from his friends and neighbors who can only be the best judges of his innocence or guilt?

Has North Carolina forgot that for such acts America took up arms against the British nation? Has she also forgot that the man and party that now suffers was her zealous defenders in the days of her greatest extremity?

Can it be possible that North Carolina is so void of understanding as to think she is so permanently fixed as not to be shaken? Has she not discovered that there is formidable and inveterate enemies around her watching to take advantage of our divisions, which I am sorry to say are too numerous? Have you not discovered that those people have it in their power to do as much at least, if not a great deal more, for the Western Americans than you can yourselves? Have you not seen the most affectionate child become sour and inveterate against the parent, when the parental and tender ties of humanity have been refused?

Is it consistent with the honor and dignity of a government, or any of her executive department, to call upon some of those miserable, detestable miscreants, who were so lately sentenced to death in the Superior Court of Morgan District for being inimical to American liberty, to have it in their power to put to death at pleasure any of your defenders, which your own records acknowledge to have been your faithful servants for a number of years past?

Or can you think that any set of men, who are daily endeavoring to irritate and disaffect at least four-fifths of the people in the Western Countries, are in fact your friends? Surely you cannot; neither can you suppose those men, who are daily wishing for a return of British government, and also making it a point to put it in the power of those who was but the other day conquered by the American arms, now to tyrannize over and treat with barbarity and wanton cruelty the warm and zealous friends to American liberty? It is not myself alone that will be disgusted at such treatment; thousands have been engaged in the same cause.

These observations may be worthy of consideration and hope I shall be thought candid when I assure the State of North Carolina I have always wished her prosperity. I have fought and suffered in her cause. It is consistent with my own honor, secret pride and satisfaction that she, as well as the whole of the Union, may always flourish and become great.

I have the honor to be with due regard and consideration, your obedient and humble servant,

JOHN SEVIER

LAST OF FRANKLIN

Many settlers, below the French Broad, had obtained land grants from North Carolina officials before moving across the mountains. Threats of removal, by these same officials, caused much resentment and concern. Along with this group was another class of families who had taken up claims, squatter style. The report of free land for the taking had brought many families into the Indian territory.

These people, wanting protection and some form of law and order, continued to function as the State of Franklin. Some writers term it "The Lesser Franklin". Their grants were maintained for a short period under that status. They cited the Dumplin Creek and Coyatee Treaties as the guarantee of their right of possession.

It was during September of 1788 that Sevier had his correspondence with the Spanish Minister, Gardoqui. Colonel Sevier was trying to arrange a loan to keep Franklin alive. Dr. James White had made contact with Sevier earlier in 1788 and explained the Spanish offers of help. The friends in the lower counties were about the only supporters Sevier had left. He had watched as his Nolichucky and Watauga friends left one by one and turned back to the North Carolina fold.

The October 15, 1788 session of the Franklin Assembly passed the following act:

In the General Assembly, State of Franklin, October 15th, 1788.
Whereas, the collection of taxes in specie, for the want of a circulating medium, has become very oppressive to the good people of this Commonwealth; and

Whereas, it is the duty of the legislature to hear at all times the prayers of their constituents and apply as speedy a remedy as lays in their power,

Be it enacted by the General Assembly of the State of Franklin, and it is hereby enacted by the authority of the same, That, from the first day of January, A. D. 1788, the salaries of the civil officers of this Commonwealth be as follows, to wit:

His excellency, the governor, per annum, one thousand deer skins; his honor, the chief justice, five hundred do. do.; secretary to his excellency, the governor, five hundred racoon do. do.; the treasurer of the State, four hundred and fifty otter do. do.; each county clerk, three hundred beaver do.; clerk of the house of commons, two hundred beaver do.; members of the assembly, three do.; justices for signing a warrant, one muskrat do.; to the constable for serving a warrant, one mink do.

Enacted into a law this 15th day of October, 1788; under the great seal of the State.

Witness his Excellency, &c.

—————————————————————————
Governor, captain-general, commander-in-chief
and admiral in and over the same State.

Ramsey indicates that the seat of the Franklin Government during these last months was Newell's Station near Seymour, Tennessee. These friends remained loyal to Sevier throughout.

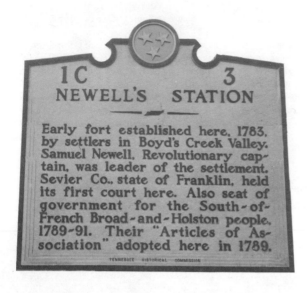

1C 3
NEWELL'S STATION

Early fort established here, 1783, by settlers in Boyd's Creek Valley. Samuel Newell, Revolutionary captain, was leader of the settlement. Sevier Co., state of Franklin, held its first court here. Also seat of government for the South-of-French Broad-and-Holston people, 1789-91. Their "Articles of Association" adopted here in 1789.

TENNESSEE HISTORICAL COMMISSION

NORTH CAROLINA ASSEMBLY 1788

The North Carolina Convention of July 1788 met, discussed, argued but failed to ratify the Federal Constitution. Congressional pressure had been exerted for help in the war debt; Franklin was asking for cession; Cumberland was requesting help and aid in their far away province. The western citizens were more disillusioned than ever with eastern politicians, who turned deaf ears to their pleas.

It must be remembered that North Carolina had voted herself out of the Union of States. They had no militia force of any great strength and not being a member of the union couldn't call on the other states for help in their domestic problems. The only gesture the Legislature made toward the closure of the Mississippi River by Spain was a declaration that the western citizens had an indisputable right to the navigation of the Mississippi.

General Daniel Smith of Sumner County wrote Governor Johnston that "many settlers were worn out with war and that North Carolina was doing practically nothing for their protection. The Spaniards had offered them protection and use of the waterways."

Cumberland was practically a state or domain unto itself as North Carolina paid little heed to her political functions. North Carolina was not a member of the Federal Union and Franklin was the step-child. The situation was a sort of stand-off. Alexander Hamilton expressed the view "that if Spain continued in her determination to bar navigation in the Mississippi, the result would be war with Spain or a separation of the western country from the seaboard states."

John Sevier had received overtures from Spanish authorities in Louisiana about aligning Franklin with Spain. There was some correspondence between Sevier and Gardoqui. A desperate people attempt desperate means. Franklin needed money and backing to survive. John Sevier tried to use the Spanish contact to borrow money for his state. In his despondent mood John Sevier even considered taking residence with the Chickasaw Indians. The Cumberland situation was getting so desperate James Robertson and other strong leaders of the Mero District went even further than Sevier in their dealing with Spain.

This was the situation when the Assembly met in Fayetteville, North Carolina November 1788. Many of the western delegates were former Franklinites in favor of separation. Senate members were: Greene, James Roddy; Hawkins, Thomas Amis; Washington, John Tipton; Davidson and Mero were represented by James Robertson. In the House: Greene, Joseph Hawkins, Alexander Outlaw; Washington, James Stuart, John Blair; Sullivan, George Maxwell, John Scott; Hawkins, Thomas King, William Outlaw; Davidson, Elijah Robertson, Thomas Hardiman; Sumner, William Walton, James Clendenning.

Willie Jones, for whom Jonesborough was named, presented a bill of oblivion and forgiveness for all citizens of Greene, Hawkins, Sullivan and Washington counties. An amendment to exclude John Sevier was introduced. During debate Thomas Amis spoke against this amendment. John Tipton spoke strongly for it. The debate led to an argument, struggle and fist fight. The participants were separated. Action was postponed until next day. James Roddy, who had attempted to soothe the argument and tempers the preceding day, was selected as the speaker against the amendment. Roddy had hardly started speaking when Tipton went for him and soon had Roddy down on the floor. Amis, standing by, admonished Roddy with "soothe him Colonel, soothe him."

The amendment, cutting Sevier out of the priviledge of turning back to Carolina allegiance, was beaten 24 to 19. In the house the pardon bill was passed 52 to 33. The Davidson and Sumner County delegates were now voting with the Franks. The North Carolina leaders were beginning to see the handwriting on the wall.

Willie Jones offered another bill that the western lands be ceded to Congress. An amendment was offered that would have made the boundary lines of the cession, the Cumberland mountains, rather than the Allegany. John Tipton seconded this motion as he felt his chances stronger with North Carolina than with the Overmountain people. This amendment was defeated. Tipton was the only westerner voting for this amendment. None the less the cession and ratification were postponed for the time being. The seaboard leaders, realizing time was running out, needed opportunity to do some political horse trading before making a final cession.

The western representatives, sensing that the tide was beginning to turn in their direction, asserted themselves with a stronger voice. The leadership of those who had split off from Franklin during the latter part of 1785 was reaching an end. The North Carolina officials were made aware that Colonel Tipton and his followers were as much to blame as John Sevier and other accused Franklin leaders for the troubles across the mountains. This was shown clearly in the appointment of officers for the militia and officials for the civil posts.

THOMAS AMIS STONE HOUSE was built by Amis 1780 on 1000 acre land grant in present Hawkins County. Note old clock and closed stairway doors. Mary Amis Rogers, daughter, married Joseph Rogers founder of Rogersville. Rogers operated blacksmith shop, corn mill, saw mill, distillery and store here with great success.

HAYSLOPE: Home of Colonel James Roddye located at Russellville, Tenn. First house built in present Hamblen County. James Roddye served with Sevier at King's Mountain, Boyd's Creek and other campaigns. Roddye was a loyal Frank; magistrate of Jefferson County during Territorial Government. Hayslope served as tavern, stage coach stop and on occasion church meetings.

LAST BATTLE OF FRANKLIN

Many friends and neighbors had gathered at Mount Pleasant to welcome John Sevier when he returned from Morganton. A real "Jubilee" was celebrated with barbecue and dancing. But there was a sad note in the air. During John Sevier's detention in Morganton the Indians had been busy. John Watts with 300 warriors had attacked Gillespie's Station, located on Little River. The undermanned station made a valiant resistance until their ammunition gave out. The warriors were able to gain entrance over the roof. 17 men and women were killed and 28 taken captive. The bodies of the 17 were burned with the fort. This successful conquest, following the others, gave the Indians fresh hopes. They felt that the victory spirit was on their side.

Richard Winn, Indian Agent from Congress, and Alexander Drumgoole, representing North Carolina made overtures to the Cherokee . They said what the Indians wanted to hear, but Dragging Canoe told them that he would keep his warriors and spies out for their own protection. The Indians still hoped to get the whites fighting among themselves.

John Watts, Bloody Fellow and Kitegisky did not return to their towns for the winter as was their custom. With several hundred warriors they set up winter headquarters along Flint Creek in Greasy Cove (Unicoi County). The location of the camp was secluded and the passes would allow bands of warriors to slip in and out, striking the unsuspecting settlements at will. They were determined to win back their hunting lands promised by the Federal Commissioners at the Hopewell Treaty.

In the meanwhile John Sevier had not been idle. Elected as President of the Franklin Safety Council he made preparations for such a move by the Indians. His scouts had kept him posted on the activities of the Indians. John Sevier set his mustering place for the men on Buffalo Creek not far from the site of Milligan College. It was extremely cold and a heavy snow lay on the ground. Following is an account of the battle by Sevier.

FLINT CREEK

(Copy of a letter from Governor Sevier to the privy council of the new State of Franklin, dated at Buffalo Creek, January 12, 1789.)

"It is with the utmost pleasure I inform your honors, that the arms of Franklin gained a complete victory over the combined forces of the Creeks and Cherokees, on the 10th inst. Since my last, (message) I received information that the enemy were collecting in a considerable body near Flint Creek, within 25 miles of my headquarters, with an intention to attack me. To improve this favorable opportunity, I immediately marched my corps towards the spot and arrived, after enduring much hardship by (reason of) the immense quantities of snow and piercing cold. On the morning of the 10th inst., we were within a mile of the enemy. We soon discovered the situation of their encampment by the smoke of their fires, which we found extended along the foot of the Appalachian Mountain. I called a council of war of all the officers, in which it was agreed to attack the enemy without loss of time; and in order to surround them, I ordered Gen. M'Carter, with the bloody rangers and the tomahawk-men, to take possession of the mountain, the only pass I knew that the Indians could retreat by while I with the rest of the corps formed a line extending from the right to the left of their wings.

"The arrival of Gen. M'Carter on the mountain, and the signal for the attack was to be announced by the discharge of a grass-hopper, which was accordingly given and the attack began.

"Our artillery soon roused the Indians from their huts; and, finding themselves pretty near surrounded on all sides, they only tried to save themselves by flight, from which they were prevented by our riflemen posted behind the trees. Their case being desperate, they made some resistance, and killed the people who were serving our artillery. Our ammunition being much damaged by the snow on the march, and the enemy's in good order, I found it necessary to abandon that mode of attack, and trust the event to the sword and the tomahawk; accordingly gave orders to that purpose. Col. Loid, with 100 horsemen, charged the Indians with sword in hand, and the rest of the corps followed with their tomahawks. The battle soon became general, by Gen. M'Carter's coming down the mountain to our assistance; death presented itself on all sides in shocking scenes, and in less than half an hour, the enemy ceased making resistance, and left us in possession of the bloody field.

"The loss of the enemy sustained in this battle is very considerable; we have buried 145 of their dead, and by the blood we have traced for miles all over the woods it is supposed the greatest part of them retreated with wounds. Our loss is very inconsiderable; it consists of five dead, and 16 wounded; amongst the latter is the brave Gen. M'Carter, who, while taking off the scalp of an Indian, was tomahawked by another whom he afterward killed with his own hand. I am in hopes this brave and good man will survive.

"I have marched the army back to my former cantonment, at Buffalo Creek, where I must remain until I receive some supplies for the troops, which I hope will be sent soon. We suffer most for the want of whiskey."

(This written account of John Sevier's report to the council of the State of Franklin as found in Williams' "Lost State of Franklin" and transcribed from the City Gazetter and Daily Advisor, of Charleston, S. C., April 21, 1789; and Augusta Chronicle, May 2, 1789.)

SITE OF THE BATTLE OF FLINT CREEK

NORTH CAROLINA PASSES CESSION BILL

During the February 1789 term of court in Greene County, John Sevier, Henry Conway, Joseph Hardin and Hugh Wear took the oath of allegiance to North Carolina agreeable to the act of that assembly. Even though there was a phrase, barring Sevier from office or public gain, in the bill little attention was given to that stipulation. The people of Greene County elected Sevier to serve in the Senate which was to convene in Fayetteville, North Carolina.

As North Carolina had not fulfilled her obligations toward the Federal debt, pressure was being exerted by Congress. Along with this demand General Joseph Martin presented his bill for the unsuccessful campaign against the Chickamauga towns. The State Council could find no means of payment of these bills other then cession of the western territory. After much debate, pro and con, the second cession act was finally passed. The wording differed little from the first bill. John Sevier was able to record his vote for this act. The Convention also ratified the Federal Constitution during this session. John Sevier a member of this body, was able to vote for ratification.

Joseph Martin, who had sided with the North Carolinians against Franklin, was not very popular with the western people. His signature on the Hopewell Treaty and other similar acts made him disliked and distrusted by the Overmountain people. The Indians were also leery of Martin. He was displaced as Brigadier-General by John Sevier. The State legislature dated Sevier's Commission back to the year 1784 when Governor Martin first made

OLD MARKET HOUSE, Fayetteville, N. C. Town first named Cross Creek; merged with Campelton, renamed Fayetteville 1783.

the appointment. General Sevier was continued in this office during the South West Territory period.

The Overmountain counties were formed into a congressional district. John Sevier was the first elected represented from the western country. Several of the former Franklin citizens prepared a petition, addressed to Senator Samuel Johnston, commending Sevier to the Federal Government. One request in the petition was that John Sevier be appointed Territorial Governor.

The State of Franklin lost its bid in the struggle to become the 14th state in the Union, but its leaders were destined to become the moulders of Tennessee, the 16th State. Deeds, marriages and other legal transactions of Franklin were, in the course of time, validated by the State of Tennessee. Many Franklin descendants, along with other Tennesseans, were destined to play prominent roles in the political affairs of the nation and the creation of other states as young America spread westward.

Today the spirit of Franklin rises up in the political spectrum of Tennessee. Many times in the past it has threatened political dictates with separation. The independent spirit of "The State of Appalachia" will continue to echo in the political halls when they feel that they are the objects of dictation.

THE FIRST TAX LIST FOR THE COUNTY OF GREENE, STATE OF TENNESSEE, 1783

This Greene County Tax List of 1783 was compiled by Louise Wilson Reynolds and published in the D.A.R. Magazine April 1919 Issue.

Allison, Robert
Allison, David
Alexander, James
Alexander, Joseph
Alexander, Ebinezer
Anderson, Daniel
Anderson, Barnibas
Armstrong, John
Armstrong, Langsnell
Atherton, Charles

Balch, Hezekiah
Ball, John
Ball, William
Ballard, Isac
Ballard, Thomas
Barham, William
Barnett, Robert
Barnett, Thomas
Barton, Isac
Barton, Robert
Basher, John
Beard, Hugh
Beard, John
Bearchett, John
Bennett, Thomas
Bennett, William
Biggs, John
Bigham, William
Billings, William
Bird, Amos
Bird, John
Bird, Joseph
Bishop, John
Bishop, Mathew
Blackwell, David
Blake, Hezekiah
Borden, Michael
Blackwell, John
Boy, Elizabeth
Box, Henry
Box, Isac
Box, Israel
Box, Joseph
Box, Robert
Boy, Ezekial
Boyd, James
Boyd, Joseph
Boyd, William
Boyd, John
Boydston, William
Brabson, Andrew
Brabson, Susan
Brandon, Barnett
Brandon, Garrett
Brandon, Thomas
Breed, Avery
Brock, George
Brown, George
Brown, James
Brown, Thomas
Brumley, Augustine
Brumley, Barnabas
Brumley, Joseph
Brumley, Thomas
Bryant, Bryan
Bryant, John
Bryant, Thomas
Bryson, Hugh
Buckingham, Thomas
Bull, John
Bullard, Isac
Bullard, Joseph
Burney, William
Burk, James
Buskin, Jonathan
Byram, Benjamin
Byram, Ebenezer
Byram, William

Cameron, James
Campbell, Alexander
Campbell, David
Campbell, James
Campbell, John
Campbell, Robert

Campbell, William
Cannon, John
Carlyle, John
Carson, John
Carson, Robert
Carter, Abraham
Carter, John
Carter, Michael
Casteel, William
Casteel, John
Casteel, John, Jr.
Chamberlin, Jane
Chamberlin, Stout
Chambers, John
Christian, Isham
Cisco, John
Claggs, William
Clowers, Jacob
Colly, James
Colton, John
Condry, Henry
Conway, Henry
Conway, Philip
Corbitt, John
Cooper, Jacob
Cooper, John
Copeland, David
Cotter, John
Cotton, Young
Cowan, Philip
Cox, Benjamin
Cox, Thomas
Cox, Ephraem
Cox, Matthew
Crabtree, James
Craddick, David
Craig, James
Craig, James, Jr.
Craig, David
Craig, John
Cravan, Robert
Crawford, John
Creamer, Daniel
Crockett, John
Crockett, Robert
Cross, Henry
Crow, James
Crow, John
Crow, Joseph
Croweon, William
Crump, Edmund
Cunningham, John
Curtis, Nathaniel
Curtis, Robert

Davis, Alexander
Davis, Nathan
Davis, James
Davis, John
Davis, Joseph
Davis, Nicholas Day
Davis, Phillip
Davis, Robert
Davis, Samuel
Davis, Thomas
Dawson, William
Delaney, Francis
Delaney, James
Delaney, John
Dillard, James
Dillon, Peter
Dixon, Samuel
Dotson, Charles
Dotson, John
Doty, Azariah
Doherty, George
Doherty, Joseph
Doherty, James
Dudley, Abraham
Duncan, Cravan
Dunham, Henry
Dunham, Joseph
Dunham, Robert
Dunn, William
Dunwoody, Samuel
Dunwoody, Adam

Dunwoody, James
Duval, Thomas

Eagleton, David
Eakin, Joseph
Edmunds, John
Eldridge, Thomas
English, Andrew
English, James
English, Daniel
English, John
English, Joseph
English, William
Epperson, David
Epperson, Joseph
Ernest, Henry
Evans, Evan
Evans, Jonathan
Eaton, James

Falls, Thomas
Fant, John
Fant Phillip
Farnsworth, Henry
Fincher, Robert
Fine Peter
Fine, John
Fine, Phillip
Forby, Henry
Frame, David
Francis, William
Furman, James
Fuston, Robert

Galbrath, Alexander
Galbrath, James
Galbrath, John
Galbrath, Joseph
Galbrath, William
Gass, John
Gass, Thomas
Gibson, Samuel
Gilbert, John
Gilbert, Richard
Gillespie, James
Gillespie, Thomas
Gilliam, Robert
Gilliand, John
Gillis, John
Gist, Thomas
Gist, Avery
Gist, Benjamin
Gist, John
Glass, Jacob
Glass Joseph
Glaze, Lawrence
Goforth, William
Godden, Benjamin
Gooden, James
Gooden, Thomas
Gorrell, David
Greene, Jacob
Griswell, Daniel
Gross, Thomas
Guthrie, James
Guthrie, William
Garrett, David
Garrett - - -

Hardin, Joseph
Hardin, John
Hamilton, Francis
Hadden, Elisha
Hale, Alexander
Hale, Shadrack
Hale, William
Hall, Alexander
Hall, Gailor
Hamilton, Isiah
Hammond, John
Hardin, William
Hawkins, Joseph
Haynie, Charles
Haynie, James
Hays, Charles
Hays, James

Hays, John
Hays, Joseph
Hays, Nathaniel
Hays, Naoma
Hayworth, Abraham
Hayworth, George
Hayworth, James
Hemile, Joseph
Henderson, Daniel
Henderson, John
Henderson, Joseph
Henderson, Thomas
Henderson, William
Henkle, Thomas
Henry, James
Herman, Robert
Hicks, Jonathan
Hightower, Richard
Hill, James
Hodges, Drury
Hodges, William
Holly, Elizabeth
Holly, Johnahan
Hood, Robert
Hopton, John
Hornback, John
Hough, John
Houston, James
Houston, Samuel
Howard, Abraham
Howard, Richard
Hubbard, Samuel
Hubbard, James
Hubbard, William
Hubbs, Caleb
Huffman, Michael
Hughes, Andrew
Hughes, Edward
Hughes, John
Hughes, Francis
Hunt, Abraham
Hunt, Thomas
Hutchins, Smith

Inman, Shadrack

Jamison, Andrew
Jamison, Benjamin
Jamison, George
Jarvis, James
Johnson, James
Johnson, John
Johnson, Joseph
Johnson, William
Jones, Evan
Jones, Henry
Jones, William

Keel, James
Keel, Robert
Kelly, John
Kelly, Johnathan
Kenedy, Daniel
Kenedy, Francis
Kenedy, Moses
Kenedy, William
Kerr, Robert, Sr.
Kerr, Robert
Kerr, William
Kesterson, John
Keykendall, James
Keykendall, John
Keykendall, Joseph
Keykendall, Mathew
Kilgore, Charles
King, German
King, James
King, Joseph
King, Robert
Kirkland, Daniel
Kirkwood, David
Kyler, Joseph

Lane, Dutton
Lane, Isac
Lawson, Anthony

Lee, Abner
Lee, George
Lee, Thomas
Leeper, Andrew
Leeper, Mathew
Leggett, John
Leming, David
Lovitt, Elisha
Lewis, Uriah
Lincoln, Mary
Lindsey, David
Lintz, Alexander
Livingston, Robert
Lonas, James
Lonas, Joseph
Long, Zopher
Loony, Richard
Lovelady, James
Lovelady, John
Lovelady, Marshall
Lusk, Joseph
Lyle, James

McAdoo, John
McAdoo, John, Jr.
McAlpin, Alexander
McBroom, William
McCall, Robert
McCartney, Charles
McCartney, John
McCartney, James
McCartney, James
McCartney, William
McClung, Hugh
McClung, John
McClung, James
McClure, Nathan
McConnell, Jacob
McCool, Gabrael
McCouglan, Alexander
McCrosky, John
McCurdy, John
McCurdy, Andrew
McCurdy, Archibold
McDowell, Ephraem
McFarland, Alexander
McFerrin, Andrew
McFerrin, James
McGaughey, William
McGhee, Terrell
McGill, James
McGill, Robert
McGill, Robert
McGuire, Cornelius
McGuire, Francis
McGuire, Francis, Jr.
McKeehan, Samuel
McMeans, Samuel
McMurry, William
McMurray, Samuel
McNew, Shadrack
McPherron, James
McPheters, Joseph
McPike, William
McWilliams, David
Martin, Andrew
Martin, George
Martin, Richard
Mathew, Phillip
Mathews, Joel
Mathews, Obediah
Mathews, Peter
Mathews, William
Mays, Samuel
Mays, Thomas
Meek, Israel
Meek, Adam
Middleton, John
Milburn, Joseph
Miller, Andrew
Millican, Alexander
Millican, James
Mitchell, Andrew
Mitchell, David
Montgomery, Alexander
Montgomery, James

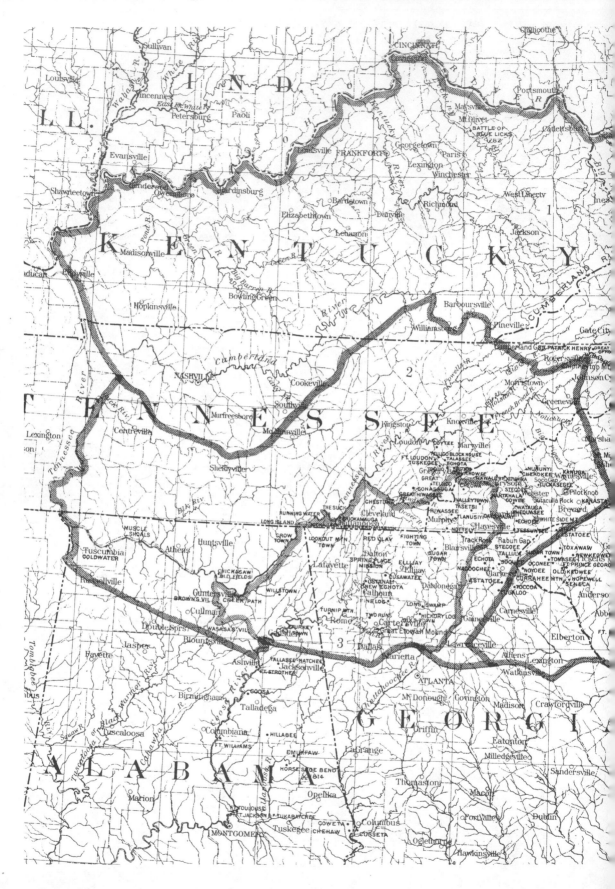

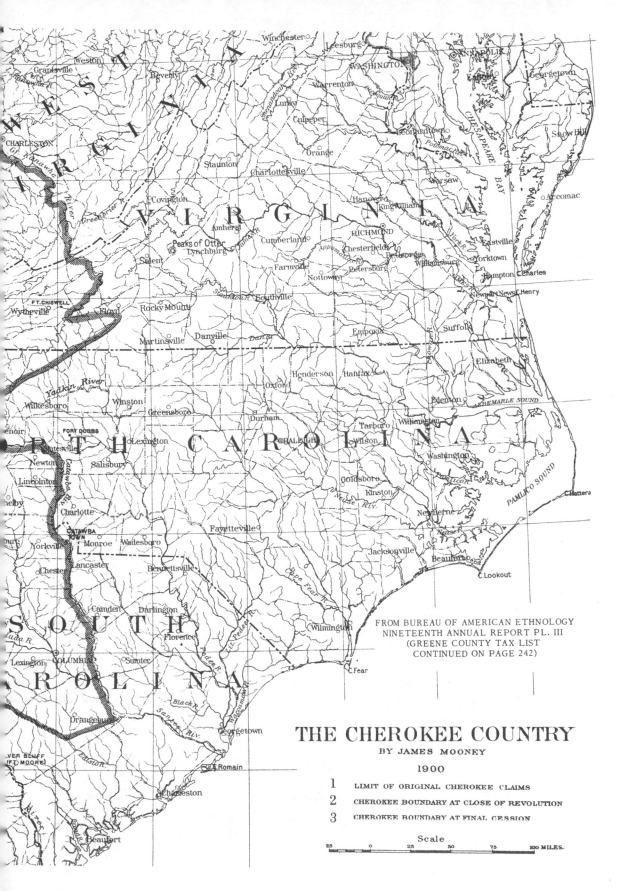

THE CHEROKEE COUNTRY

BY JAMES MOONEY

1900

FROM BUREAU OF AMERICAN ETHNOLOGY
NINETEENTH ANNUAL REPORT PL. III
(GREENE COUNTY TAX LIST
CONTINUED ON PAGE 242)

1   LIMIT OF ORIGINAL CHEROKEE CLAIMS

2   CHEROKEE BOUNDARY AT CLOSE OF REVOLUTION

3   CHEROKEE BOUNDARY AT FINAL CESSION

Scale

25   0   25   50   75   100 MILES.

Montgomery, Thomas
Mooney, George
Moore, Anthony
Moore, Hugh
Moore, James
Moore, John
Moore, Moses
Moore, Mary
Moore, Robert
Moore, Samuel
Moore, William
Morgan, Adonijah
Morgan, Levi
Morgan, Thomas
Morris, Gideon
Morris, John
Morris, Shadrack
Morrison, Patrick
Morrow, William
Mulholland, William
Murphy, John
Murphy, William

Neas, Peter
Neil, Mathew
Neil, Nicholas
Neil, Walter
Nelson, James
Nelson, Joseph
Nelson, William
Nelson, William
Newby, James
Newby, Joseph
Newman, John

Oliphant, John
O Neal, Bartholomew
O Neal, Cornelius
O Neal, Robert
O Neal, William
Oren, David
Oren, Thomas
Orphan, Thomas
Owens, John
Owens, William

Painter, Adam
Parker, William
Parks, James

Parker, William
Paris, Robert
Parton, Samuel
Pate, Mathew
Patterson, James
Patterson, John
Pennington, Absalom
Perciful, Thomas
Perkins, James
Perkins, Joseph
Phillips, Thomas
Posey, Abraham
Pickens, James
Pierce, James
Piper, Martha
Poor, Moses
Posey, Abraham
Prather, Alexander
Prather, Thomas
Prewitt, David
Prewitt, Martin
Prewitt, William
Price, John
Pryor, John
Pryor, Richard
Perciful, Thomas

Rankin, David
Rankin, Thomas
Rankin, William
Rawlings, Ashahel
Ray, Benjamin
Ray, William
Reece, John
Reece, Abraham
Reece, John
Reed, David
Reed, George
Reed, John
Ray, Thomas
Reed, Michael
Renfro, Samuel
Reynolds, David
Reynolds, Henry
Reynolds, Job
Reynolds, William
Richison, Abel
Richison, James
Richison, John

Richison, William
Richey, Gideon
Richey, Thomas
Ricker, John
Riggs, Edward
Riggs, Jenny
Riggs, Reuben
Right, James (Wright)
Rightsell, George
Ringo, Cornelius
Ripper, Hardy
Roberts, Barnard
Roberts, Edward
Roberts, John
Roberts, Jonathan
Rodgers, James
Robertson, Charles
Robertson, Francis
Robertson, James
Ross, John
Rowan, Charles
Rowan, Francis
Rudder, James
Running, Isac
Russell, David
Russell, Thomas
Russell, John
Rutherford, Thomas
Ryan, William

Samples, Samuel
Sampson, Anthony
Serratt, Joseph
Serratt, Elisha
Scott, Adam
Seaton, Isiah
Seaton, Jacob
Sellers, Sebert
Sheffy, John
Shelly, Luke
Sherrell, Adam
Sherrell, John
Sherrell, Phillip
Sherrell, Samuel
Sherrell, Samuel, Jr.
Shores, Alexander
Simpson, Andrew
Simpson, James

Simpson, Mary
Simpson, Reuben
Sloan, John
Smiley, Jacob
Smith, Alexander
Smith, Francis
Smith, John
Smith, Thomas
Smith, Turner
Stanfield, Thomas
Starnes, Adam
Starnes, James
Steel, James
Steel, Richard
Steel, Robert
Stephenson, John
Stewart, Benjamin
Stewart, Robert
Stockton, William
Stone, John
Stone, William
Stuart, Benjamin
Stuart, James
Stewart, Joseph
Swaggerty, Abraham
Swaggerty, Frederick

Tadlock, Jeremiah
Tadlock, John
Tadlock, Josiah
Tadlock, Mathias
Tadlock, Thomas
Tate, Thomas
Taylor, Isac
Temple, James
Temple, Major
Temple, John
Temple, William
Thomas, Andrew
Thompson, William
Tidence, Emanuel
Toby, Henry
Teny, Zopher
Tool, John
Totten, John
Trimble, John
Trimble, Moses Tye John

Vance, Samuel

Vance, John
Vanhooster, John
Veatch, Amos
Veatch, Elijah
Veatch, Josiah
Veatch, Jeremiah
Veatch, Nathan

Walker, Joseph
Wallace, Samuel
Ward, James
Wear, Samuel
Wear, John
Wear, Hugh
Webb, George
Webb, Richard
Wells, Henry
Wells, Thomas
Welty, John
West, Thomas
Whittenburg, Frederick
Whittenburg, Henry
Whittenburg, James
Whitson, Henry
Wilhoit, Adam
Williams, James
Williams, John
Williams, Joseph
Williams, Thomas
Williamson, William
Willis, Joseph
Willson, Alexander
Wilson, Ephraem
Wilson, James
Wilson, John
Wilson, Joseph
Wilson, Robert
Wilson, William
Winningham, John
Wood, John
Woodward, John
Woods, Richard
Woolsey, John
Wright, James
Wyatt, Samuel
Wyatt, William

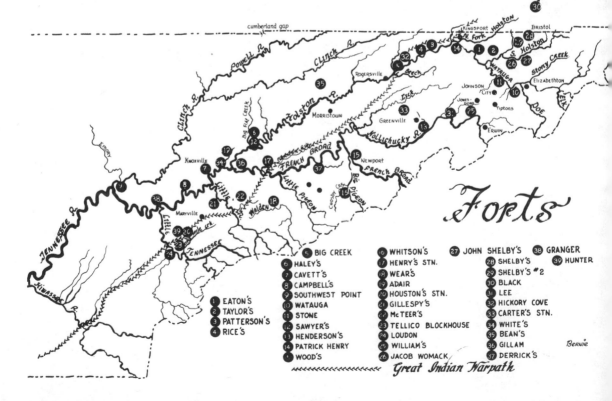

Forts

1 EATON'S
2 TAYLOR'S
3 PATTERSON'S
4 RICE'S
5 BIG CREEK
6 HALEY'S
7 CAVETT'S
8 CAMPBELL'S
9 SOUTHWEST POINT
10 WATAUGA
11 STONE
12 SAWYER'S
13 HENDERSON'S
14 PATRICK HENRY
15 WOOD'S
16 WHITSON'S
17 HENRY'S STN.
18 WEAR'S
19 ADAIR
20 HOUSTON'S STN.
21 GILLESPY'S
22 McTEER'S
23 TELLICO BLOCKHOUSE
24 LOUDON
25 WILLIAM'S
26 JACOB WOMACK
27 JOHN SHELBY'S
28 SHELBY'S
29 SHELBY'S #2
30 BLACK
31 LEE
32 HICKORY COVE
33 CARTER'S STN.
34 WHITE'S
35 BEAN'S
36 GILLAM
37 DERRICK'S
38 GRANGER
39 HUNTER

Great Indian Warpath

Bernie

APPENDIX

THE CONSTITUTION OF THE STATE OF FRANKLIN

Your committee appointed to collect and adjust the reasons which impel us to declare ourselves independent of North Carolina, report as follows, to-wit:

WHEREAS, we, the freemen inhabitants of part of the country included in the limits of an Act of North Carolina ceding certain vacant territory to Congress, having declared ourselves independent of North Carolina, a decent respect to the opinions of mankind made it proper that we should manifest to the world the reasons which induced us to a declaration, which are as follows:

FIRST. That the Constitution of North Carolina declares that it shall be justifiable to erect new States whenever the consent of the Legislature shall countenance it, and this consent is implied, we conceive, in the cession act which has thrown us into such a situation that the influence of the law in common cases was almost a nullity, and in criminal jurisdiction had ceased entirely; which reduced us to the verge of anarchy.

SECOND. The Assembly of North Carolina have detained a certain quantity of goods, which was procured to satisfy the Indians for the lands we possess, which detainure we fully conceive has so exasperated them that they have actually committed hostilities upon us, and we are alone compelled to defend ourselves from these savages.

3RDLY. The resolutions of Congress held out from time to time, encouraging the erection of new States, have appeared to us ample encouragement.

4THLY. Our local situation is such that we not only apprehend we should be separated from North Carolina, but almost every sensible, disinterested traveler has declared it is incompatible with our interest to belong in union with the eastern part of the State; for we are not only far removed from the eastern parts of North Carolina, but separated from them by high and almost impassable mountains, which naturally divide us from them, which have proved to us that our interest is also in many respects distinct from the inhabitants on the other side, and much injured by union with them.

5TH AND LASTLY. We unanimously agree that our lives, liberties and property can be more secure and our happiness much better propagated by our separation; and consequently that it is our duty and inalienable right to form ourselves into a new and independent State.

A DECLARATION OF RIGHTS MADE BY THE REPRESENTATIVES OF THE FREEMEN OF THE STATE OF FRANKLIN

Section 1. That all political power is vested in and derived from the people.

Sec. 2. That the people of this State ought to have the sole and exclusive right of regulating the internal government and police thereof.

Sec. 3. That no man, or set of men, are entitled to exclusive or separate emoluments or privileges from the community, but in consideration of public services.

Sec. 4. That the legislative, executive and supreme judicial powers of government ought to be forever separate and distinct from each other.

Sec. 5. That all powers of suspending laws or the execution of laws, by any authority, without the consent of the representatives of the people is injurious to the rights, and ought not to be exercised.

Sec. 6. That elections of members to serve as representatives in General Assembly ought to be free.

Sec. 7. That in all criminal prosecutions every man has a right to be informed of the accusation against him, and to confront the accusers and witnesses with other testimony, and shall not be compelled to give evidence against himself.

Sec. 8. That no freeman shall be put to answer any criminal charge but by indictment, presentment or impeachment.

Sec. 9. That no freeman shall be convicted of any crime but by the unanimous verdict of a jury of good and lawful men in open court, as heretofore used.

Sec. 10. That excessive bail should not be required, nor excessive fines imposed, nor cruel and unusual punishments be inflicted.

Sec. 11. That general warrants, whereby any officer or messenger may be commanded to search suspected places, without evidence of the fact committed, or to seize any person or persons not named whose offense is not particularly described and supported by the evidence, are dangerous to liberty and ought not to be granted.

Sec. 12. That no freeman ought to be taken, imprisoned or disseized of his freehold, liberties or privileges, or outlawed or exiled, or in any manner destroyed or deprived of his life, liberty or property, but by the laws of the land.

Sec. 13. That every freeman restrained of his liberty is entitled to a remedy to inquire into the lawfulness thereof and to remove it, if unlawful; and that such remedy ought not to be denied.

Sec. 14. That in all controversies at law respecting property, the ancient mode of trial by jury is one of the best securities of the rights of the people, and ought to remain sacred and inviolable.

Sec. 15. That the freedom of the press is one of the greatest bulwarks of liberty, and therefore ought never to be restrained.

Sec. 16. That the people of this State ought not to be taxed, or made subject to the payment of any impost or duty without the consent of themselves or their representatives in General Assembly freely given.

Sec. 17. That the people have a right to bear arms for the defense of the State; and as standing armies in times of peace are dangerous to liberty, they ought not to be kept up, and that the military should be kept under strict subordination to and be governed by civil power.

Sec. 18. That the people have a right to assemble together to consult for their common good to instruct their representatives, and to apply to the legislature for redress of grievances.

Sec. 19. That all men have a natural and inalienable right to worship God Almighty according to the dictates of their own conscience.

Sec. 20. That for redress of grievances and for amending and strengthening the laws, elections ought to be often held.

Sec. 21. That a frequent recurrence to fundamental principles is absolutely necessary to preserve the blessings of liberty.

Sec. 22. That no hereditary emoluments, privileges, or honors ought to be granted or conferred in this State.

Sec. 24. That retrospective laws punishing acts committed before the existence of such laws, and by them only declared criminal, are oppressive, unjust and incompatible with liberty; wherefore no *ex post facto* law ought to be made.

Sec. 25. That the people have a right by their representatives to enact laws to encourage virtue and suppress vice and immorality.

THE CONSTITUTION AND FORM OF GOVERNMENT

AGREED TO AND RESOLVED UPON BY THE REPRESENTATIVES OF THE FREE MEN OF THE STATE OF FRANKLIN, ELECTED AND CHOSEN FOR THAT PARTICULAR PURPOSE, IN CONVENTION ASSEMBLED, AT JONESBOROUGH, THE 17TH DECEMBER, ANNO. DOM. 1784.[2]

Section 1. That the legislative authority shall be vested in two distinct branches, both dependent on the people, to-wit: a Senate and a House of Commons.

Sec. 2. That the Senate shall be composed of three representatives annually chosen by ballot from each County[3] until there be ten Counties in the State, after that period, one from each County.

Sec. 3. That the House of Commons shall be composed of representatives chosen by ballot, four[4] for each County, until there be ten Counties within the State, and after that period, two for each County.

Sec. 4. That the Senate and House of Commons assembled for the purpose of legislation shall be denominated the General Assembly.

Sec. 5. That each member of the Senate shall have usually resided in the County in which he is chosen for one year immediately preceding his election, and for the same time shall have possessed and continued to possess in the County in which he represents not less than one hundred acres[5] of land in fee.

Sec. 6. That each member of the House of Commons shall have usually resided in the county in which he is chosen for one year immediately preceding his election.[6]

Sec. 7. That all freemen of the age of twenty-one years who have been inhabitants of any one County within the State twelve months immediately preceding the day of any election, and possessed of a freehold within the same County of fifty acres of land for six months next before and at the day of election shall be entitled to vote for a member of the Senate.

Sec. 8. That all freemen of the age of twenty-one years who have been inhabitants of any County in this State twelve months immediately preceding the day of any election, and shall have paid public taxes, shall be entitled to vote for members of the House of Commons for the County in which he resides.

Sec. 9. That all persons possessed of a freehold in any town in this State having a right of representation, and also all freemen who have been inhabitants of any such town twelve months next before and at the day of election, and shall have paid public taxes, shall be entitled to vote for a member to represent such town in the House of Commons; provided always, that this section shall not entitle any inhabitant of such town to vote for members of the House of Commons for the County in which he may reside, nor any freeholder in such County who reside without or beyond the limits of town to vote for a member of said town.

Sec. 10. That the Senate and House of Commons, when men, shall each have power to choose a speaker and other officers, and shall be judges of the qualifications and election of their members, sit upon their own adjournment from day to day, and prepare bills to be passed into laws. The two houses shall direct writs of election for supplying intermediate vacancies and shall also jointly by ballot adjourn themselves to any future day.

Sec. 11. That all bills shall be read three times in each house before they pass into laws, and be signed by the speakers of both houses.[7] On motion and second, the yeas and nays shall be taken on the passing of any act, and printed with the same.

Sec. 12. That every person who shall be chosen a member of the Senate or House of Commons, or appointed to any office or place of trust, before taking his seat or entering upon the execution of his office, shall take an oath to the State, and all officers also shall take an oath of office.

Sec. 13. That the General Assembly by joint ballot of both houses shall appoint Judges of the Supreme Courts of Law and Equity and Attorney General, who shall be commissioned by the Governor and hold their offices during good behavior.

Sec. 14. That the Senate and House of Commons shall have power to appoint the general and field officers of the militia and all officers of the regular army of the State.

Sec. 15. That the Senate and House of Commons jointly at their first meeting after each annual election shall by ballot, elect a Governor for one year, who shall not be eligible to that office longer than three years in six successive years; that no person under thirty years of age and who has not been a resident in this State above one year and shall not have in the State a freehold in land and tenements above the value of two hundred and fifty pounds, shall be eligible as Governor.

Sec. 16. That the Senate and House of Commons jointly at their first meeting after each annual election shall by ballot elect five persons to be a Council of State for one year, who shall advise the Governor in the execution of his office, and that three members shall be a quorum. Their advice and proceedings shall be entered in a journal to be kept for that purpose only, and signed by the members present, to any part of which any member present may enter his dissent; and such journals shall be laid before the General Assembly, when called for by them.

Sec. 17. There shall be a seal of this State, which shall be kept by the Governor and used by him as occasion may require, and shall be called the great seal of the State of Franklin, and be affixed to all grants and commissions.

Sec. 18. The Governor for the time being shall be Captain General and Commander in Chief of the Militia and in the recess of the General Assembly shall have power by and with the advice of the Council of State, to embody the Militia for public safety.

Sec. 19. That the Governor for the time being shall have power to draw for and apply such sums of money as shall be voted by the General Assembly for the contingencies of government, and be accountable to them for the same; and he also may, by and with the advice of the Council of State, lay embargoes or prohibit the exportation of any commodities for any term not exceeding thirty days at any one time in the recess of the General Assembly; and shall have the power of granting pardons and reprieves, except where the prosecutions shall be carried on in the General Assembly or the law shall otherwise direct. In such case, he may in the recess grant a reprieve until the next sitting of the General Assembly; and may exercise all other executive powers of government, limited and restrained as by the State; and on his death, inability or absence from the State, the Speaker of the Senate, for the time being, and in case of his death, inability or absence from the State, the Speaker of the House of Commons, shall exercise the powers of government, after such death or during such absence or inability of the Governor or Speaker of the Senate or until a new nomination is made by the General Assembly.

Sec. 20. That in every case where any officer, the right of whose appointment is made by this Constitution vested in the General Assembly, shall during their recess die, or his office by other means become vacant, the Governor shall have power, with the advice of the Council of State, to fill up such vacancy by granting a temporary commission, which shall expire at the end of the next session of the General Assembly.

Sec. 21. That the Governor, Judges of Supreme Courts of Law and Equity and Attorney General, shall have adequate salaries during their continuance in office.

Sec. 22. That the General Assembly shall by joint ballot of both houses annually appoint a Treasurer or Treasurers for this State.

Sec. 23. That the Governor or other officers offending against the State by violating any part of this Constitution, maladministration or corruption, may be prosecuted on the impeachment of the General Assembly, or presentment of the grand jury of any court or supreme jurisdiction of this State.

Sec. 24. That the General Assembly shall by joint ballot of both houses, triennially appoint a Secretary for this State.

Sec. 25. That no persons, who heretofore have been or hereafter may be receivers of public monies, shall have a seat in either house of General Assembly, or be eligible to any office in this State, until such persons shall have fully accounted for and paid into the treasury all sums for which they may be accountable and liable if legally called upon.

Sec. 26. That no Treasurer shall have a seat in either Senate, House of Commons or Council of State during his continuance in that office, or before he shall have finally settled his accounts with the public for all monies which may be in his hands at the expiration of his office belonging to the State and have paid the same into the hands of the succeeding Treasurer.

Sec. 27. That no officer in the regular army or navy in the service and pay of the United States, of this or any other State, nor any contractor or agent for supplying such army or navy with clothing or provisions, shall have a seat either in the Senate, the House of Commons, or the Council of State, or be eligible thereto; any member of the Senate, House of Commons or Council of State being appointed to and accepting of such office shall thereby vacate his seat.

Sec. 28. That no member of the Council of State shall have a seat either in the Senate or the House of Commons; provided, nevertheless, that the Governor and Council shall attend the General Assembly during the sitting of the same, and that it shall be a part of their official duty to revise all bills before they can be passed and recommend such amendments as they think proper.

Sec. 29. That no Judge of the Supreme Court of Law or Equity shall have a seat in Senate, House of Commons or Council of State.

Sec. 30. That no Secretary of this State, Attorney General or clerk of any court of record shall have a seat in the Senate, House of Commons or Council of State.

Sec. 31. That no clergyman or preacher of the gospel of any denomination shall be capable of being a member of either the Senate or House of Commons while he continues in the service of the pastoral function.

Sec. 32. That no person shall deny the being of a God or the truth of the Protestant religion or the divine authority of the Old or New Testament, or who shall hold religious principles incompatible with the freedom and safety of the State, shall be capable of holding any office or place of truth or profit in the civil department within this State.

Sec. 33. That the Justices of the Peace within their respective Counties in this State shall in the future be recommended to the Governor for the time being by the representatives in General Assembly, and the Governor shall commission them accordingly, and the Justices commissioned shall hold their office during good behavior, and shall not be removed from office by the General Assembly unless for misbehavior, absence or inability.

Sec. 34. That there shall be no establishment of any religious church or denomination in this State in preference to any other, neither shall any person on any pretense whatever be compelled to attend any place of worship contrary to his own faith or judgment, nor be obliged to pay for the purchase of any glebe of the building of any house of worship or for the maintenance of any minister or ministry contrary to what he believes right, or has voluntarily and personally engaged to perform; but all persons shall be at liberty to exercise their own mode of worship; provided that nothing therein contained shall be construed to except preachers of treasonable or seditious doctrines from legal trial or punishment.

Sec. 35. That no person in the State shall hold more than one lucrative office at any one time; provided that no appointment in the militia of the office of a Justice of the Peace shall be considered as a lucrative office.

Sec. 36. That all commissions and grants shall run in the name of the State of Franklin and bear test and be signed by the governor; all writs shall run in the same manner that bear test and be signed by the clerks of the respective courts. Indictments shall conclude against the peace and dignity of the State.

Sec. 37. That the delegate for this State to the Constitutional Congress, while necessary, shall be chosen annually by the General Assembly, by ballot, but may be superseded in the meantime in the same manner; and no person shall be elected to serve in that capacity for more than three years successively.

Sec. 38. That there shall be a sheriff , coroner or coroners and constables in each County within the State.

Sec. 39. That the person of a debtor, where there is not a strong presumption of fraud, shall not be continued in prison after delivering up *bona fide* all his estate, real and personal, for the use of his creditors, in such manner as shall be hereafter regulated by law. All prisoners shall be bailable by sufficient sureties, unless for any capital offenses, when the proof is evident or presumption great.

Sec. 40. That any foreigner who comes to settle in this State, having first taken an oath of allegiance to the same, may purchase or by other means acquire, hold and transfer land or other real estate; and after one year's residence shall be deemed a free citizen.

Sec. 41. That a school or schools shall be established by the legislature for the convenient instruction of youth, with such salaries to the masters, paid by the public, as may enable them to instruct at low prices; and all useful learning shall be duly encouraged and promoted in one or more universities.

Sec. 42. That no purchase of lands shall be made of Indian natives, but on behalf of the public, by authority of the General Assembly.

Sec. 43. That the future Legislatures of this State shall regulate entails in such manner as to prevent perpetuities.

Sec. 44. That the Declaration of Rights is hereby declared to be a part of the Constitution of this State, and ought never to be violated on any pretense whatsoever.

Sec. 45. That any member of either house of the General Assembly shall have liberty to dissent from and protest against any act or resolves which he may think injurious to public, or any individual, and have the reasons of his dissent entered on the journals.

Sec. 46. That neither house of the General Assembly shall proceed upon public business unless a majority of all the members of such house are actually present; and that upon motion made and seconded, the yeas and nays upon any question shall be taken and entered on the journals and that the journals of the proceedings of both houses of the General Assembly shall be printed and made public immediately after adjournment.

This Constitution is not intended to preclude the present Convention from making a temporary provision for the well ordering of this State until the General Assembly shall establish government agreeable to the mode herein described.

Resolved, That this Convention recommend this Constitution for the serious consideration of the people during six ensuing months, after which time and before the expiration of the year, they shall choose a Convention for the express purpose of adopting it in the name of the people, if agreed to by them, or altering it as instructed by them. A true Copy, test:

THOMAS TALBOT, Clk.

PETITION OF THE INHABITANTS OF THE WESTERN COUNTRY

The Honourable, The General Assembly of North Carolina now sitting:

The Inhabitants of the Western Country humbly sheweth:

That it is with sincere concern we lament the unhappy disputes that have long subsisted between us and our Brethren on the Eastern side of the Mountains, respecting the erecting of a new Government. We beg leave to represent to your Honourable body, that from Acts passed in June 1784, ceding to Congress your Western territory, with reservations and conditions therein contained; also from a clause in your wise and mild Constitution, setting forth that there might be a State, or States, erected in the West whenever your Legislature should give consent for same; and from our local situation, there are numberless advantages, bountifully given to us by nature, to propagate and promote a Government with us. Being influenced by your Acts and Constitution, and at the same time considering that it is our undeniable right to obtain for ourselves and posterity a proportionable and adequate share of the blessings, rights, privileges, and immunities allotted with the rest of mankind, have thought that the erecting of a new Government would greatly contribute to our welfare and convenience, and that the same could not militate against your interest and future welfare as a Government. Hoping that mutual and reciprocal advantages would attend each party, and that cordiality and unanimity would permanently subsist between us ever after, we earnestly request that an impartial view of our remoteness be taken into consideration; that great inconveniency attending your seat of Government, and also the great difficulty in ruling well and giving protection to so remote a people, to say nothing of the almost impassable mountains Nature has placed between, which renders it impracticable for us to furnish ourselves with a bare load of the necessaries of life, except we in the first instance travel from one to two hundred and more miles through another State ere we can reach your Government.

Every tax paid you from this country would render us that sum the poorer, as it is impossible from the nature of our situation, that any part could return into circulation, having nothing that could bear the carriage, or encourage purchasers to come so great a distance; for which reasons were we to continue under your Government a few years, the people here must pay a greater sum than the whole of the medium now in circulation for the exigencies and support of your Government which would be a sum impossible for us to secure, would we be willing to give you our all; and of course we must be beholden to other States for any part we could raise; and by these means our property would gradually diminish, and we at last be reduced to mere poverty and want by not being able equally to participate with the benefits and advantages of your Government. We hope that having settled West of the Appalachian Mountains ought not to deprive us of the natural advantages designed by the bountiful Providence for the convenience and comfort of all those who have spirit and sagacity enough to seek after them. When we reflect on our past and indefatigable struggles, both with savages and our other enemies during our late war, and the great difficulty we had to obtain and with-hold this Country from those enemies at the expense of the lives and fortunes of many of our dearest friends and relations; and the happy conclusion of peace having arrived, North Carolina has derived great advantages from our alertness in taking and securing a County, from which she has been able to draw into her Treasury, immense sums of money, and thereby become enabled to pay off, if not wholly, yet a great part, and sink her national debt. We therefore humbly conceive you will liberally think that it will be nothing more than paying a debt in full to us for only to grant what God, Nature, and our locality entitles us to receive. Trusting that your magnanimity will not consider it a crime in any people to pray their rights and privileges, we call the world to testify our conduct and exertion in behalf of American Independence; and the same to judge whether we ask more than free people ought to claim, agreeable to Republican principles, the great foundation whereon our American fabric now stands. Impressed with the hope of your great goodness and benevolent disposition that you will utterly abhor and disclaim all ideas of involving into innumerable, disagreeable and irksome contentions, a people who have so faithfully aided and supported in the time of imminent and perilous dangers; that you will be graciously pleased to consent to a separation; that from your paternal tenderness and greatness of mind, you will let your stipulations and conditions be consistent with honour, equity and reason, all of which will be cheerfully submitted to; and we, your petitioners, shall always feel an interest in whatsoever may concern your honour and prosperity. Lastly, we hope to be enabled by the concurrence of your State to participate in the fruits of the Revolution; and to enjoy the essential benefits of Civil Society under a form of Government which ourselves alone can only calculate for such a purpose. It will be a subject of regret that so much blood and treasure have been lavished away for no purpose to us; that so many sufferings have been encountered without compensation, and that so many sacrifices have been made in vain. Many other considerations might be here adduced, but we hope what hath been mentioned will be sufficient for our purpose, adding only that Congress hath, from time to time, explained their ideas so fully and with so much dignity and energy that if their arguments and and requisitions will not produce conviction, we know of nothing that will have a greater influence, especially when we recollect that the system referred to is the result of the collected wisdom of the United States, and, should it not be considered as perfect, must be esteemed as the least objectionable.

John Corson	James Shanks	James Mitchell	Anthony Kelly
James English	David Robinson	David Gemel	Thos. McMackin
William Hannah	Robert Allison	Thomas Bell	George Davies
Peter McNamee	Isaac Davis	Thomas Rodgers	Nathaniel Davies

Samuel Davies
John Lowe
Joseph Wilson
David Brown
William Brown
Jas. Henry
Alexr. Potter
William Reynolds
David Reynolds
Aaron Been
William Wilson
This. Thomson
David Rankin
John Lee
Sam'l Vance
Rd. Kerr
Samuel McPherson
Matthew Rue
Joseph Lusk
Andrew Jackson
Jos. Gest
Jos. Newberry
Joseph Blair
Thomas Williams
Henry Styers
   his
Thomas x Tadlock
   mark
William McPick
Botholmu Odeneal
   his
Shadrack x Hale' Jr.
   mark
Daniel Denny, Jr.
John Wear
Ashael Rawlings
Henry Earnest
James Patterson
Francis Hughes
Robert Hood
   his
Wm. x Francis
   mark
   his
Patrick x Kirkpatrick
   mark
John Tadlock
James Davis
Benn Brumley
Mary Webster (?)
George Kirkpatrick
Thomas Jones
William Jones
Reuben Simmon
Archibel Alexander
Moses Kelsay
Robert McCall
Joseph Alexander
Wm. Cocke
Archibald Roan
Elias Witt

James Stinson
Alexander Street
James McPherson
John Prim
Jacob Smelser
Joshua Kidwell
Samuel Jameson
John Brumley
William Davidson
Wm. Boyd
Benja. Gist
Thos. Bromley
Hugh Beard
Samuel Beard
James Millikin
Robert Orr
Searling Bowman
Rich'd Woods
Robert McCall
John Galbreath
   (Illegible)
James Watson
   (Illegible)
William Goings
James Hays
David Carr
Joseph Garrison
William Gillehan
Stephen Strong
Michael Rawlings
Donnell Cremor
Nath. McMeno.
William La''' (?)
   (Illegible)
Nathaniel Witt
Rich'd Dunn
Wm. Dunn
Thomas Call
H. Call
Joseph N. Newport
Wm. W. Newport
John Greer
Absolem Greer
Thomas Springer
Levy Springer
Thomas Wolfe
Conrad Wilfe
Phillip Guibb
Henry Easter
William Eats
Simeon Craine
Harmon Nowel
James Patton
Robert Patton
John Fout
Peter Fout
Harmon Kennedy
Moses Long
Coonnas Miller
Thomas McKee
And. Wray

Phillip Rudolph
Wm. Stubblefield
Thomas Baits
John Keller
Moses Keller
William Fergosen
Wm. Morrow
Charles Ramsey
   (Illegible)
John R. ''' (?)
Peter Nowels
James Millikan
Thomas Millikan
Thomas Dicson
Redman McDaniel
Samul Gilbertson
Samul McMinn
Auborn ''' (?)
Anson Rit
Nuness Potter
John Noman (?)
Peter Nuless
James W. Begses (?)
Dalton Ridgs
James Jack
John Adkins
Adword Adword
Henry Brumley
Simon Ridgs
Joseph Donn
Allen Bellew
Rows Potter
John Norton
Aaron Norton
Aaron Rider
John Jameson
Dan'l Rawlings
William Jinkins
Robert Smith
Wm. Howard
Joshua Tadlock
Robert Hayes
Thomas Johnson
Francis Johnson
   his
Js. x Huston
   mark
   his
John x Huston
   mark
Lanry Armstrong
William Hennidge
John Armstrong
Andrew English
Nathaniel Hayes
Daniel Leming
John Williams
   his
Robert x Miller
   mark
   (Illegible)

   his
Thomas x Baley
   mark
Moses Moore
Adam Fergosen
Ralph Hogan
William Hogan
Richard Webb
Josiah Epperson
Humph'y Montgomery
Carmack George
Charles Willson
John Johnson
Wm. Magill
Oton Clark
John Gibson
Reuben Gibson
William Adkins
Thomas Fryar
John Lyon
William Brownin
Rich'd Wood
James Pickins
Robert Bettey
George Black
Reuben Riggs
George Hayes
William Hill
Henry Richardson
Shiffell Goodlop
John Shane
Miller Doget
Christy Miers
John Miers
William Owins
Thomas Owins
John Jarrett
Thomas Pickny
James Stump
Leonard Hopkins
Martha Gahee
Patrick Gahee
Jeremiah Smith
Robert Sample
Anthony Moore
James McCammis
Thomas McCammis
William McCammis
Adam McCammis
Henry H. Hammer
Frenses Castel
Jacob Meek
Thomas Miller
Robert Pain
Joseph Hamilton
Robert Kerr
John Sellars
Benj. Wray
Wm. Moore
Joseph Ray
Joseph Lachlen, Sen.

Thomas Witt	Wm. Wood	his	Joseph Lachlen, Jur.
Alex. Lowry	Gordon Potter	William x Hust.	Edward Crunt (?)
Jno. McClelland	Wm. Peck	mark	James Crunt
Solomon Reed	Thomas Mosely		
Uriah McClellennon	Henry Mosely		

The following names are taken from the back of the petition:

Nicholas Hayes	James Richardson	James Wheeler	James Arbutton (?)
Sam'l Hayes	David Taylor	John Cottrell	Martin Roller, Jr.
Jno. Mitchell	Benja. Gist	Hugh Gentry	Joseph Blair
James Hammer	Joseph Huson	Valentine Rose	David Arwin
Henry Hokimer	Mikill Borders	Eli Shipley	William '" (?)
Geo. Martin	Alx. Pethrow	Thomas Shipley	Thos. Taylor
David Moore	Oystan Hewtower	William Childress	Adam Stoaks
Henry Winterberger	Wm. Davies	Joshway Hampton	Joseph Waldrep
Jos. Winterberger	John Noris	Christurphur Cross	Mattw. Caruthers
Sam'l Winterberger	Robert Hayes	Benjamin Aze	Gilbert Christian
Joseph Lusk	James Hayes	Reuben Hunt	John Pryor
Thos. Wood	William Sippard	Ellecander Moore	Moses Looney
Joseph Gest	Alexander Cavitt	Martin Roller	Macajah Adams
William Gest	Moses Cavitt	John A. Caft	James McLern
Joshua Kidwell	Jacob Jobe	D. Wright	Alexander Caright
Thomas Davie	Nathan Jobe	Adam Stake	Benj. Burdwell
John Kidwell	Joseph Birdwell	William Shewmaker	John Dean
Charles Kidwell	Geo. Birdwell	Gabriel Goad	William Holland
Whaley Newby	James Smith	Peter Easley	William Morroson
Craven Dunear	Moses Russel	Jacob Cox	John Morroson
Alexr. Lowrey	Conrad Shepley	William Bucknell	James Morroson
James Stitson	John Comin	Haley Bucknell	Samuel Bofman
Adam Guthrey	Walker Barren	Preley Bucknell	David Merryon
Wm. Craige	John Bell	Shadrick Haile	Richard Morell
Benjamen Henslee	William Carson	Forrester Mercer	Dudley Rutherford
Abel Morgan	Robert Christian	Bryce Russell, Sen.	John Bradford
Thomas Vincent	Abraham Tittsworth	Bryce Russell, Jr.	Peter Fin
Jno. Chester	Benjamin Walb'" (?)	James Pickens	John Hunt
Patrick Morrison	Green Chote	Phil. Grafford Pierce	William Bailey
Stephen Easley	John Goad, Jun.	William Gewil	George Smith
Jackal Light	George Vincent	Charles Parker	Jacob Joab
Robert Easley	Henry Heckey	Antony Agee	William Cooper
Henry Sullivan	Owen Atkin	John Sawyer	Wm. Jackson
John Light	Nicholas Mercer	Joseph Moore	Ephraim Joab
Moses Robinson	Richard Mercer, Sen.	Joseph Yancy	William Mehallm
William Light	Arch'd McHaughan	Richard Shipley	Charles Bacon
William Light, Sen.	Edward Mercer	W. Cage	John French
Thomas Easley	John Black	Timothy Huff	John Bilensy
William Goad	John Hunt, Jr.	George Christian	William Combs
Jesey Holland	Basset Hunt	Deness Murfee	William Combs, Jr.
James Walb'" (?)	Reuben Hunt	Isaac Thomas	Henry Combs
William Wilson	Thomas Tipton	William Massengill	William Stacey
Moses Kennedy	Jonathan Hunt	John Tulley	Adam Coumb
Hermon King	James Cooper	Thos. Easterlin	Daniel Agee
Joseph Screat	Isaiah Waldrew	William Copeland	John Comay
Lewis Tadlock	Lewis Hunt	Rich'd Gamon	James Peterson
Thomas Tadlock	James Smart	John Spurgin	Jeremiah Taylor
Joshuaway Padfield	James Smith	Thos. King	Joseph Taylor
his	Joseph Smith	Roger Gibson	Stephen Taylor
Thomas x Bennet	John Duncan	James Adam	Isaac Taylor
mark	Wm. Berry	Geo. Gabriel (black)	John Chisholm
Moses Kelsay	Isaac White	John Yokley	Edward Tule
John Anderson	Samuel Cox	John Woolsey	Nathaniel Tule

Endorsement:
Petition of the Inhabitants of the Western Country, December, 1787.
In Senate, December, 1787. Read and referred to Court on Public Bills. (N.C.St.Rec., XXII,705-714).

EARLY CHURCHES

The Overmountain frontiersmen, along the Holston, Watauga and Nolichucky valleys had little time for religion during those early years. Those hardy pioneers were busy with taming the wilderness and combating Indian assaults. Much of the 'preachin' was done by settlers who felt the call to exhort their brethren. They worked their land claims during the week and would often ride many miles to preach on Sunday.

The Presbyterians were among the first to brave the wilds. Charles Cummings started a church in Abingdon, Virginia as early as 1772. Joseph Rhea, who settled near Blountville, Tennessee, is said to have been the first Presbyterian to preach in the environs of Tennessee. Samuel Doak started preaching and teaching at Salem, (Washington College Academy) 1780. Samuel Houston, Samuel Carrick, James and Hezekiah Balch, Samuel Henderson and Gideon Blackburn arrived in the early 1780's. By 1790 there were reported to be 23 or 24 Presbyterian Churches in Tennessee country.

OLD IRELAND: Home of the Rhea's in Blountville, Tenn. Was built in 1800 by Joseph Rhea Junior, son of Joseph Rhea said to be the first Presbyterian Preacher to visit country now Tennessee 1775.

The Baptists also arrived during the 1770's. A preaching revival was held in the home of Charles Robertson on Sinking Creek (Johnson City, Tenn.) during the winter of 1775. Two brothers, John and Charles Chastain, did the preaching. Mathew Talbot continued these services in an infrequent manner, for 7 or 8 years. A church, listed in Baptist records, was called "Watauga River Church". It is said that this church became Sinking Creek Baptist Church.

SINKING CREEK BAPTIST CHURCH restored by Watauga Baptist Association (one of oldest churches in state).

Tidence Lane, pastor of Buffalo Ridge Baptist Church 1778, was also the moderator of the Holston Baptist Association, organized at Cherokee Meeting House, near Jonesborough, Tennessee, October 30, 1786. Churches listed in the Association were: Kendricks Springs (Double Springs); Bent Creek, (Whitesburg) Beaver Creek, Greasy Cove, (Erwin, Tenn.); North Fork of Holston, (Kingsport); Lower French Broad, (Dandridge). There were reported 10 Baptist churches in 1788.

A Methodist circuit was organized in 1783. This included part of southwest Virginia as well as the area of present east Tennessee. Jeremiah Lambert was the first circuit rider, then came Henry Wills, Richard Swift and Michael Gilbert.

Thomas Ware was sent into Franklin 1787. Other Methodist preachers of the time were John Tunnel, Jeremiah Martin, Nathaniel Moore and Micajah Tracey.

The Holston Conference of the United Methodist Church is sponsoring restoration and maintenance of the Edward Cox home.

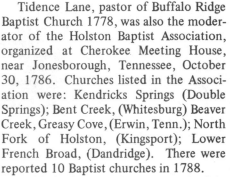

RICHARD CASWELL

Richard Caswell was elected to 7 different terms as North Carolina Governor. The first temporary term was from December 17, 1776 to April 18, 1777. The second term was for one year April 18, 1777 to April 18, 1778. Third term April 18, 1778 to May 4, 1779. Fourth term May 4, 1779 to April 1780. Fifth term April 1, 1785 to December 12, 1785. Sixth term December 12, 1785 to December 23, 1786. Seventh term December 23, 1786 to December 20, 1787.

Richard Caswell was active in the politics of his state and participated in the organization of the first Provincial Congress. He was never acclaimed a military genius even though he was an officer and participated in many Revolutionary War battles. Caswell was involved in many land speculation ventures in North Carolina and the Tennessee territory. Many historical places have borne his name. Fort Caswell, better known as Fort Watauga; Caswell County of the State of Franklin, now Jefferson County. Many sites in North Carolina bear his name. He died practically broke at the age of 60 while serving as President of the North Carolina Senate, convening in Fayetteville, November 10, 1789. This was the session that John Sevier attended after the demise of Franklin. Following is an account of the funeral.

Newspaper Reports of Caswell's Death   Newspaper Reports of Caswell's Death
The State Gazette of North Carolina, Thursday, Dec. 3, 1789, p. 4:

Extract from the Journal of the Senate for Friday, November 6, [1789]. "Mr. Bloodworth informed that the Honorable Richard Caswell, Esquire, had departed this life: This House having received information of the decease of the Honorable Richaed Caswell, Esquire, their late Speaker, propose that a joint committee be appointed to direct and conduct the mode and order of his interment, and have appointed on our part, for this purpose, Mr. Blount, Mr. Skinner, and Mr. Bloodworth."

Received from the House of Commons the following message: "Mr. Speaker and Gentlemen: This House have received the message of your's containing the information of the much to be lamented death of your late Speaker and concurred with your proposition for a committee to direct the mode of his interment and have appointed Mr. Davie, Mr. Stokes, Mr. Thomas Blount, Mr. Lock, Mr. Hawkins, and Mr. Person, a committee on our part for this purpose."

Wednesday, November 11 [1789]: Mr. Blount, from the committee appointed to conduct and direct the mode and order of burial of the corpse of the Honorable Richard Caswell, Esq., late Speaker of this House, delivered the following which was agreed to; vis.
"The clergymen and Doctors precede the corpse
The CORPSE
The relations of the deceased as chief mourners
The members of the Senate, two and two
The members of the House of Commons, two and two
The Governor and the Secretary of State
Treasurer and Comptroller
Clerks of the General Assembly
Other persons attending, two and two
That the General Assembly go into mourning one month."

The deceased being the most worshipful Grandmaster of the Grand Lodge of the Most Ancient and Honorable Fraternity of the Free and Accepted Masons, the Officers and Members of the Grand Lodge, and the Officers and Brethren of the different Lodges present, attended the procession in their Masonic dress and orders. The pall was supported by six members of the Grand Lodge, who were also members of the General Assembly, and all the usual ceremonies and forms were duly observed.

The order of procession was strictly attended to, and closed by a very respectable and numerous body of citizens.

This gentleman was a member of the first Congress in the year 1775 — was the first Governor under the present Constitution, and at all times since, when the Constitution would permit. He came early to the Legislature, and was 35 years in succession a member, except when he was in the more Honorable station of Governor and ever walked among the first patriots and the best of men.

SOUTHWEST TERRITORY

HOLSTON RIVER enters the historical picture early in the white man's westward expansion. Settlers were staking claims along the headwaters of the Holston River before the French-Indian War. Some grants were dated 1753. One such grant became the Shelby Home, "Sapling Grove", Bristol, Tenn.-Va. Holston River furnished transportation for the Indians; armies to attack the Indians; Donelson's flotilla; commercial ventures. Kingsport was named for King's Port on the Holston.

The Isaac Hammer House was built in 1793 on the Old Stage Road. Isaac Hammer was a pioneer preacher of the Church of the Brethren. The renovated log building is now owned and occupied by Mr. and Mrs. Sam Humphreys. The house is a two story structure with a basement.

SOUTHWEST TERRITORY

"Time out of mind, these lands have been the hunting grounds of the Cherokees," spoke Attakullakulla at the Sycamore Shoals Treaty of 1775. 61 years later, Speckled Snake, Creek Chief, spoke of the Indian's past and predicted the white man's continuing drive to the West. His words at the Creek National Council in 1836 were recorded by Blake:

Brothers, we have heard the talk of our Great White Father; it is very kind. He says he loves his red children. Brothers, when the white man first came to these shores, the Indians gave him land, and kindled fire to make him comfortable. When the Pale Faces of the South (Spaniards) would have taken his scalp, our young men drew the tomahawk and protected him.

SMOKE SIGNALS

But when the white man had warmed himself at the Indian's fire, and had filled himself with the Indian's hominy, he became very large. He stopped not at the mountain tops, and his foot covered the plains and valleys. His hands grasped the eastern and western seas. Then he became our Great Father. He loved his red children, but said, 'you must move a little farther, lest by accident I tread upon you.'

With one foot he pushed the red men across the Oconee, and with the other he trampled down the graves of our fathers. But our Great Father still loved his red children, and soon made them another talk. He said much, but it all meant, 'Move a little farther; you are too near me.'

Brothers, I have heard many talks from our Great Father, and they all began and ended the same. When he made us a talk on a former occasion he said, 'Get a little farther; go beyond the Oconee and the Ocmulgee, -- there is a pleasant country.' He also said, 'It shall be yours forever.'

Now he says, 'The land you live upon is not yours. Go beyond the Mississippi: there is game; there you may remain while the grass grows and the rivers run.'

Brothers, Will not our Great Father come there also? He loves his red children, and his tongue is not forked.

This greedy push of the white man onto Indian lands increased the red man's resentment and brought much death and suffering to the frontiers of the young republic. During the six years following the Revolutionary War, each state handled its own Indian problems, sometimes very badly. The Hopewell Treaty of 1785 was an attempt to bring peace to the southern frontier, but at best it was a bungled affair. The Spanish, still hoping to control the Mississippi Valley, used these years to good advantage.

North Carolina, tired of the constant demands of the Overmountain People decided to let Congress have the Territory. Most of the good land having already been taken up, they had nothing to lose but the responsibility. The Northwest Tribes, encouraged and supplied by British-Canadian leaders, were forming a federation with plans to fight the Americans. President Washington, tired of war, wanted to bring peace to the Country. He was making efforts to satisfy the complaints and grievances of the Tribes, North and South, and at the same time to restrain the frontiersmen from an all out war against the red man.

The North Carolina Legislature finally voted to ratify the United States Constitution, November 21, 1789. Neither North Carolina nor Rhode Island was eligible to vote when General George Washington was elected President. It was during this same 1789 Assembly session that North Carolina passed the second cession act, ceding the territory now Tennessee to the Federal Government. The deed giving Congress control over the Territory was signed and executed February 15, 1790, by Samuel Johnson and Benjamin Hawkins. The document was worded with provisions similar to the one passed in 1784.

Congress voted acceptance and the act was signed into effect by President Washington on May 16, 1790. The official title, "The Territory of the United States south of the River Ohio," is misleading and confusing. Virginia claimed the Kentucky country, admitted as a State June, 1792. Georgia claimed the land that is now Alabama and Mississippi, and did not cede this territory until 1802. This left the area approximately within the present boundaries of Tennessee as the Southwest Territory.

Joseph Martin and William Blount sought the post of Territorial Governor. Martin had the backing of Patrick Henry and other influential men. William Blount had more political acumen and was nominated for the post of Territorial Governor and received his official commission from President Washington August 7, 1790.

PRESIDENT GEORGE WASHINGTON

Many of the Representatives from the western country had been associated with Blount in the North Carolina Legislature and their recommendations possibly carried weight. Blount's experience in the political, educational and financial world qualified him for the position.

GOVERNOR WILLIAM BLOUNT

General plan being followed in Territorial Administration called for three stages of government: First, it was to be administered by a governor, territorial secretary, judges, district militia and local county officials. Second stage would be put in motion when a census showed 5000 land-owning, free males of voting age living in the territory. At this stage they could elect their own assembly to administer state affairs. Third phase, statehood. When a Territory showed 60,000 free citizens living within its boundaries, the citizens could request Congress for the status of a State.

When Blount was appointed Governor, Congress asked that he assist Thomas Jefferson in making a survey of the Territory to determine the amount and location of available land for Federal use. On investigation, it was discovered that there was so little unclaimed land that a Federal Land Office was never opened in the Territory.

Governor Blount arrived in the Overmountain Country October 10, 1790. He made his official residence and headquarters at the William Cobb home, Rocky Mount. The Governor immediately began his duties. In Washington District he nominated Colonel John Sevier as Brigadier-General. He presented the name of Colonel James Robertson for the same position in Mero District. Judges nominated were David Campbell, John McNairy and Joseph Anderson. Daniel Smith was selected as Territorial Secretary. These nominations were later confirmed by President Washington. All other county officials were appointed by the Governor.

ROCKY MOUNT, Original U. S. Territorial Capital Building of The Territory of the United States of America South of the River Ohio. Home of William Cobb; stage coach stop; United States Post Office; Museum of Pioneer History.

William Blount and his brothers had acquired over a million acres of land in the Territory, now Tennessee. He is supposed to have remarked to a friend, *"My western lands had become so great an object to me that it had become absolutely necessary that I should go to the western country to secure them."*

The Indians were vigorously protesting the land grabbing tactics of the white people. Treaty lines were ignored as landhungry immigrants erected new cabins on Cherokee land. The Indians resented these imposters and the two-faced talk of the officials. Unable to get satisfaction, they followed their own code rather than the white man's law. They retaliated by raiding, stealing, killing and scalping.

Governor Blount's position automatically carried the Office of the Superintendent of Indian Affairs. This two-sided duty made his task difficult. He made attempts to satisfy the disgruntled settlers who would not, or could not, understand the Indian's viewpoint or philosophy. On the other hand, he was pressured by the Federal Government to satisfy the complaints and grievances of the resentful Indians.

In 1790, one of the most colorful figures of the southern tribes traveled to New York to see President George Washington. Alexander McGilivray, the outstanding Creek Chief, was a strong and powerful leader of this southern tribe occupying the territory now Alabama and part of Georgia. He was well educated, could speak seven languages and carry on correspondence with the leaders of many nations. He was a mason and a partner in a profitable business. He refused to talk with the commisioners sent by Congress. He was persuaded to make the trip to New York and talk with the head of the American people. He and his retinue of Chiefs made the trip on horseback. They were greeted enroute by large enthusiastic crowds. President Washington received the Creek Delegation with the ceremonial welcome extended kings. Chief McGilivray made a treaty with Washington and promised to use his influence in keeping the Creek Nation out of the open conflict. The Chief was playing both sides of the fence hoping to be on the winning side. He accepted a salary from the United States, while at the same time he was in the pay of the Spaniards. President Washington sent the Chief and his party home on a United States Warship.

As the settlements continued to spread along the frontier, crude forts and stations were built as havens of safety from the frequent Indian attacks. During much of the early territorial period, these fortifications were crowded. Small bands of warriors constantly prowled the countryside. Any isolated cabin, party or individual was soon made aware of the ever present menace. Most of the massacres were commited by the Chickamaugas and dissident Creeks. The Spanish Officials furnished free guns and ammunition to these war parties and encouraged them to harass the whites.

The Cherokees in the Upper Towns, under Chief Hanging Maw, were living more peacefully with the frontiersmen. A few of the younger braves had followed Dragging Canoe, but mainly the Overhill towns observed treaty agreements. This would work a hardship on them as resentments increased.

Hector, Baron de Carondelet, appointed to replace the deceased Miro as Governor of the Spanish Province, was far more vigorous in his fight against the western settlers than Miro had been. He outbid the frontiersmen in efforts to lure the southern Indians into the Spanish influence. With supply depots located at Baton Rouge, Pensacola, Mobile and St. Augustine, his deputies were able to furnish the constant needs of the red men. These Spanish Deputies encouraged the Chiefs in their holy war to regain their lands. The Indians didn't like the Spaniards but wanting supplies they went to the source that could supply them.

Many of the Indians enjoyed the use of slaves. Some employed captured Negro slaves and white captives in this role. They were following the white man's precedent in this practice. Many settlers brought their Negro slaves to the new country to build cabins, clear lands and till the soil. The Territory Census taken 1791 showed a population count of 35,691. Of this group, 3,417 were Negro slaves. In many sections, slave owners had to organize patrols to ride the roads at night on the watch-out for escaping slaves. Any black men out after dark needed a pass from his master showing cause. These patrol groups were soon called the "Pattyrollers," giving rise to the song, "You'd better watch out or the Pattyrollers will get you."

The long, exposed border was an open invitation to the Indians who were quick to take advantage of this weakness. North Carolina's refusal to acknowledge the "Dumplin Creek Treaty," made by the Franklin Government, placed many cabins below the Hopewell Treaty line. Knox insisted that these settlers move back within the agreed boundary. They refused. Situations of this nature made Blount's duties tricky. The Indians had a legitimate cause for complaint. Both the whites and red men felt that they were being double-crossed. All of this had added fuel to the fires on both sides; Secretary Knox directed Blount to arrange a treaty and work out the differences.

Another matter that inflamed the Indians was the revival of a plan to settle Muscle Shoals. Many attempts had been made to take over this Big Bend property. The State of Georgia, by legislative act, had transferred more than 300,000 acres to a group called the Tennessee Company. This Big Bend territory had been guaranteed to the Indians permanently in every treaty, but the whites wanted that land. Zachariah Cox and Thomas Carr, agents for the Tennessee Company, were offering 500 acres free to each family if they would help settle the Muscle Shoals country. A large armed force was promised.

When informed of this scheme, President Washington and Secretary Knox issued a proclamation forbidding the settlement. Colonel Hubbardt, Peter Bryant and some 30 others decided they would go with Cox and chance the undertaking, despite the governmental edict.

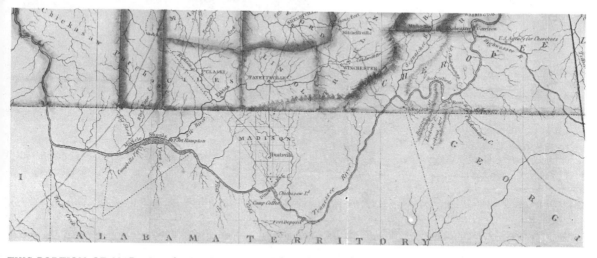

THIS PORTION OF MAP taken from one constructed from John Strothers map and other documents by John Melish, published in 1818.

The party of 30 men, with their supplies and tools, embarked from Mouth of Dumplin Creek in three boats, January, 1791. All caution was observed as they moved downstream. The Indians, who had learned of the venture, posted watch-outs all along the route. Word of the boats progress was relayed from point to point. At one place, several canoes loaded with warriors paddled out to make talk with the white party. The show of rifles discouraged a close approach so the canoes returned to shore. At night campfires dotted the north shoreline and braves could be seen watching from the banks. The three boats stayed close to the south bank of the stream throughout the nights and moved out to midstream each morning at daybreak. For three days and nights the Muscle Shoals-bound party never left their boats. Although there was much tension, caused by the expectation of an attack, the three boat loads of adventurers reached their destination without an actual skirmish.

On arrival, the men erected a blockhouse with some palisades. Other structures were started, but never completed. Chief Glass, with 60 warriors, appeared one day and told them to leave or face death. The party, still uneasy and afraid because of the experience coming downriver, were not long in packing their belongings and departing. They were barely out of sight when the blockhouse and other physical structures were destroyed by fire.

When the result of the 1791 Census was reported, it showed that the Territory was eligible to elect its own Assembly. Governor Blount delayed in arranging the organizational machinery for an election. Besides enjoying the prominent role and power that the Governor's position gave him, he feared that taxes on his vast holdings would be increased. He also, most likely, was trying to evaluate his future role in the political developments of the Territory.

Secretary Knox sent urgent instructions to Blount to solve the conflicts between the Indians and the white settlers. The Governor sent James Robertson and Joseph Martin to talk with the various Chiefs and arrange such a Treaty-Meet. White's Station was selected as the site as it was a convenient location and Blount planned to move the Territorial Headquarters here as soon as feasible.

July 2, 1791, some 40 Chiefs and 1200 Indians arrived for the Treaty. The occasion is said to have been an elaborate affair. A marquee, or tent was set up near the Holston River, as Headquarters. Governor Blount, in full military dress, was seated just outside the tent. Each Chief was presented individually by name to the Governor. Trooper James Armstrong served as Master of Ceremonies. No soldiers were present by design, but a large number of settlers and visitors attended.

HOLSTON TREATY

Governor Blount had been instructed to give the Indians presents and a guarantee of $1,000 a year for land to be included in the treaty. The Cherokees had looked forward to this occasion, thinking that at last Congress was going to treat them as people and restore their rights. Instead of this, the whites asked for more land.

From Brown's "Old Frontiers," we quote:

John Watts spoke, 'I know that the North Carolina people are headstrong. Under the sanction of a flag of truce, they laid low my Uncle, Old Tassel. It is vain for us to contend about a line. The North Carolina people will have their way, and will not observe the orders of Congress or anyone else. I wonder that you, Governor Blount, should be appointed to settle such a matter, being a North Carolinian. When you North Carolinians make a line, you tell us it is a standing one, but you are always en-croaching on it and we cannot depend upon what you say. We will, notwithstanding, make you an offer of a line.'

Blount replied, 'The lands were taken from the Cherokees in time of war, and I do not consider the settle-ments to be encroachments.'

WHITE-KENNEDY HOUSE: Log block house said to have been built by James White, founder of Knoxville. Purchased by James Kennedy Jr. who built several rooms and porches around log structure. House destroyed soon after Civil War.

The Treaty-Meet lasted seven days with little progress. Some of the Chiefs wanted to talk with the President, in person, before signing. Blount was able to out talk the Indians and they reluctantly signed the document. The Cherokees left the Holston Treaty in a bitter mood.

Determined to present their complaints to the President, they sent a delegation composed of Bloody Fellow, Kingfisher, The Northward, Kitigiski the Prince, and Testeekee to Philadelphia. George Miller and James Carey went along as interpreters. The visit was a surprise to Knox, who arranged a meeting with President Washington. About the only result of this conference was to raise the annual payment to $1500 per year.

Another event of outstanding importance during 1791 was the publication of Tennessee's first newspaper, November 5th. George Roulstone set up his press at Rogersville, Hawkins County. The paper was called the "Knoxville Gazette." Hawkins County at this time included the present Counties of Jefferson, Grainger and Knox. Roulstone moved the paper to Knoxville the next year and located his press in a log cabin on the street now called Gay. Factual news of the day was printed; the Editor did not attempt to editorialize. Much important data has been preserved from his columns.

COPY FOR TENNESSEE'S FIRST NEWSPAPER was prepared on this table by George Roulstone and Robert Ferguson, Nov. 5, 1791 at Rogersville. The Cartwright kettle arrived in Nashborough on board The Adventure. Items on display at the Tennessee State Museum.

New settlers were arriving almost daily in the White's Station vicinity. James White, anticipating future prospects when the Territorial Capital would be moved there, began laying off lots for a town. Some 64 were sold during 1791, but little in the way of building was started before 1792. Blount and his leaders decided that the new County and Town to be erected would be named after Secretary of War General Henry Knox. Thus the County and its seat of government bear the name of Knox.

Knox and Jefferson Counties were, by ordinance cut off Hawkins County in June, 1792. Courts of Pleas and Quarter Sessions were set to convene in the new Counties. The first Court of Jefferson County named after Thomas Jefferson, met at the house of Jeremiah Mathews. Knox County Court met at White's Station, now Knoxville. The two new Counties were designated as the Judicial District of Hamilton. This honored Alexander Hamilton, another member of President Washington's Cabinet.

Records of the first Sessions of both County Courts are quoted as taken from Ramsey's Annals:

KNOX COUNTY COURT

1792, June 16 - James White, John Sawyers, Hugh Beard, John Adair, George McNutt, Jeremiah Jack, John Kearns, James Cozby, John Evans, Samuel Newell, William Wallace, Thomas McCulloch, William Hamilton, David Craig and William Lowry, presented a Commission from Governor Blount, appointing them Justices of the Peace for Knox County and, appeared before the Honourable David Campbell, Esq., who, in the presence of Governor Blount, administered to each of them an oath to support the Constitution of the United States, and also an oath of office.

Charles McClung also produced a Commission from the Governor, appointing him Clerk of Knox County, and he was in like manner qualified.

Thomas Chapman, also, as Register.

June 25 - Robert Houston, in like manner, was commissioned and qualified as Sheriff.

It was ordered by the Court, that the Sheriff make proclamation for the opening of a County Court, at the house of John Stone, in the town of Knoxville, and that Charles McClung be admitted Clerk to record the same.

Whereupon, the said Robert Houston, having solemnly proclaimed for that purpose, it is ordered, that the said Court be considered open for the purpose of dispatching public business, and be ordered of record accordingly.

The first Court held, was on the 16th of July 1792. Present - James White, Samuel Newell, David Craig and Jeremiah Jack. James White was appointed chairman.

June 16 - Luke Bowyer, Alexander Outlaw, Joseph Hamilton, Archibald Roane, Hopkins Lacy, John Rhea and Jame Reese, Esquires, were qualified and admitted to practice law in this Court.

William Henry obtained leave to build a mill on Rosebury's Creek.

Ordered, that Alexander Cunningham have leave to keep a public ferry at his landing opposite Knoxville.

Roads were also ordered to be laid out, from Knoxville to Col. Alexander Kelley's Mill; and to David Craig's, on Nine Mile Creek.

June 17 - John Rhea was commissioned by the Governor, Solicitor for Knox county.

A public road was ordered to be laid off from Knoxville to the Ford on Clinch, and from Knoxville to Campbell's Station.

Oct. 23 - A public road was ordered to be laid out from Knoxville to the mouth of French Broad.

The Sheriff appeared and protested against the Jail of Knox County.

1793, January 26 - Commissioners were appointed to contract for the building of a jail. Its dimensions were, sixteen feet square; the logs to be one foot square, the lower floor to be laid of logs of that size, to be laid double and crosswise; the loft to be laid also with logs, and covered crosswise with oak plank, one and a half inchest thick, and well spiked down.

The same Commissioners were also authorized to contract for building a Court House.

1793, May 6 - John Sevier produced a license from Governor Blount to practice law, and was admitted.

JEFFERSON COUNTY

July 22 - JEFFERSON COUNTY COURT first held. - It met at the house of Jeremiah Mathews, (now Reuben Zirkles, four and a half miles west of Dandridge, near the river). The magistrates had been commissioned and qualified.

June 11 - The following gentlemen appeared and took their seats viz: Alexander Outlaw, George Doherty, James Roddye, John Blackburn, James Lea, Josiah Wilson, Josiah Jackson, Andrew Henderson, Ams Balch and Wm. Cox.

Joseph Hamilton was commissioned Clerk.

Robert McFarland, Sheriff, James Roddye, Register.

Luke Bowyer, Wm. Cocke, John Rhea, Alexander Outlaw, James Reese, Archibald Roane and Hopkins Lacy, were admitted as Attornies.

ALEXANDER HAMILTON served on General Washington's staff as Lieut-Col.; was appointed Secretary of Treasury; worked to establish U. S. Credit.

HENRY KNOX, Secretary of War under Washington, Knox County and Knoxville, Tennessee were named in his honor.

Blount Mansion in Knoxville, Tennessee was the first frame house built west of the Appalachian Mountains. It served as residence and official headquarters for Governor William Blount when he moved from Rocky Mount to White's Fort.

THOMAS EMBREE HOUSE; Thomas was Quaker father of Elihu Embree, publisher of first Abolitionist Paper in Tennessee, and Elijah Embree early ironmaster, House near Telford built 1791.

Governor William Blount moved his official residence and headquarters to Knoxville, January, 1792. His family did not join him until sometime in March. Blount's home was completed later in the same year. The restored building is known today as "Blount Mansion." It is said to be the first frame house west of the mountains.

Not much has been said concerning the growth and economic development in the older settlements of the Holston, Watauga and Nolichucky. Although they suffered occasional raids by small bands of Indians, they were largely removed from the almost daily killing occurring on the western frontier. The citizens of this area were busy getting their homesteads to produce. Larger and more permanent buildings were being erected, some of which are still in good repair.

Seth Smith, a stonemason who had moved into the Washington District, was employed to build a stone house for Elihu Embree during 1791. The house is located near Telford, Tennessee. Smith also built another stone building for George Gillespie at Limestone. This building was erected in 1792 on the site where Fort Lee stood in 1776. The Fort was never completed as the Indians destroyed it during their July attack on the settlements. Washington District included the Counties of Sullivan, Hawkins, Washington and Greene. Space does not allow much of the political and economic activities of individual counties during the territory period to be recorded in this volume.

GILLESPIE STONE HOUSE: Built 1792 at present Limestone, Tenn. Purchased by Jacob Klepper 1842. The H. M. Kleppers own and live in house at this writing.

MARBLE SPRINGS: Renovated John Sevier home near Knoxville. Known as "Governor's Old Place." Originally a frontier station used by emigrants.

TOMAHAWKS — MUSKET—BALLS — BAYONETS

Indian Treaties of 1790 and 1791 did not bring the expected peace on the frontiers. The lower Cherokees and dissident Creeks continued their raids. One such recorded attack was on a cabin some ten miles from the site of the Town of Maryville. Several families, warned of Indian bands in the vicinity, gathered in this cabin for protection. Portholes had been cut in the cabin logs and the door could be barricaded. The seven men able to handle guns planned their strategy well. The Indian force of some 200 approached the log house expecting little resistance. When in good gun range, the seven guns fired a broadside into their unsuspecting ranks, then, quickly reloading, they sent another effective charge at the redskins before they could recover from their surprise. The startled warriors quickly gathered their dead and wounded and departed. They evidently thought the cabin filled with frontier riflemen and not worth the risk.

Indian unrest and assaults on the pioneer settlements of the Northwest Territory were increasing. These Tribes, encouraged and supplied by British-Canadian fur traders, formed a confederacy. The British, with the help of the Indians, hoped gradually to gain control over the Mississippi Valley.

In the fall of 1790, President Washington had sent General Josiah Harmar and 1500 militia to destroy the Indian Towns along the Maumee. This task accomplished, General Harmar was returning to his base camp when a large force of warriors ambushed him at Chilicothe. Harmar suffered a humiliating defeat. Several Overmountain men were with General Harmar on this campaign.

Colonel Hardin was later lured into a similar ambush at Maumee Ford. He suffered an even worse defeat. Historic descriptions relate that you could walk across the river dryshod on the bodies of his men killed in this action.

Governor Arthur St. Clair, Governor of the Northwest Territory, appealed to President Washington for help. Washington, realizing that the uprising must be put down, sent out a call for volunteers. 300 men were requested from Washington District, (east Tennessee) and it is assumed that a like call was sent to Mero, (middle Tennessee). The response was slow. The Southwest people did not take too kindly to this call. They remembered the many times they had sent requests for help and how their cries were ignored.

Governor Blount turned this task over to General John Sevier. Sevier was attending session of Congress at the time. He started home but was taken sick in Richmond, Va. He sent instructions for the muster and

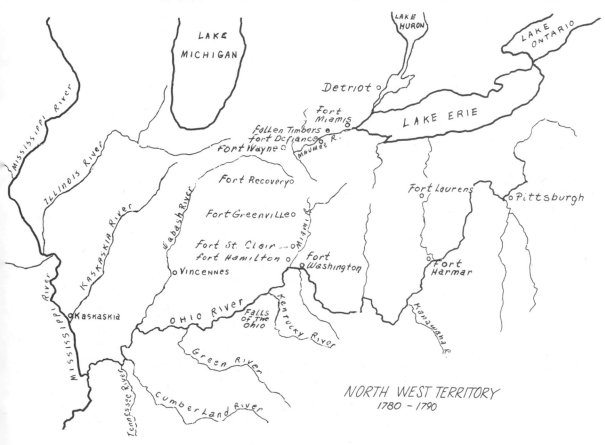

NORTH WEST TERRITORY
1780 ~ 1790

200 men from Washington District were enlisted. They mustered at Jonesboro during June or July, 1791. Major Mathew Rhea was placed in command. One company was under Captain Jacob Tipton.

The Mero District, as far as is known, did not send any whites. Chief Piomingo was persuaded to take some 50 of his Chickasaw warriors to serve as scouts. This band of braves was outfitted at the home of General James Robertson, near Nashville, Tennessee. Piomingo, disgusted with St. Clair's careless, unorganized campaign, left November 3, for home. Whole companies deserted. St. Clair sent other companies after them in an effort to force these groups to return. This merely weakened his already inadequate force.

The Northwest Tribes had laid aside their differences and united under Chief Little Turtle. This shrewd

CHIEF LITTLE TURTLE

Miami Chief knew every move and plan of the St. Clair camp. He had watched Piomingo and his braves depart homeward. His spies reported the deserting groups and he knew the laxity of outposts. The attack of Little Turtle was well organized and he had a large force to back up his plan. The Indians charged early morning, November 4, 1791, as the Americans were breaking camp. The young, raw militia were completely routed. Some fled in confusion and fright, casting aside their guns as they ran. Some of the more disciplined companies were able to break through the Indian lines and escape toward Fort Washington. It is estimated that about 500 reached safety.

The Indians killed and scalped over 600. The defeat was as bad as, or worse than, that suffered by Braddock in 1755. President Washington had warned Governor St. Clair against the possibility of such a catastrophe. The elderly General, of the old school and sick at the time, paid little heed to the advice. The only reasons that the 500 escaped were the Indians' lack of discipline in crucial moments of battle and their intense love of horses and plunder, which took their attention away from pursuit. They were too occupied with grabbing guns, axes, clothing, tents, blankets, scalps and horses to chase the fleeing men. The debacle was to sound a note of triumph through all Indian tribes.

One of the casualties of the battle was Captain Jacob Tipton of Washington District. He was the son of Colonel John Tipton. Tipton County, Tennessee, was named in his honor. He was a member of the party that escorted Colonel John Sevier to Morganton after his arrest.

A CHEROKEE PATRIOT

After the victory, emissaries from the northern tribes visited the southern nations in an effort to form a joint confederation and plan a coordinated attack along the entire Mississippi Basin. The Badger, a Cherokee Chief and Brother of Dragging Canoe, returned home with his 30 braves boasting of the great victory, "It is nothing to meet the Americans in Regimentals." Dragging Canoe immediately visited the neighboring tribes with talks of a Southern Federation. The Creeks and Choctaws joined with a pledge of cooperation. The Chickasaws refused to take part.

Raids, by "Glass" in the Cumberlands and "Turtle at Home," in Kentucky country, furnished fresh scalps to be displayed during the festival celebrations. War against the whites was being talked in every Council. Big war dances were going full blast in all Chickamauga Towns. Dragging Canoe, back from his successful talks, took a party of braves and went to Lookout Mountain to join the celebration. The great War Chief, 60 years old, danced with savage ferocity. His hope and determination to drive the hated, landstealing pioneers from the Indian hunting grounds seemed to be maturing. The great victory over St. Clair was the spark needed to unite the southern tribes and start them on a real war path.

The next day, March 1st, 1792, Dragging Canoe was dead. It could have been the exertion of the all night dancing, or it could have been the result of wounds received in past battles. The great Cherokee patriot was gone. He never wavered from his purpose of driving the Americans from Cherokee land. He had consistently refused to sign treaty deeds or barter the land of his people. He had predicted, "a dark and bloody settling," and lived up to his word. Governor Blount, when told of Dragging Canoe's death, said.

Dragging Canoe stood second to none in his nation."

It is surmised that the War Chief was given burial rites accorded to ranking Chiefs who died a natural death. From Adair, a summary of a burial ceremony of a Chief's ritual.

The body is washed and clothed in the Chief's best garments. The hair is anointed with bear's oil and the face painted red. The body is seated, on animal skins, outside his winter home, facing west. His most cherished possessions are placed around him. A prominent headsman, usually a kinsman, delivers an eulogy on the achievements and deeds of the dead leader. Then the body is borne three times around the place of internment with the Medicine Man leading the procession. The relatives and friends follow behind. At each complete round the Medicine Man pauses and commends the body to the Master of Life. When this part of the ceremony is finished the dead Chief is placed in his grave or tomb, in a seated position, facing east. His gun, bow, and quiver, made of panther skin, is filled with arrows, pipe, tobacco, and other useful articles, along with food for the journey are placed in the grave. His widow visits the grave daily, during the first month, to mourn his going.

At the time of Dragging Canoe's death, Watts was at Chote making talks with Governor Blount. Every effort was being extended by United States Government Officials to win back the Lower Towns. The Governor invited John Watts and the other Chickamauga Chiefs to attend the Coyatee meet in May and receive their part of the annual allowance from Congress.

Two messengers arrived in Chote during this conference to inform John Watts that the Council of Headmen of the five Lower Towns had chosen him as War Chief to succeed Dragging Canoe. The Council requested his immediate return.

John Watts, although a half-breed, was all Indian. The red man's code, law and practice were the governing forces in his life. Watts had a fair education for the times and had learned the ways of the white man's diplomatic dealing. Chief Watts was one of the greatest Cherokee speechmakers, but he had also learned the art of listening. The new War Chief was to demonstrate his leadership and organizational ability at the Coyatee meet.

COYATEE MEET

The Coyatee reception started May 20th, 1792. The Governor and his party were stopped before reaching the town and the site of the meet. His escorts merely told Blount that a few arrangements were necessary before proceeding further. Soon the word was brought by messenger to proceed.

It was one of the memorable occasions of Territorial history. The 2000 or more warriors had been arranged in two parallel lines, forming a long lane through which the official party was to pass. In the middle of the ceremonial ground, at the end of the two lines, a pole had been erected from which an American Flag had been raised. As the Governor's party was escorted down this array of Cherokee Warriors, shouts of welcome and the salute of guns were loud in every quarter. The Territory Officials, hearing the wild cheers, felt that the talks ahead might put an end to the frontier warfare. As they reached the foot of the flagpole and dismounted, handshakes were exchanged between the two races of people. It seemed a happy occasion.

This ceremony took place about noon. The remainder of the day was spent eating, drinking and making light talk. Early next morning, Chief Bloody Fellow suggested that the official talks be postponed another day and that Governor Blount and his party enjoy the day with eating, drinking and watching ball play. This the Governor agreed to do. Bloody Fellow had made rather heavy bets on the game and he was much concerned with the play, but it was to prove a bad day as he lost his wager.

Early Tuesday, the Chief asked Blount to delay the talks yet another day. The Chief gave as a reason heavy drinking the night before. It was also rumored that Bloody Fellow had given much drink to the opposing team in an effort to recuperate his losses. Thus Tuesday was spent pretty much as Monday, the exception being that the Chief's team won and he recovered his losses and his clothes.

On Wednesday, the headmen assembled at the place designated for the talks. After apologies for the delayed session, discussions of state affairs began. Governor Blount thanked the Chiefs for their warm, congenial reception and the hospitality during his stay. He called attention to the many whites killed since the signing of the Holston Treaty. He spoke of the 200 or more horses stolen from the Cumberland settlements during that same period. He reminded them that the white captives had not been returned.

Hanging Maw, Chief of the Upper Towns, announced that the National Council would meet in 30 days at Ustanali and a report would be made known to Governor Blount and the other Government Officials.

Governor Blount at this time announced that Bloody Fellow's name would be changed, by President Washington's direction. From henceforth he would be called, "Eskaqua," meaning, "Clear Sky." The Governor also announced the appointment of James Carey as Official Interpreter for the Nation.

The distribution of presents and goods sent by Congress brought forth a suggestion from the Badger. He requested that as the Lower Towns had not participated in the distribution for many years, they should be entitled to a greater portion. The Chiefs of the Upper Towns gave their consent as an inducement to the younger braves and chiefs to keep the peace.

Governor Blount returned to Knoxville feeling that peace had been restored to the frontier. The Indians had learned well their forked tongue way of talking from their white fathers. "Tomahawk diplomacy"

became their mode of procedure during meets. "Cover the tomahawk with a blanket while you talk peace." They had insisted that the Cumberlands belonged to all the tribes as a communal hunting ground. They wanted every white off and the forts and cabins burned. They felt that they had a right to steal and plunder the Cumberland intruders and, if opposed in this practice, they had a right to kill.

GITLU—ALE—TSAQWALI

The Indians called the Cumberland Settlements, "Gitlu-ale-tsaqwali," which meant "Hair and Horses." The Cherokees and Creeks found horses and scalps easier to obtain in this horse country than in Virginia. They used the animals for barter with some of the Carolina border traders. It has been reported that during the year 1792 over 500 horses were stolen in the Cumberlands. The Middle Tennessee country became known as the "Horse Stamp."

The Spanish, also alert to the change in Chickamauga leadership, invited John Watts to visit them in Pensacola. William Panton was host to the Chief and his party. The Cherokees were promised unlimited supplies of arms in their war to hold their lands. They urged Chief Watts to strike while the Creeks and Choctaws were in the spirit and willing to cooperate.

John Watts returned to Willstown, where the council was in progress. He related the talks with the Spanish and their promise of guns and supplies. A Council vote was taken — the verdict: War. In September, 600 Cherokees, Shawnee and Creek warriors assembled to march against Nolichucky and Holston Settlements. A spy reported these people had been warned. Eskaqua had brought Leonard Shaw to show the Indians the white man's way of farming. Shaw, married to a Chief's daughter, had sent word to Blount of the impending attack.

Watts shifted the direction of his campaign toward Nashville. Messengers from Blount had also carried news of the Indian plans to Robertson. Scout Abraham Castlemen had discovered signs of Indian parties at Fox's Camp in the vicinity of present Murfreesboro. He had warned the Cumberland people of Indian presence.

General Robertson mustered out the Militia. They made camp at Rains Springs, about two miles from Nashville. After several days, with no Indians seen or reported, the men became restless. It looked like a false alarm. They abused Castleman and other scouts who had reported Indian signs. General Robertson finally dismissed the men.

Castleman, angry at the abuse and at having his report ignored, took his gun and bullets and left for Buchanan's Station four miles south of the Bluffs. Robertson, to be on the safe side, sent Jonathan Gee and Seward Clayton out on a scouting mission. Captains Rains and Kennedy were directed to cover the Indian trails in another section. Rains and Kennedy found no Indians or signs on their trip. Gee and Clayton never returned.

John Watts also had scouts checking the countryside and movements of the whites. Two of his half-breed warriors, dressed in white man's clothing, were following Gee and Clayton. The two white scouts were keeping contact with each other by using a country halloo. The two Indian scouts imitated the whites' call and thus lured them to their death. Through such vigilant means, Watts had been able to reach the Cumberlands undetected.

A short distance from Buchanan's Station, the Chiefs held a council to plan their attack. An argument started between Watts and Taloliskee, Creek Chief, over which place to attack first. Watts wanted to bypass Buchanan's and strike Nashville. The Creek Chief wanted to take the smaller station first. Watts lost. The weakness of Indian strategy was again demonstrated, in that each Chief was a law unto himself. He was in supreme command of his band. Unless all were in agreement, a coordinated effort was difficult. The argument between the two Chiefs lasted into the night. Taloliskee won and they headed for Buchanan's. Watts said that he would stay in the background and watch the Creeks capture the fort, but when the heat of the fighting began, Watts was right in the middle of the conflict.

BUCHANAN'S STATION

The 15 men in the station were on the alert. The nervous movements and sounds of the cattle had warned of Indian presence. In spite of this, the Indians were within 30 feet of the gate before being discovered by sentry John McRory. His first shot killed a Shawnee and alerted the men. The battle lasted about an hour. Several Indians were killed and many wounded. John Watts was seriously wounded.

From Blount's papers has come this description of the battle as taken from Ramsey's Annals:

On the 30th September, about midnight, John Buchanan's Station, four miles south of Nashville, (at which sundry families had collected, and fifteen gunmen) was attacked by a party of Creeks and lower Cherokees, supposed to consist of three or four hundred. Their approach was suspected by the running of cattle, that had taken fright of them, and, upon examination, they were found rapidly advancing within ten yards of the gate; from this place and distance they received the first fire from the man who discovered them (John McRory). They immediately returned the fire, and continued a very heavy and constant firing upon the station, (blockhouse, surrounded with a stockade) for an hour, and were repulsed with considerable loss, without injuring man, woman, or child, in the station.

During the whole time of the attack, the Indians were not more distant than ten yards from the block-house, and often in large numbers around the lower walls, attempting to put fire to it. One ascended the roof with a torch, where he was shot, and falling to the ground renewed his attempts to fire the bottom logs, and was killed. The Indians fired thirty balls through a port-hole of the overjutting, which lodged in the roof in the circumference of a hat, and those sticking in the walls, on the outside, were very numerous.

Upon viewing the ground next morning, it appeared that the fellow who was shot from the roof, was a Cherokee half-breed

BUCHANAN STATION: The log building in the foreground is said to be part of the original Blockhouse. The brick house was later home of John Buchanan.

of the Running Water, known by the whites by the name of Tom Tunbridge's step-son, the son of a French woman by an Indian, (His Indian name was Kiachatalee), and there was much blood, and signs that many dead had been dragged off and litters having been made to carry their wounded to their horses, which they had left a mile from the station. Near the block-house were found several swords, hatchets, pipes, kettles, and budgets of different Indian articles; One of the swords was a fine Spanish blade, and richly mounted in the Spanish fashion. In the morning previous to the attack, Jonathan Gee and Seward Clayton were sent out as spies, and on the ground, among other articles left by the Indians, were found a handkerchief and a moccasin, known one to belong to Gee and the other to Clayton, hence it is supposed they are killed.

An interesting story is told about a young lad named Jimmy O'Connor. He had no gun but wanted to aid in the defense of the station. Buchanan handed him an old and heavy blunderbuss that hung near the main porthole. This unhandy type of gun was used only in fort defense. Young O'Connor loaded the gun stuck it through a porthole and pulled the trigger. With heavy firing inside and out, Jimmy thought his gun had fired. He pulled his gun back and put another load into the barrel. Again he pulled the trigger. He took the gun out and put in yet another charge of shot and powder. The third time he placed the gun in the porthole and aimed at a large body of Indians; he pulled the trigger and the gun fired. The heavy blast of powder and shot cut a wide lane through the savage lines. The heavily-loaded gun also played havoc with poor Jimmy. He was thrown across the room and under the bed by the kick of the heavy discharge.

Before starting on the campaign, Chief John Watts had assigned two different war parties to cover roads leading toward Nashville. Doublehead was sent to scout the road through Kentucky, and Middlestriker was to cover the Walton Road. (The Walton Road was started by Major John Evans from Clinch River, near present Kingston, through Crab Orchard, Crossville, Carthage and Bledose's Lick to Nashville. William Walton was given the contract in 1790 to finish and improve the road.)

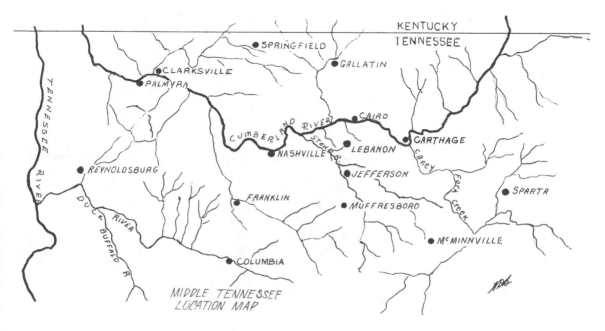

MIDDLE TENNESSEE LOCATION MAP

Doublehead took his 60 warriors and hurried to the Wilderness Road in Kentucky. He met a party of six whites, took one scalp. This ambitious Chief, resentful at being left out of the Nashville action, started immediately down the trail toward the Bluffs. Needing food, he made camp on Caney Fork River. While the Chief and his warriors were out hunting, Lieutenant William Snoddy and a Sumner County Company of 34 men out on patrol, accidentally stumbled on the empty camp. 62 war packs, each consisting of blanket, bearskin and extra lead, were captured. Snoddy decided to camp near, and wait for the return of the party. He chose a bluff on the river that was suitable for his purpose.

Doublehead was very angry to find his camp discovered and war packs gone. His scouts soon located Snoddy's position. The Chief assembled his men on Rook Island, nearby, to work out a plan to retake his war packs and kill the white soldiers. Snoddy's men were alert to the moves of the Indians. With guns loaded, they listened to the Indians, signaling each other as they maneuvered to designated spots. The night was cold, wet and foggy.

The Cherokees approached to within 40 yards of the white camp before charging, with loud warwhoops and blazing guns, the Sumner County Militia. It was a desperate struggle with both sides showing great bravery. Many of the fights were hand-to-hand struggles. Finally, Doublehead's warriors gave way and fled He blamed Martin Harpool, a Dutchmen with a big English musket, for the defeat. Harpool would shoot his scatter gun into the ranks of the braves with loud shouts. His Dutch-English gibberish frightened the Indians. They thought maniacs were being loosed against them. They also disliked his scatter gun that seemed to shoot in all directions, and everywhere at the same time.

Snoddy lost two men. The Indians had 13 killed and many wounded. Doublehead, the scourge of the frontier, was outdone. He had lost his warpacks and a battle. He led his warriors toward Nashville. At Walton's Road, he learned of John Watts' disasterous defeat. The Indian scouts who reported the defeat also reported that Watts had been mortally wounded. Doublehead vowed that he would avenge his nephew's death. He told his men to divide into small groups, obtain more food and supplies from home and meet him at Short Mountain.

Meanwhile, Middlestriker had placed his men in an ambush arrangement near a much-used spring close to Spencer's Hill. Captain Samuel Handley had been sent by Governor Blount, with a company of 42 men, to assist in the defense of Nashville. As the company approached the spring, they were met with heavy fire from the concealed warriors. Some of the unseasoned militia ran when this ambush caught them unprepared for a fight. Several horses were shot, one belonging to Leiper. Captain Handley went to his rescue and his own horse was shot from beneath him. He was captured and forced to watch while the savages brutally murdered and scalped Leiper.

Handley's capture was a great event as he was one of their most wanted whites. Handley had served, as Colonel John Sevier's aid, on many Indian campaigns. This made him a marked man in Indian country. The

Captain was taken to Willstown, home of Chief John Watts. The Chief was at home recovering from the serious wounds received at Buchanan's.

A Council of the Chieftains was held and lasted three days. Handley, condemned to death by fire, was made to run the gauntlet before being tied to the stake. Severe injuries received in this ritual caused the death-by-fire ceremony to be postponed until the Captain recovered enough to stand up. Again all was prepared for the fire death. Handley was tied to the stake, insulted, and objects of filth were thrown into his face by the squaws. The fire was lighted and Handley, hoping to taunt the warriors into shooting him, called them old women, cowards and every insult thinkable. This had no effect; the fire burned on. A sudden thunderstorm and a heavy downpour of rain put out the fire, causing the second postponement.

When the weather cleared, Captain Handley was again tied to the stake for execution. The fagots were lighted around the bound man. Chief Watts, now able to leave his couch, came outside to witness the death ceremony. Handley began to talk to Watts. Here is a quote from Brown's, "Old Frontiers."

'You are a brave Chief, and the white men love a brave man, and all of them love John Watts. They regret they must fight him. I am John Sevier's aid and he often talks of the brave Chief Watts. But you have a cowardly set of warriors. They are old women; if they were not they would shoot a warrior.'

Watts, greatly moved, had Handley released and took him by the hand. Other headmen followed his example. Watts took Handley home with him, where he was fed, clothed and made a member of the Wolf Clan. Colonel Sevier wrote Watts that if Handley were injured by any torture, he would treat his Indian captives in the same manner. Handley was allowed to write a letter to Colonel James Scott. Watts, himself, wrote a message to Governor Blount. A messenger took the two letters for delivery December 10, 1792.

It is well to know that many times the lives of Col. John Sevier's family, as well as his own, had been threatened. Nine different parties had left the Indian towns for that specific purpose. Some unforeseen circumstance each time had prevented the actual deed. Twice they had reached Sevier's neighborhood and killed other families, but did not locate the Sevier home.

Captain Handley returned to Knoxville, January 24, 1793. He was accompanied by Middlestriker, Candy and eight warriors. Governor Blount received the group with proper ceremony and gave presents to each, consisting of a blanket, shirt, leggings, flap and match coat. Captain Handley's hair had turned white during the three months of captivity. He advised the Governor that Watts wanted peace with the Holston-Nolichucky settlements, but that the Cumberland imposters must be removed or destroyed.

These peace overtures by Watts were but a cover-up. He had learned his diplomatic lessons well and copied the white man's way. His credo: make treaties, lull their suspicions and hit again. Treaties always cost the Indians as the more astute white could out talk, and out bargain, the red man as he took and took of the Indian land. The whites made treaties but did not observe them; why should the Indian not do the same. The Indians were only defending their right, but this made the aggressive Americans angry.

Chief Watts wrote Carondelet a letter telling of their recent misfortunes and their need of more supplies. The Spanish Governor was prompt in promising and furnishing more aid.

Governor Blount went to Philadelphia to confer with Secretary of War Henry Knox. He tried to use the Buchanan Station Attack as a lever in obtaining permission to employ Federal Troops against the Indians. He was almost successful in talking Knox into granting the request, when events caused Secretary Knox to revert back to, and become more adamant in, his opposition to the plan. He reaffirmed his position that only defensive measures would be countenanced. General Knox, uncertain of Blount, felt that the Governor's political ambitions and vast land interests influenced his attitude and actions.

Until the unexpected death of Alexander McGilivray, the strong Creek Chief, most of the southern Creek warriors and their Chiefs had restrained from much active participation in the frontier attacks. The ones that had been guilty were of the Upper Creek Towns, located near the Chickamauga towns, around Lookout Mountain.

Chief McGilvray died February 17, 1793, while on a trip to Pensacola. He was buried, with full masonic honors, in William Panton's Gardens. Panton and McGilivray had been business partners and close friends. Charles Weatherford, a brother-in-law, succeeded him as head of the Creek Nation. A weak leader, Chief Weatherford was unable to unite the Creeks. More of the clans pulled away and joined the Chickamaugas in their raids.

CAPTAIN BEARD ATTACKS COYATEE

The circumstances surrounding the division of the Cherokee Nation made treaty settlements difficult. Hanging Maw, Head Chief of the Upper Towns, had been able to keep his people at peace with the whites. Dragging Canoe had often called these people old women in his derisive talks. These Upper Town Indians resented the large share of gifts and goods that the Government officials gave to the towns that were doing the killing and stealing, while they, were the ones who had been keeping the peace.

Opposition was growing more violent on both sides. The frontier settlers crowded into the stations and forts for safety, resented the restrictions more and more. Small parties of whites going out would vent their frustration on any innocent Indian, man, woman or child. This placed Generals Sevier and Robertson in a difficult position, as they had to obey orders issued by President Washington and Secretary Knox.

The event, that prevented General Knox from sending Federal Troops against the southern Indians, occurred while Blount was enroute to Philadelphia, to confer with Federal Officials. Blount did not learn of the massacre until his arrival at the Capital. Thomas Gillam and son, James, were killed in Raccoon Valley, not far from Knoxville. War clubs left near the bodies indicated that Shawnees were the culprits. This happened in May, just as Blount was leaving for Philadelphia. The Governor had directed Captain John Beard to follow the War Party, but not to cross the River. Secretary Daniel Smith was left in charge during Blount's absence.

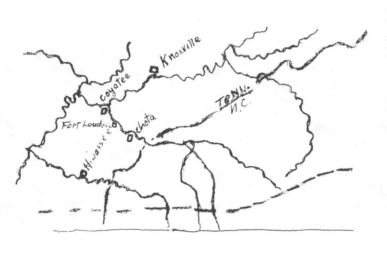

Captain Beard, with his mounted command, followed the Shawnee trail, which led to and crossed Little Tennessee and passed through Coyatee. Hanging Maw's son, contrary to orders, had bought two of the stolen horses from the renegade band. Captain Beard disobeyed orders, crossed the River and attacked Coyatee. Hanging Maw, his wife and a daughter of Nancy Ward were seriously wounded. Fool Charles, Betty, daughter of Kitegista, a white man and four others were killed.

Hanging Maw and his people, who had been friendly to the United States, were innocent of the deed committed by the Shawnee. Unfortunately, Captain Beard and many of his men were in the mood to vent their feelings on any Indian.

Hanging Maw sent a messenger to Secretary Knox telling him of the massacre of his people. Secretary Smith, Governor Pro Tem, investigated and wrote Knox the details. Smith ordered Captain Beard to a Court Martial and requested that he give up his command, but Beard ignored both orders. Smith also wrote Hanging Maw, Doublehead and the others saying that Captain Beard would be punished. This was one of the events that caused Knox to refuse Blount's request. Captain Beard was tried, but a partisan jury acquitted him.

The Coyatee massacre served Chief John Watts in an unexpected way: it united the whole Cherokee nation. He was able to win the active cooperation and support of practically all the Chiefs and Headmen. In September of 1793, Watts assembled 1000 warriors with the intent of assaulting Knoxville. When news of the contemplated march reached the settlers, plans for defense were worked out. General John Sevier was encamped with 400 men at Ish's Station. Chief Watts had sent two scouts to watch Sevier's movements. They were Pumpkin Boy, brother of Doublehead, and Nettle Carrier. Pumpkin Boy, exposing himself too much, was killed by Sentry Thomas Mains. Nettle Carrier, though wounded, was able to reach the Indian camp.

The Chiefs held a council a short distance from Knoxville. They were divided in their ideas of how the attacks should be made. John Watts wanted to attack Knoxville directly. Doublehead, his uncle, angered by Pumpkin Boy's death, wanted immediate revenge on any nearby family. As frequently happened during a major Indian campaign, each Chief and Headman wanted his own way. Each clan head was a law unto himself: his nature, tradition and training making him completely individualistic. A Chief earned his position by displaying personal ability and achievement. This encouraged him to follow his own dictates,

THE FEDERAL BARRACKS, early Knoxville Fort constructed to house Federal Troops posted there for defense. Picture from a painting by Lloyd Branson that hangs in Lawson-McGhee Library, Knoxville, Tennessee. Courtesy of Pollyanna Creekmore.

inclinations and hunches. Thus, once again a concerted battle front proved futile. This was an underlying cause of the Indians' inability to win victories in battles against the white men.

Again, John Watts, a capable leader, was frustrated in his plans to overcome a white stronghold. The surprise element was lost because of the prolonged council. Morning came and they were still some distance from their objective. The United States Troops, quartered in the barracks at Knoxville, were accustomed to firing a cannon signaling sunrise each day. When the Indians heard the shot, on this morning of September 25, 1793, they were sure that their nearness to the settlement had been discovered and that the cannon was a signal. They halted their forward progress and vented their disappointment on the nearest cabin, which happened to be that of Alexander Cavett.

They surrounded the Station containing 13 people. Only three could handle guns. During the first attack, five Indians were killed. The Indians withdrew for another pow wow. They decided to parley because it was less dangerous. The three gunners inside were doing too much damage. Chief Bench, who could speak English well, was chosen as the emissary. Watts had agreed to this action. Bench told the Cavetts that their lives would be spared if they surrendered. These people, knowing they could not withstand so large a force, agreed to the terms.

Doublehead, still angry, had not taken part in the council talk. When the gates were opened he sounded a loud warwhoop and fell on the helpless men, women and children with his tomahawk. All were killed and scalped except one small boy who John Watts slipped away. This boy was killed by his Creek guard three days later. The station was burned to the ground.

General John Sevier, learning of the large Indian force nearby, sent Captain Harrison with a company of men to scout the area. Captain Harrison found the burning embers of the station and the mangled bodies of the Cavetts. General Sevier, despite the urging of many followers, had restrained his various commands from offensive forays into Indian towns. But now that the situation was getting out of hand, something had to be done.

271

Sevier sent a report of the Cavett massacre to acting Governor Daniel Smith and asked permission to give chase to the Indians. Following is Smith's reply to Sevier as quoted from Brown's, "Old Frontiers":

In answer to yours of the 27th, I hold it would be proper to follow the trail of the large party of Indians who murdered Cavett's family on the 25th instant, and if possible inflict punishment upon them. The country is to be defended in the best manner we can, comporting with my general instructions to you of the 17th.

John Sevier's philosophy, that the best defense was an effective offense, put the wheels in motion for a push into Indian territory. He sent a call for additional men from both Washington and Hamilton Districts. Colonel John Blair commanded the Washington reinforcements and Colonel Gilbert Christian lead the Hamilton force. Major George Elmholm served as aid to General Sevier. The force now numbered over 700 mounted riflemen.

This Southwest Army followed the Great War Path across Hiawassee to the Indian Town of Oostinaula. Finding supplies of grain and meat here, the force stayed two or three days waiting for the report of scouts. They burned the deserted town before leaving, then made camp on the banks of the Oostinaula River. The Indians were all around the camp. The posted sentries could hear their movements in the tall grass. The Army guarded their horses carefully and Sevier's men slept on their arms at night. Two or three skirmishes occured, but only one slight wound was suffered. The Indians, realizing the strength of the force and who the commanding officer was, pulled back hoping for a better opportunity.

The night after the skirmishes, Sevier moved his army. He left the campfires burning brightly, hoping the Indians would not suspect the departure of the troops. The Indians returned and fired into the empty camp before learning of their mistake.

The forward march led the white army to the Coosawatie River. The Indians had prepared defenses on the opposite banks where the whites had to cross. Sevier called his Officers for a council to make other plans. Scouts had observed many small openings along the bank nearest the Village. The Indians had dug cavities, each large enough for one warrior and his gun. Each brave concealed in this spot could cause much damage without exposing himself to the trooper fire.

Sevier realized that his men would suffer heavy casualties if he undertook to cross the river at this location. He ordered Colonel Kelly and his Knox County Company to locate another crossing. Such a spot was found about half-a-mile downstream. Some of the horsemen pushed their horses out into the stream to check on its depths and bottom, and some crossed the river. The Indians thought they were being flanked by the force moving downstream for the crossing. They hastily left their places of concealment to oppose this new threat. When the defense was weakened at the regular ford, Sevier quickly led his men across with very little opposition.

The Indians now found themselves caught between the white army and the river. The red warriors put up a brave battle under the leadership of Kingfisher, but were no match for Sevier's force. They managed to escape into the hills along a secret route known only to them. Sevier wanted to follow, but his scouts advised against this course.

The Battle of Etowah was fought near the site of the present town of Rome, Georgia. Sevier tried to keep the killing to a minimum. Most of the Squaws and children were allowed to escape. All structures in the Indian town of Etowah were destroyed by fire.

This was General John Sevier's last battle. He had fought Indians, Tories and British during a span of some 20 years. He never lost a battle, and only 58 of his command were killed during his military career.

GENERAL "MAD" ANTHONY WAYNE was a very successful officer though unsuccessful in financial ventures. The many sections of country that saw his service during Revolutionary War responded by naming county, town or fort in his honor. Courtesy Yorktown Nat. Military Park.

GENERAL "MAD" ANTHONY WAYNE

Shortly after Sevier's victory at Etowah, John Watts and several other Chiefs took their troubles and requests for supplies to the Spanish Officials. The Spaniards, who were having their own problems and economic difficulties, felt neither able nor inclined to continue financing a losing cause. They advised the Indians to make their peace with the Americans and get off the warpath.

About this time, President Washington appointed General Anthony Wayne to direct a campaign against the Tribes of the Northwest Territory. These Indians, influenced by English Agents, were causing more and more bloodshed in the Northern Territory. After the defeats of Harmar, Hardin and St. Clair, the tribes were louder and stronger in their anti-American attitudes. More and more massacres and attacks were occurring.

General Wayne took the remnants of the St. Clair force and the many raw recruits enlisted by Congress, and began the enormous task of training them into an efficient army. His rigid discipline and long hours of drilling nearly drove his men to exhaustion. Colonel James Wilkerson, a member of his staff, was one of his biggest hindrances and critics. Wilkerson resented that Wayne was given the command that he coveted. While professing American patriotism, Wilkerson was in the pay of the Spanish.

The rigid training of General Wayne paid off. His force of 3000 disciplined troops was called, "Wayne's Legions." Keeping scouts and spies out in all directions, General Wayne marched his men into the heart of Indian Country. The Indian Chiefs had vainly watched for an opportunity to ambush the American Force. General Wayne met the Indians in battle at Fallen Timbers, August, 1794. Blue Jacket, Shawnee Chief who led the attack against Wayne, had been advised by Little Turtle, Miami Chief, against the confrontation as Wayne had offered them a choice of peace or war. The Indians were beaten disasterously. Their towns and supplies were burned. The British Agent's home was burned, as was Fort Campbell. After the battle, the General built Fort Wayne where St. Mary's and St. John's Rivers merge.

The result of this battle inflamed the Indians against the British, who had promised supplies and military help that never came. Some 300 Cherokees assisted in the battle against Wayne. The Chiefs were told to report to Greenville for a treaty meet in the spring of 1795.

States bordering Tennessee all have a county named Wayne in honor of General Anthony Wayne. This outstanding historical General of the Revolutionary War was brave, at times reckless, and bold in his victories. He oftimes attempted the impossible and won, which gave rise to the nickname, "Mad." He was a surveyor turned soldier and general. His successes in northern battles influenced General Washington in sending him to assist General Lafayette in the Virginia Campaign, just months before the surrender of General Cornwallis at Yorktown. Later Washington sent him to assist General Greene in mopping up the Tory and British pockets of resistance in South Carolina and Georgia.

The Georgians liked General Wayne so well that they gave him a rice plantation near Savannah. With visions of wealth, Wayne arranged, through Robert Morris to finance improvement and operation of the plantation. The rice crops failed and Wayne, badly in debt, had to sell his property to pay off his obligations. Learning that President Washington was looking for someone to lead the Northwest Campaign, Wayne applied for the job. The President gave Wayne the command and appointed him Commander-in-Chief of the American Army.

General Wayne lost his wife during this campaign and was sick the day of the battle. He died December 15, 1796, and was buried at Presque Isle, Lake Erie. Many patriots of Tennessee, Kentucky, Virginia, North Carolina, South Carolina and Georgia served under Wayne at one time or another. His name is synonymous with history in all states east of the Mississippi River.

TERRITORY'S FIRST ASSEMBLY

JAMES WINCHESTER arrived on Cumberland 1785; prominent in early government. His son Marcus opened first store in Memphis 1819; postmaster 1821-1849; first Mayor of Memphis 1827-29; close friend of Davy Crockett.

When the results of the 1791 Census were reported in September of that year, they showed that the citizens of the Territory were entitled to elect their own Assembly. Governor Blount delayed calling this election until the summer of 1793. The public clamor was so great that he was forced to arrange for the legislative polls. The heads of local militia, in the several counties, were designated to hold the elections October and December of 1793.

The elected members of the first Territorial Legislature were; Knox County, Alexander Kelly and John Baird; Jefferson, George Doherty and Samuel Weir; Greene, Joseph Hardin; Washington, Leroy Taylor and John Tipton; Sullivan, George Rutledge; Hawkins, William Cocke and Joseph McMinn; Davidson, James White; Sumner, David Wilton; Tennessee, James Ford. These elected representatives met in Knoxville, January, 1794. David Wilson was appointed Speaker and Hopkins Lacey, Clerk. They elected ten persons, out of which five would be chosen for the Upper House. Those appointed by President Washington were Griffith Rutherford, John Sevier, James Winchester, Stockley Donelson and Parmenas Taylor.

Both houses of the Territorial Legislature met at Knoxville, August 25th, 1794. Griffith Rutherford was elected Chairman of the Upper House; George Roulstone, Clerk; and Christopher Shoat, Doorkeeper. The many acts of this Session cannot be recorded here, but a few outstanding ones were Legal Incorporation of the Town of Knoxville; Creation of Sevier County; Chartering two colleges, namely Tusculum College, near Greeneville, and Blount College at Knoxville. Dr. James White was appointed as a non-voting Representative to Congress. The last day of this Session was September 30th. The Assembly voted to adjourn and set the next meeting for the first Monday in October, 1795.

Sevier County, named for Colonel John Sevier, was included in the Hamilton District. The first Sevier Court met November 8th, 1794, in the house of Isaac Thomas. Magistrates present were Samuel Newell, Joseph Wilson, Joshua Gist, Peter Bryant, Joseph Vance and Andrew Evans. Absent, M. Lewis and Robert Pollock.

NICKAJACK AND RUNNING WATER

The newly elected House of Representatives of the Territory prepared a written paper that was presented to Congress by Dr. White. The paper listed the 200 persons killed since 1791, and property losses estimated at some $100,000. The Federal Government was so heavily involved with the Northwest Campaign under General Wayne that the policy of defense, rather than offense, was continued for the Southwest Territory Defense fortifications were authorized at Southwest Point (Kingston), Fort Grainger (Lenoir City) and Tellico Blockhouse (near site of Fort Loudon).

During this year, Secretary Knox received delegations from the Southern Tribes. He presented Doublehead, self-chosen emissary, with gifts and raised the annual payment to $5,000 per year. Nevertheless raids continued on the frontier. Accounts of more than 40 raids are listed in Haywood's chronicle of the Cumberland Territory during 1794.

General Robertson, after a secret conference and understanding with Governor Blount, made plans of his own regarding defensive warfare against the Chickamaugas. He sent Sampson Williams into Kentucky

Country to seek help in recruiting an armed force. These people, also suffering from Indian attacks, responded by sending 150 volunteers under the command of Colonel William Whitley. Colonel John Montgomery recruited a company of riflemen from the Clarksville area. Colonel Ford enlisted another company from the Nashville settlement and placed Captain Miles in command. These armed groups quietly rendezvoused at a blockhouse near Buchanan's Station, four miles from Nashville.

Meanwhile, Governor Blount had ordered Major James Ore to march toward Nashville with 69 men, on a scouting expedition. He was to report to General James Robertson. When all the companies had assembled in Davidson County, final plans for a campaign were made. Robertson wanted to make the project as official as he legally could, so he placed Major Ore, the only officer present with official status, in command of the 550 mounted riflemen. When arrangements were completed and all was in readiness to march, Robertson gave the Major the following written orders:

The object of your command is to defend Mero District against a large body of Creeks and Cherokees of the Lower Towns, which I have information is about to invade it; also to punish in any exemplary manner such Indians as have recently committed depredations in this District.

The second part of the orders were contrary to instructions from Congress, Secretary Knox and Governor Blount.

You are to proceed along Taylor's Trace toward the Chickamauga Towns in which you are momently to expect a large party of Creeks and Cherokees advancing to invade this District. If you do not meet this party before you reach the Tennessee River, you will cross it and destroy the Lower Towns, which must serve as a check to the expected invaders.

Major Ore led his force toward Lookout Mountain Country. Scouts on an earlier trip had located a practical route that allowed the Cumberland Army to reach the Tennessee, near mouth of Sequatchie (South Pittsburg), undetected. Using crude oxhide boats and other improvised means, about half of the force was able to cross the River by daybreak. The leaders decided to march against Nickajack before the Indians could learn of their nearness.

The element of complete surprise was aided by a foggy atmosphere which hid the three companies as they maneuvered around the log cabins to their positions. The bewildered warriors offered little resistance as the companies charged from all sides. Some tried to escape to the river, but were shot down. 70 braves were killed as the attack became a massacre. Chief Breath was among the casualties. 20 women and children were taken captive to be used as hostages in a prisoner exchange.

The Town of Nickajack was completely destroyed by fire. Major Ore immediately marched his men toward Running Water three miles away. Encoute, they met a force of braves coming to the aid of their brothers at Nickajack. A short, desperate struggle took place at the Narrows. The Indians, unable to compete with the mounted riflemen fled into the hills. They did not inflict much damage on the white force, but delayed it long enough for their women and children to escape into the forest. The Running Water Town was also burned to the ground.

Having accomplished this mission, Major Ore led his men back across the River to rejoin their comrades. The return march was begun immediately. Before reaching Nashville they met a friendly band of Chickasaws who told them about General Wayne's victory in the Northwest. The trip to Nickajack and return took ten days. Joshua Thomas was the only casualty.

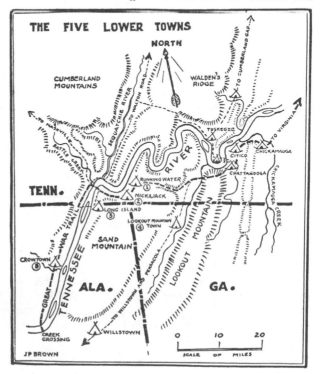

THE FIVE LOWER TOWNS

General Robertson wrote out his report of the campaign and sent it to Governor Blount by express messenger, James Russell. He also sent Blount his resignation as Brigadier-General of Mero District. Russell, the messenger, was attacked by Indians near Southwest Point. Mr. Shannon carried the bloodied document to the Governor because Russell was confined to the fort with his wounds. Messengers were charging $50.00 per trip from Nashville to Knoxville. Blount officially made a great show of anger and publicly blamed Robertson, but actually was very pleased with the results. General Robertson's resignation was never accepted.

The bitterness of defeat, loss of two main towns, the refusal of the Spaniards to furnish more supplies and the news of the defeat of his northern allies by Wayne all bore heavily on John Watts. He could see the gradual disintegration of his people. Circumstances were forcing him to bow his head in humiliation to the white imposters. In his anguish, the proud Chief asked Governor Blount to meet him for a peace conference. Watts requested that the meet be held outside Knoxville.

TELLICO TREATY

Tellico Block House was selected as the site. Many of the Chickamauga Chiefs attended this preliminary discussion of the situation. A treaty meet was then scheduled at the same place for November 7, 1794, when the Chieftains of all the Cherokee Nation would be present.

It was quite a colorful occasion as John Watts, flanked by Bloody Fellow, Middlestriker, Richard Justice, Glass, Tatlanta, and the Crier, sat down with The Little Turkey, Long Warrior of Turnip Mountain, Standing Turkey of Ustanalie, Dreadful Water of Elijay, Pathkiller of Cotokoy, Stallion of Chenee, Bold Hunter of Connasauga, and Tuckasee of Etowa (son of the old Chief Oconostota). The Upper Towns of the Overhills were represented by Hanging Maw of Coyatee, Oconostota of Hiwassee, Will Elder of Toquo and others.

Governor Blount was accompanied by Silas Dinsmoor, United States Agent to the Cherokees; John McKee, Deputy Agent; Colonel S. R. Davidson, Tellico Block House Garrison Commander; General John Sevier and other officials of the Territory Government.

MANSION HOUSE: This house, located near Athens, Tenn., is said to have been a blockhouse built on the Tellico River by General Sevier's direction, and similar to the Federal constructed Tellico Blockhouse. The log structure and site purchased 1824 by a Mr. Johnson who built 9 rooms around the square building. A secret passage leads underground from the house to the river. This afforded means of escape during Indian attacks.

These items are taken from Brown's Old Frontiers in the form reproduced from the American State Papers, Indian Affairs.

John Watts, leading War Chief of the Cherokee, spoke with finality as he presented a string of white beads to Governor Blount, saying, "This meeting seems to have been ordered by the Great Spirit." Then, turning to Hanging Maw, he continued:

There is Scolacuta, He is old enough to be my father. From my infancy he was a great man, and he is now the Great Chief of the Nation. In the spring of this year, he sent a talk to the Lower Towns, telling them that he and his Upper Towns had taken the United States by the hand, and inviting the Lower Towns to do the same.

Just before Running Water and Nickajack were destroyed, I went to those towns, as well as to Lookout Mountain, and exerted myself for the restoration of peace. I verily believe that these towns had heard my talk and were determined for peace. I do not say that these towns did not deserve the chastisement they received, nevertheless, it so exasperated those who escaped from the ruins that for a time I was compelled to be silent myself. But the Running Water people told the Glass that notwithstanding the injury they had received, they remembered my good talks and held them fast, and desired me to take measures for the recovery of their prisoners. I deliver to you this string of beads as a true and public talk from the Lower Towns. Scolacuta, the head of the Nation, is sitting beside me. The Lower Towns instructed me to request him not to throw them away, but to come with me and present this talk to you.

Hanging Maw replied in turn:

I too have had a talk with the Lower Towns. They were once my people, but not now, yet I cannot but think much of the talk I have now received from Watts. Before anything happened to Nickajack and Running Water, I sent those towns many peace talks which they would not hear. Now since their destruction by Major Ore, they send me to make peace for them, together with Watts. I am the head man of my Nation, and Governor Blount is the head of the white people. It is not the fault of either that those towns were destroyed, but their own bad conduct brought destruction upon them.

All last winter, I was compelled to live in the woods by the bad conduct of my people drawing war upon us. In the spring you invited me to meet your deputy, John McKee. He assured me of the disposition of the United States for peace, and told me and my party to return to our houses and fields. I could hear threats against my life from several parts of the Nation. I then asked that this fort should be built, to protect me and my party as well as the frontier inhabitants. I still hear murmurings from several parts of the Nation that they would have nothing to do with this fort; but I see standing around me many of those very people, who are now glad to come to it.

The above quotations appear in the American State Papers, Indian Affairs.

A partial exchange of prisoners was made, and arrangements for others at an early date. Hanging Maw died not long after the Tellico Treaty. He was succeeded by Little Turkey.

Doublehead did not attend the Tellico Treaty Meet. He had just returned from Philadelphia with the $5,000 in goods, the advanced payment by President Washington. The goods were distributed at Oconee Mountain to those present, Doublehead keeping the major share for himself and his followers. Hanging Maw, before his death, had complained to Deputy McKee about this practice:

Are these goods to be delivered to Doublehead and his band of murderers, or to that part of the Nation that has given proof of friendship to the United States by taking one Creek and killing two others? If they are, the friendly part of the Nation will know how to insure the reward of the United States for their services.

THE VALENTINE SEVIER MASSACRE

Doublehead had left with a party of his braves for a hunting trip in the Cumberland country. He stopped at Nashville and smoked the pipe with General Robertson, telling of his trip to see President Washington. He continued down the Cumberland to Clarksville, where he stopped at the home of Colonel Valentine Sevier. Charles Snyder, Sevier's son-in-law, repaired several of the warrior's guns. A few miles downriver, Doublehead met a Creek Band bent on a raiding trip through the area. After much discussion and argument, they joined forces and returned to the Sevier Home. Any Sevier was a marked person by Cherokee Indians, who remembered the many battles Colonel Valentine Sevier had participated in with "Chucky Jack," John Sevier. Doublehead saw an easy opportunity to get a Sevier.

Colonel Valentine Sevier,II and Wife Naomi Sevier were parents of 14 children. Colonel Sevier moved his family to the Cumberland Settlements soon after the collapse of the Franklin Government in 1789. Recorded deeds indicate that he purchased several lots in Nashville and tradition says he lived there a short period. His youngest son, it is said, was born there.

The Seviers moved to Clarksville during 1791. He purchased a 640 acre farm near mouth of Red River from George Cook. He built a two-room, stone blockhouse, with portholes for safety should Indians raid. Several cabins were clustered around the stone house.

His son-in-law, Thomas Grantham, was killed in 1791 at a nearby pond while deer hunting. Twins, Robert and William, 17 years old, were ambushed near the mouth of Blooming Grove Creek late in the afternoon of January 15, 1792. Valentine, III, was killed the following morning near the same spot. They had been on a mercy mission delivering supplies to immigrants.

November 11th, 1794, James Sevier, brother-in-law John King, and a Negro man were harvesting corn in a nearby field. Charles Snider, husband of Betsy Sevier, was working in the blacksmith shop. Joseph Sevier, Valentine's young son, was helping.

VALENTINE SEVIER STONE FORT; built 1791. Scene of Sevier Massacre 1794. Near Clarksville.

The sudden, surprise attack allowed no opportunity for the victims to reach the stone house. Ann King, her infant son James, Betsy Snider and son John Charles Snider and Joseph Sevier were all killed. Rebecca, 12 year old daughter, was scalped, but lived. Benjamin Lindsay, Snider's helper, managed to escape. Colonel Valentine, his wife and some of the smaller children were able to reach the stone house and barricade the door. The Colonel was able to do some damage with an old blunderbuss before the Indians left. The kick of the blunderbuss injured his face and shoulder. The men working in the cornfield nearby rushed toward the house. Having no weapons, they were unable to fight the Indians. They started toward Clarksville to get help. Two men, hearing the gunfire, had started to give aid, but were too late. The Indians had gone.

The Valentine Seviers buried their dead and moved back to Nashville. Colonel Valentine sold the farm, site of the massacre. In 1796, it is said that he returned to Clarksville and lived there until his death, February 23, 1800.

The 20 years of frontier bloodshed were drawing to a close. The Cherokees, after signing the Tellico Treaty, were relatively quiet. They spent their time mastering farming skills instead of scalping. Fruit trees were set out under white man's guidance. Bees were housed in gums made of hollow trees. Some raised cattle and horses. Hunting and trapping were still important and required much of their time.

At the close of the frontier wars, the Cherokees owned much land in Tennessee, North Carolina and Georgia. This land was guaranteed to them forever by solemn treaty. Land-hungry Americans paid no attention to treaty or boundary lines; as there was no standing army to patrol the boundaries, nor a national guard to protect the Indians' rights, the whites just took the land.

North Carolina began to settle its Revolutionary Claims by grants issued for land in present Tennessee. It made no difference that many of these grants were on lands guaranteed to the Indians.

THE COLERAIN TREATY

The Creeks continued their harassments of the Cumberland people during 1795. Mostly small bands stole and killed when the opportunity was to their advantage. This southern tribe was persuaded to sign a Treaty during 1795. United States Commissioners Benjamin Hawkins, George Clymer and Andrew Pickens met the Creeks at the military post of Colerain June 14, 1796. From the American State Papers, Indian Affairs, come this description of the meet:

The kings, head men, and warriors, to the number of four hundred, marched under the flag of the United States to the spot where the commissioners, attended by the officers of the garrison, were seated. As they marched, they danced the Eagle Tail dance, and the four dancers at the head of the chiefs waved the Eagle Tail six times over the heads of the commissioners.

Six of the principal chiefs came up and took the commissioners by the hand. Then they handed them their pipes and held out fire which they had brought from their camp. The commissioners lit the pipes and smoked. There was a short pause between each dance, and the waving of an Eagle Tail, and the same interval in the shaking of hands, and lighting the pipes.

Thus with this ceremonial the Creeks signified that their warriors had come to "Ulawistu-Nunnehi," "The End of the Trail."

The following paragraph from a letter written by Secretary of War Henry Knox to President George Washington, dated June 15, 1789, demonstrates the policy of the Federal Government toward the Indians then and now:

As the settlements of the whites shall approach near to the Indian boundaries established by the treaties, the game will be diminished, and the lands being valuable to the Indians only as hunting grounds, they will be willing to sell further tracts for smaller consideration.

(The above taken from American State Papers, Indian Affairs.)

A letter from Knox to James Robertson clarifies the price paid to the Indians for these lands: *"The average price paid for Indian lands in various parts of the United States within the past four years does not amount to one cent per acre."*

During the Colerain Treaty a Creek Chief made answer to this attitude of the United States Officials and their statements that to the Indians the land was useless. Found in the American State Papers, Indian Affairs, the Chief said:

Upon this land, there is a great deal of timber, pine and oak, which are of much use to the white people. They send it to foreign countries, and it brings them a great deal of money. On this land there is much grass for cattle and horses, and much good food for hogs. On this land there is a great deal of tobacco raised, which likewise brings much money. Even the streams are found valuable to the white men, to grind the wheat and corn that grow on these lands. The pine trees, when they are dead, are valuable for tar.

All these are lasting profits; but if the Indians have a little goods for their lands, in one or two seasons they are rotten and gone for nothing. We are told that our lands are of no service to us, but still, if we hold our lands, there will always be a turkey or a deer, or a fish in the streams, for the younger generation that will come after us. We are afraid that if we part with any more of our lands, the white people will not suffer us to keep as much as will be sufficient to bury our dead.

END OF AN ERA

The days of the Territorial Government were drawing to a close. The Territorial Assembly existed only two years. The second session, due to meet in October, was called by proclamation for June 29, 1795. During this session, General John Sevier presented a bill to convert Doak's Martin Academy, at Salem, into a college, namely Washington College. The main purpose of the Assembly was to plan a census listing of the Territory, anticipating a sufficient number of citizens to sue for statehood.

Blount County was cut off Knox during this session. Other items attended to were the chartering of Blountsville in Sullivan County, Seviersville in Sevier County, Greeneville in Greene County and Clarksville in Montgomery County. These towns were, and are, the official seats of the county governments. The session having accomplished its main purpose, adjourned after 13 days.

From Ramsey, we list the tabulated results of the Census taken and forwarded to President Washington by Governor Blount.

TERRITORY OF THE U. STATES OF AMERICA SOUTH OF THE RIVER OHIO.

Schedule of the aggregate amount of each description of persons, taken agreeably to "An act providing for the enumeration of the inhabitants of the Territory of the United States of America south of the River Ohio;:: passed July 11, 1795.

COUNTIES	Free white males, 16 years and upwards, including heads of families	Free white males under 16 years	Free white females including heads of families	All other free persons	Slaves	Total amount	Yeas	Nays
Jefferson	1706	1225	3021	112	776	7840	714	316
Hawkins	2666	3279	4767	147	2472	13331	1651	534
Greene	1567	2203	3350	52	466	7638	560	495
Knox	2721	2723	3664	100	2365	11573	1100	128
Washington	2013	2578	4311	225	978	10105	873	145
Sullivan	1803	2340	3499	38	777	8457	715	125
Sevier	6888	1045	1503	273	129	3578	261	55
Blount	585	817	1231	00	183	2816	476	16
Davidson	728	695	1192	6	992	3613	96	517[
Sumner	1328	1595	2316	1	1076	6370	00	00
Tennessee	₊380	444	700	19	398	1941	58	231
	16179	19944	29554	973	10613	77262	6504	2562

I, WILLIAM BLOUNT, Governor in and over the Territory of the United States of America south of the River Ohio, do certify that this schedule is made in corformity with the schedules of the sheriffs of the respective counties in the said Territory, and that the schedules of the said sheriffs are lodged in my office.

Given under my hand, at Knoxville, November 28, 1795.   WILLIAM BLOUNT

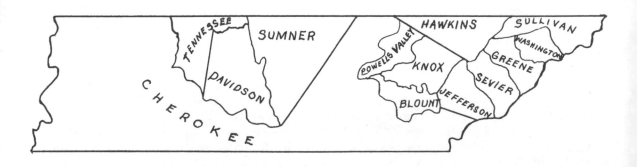

When the total results of the Census were known, the several Counties, determined on statehood, elected their legislative body. Members of the first election, held by counties, met in Knoxville on January 11, 1796. The following elected members assembled in Knoxville, produced their credentials, and took their seats:

BLOUNT COUNTY: David Craig, James Greenaway, Joseph Black, Samuel Glass, James Houston.

DAVIDSON COUNTY: John McNairy, Andrew Jackson, James Robertson, Thomas Hardemen, Joel Lewis.

GREENE COUNTY: Samuel Frazier, Stephen Brooks, William Rankin, John Galbreath, Elisha Baker.

HAWKINS COUNTY: James Berry, Thomas Henderson, Joseph McMinn, William Cocke, Richard Mitchell.

JEFFERSON COUNTY: Alexander Outlaw, Joseph Anderson, George Doherty, William Roddye, Archibald Roane.

KNOX COUNTY: William Blounte, James White, Charles McClung, John Adair, John Crawford.

SULLIVAN COUNTY: George Rutledge, William C. C. Clairborne, John Shelby, Jr., John Rhea, Richard Gammon.

SEVIER COUNTY: Peter Bryan, Samuel Weir, Spencer Clark, John Clack, Thomas Buchenham.

TENNESSEE COUNTY: Thomas Johnston, James Ford, William Fort, Robert Prince, William Prince, Robert Prince.

WASHINGTON COUNTY: Landon Carter, John Tipton, Leroy Taylor, James Stuart, Samuel Handley.

SUMNER COUNTY: D. Shelby, Isaac Walton, W. Douglas, Edward Douglas, Daniel Smith.

William Blount was elected President of the Legislative Body; William Maclin, Secretary; John Sevier, Jr., Clerk; John Rhea, Door-Keeper.

The House appointed two members from each County as a Committee to draft a state constitution.

Daniel Smith was elected Chairman of the Constitution Committee. The writers of the original Tennessee document borrowed heavily from other state constitution provisions. This caused many inconsistencies in application during later years. The Pennsylvania document strongly influenced some of the provisions. The preamble contains expression similar to those found in the written articles of the Watauga Association, Cumberland Compact, the Notables and the State of Franklin.

When a name was proposed for the new State, it was Daniel Smith who submitted the name Tennessee. The County by that name agreed to relinquish its name to the State. The original County of Tennessee became Montgomery, named in honor of Colonel John Montgomery killed by Indians in 1794, and Robertson County, named for General James Robertson.

Tennessee was admitted to the Union of States when the Act was passed by Congress, May 31, 1796, and signed into effect by President George Washington. As the Sixteenth State, Tennessee, began its role as a member of the United States of America, John Sevier was elected its first Governor, William Blount and William Cocke its first Senators, and Andrew Jackson its first Congressman. These elected members were not allowed seats during their first sessions, but were permitted to watch proceedings from the sidelines.

The 36 years of eventful happenings, starting with Daniel Boone and the Long Hunters in 1760, emerge into a new horizon as Tennessee becomes the gateway for western migrations. Many leaders of future states and territories and the federal government could trace their origins back through the geneological trails of the Cumberlands, State of Franklin, Holston and Watauga people.

W. C. C. CLAIBORNE: Private secretary to Thomas Jefferson; received law license in Sullivan County 1794; brigade major under Sevier 1795; Governor Mississippi Territory; Governor Orleans Territory 1812-15.

DAVID FARRAGUT, First Admiral United States Navy.

PETER HARDEMAN BURNETT, born Nashville, Tenn. 1807. Elected first Governor of California 1849. Lawyer, banker and statesman.

ARCHIBALD ROANE; Soldier, Judge and second Governor of Tennessee.

JOSEPH McMINN: Settled in Hawkins County 1787. Governor 1815-1821.

SAM HOUSTON: Nephew of Rev. Samuel Houston; born in Va.; moved to Tenn.; School teacher, Indian fighter, and for a period lived with the Cherokee. U. S. Congressman; Gov. of Tenn. 1827, resigned and moved to Texas. Led Texas army to victory over Mexico; elected first President Texas Republic.

JAMES SEVIER CONWAY, First Governor of Arkansas.

HUGH LAWSON WHITE: Son of Colonel James White, founder of Knoxville. Served as secretary under Blount during Territorial period; elected Tenn. Judge 1802; banker; appointed to complete Andrew Jackson's term in U. S. Senate 1825; refused cabinet post under Jackson; speaker pro-tem in senate; co-sponsored, with Congressman Bell of Nashville, Andrew Jackson's Cherokee removal bill. Nominated for President 1835.

JAMES PARK HOME: Foundation and part of wall built by John Sevier. Governor Sevier didn't have money to finish building. He sold the site, foundation and plans to James Park 1812. It is said Park used Sevier's plans and specifications in completing the house.

BEAN STATION; Site, now under water, first settled by Jesse and Robert Bean 1776. Picture shows Tavern moved by T.V.A. before water covered location.

RAMSEY HOUSE; Known as the Stone House. Built around 1797 by F. A. Ramsey father of the historian Dr. J. G. M. Ramsey. Is located near Knoxville, Tenn.

ROCKWOOD OAK: This is site of Indian tollgate placed across the white man's trail from Watauga Settlements to Cumberland Valley. The Indians used this plan in imposing the 5th section of the Holston Treaty. James Glascow, John Hackett and Littlepage Sims, agents for Elizabeth Donelson, treated with the Indian Chief on this spot. Indian Chief Tullentuskee and the three men planted this tree at the door of the Chief's wigwam as symbol of the Treaty.

BIBLIOGRAPHY

James Adair, *History of The American Indian*

John Allison, *Dropped Stitches In Tennessee History*

Zella Armstrong, *Notable Southern Families*

John P. Brown, *Old Frontiers*

Howard Earnest Carr, *Washington College*

Tennessee Daughters of the American Revolution, *Various Publications*

The East Tennessee Historical Society, *The East Tennessee Historical Society's Publications*

Garrett and Goodpasture, *History of Tennessee*

John Haywood, *The Civil and Political History of The State of Tennessee*

_____ *Natural and Aboriginal History of Tennessee*

Archibald Henderson, *Conquest of The Old Southwest*

Kentucky Historical Society, *Various Publications*

Robert L. Kincaid, *The Wilderness Road*

North Carolina Records, *Publications of the Historical Commission*

John Parris, *Oconaluftee*

William S. Powell, *The War of The Regulations and The Battle of Alamance*

Thomas W. Preston, *Historical Sketches of Holston Valley*

J. G. M. Ramsey, *The Annals of Tennessee History*

Emmet Starr, *History of The Cherokee*

Lewis P. Summers, *History of Southwest Virginia*

Oliver Taylor, *Historic Sullivan*

Tennessee Historical Society, *Tennessee Historical Magazine*

Scates, *A School History of Tennessee*

Samuel Cole Williams, *Early Travels In Tennessee Country*

_____ *Dawn of Tennessee Valley and Tennessee History*

_____ *William Tatham, Wataugan*

_____ *Memoirs of Lieutenant Henry Timberlake*

_____ *Tennessee During The Revolutionary War*

_____ *The Lincolns and Tennessee*

Robert H. White, *Tennessee It's Growth and Progress*

Folmsbee-Corlew-Mitchell, *History of Tennessee*

A. W. Putnam, *History of Middle Tennessee*

Mary U. Rothrock, *This Is Tennessee*

Sevier-Madden, *Sevier Family History*

George C. Mackenzie, *King's Mountain*

Malcolm Fowler, *They Passed This Way*

Lyman C. Draper, *King's Mountain and its Heroes*

Daughters Of The American Revolution, *Various Publications*

Tennessee Historical Society, *Various Publications*

Katherine Keogh White, *The King's Mountain Men*

Sara Sullivan Ervin, *South Carolina In The Revolution*

Lucian Lamar Knight, *Georgia's Roster Of The Revolution*

D. A. R., *Roster of Soldiers From North Carolina In The Revolution*

Courtland T. Reid, *Guilford Courthouse*

Charles E. Hatch, Jr., *Yorktown and Siege of 1781*

PICTURE CREDITS

Tennessee Department of Conservation, 52, 143, 147, 152, 163, 176, 177, 180, 214, 252, 253, 274, 282

Tennessee State Library, 146, 164, 167, 180, 186, 195, 232, 235, 250, 258, 266, 267

Tennessee Conservationist, 36, 127

Tennessee State Museum, 115, 157, 159, 258

Tennessee Game and Fish Commission, 195

King's Mountain Military Park, 81, 88, 92, 93, 97, 104, 105, 106, 116, 130, 134

Mrs. Mary K. Savage, Clarksville, Tennessee, 278

North Carolina State Department of Archives and History, 20, 35, 39, 88

John P. Brown "Old Frontiers", 110, 111, 171, 275

Charles Pugh, 74, 85

Carolina Press, 67, 231, 238

Randy Norton, 223, 260

ILLUSTRATIONS

Bernie Andrews, 6, 7, 8, 10, 12, 13, 14, 15, 16, 18, 21, 22, 24, 25, 26, 30, 31, 32, 33, 34, 38, 41, 42, 44, 46, 48, 49, 50, 51, 81, 155, 172, 210, 222

Kenneth Ferguson, 148, 149, 150, 151, 153, 157, 160, 166, 168, 169, 172, 174, 177, 228, 263, 264, 265, 267, 268, 279

John Alan Maxwell, bottom 224

Edyth Price, 72, 90, 91, 106, 138

William D. Bowman, (maps) 129, 145, 153, 185, 261, 267, 280

Robert Pannell, 132, 140, 189

ACKNOWLEDGMENTS

The author wishes to thank all who have assisted in preparing the materials in "The Overmountain Men." Especially, Attorney Charles Crockett and Judge Ben Allen, Elizabethton. Judeth Ideker, Linda Bailey and Lana Bowman, Erwin, Tennessee. Judy Blevins, JoLinda Blevins, Jack Lane, Dean Hensley, Nan Cocke and Mrs. Mary McCown, Johnson City. Paul Fink, Jonesboro. The Tennessee Historical Commission. The Watauga Regional Library Staff: Mrs. Novella Quillen, Mrs. Robert Shepard, Bonnie Cox, Kathy Patrick. The Unicoi County Public Library, Jane Barnett Librarian. The Tennessee State Library and Archives. Special thanks to Mrs. Olivia Young, Tennessee State Library Consultant.

Any credit not acknowledged is unintentional. Credits omitted in above list include Bureau of American Ethnology, Valley Forge from Ayers Collection New Berry Library, Williams "Dawn of Tennessee Valley".

SPONSORS

Mrs. Blanche Armentrout
W.F. Alexander
Mrs. O. E. Bergendahl
Mrs. Hustin Bacon
Dr. & Mrs. Horace B. Cupp Jr.
Mrs. Ellis Caudle
Att. Charles & Hannah Crockett
Dr. & Mrs. Burgin C. Dossett
Dr. Robert S. Hines
Fred H. Hoss
Woodrow W. Jacobs
W. E. King Jr.
Mr. & Mrs. P. O. Liken
Mrs. Mildred Nelson
Mrs. John Rainero
Mr. & Mrs. Harry Range
Mrs. Anna Setzer
Mrs. Grace Shell
Mrs. Evelyn Trivette
Mr. & Mrs. Kelly Vaughan
Eugene & Edyth Price

Miss Grace Alderman
Dr. & Mrs. M. J. Adams
James & Anna Burn
Hoyle Bingham
Mr. & Mrs. George Ed. Coward
Mrs. Margaret Crumley
Decatur Genealogical Society, Ill.
Dan & Mary Davis
Mrs. Volney Harrison
Mrs. Lela Hoffman
Mr. & Mrs. Mickey Jilton
Mrs. Elizabeth W. King
Mr. & Mrs. L. W. McCown
Burgett W. & Ethel S. Piper
Miss Mary U. Rothrock
Walter A. Soefker Jr.
John and Herma Shearer
Mrs. Hilda Thorp
Mr. & Mrs. Larry K. Tittle
Mr. & Mrs. Sherman Williams

Verna Blow Alderman
Mrs. Retha Bayless
Archer & Judy Blevins
Burt & Mabel Cash
Mrs. Moses Cantor
Dr. & Mrs. D. P. Culp
Daniel Boone Campers
Franklin Chapter D.A.R. Jonesboro
Mrs. Grace Hensley
Mr. & Mrs. John Howze
Mrs. Pauline Kelly
Marie Maxwell Long
Mrs. Elsie Meredith
Dr. & Mrs. Charles O. Parker
Mrs. William Irving Reilly
Mrs. Clyde Smith
Dr. & Mrs. Merritt Shobe
Mrs. Wallace C. Tilden
Mrs. Mary Lou Underwood
Bert & Louise Walton
Mr & Mrs. R. R. Gray

LIBRARIES

Blue Grass Regional Library
Elizabethton, Tennessee Public Library
Hamilton County-Wide Library
Linebaugh, Tennessee Public Library
Nolichucky Regional Library
Sullivan County Public Library, Blountville
Watauga Regional Library

Clarksville—Montgomery Public Library
East Tennessee State University
Public Library of Knoxville and Knox County
Muscle Shoals Regional Library, Alabama
Nashville, Tennessee Public Libraries
Unicoi County Public Library

SCHOOLS

Athens Junior High School
Decaturville Elementary School, Decaturville
H. G. Hill School, Nashville
Johnson County Schools, Mountain City
McMinn County Board of Education
C.H. Moore Elementary School, Clarksville
Onieda High School Library
Sulphur Springs High School
Unicoi County High School
Unicoi County Board of Education
Valley Forge Elementary School

Carter County Board of Education
Fairmont Elementary School, Johnson City
Johnson City Board of Education
Lookout Mountain Schools, Lookout Mountain
Madison County Schools
Niota Elementary Schools
Powell Elementary School, Powell
I.B. Tigrett Junior High School, Jackson
Unicoi County High School Library
Unaka Elementary School, Carter County

CIVIC GROUPS

Greeneville Chamber of Commerce
Elizabethton Rotary Club
Town of Elizabethton
Erwin Kiwanis Club
Erwin Jaycees
Erwin Woman's Club
Brownie's Restaurant, Erwin
Roller Drug Store, Erwin
Tipton's Cabinet Shop, Erwin
Wolf Laurel at Big Bald Mountain, Mars Hill, N.C.

Elizabethton Chamber of Commerce
Elizabethton B. and P.W. Club
Erwin Civitan Club
Erwin Y's Men's Club
Erwin B. and P.W. Club
Elms Restaurant, Erwin
Publix Supermarket, Erwin
Clinchfield Drug Store, Erwin
Tri-Cities Lithographing Co., Johnson City
First Federal Savings and Loan Assn. of Erwin

NAME INDEX

NAME INDEX

NAME INDEX

PLACE INDEX